W9-AQJ-406

COSTUME DESIGN

Barbara and Cletus Anderson

Carnegie-Mellon University

COSTUME

DESIGN

Holt, Rinehart and Winston

New York   Chicago   San Francisco   Philadelphia
Montreal   Toronto   London   Sydney
Tokyo   Mexico City   Rio de Janeiro   Madrid

Publisher: Susan Katz
Acquiring editor: Anne Boynton-Trigg
Senior Project editor: H. L. Kirk
Production manager: Annette Mayeski
Photo research: Joe Samodulski

Library of Congress Cataloging in Publication Data

Anderson, Barbara (Barbara Benz)
  Costume design.
  Bibliography: p.
  Includes index.
  1. Costume design. 2. Costume. I. Anderson,
Cletus. II. Title.
TT507.A66 1984   792'.026   83–12627

ISBN 0-03-060383-8

Address correspondence to:
  383 Madison Avenue
  New York, N.Y. 10017

  4 5 6 7 016 9 8 7 6 5 4 3 2 1

CBS COLLEGE PUBLISHING
  Holt, Rinehart and Winston
  The Dryden Press
  Saunders College Publishing

ILLUSTRATION CREDITS

Art Resource, Inc.: p. 3; Figures 1-2, 1-3, 1-20, 1-23, 1-25 right, 1-26, 4-65, 4-66, 4-69, 4-75 **Beinecke Rare Book and Manuscript Library, Yale University:** p. 77 **Bettmann Archive:** Figures 1-17, 1-19, 1-22, 1-24, 1-27, 1-30, 1-31, 3-23, 4-67, 4-68, 4-70, 4-73 **Performing Arts Research Center, New York, Public Library at Lincoln Center:** Figure 1-5 **Julian Wasser/***Time* **Magazine:** Figure 1-28 **Wide World Photos:** Figure 1-24

Figure 1-25 (left) by permission of Katharine Hepburn Figure 1-44 courtesy Bergdorf-Goodman, New York Figure 3-30 (right) from *Vecellio's Renaissance Costume Book* (New York: Dover Publications, 1976), by permission of the publisher Figure 4–74 courtesy the Picture Collection, Cooper-Hewitt Museum Library

Cover: Costume sketch by Cletus Anderson

To Cathy and Chris
our often delightful offspring

PREFACE

Costume design is both an art form and a practical craft, a duality that makes the field somewhat difficult to master and equally elusive to explain to others. The craft cannot be defined in absolutes that will provide clear answers to all questions, nor can the theatre costume designer indulge in the complete freedom of expression available to the fine artist. But an intelligent, sensitive, informed method of working can help those interested in the field develop the design ideas for a production. *Costume Design* offers a logical approach, starting with thoughts on the beginnings of costumes and the psychology of clothes, moving on to developing the ideas and sketching them, and finishing with techniques and patterns to use when actually building the costumes.

The first three chapters, "Costume Design: What It Is and What It Does," "The Costume Approach," and "Developing the Basic Concept," help the novice designer understand the field and the steps that must be taken to develop the costume ideas. We urge designers to communicate with others involved on the project in a creative way so that ideas can be exchanged and encouraged to grow. This interchange of ideas is a unique aspect of theatre, for it is through the collaboration of a number of artists involved in the different aspects of the production that an exciting piece is created for the audience. This book presents a way of working that will be creative and constructive, one that will guide the designer to be efficient and capable while encouraging good communication, for an effective collaboration is a rewarding experience.

Costume ideas cannot exist solely in the designer's head, so

Chapters 4, 5, and 6, "Developing the Line," "Designing the Costume: Color Control," and "Costume Presentation: Rendering or Final Sketch," offer the beginner ways that can be used to present the work. They provide a basic guide to the figure, suggest different materials and techniques that may help the ideas travel from head to paper, and explain the basic principles of line and color and how to apply them to costumes. Also included are a variety of sketches that can be used for reference and that may suggest directions beginning designers will want to pursue. The purpose of *Costume Design* is to open doors to myriad possibilities, not to decree what is right or wrong in the field. A good designer develops because the mind and imagination can work, not simply because he or she has learned a set of rules.

The final two chapters, "Costume Construction" and "Patterning and Building the Costume," provide a basis for converting the sketch to the actual costume. A handsome sketch can communicate ideas to others involved with the production, but the final result must be an effective costume presented to the audience. Not all designers have the manual dexterity to actually construct costumes, but they must know the principles of good construction to guide those who will be working with them effectively. The brief guide to costume history and list of source books and artists at the end of the book can be used as a springboard when the designer begins research for a project.

Many people encouraged and helped us as we set about to get these ideas onto paper, and we are very grateful to them all. We wish particularly to thank Phillip Graneto for his time, patience, and wonderful ability to clarify a thought, and Ainslie Bruneau for her companionship and assistance in developing the patterns and checking over the manuscript. We also wish to thank all of the colleagues, students, and former students who allowed us to use some of their work and Stacy Eddy and Kevin Ritter for their assistance with the pictures for Chapter 8. And we are very grateful to those reviewers who read and critiqued the manuscript: Alan Armstrong, UCLA; Alexandra Bonds, University of Oregon; Leon Brauner, Indiana University; Gail Crellin, University of Minnesota; Alicia Finkel, University of Connecticut; Phil Graneto, Glassboro State College; Barbara Mendlicott, University of Houston; Paul Reinhardt, University of Texas, Austin; and Al Tucci, West Virginia University.

CONTENTS

COSTUME DESIGN

Introduction

There are no absolutes in costume design for the theatre. Life would be much easier if there were. But there is certainly a logical way to approach the work so designers can develop both a basic understanding of the field and guidelines that will allow them to grow and expand their capabilities with each project. In any collaborative art talent is very useful, but knowing how to get the job done efficiently and in the way that is most beneficial to others with whom one works is a tremendous asset. And a well-balanced combination of talent, know-how, dependability and skill in communicating is almost unbeatable. This book is designed to help develop this combination of skills.

Good costume designers must know a tremendous number of things about a great many subjects. They need to know about drama as literature and as a performing art, and about the physical makeup of theatre. They must understand people and what makes them tick. They need to know about drawing and painting and the history of art. They must be knowledgeable about social history, both past events and what people wore in other eras. They should have a working knowledge of fabrics and sewing, how to drape and lay out patterns, and how to construct a great variety of ideas from the sublime to the ridiculous. They must be constantly open to all kinds of stimuli: a designer never knows what information will be valuable on jumping into the next project. For example, we remember one time when we were in desperate need of a heavy, important necklace and crown for King Arthur in the PBS production of *A Connecticut Yankee in King Arthur's Court*. We wanted them to be a series of medallions with the necklace extending out over the shoulders but we could find nothing in our locality or in

A practical approach to designing can help make creating a costume such as this one for Beulah in *Merton of the Movies* a fun and satisfying experience. Design for a 1982 production at Carnegie-Mellon University by Cletus Anderson. Pencil sketch.

Materials for a crown for King Arthur in Once Upon a Classic's *A Connecticut Yankee in King Arthur's Court* came from a specialty hardware store and include ornate drawer pulls. Arthur's necklace is drapery chain. Design by Barbara Anderson. Photo by Bob Breene. © Metropolitan Pittsburgh Public Broadcasting, Inc., 1977.

New York City. Then we remembered a decorative hardware supplier we had once visited and constructed both quite effectively out of drawer-pull backings and drapery chain obtained from him.

This book presents practical information in the areas mentioned above. It gives just a taste of some of them, some it will explore in depth. But it does give a working knowledge of the field so designers can then search and grow on their own. In an ever-changing field such as theatre no book should try to be the last word. It can nevertheless form a foundation and open doors: there is a vast world of information out there for designers to use. If they understand their field and know where to head, each project can be an enriching experience and new vistas will spread out as they discover more and more places to find the information they need.

Costume Design gives the designer a basic understanding of what costumes are and what they do, beginning with a brief description of how costumes developed in the past. Since costumes are based on the clothing people wear, designers must think about what is worn by

Bonnet Anglo-américain

High fashion is not always sensible, offstage or on. A 1780 "Anglo-American bonnet."

whom, why they wear it, and what others think about it. They must develop a feeling for why people dress the way they do today and know how to translate that back to other eras. They must recognize all the information costumes can convey and know how to deal with a script to realize which will best fill out all the characterizations present in it.

We believe that the primary function of the costume is to enhance the characterization of a role. "Nobody ever goes away humming the costumes," but well-thought-out costumes can certainly give a zest to a production. Developing the character feeling is much easier if a designer has a knowledge of the psychology of clothes, so Chapter 1 includes a section on this. (It would be convenient if one could simply say "This type of clothing was worn for reason A." Unfortunately, it's not that simple, for many times what people wear is neither sensible nor easily explained.) There is more than a little craziness in the clothes of everyday life and costumes in the theatre, so a well-developed sense of humor never hurt any designer. It comes in handy in more ways than

A costume sketch may indicate the mood of the play but must clearly show the costume. Jean in John Whiting's *The Devils*, produced at Carnegie-Mellon University, 1976. Done in acrylic by Cletus Anderson.

Soldiers in *Macbeth* wore quilted tunics and gauntlets in costumes designed by Cletus Anderson for the 1980 Pittsburgh Public Theatre production. The quilting and helmet-mask added bulk and menace to the figure.

being able to keep smiling at some of the silly things people put on their bodies. Actors are usually quite concerned with their physical appearance in a role, and an open, friendly approach can often soften rough spots. Directors have many things to think about, and designers who can keep their wits and wit about them make much better collaborators. Fellow workers in a costume shop will feel a lot more like working for a designer who is up and cheery than for a cloud of doom that descends on the cutting table.

So there is perhaps one absolute after all: Costume designers who know how to approach their work and know what they should do to achieve the goals decided on for a production will instill confidence in all those who work with them. The first three chapters of this book present a step-by-step method of approaching the project, defining the objectives, and determining the methods that can best be used to achieve the goals. They explore the areas that must be considered in terms of different situations. They present the aesthetic decisions designers must make and guide them through the practical questions that must be answered, even providing a guide to estimating the yardage needed and a way to budget the show.

The ability to put ideas down almost effortlessly is a basic tool the designer must master. Actually putting pencil to paper to begin drawing the costumes is a step that is sometimes difficult to take. We have provided a guide to the figure, an approach to the body areas, and ways to deal with them to achieve specific design effects. Also included are basic design principles and how they apply to the body and the costume, with encouragement to draw and draw and draw so the designer can get over that procrastination hump. Designers will be able to get to work because they are confident that they can get what is in their heads down on the paper before them. They must also believe in what they do and not try to hedge their bets. A sketch cannot be presented with the old dodge: "Well, what I really wanted was. . . ." What is really wanted should be there. It does not have to be a work of art, but it needs to be clearly presented and as attractive as possible. We go into detail on how to do the actual costume rendering, how it should be laid out, what it should show, how the color can be applied. A rendering is not expressing "five yards of emotion"; one cannot build or wear that. It should be a clear presentation of what the costume will be, one that can be easily read by the director, actors, and those in the shop who will build it.

Producing costume sketches and renderings requires an understanding of such materials as papers, pencils, paints, and pastels. These are explained, as is color theory. Color control is a primary factor in costume design. Color registers on the audience before anything else. The designer must know what range of color is available, what effect it may have, and how it reacts to other colors around it. (A red dress in a chorus of pinks and maroons is one thing. A red dress when everyone else on stage is wearing black is something else indeed. And just what is red? The variations are endless.)

Producing an effective costume rendering is indeed a wonderful thing, but since that costume plate won't be onstage it can be a mere academic exercise if the designer doesn't know how to translate it into an actual costume. And it's usually not just one plate. It's a whole show

The Purple Panda in *Mister Rogers' Neighborhood* wore this dinosaur suit designed by Barbara Anderson. Photo by Lilo Guest. Courtesy Family Communications, Inc.

full of drawings that must become real clothes on real people. We explain how to develop a point of view for building the show and how to take the costume plate and accurately interpret the areas to three-dimensional form. The world of fabric is also explored in Chapter 7: what it is, where it comes from, how it is put together. This is all good background, but of course a real feel for fabric comes with a lot of actual handling and playing with it. Designers should not be able to keep their hands off an interesting piece of cloth. It's not only a means of realizing a sketch, it can also provide initial inspiration for a design. Even while putting down the first quick impression designers can sense the idea growing as they think of how it will work in a heavy, nubby tweedy wool or a lightly flowing chiffon.

Most people who regularly attend the theatre never consider the fact that to build a costume you first have to develop the pattern for it. A thorough investigation of patterning would fill volumes, but this is not necessary here. We explain the principles of developing the pattern and include layouts for the basic shapes of the most-used elements, with illustrations of what they will look like when made up. This book gives the designer a way to work so they can tackle any problem because they understand what fabric can do and aren't afraid to keep trying things until they achieve the shape they want. This is done with a combination of flat patterning and draping. Those who insist that one method is better than the other and the truly "proper" way to work are doing the field a disservice. There are many variables in costume design and someone in charge of building the clothes must be flexible and be able to pick the method or combination of methods that will produce the best results in the shortest time. Within a space of a few months recently we designed and built a production of *Macbeth* for the Pittsburgh Public Theatre that included intricate quilting and draping; a dinosaur costume for a man in a purple panda suit for *Mister Rogers' Neighborhood;* and the costumes for the motion picture *Knightriders,*

The costume for Nathan Grantham after he has been dead for seven years required a somewhat unorthodox approach. Designed for the George Romero film *Creepshow* by Barbara Anderson. Make-up by Tom Savini. Photo courtesy Laurel-Show, Inc., New York.

which included an entire motorcycle gang doing elaborate stunts clad in medieval armor. This certainly required variation in approach and a willingness to try new things.

The best research material for a designer to use involves primary sources—sources created during the span of the historical period—but it is often difficult to know just what is being presented in these sources. Appendix A is a guide to the history of costume. It gives the designer the basic shapes of each period with a feeling for how they develop and how they are worn. It is a concise starting point for the understanding of the history of clothes and includes a period-by-period list of sources to go to for a more in-depth look at any era.

Costume design is a delightful and challenging field. It certainly isn't an area for those of faint heart who yearn for a serene life and ten hours of sleep a night. Problems run rampant, deadlines are always too near, and just as one need is met another jumps up to take its place. But the rewards can outweigh all these, for it is a field that keeps one involved, communicating, thinking, and growing. And it can be a lot of fun.

1

Costume design: what it is and what it does

Costume design must encompass both the past and the present and be built on a knowledge of both theatre and the real world from which it springs. It must be predicated on an understanding of theatrical characters created for the entertainment of others and of the actual people who provide the background for drama and its roles. Any potential designer needs an awareness of these integral components of costume design. As in any human endeavor, the past influences the present and the potential for the future, so this book begins with a brief look at the development of theatrical costuming and defines what a costume is.

Many theatrical costumes are based on everyday clothes, and the characters in a presentation may be defined largely by their garments. Some knowledge of the psychology of clothing gives designers a background that will help them begin actual work on a play so they can explore the dramatic ideas and find ways that costumes will help develop the characters and present the ideas of the script. Costume designers can bring a great deal to any production, but they do not work on their own. Theatre is made up of many people exchanging ideas and combining talents to produce an event for those who will view it. This chapter explains how this collaboration begins and develops.

Hand in hand with the development of drama, the desire to create a heightened dramatic effect through physical adornment has made the theatrical experience increasingly more exciting to the audience. Costuming for theatrical effect is thus as old as drama itself, but costume design as an element planned to help delineate the character and further the interpretation of the play as a whole is a relatively new development. Today's costume designer is a theatre artist who enriches the production by selecting the underpinnings, garments, and accessories that will best suit the actors in their roles and at the same time reinforce the flavor of the whole presentation.

Early theatrical costuming

A style of costume that added importance to the figure and gave more visibility to the actor was well established by the time of Aeschylus (525–456 B.C.) and the great Greek tragedies. Performing in a huge outdoor amphitheatre, the actor became larger than life with the aid of ample, padded robes, thick-soled boots called *cothurni*, and masks constructed to amplify the voice. The masks were not only practical; they did much to heighten the spectacle and the appearance of the actors, for they were often adorned with the *onkus*, a lofty headdress. Stock character masks were common in Greek and Roman tragedies and comedies, allowing the audience to identify the type of role played

Figure 1-1 Greek and Roman actors became larger than life with the aid of *cothurni*, mask, and *onkus*. This ivory statuette of a tragic actor, probably Roman, is in the Musée du Petit Palais, Paris.

Preceding page: A costume that is a symbol may be just right. All the audience really needs to know about this character is that she is a maid. Costume design for *The Sea Gull.* Watercolor by Cletus Anderson.

Figure 1-2   Comedy and Tragedy. Masks in a mosaic now to be seen in the Capitoline Museum, Rome.

by the actor easily. In the comedies much humor came from these exaggerated headpieces, and the colorful costumes were made ludicrous by dangling appendages.

Costuming began cautiously as drama slowly re-emerged in Western Europe at the end of the early Middle Ages (roughly A.D. 475 – 1000). The Mystery and Miracle plays started in the church, and the costumes for these were inspired by church vestments, which have always had a certain theatricality. As presentations moved from the church precincts to the marketplace the scope of the pageants widened and more contemporary characteristics and flair were incorporated into the performance to help capture the attention of the gathered populace. Much of the art of the early Middle Ages was based on religious themes, with the artists depicting the biblical characters in robes with simple lines. The style of these illustrations influenced the garments first used for the drama, but this trend was soon reversed. The presentations became more theatrical, the characters acquired more extraordinary accoutrements that would heighten the dramatic effect, and the artists soon followed along, depicting the figures in their paintings in a much more theatrical manner. From simple beginnings the human desire to adorn the body and entertain others won out again. This was particularly evident in the character of the Devil—who, aided by

Figure 1-3 The costumes for the *commedia dell'arte* during the Italian Renaissance were not as elaborate as those in the formal productions, but could be quite theatrical, particularly for the stock characters who provided most of the humor. The young lovers often wore garments very much like the actual clothes of the period. Museum of La Scala, Milan.

fantastical masks, costumes, and accessories, tended to run away with the show.

The desire for extravagant and lavish costuming in their theatrical presentations was quite compatible with the richness of the extraordinary fashions of the nobles of the time of the Italian Renaissance. This delight in spectacle was paramount, though to the modern eye it might seem a bit misplaced, as in the case of a production of *Oedipus Rex* staged at the Teatro Olimpico at Vicenza in 1585, with the king's retinue of twenty-four archers dressed in Turkish fashion. This excerpt from Sabbattini's *Practica*, published in 1638, expresses the philosophy behind the rich presentations of the time:

VERIDICO: I tell you especially that I make efforts to dress the actors always in as noble a fashion as is possible for me, but in such a manner that there is a sense of proportion among them, in view of the fact that the rich costume . . . particularly in these times when pomp is at its highest peak, adds much reputation and beauty to comedies, and even more to tragedies. I would not hesitate to dress a servant in velvet or colored satin, as long as his master's costume were embroidered or decorated with gold, so rich that there would be maintained the proper proportion between them. But I would not clothe a housemaid with a torn old skirt, or a servant with a torn doublet; on the contrary, I would have her wear a nice skirt and him a showy jacket, and I would add so much nobility to the clothes of their masters as to allow for the beauty of the servants' costumes.

MASSIMIANO: There is no doubt that the sight of the rags which others put on a miser's back, or on a servant's, detracts much from the dignity of a play.

VERIDICO: One can very well clothe a miser or even a peasant with costumes which have a certain degree of richness about them, without being unnatural.

Spectacle was often also the primary function of costumes in Elizabethan and Jacobean England, particularly in the court masques shown in the sketches of Inigo Jones (1573–1652). The basic silhouette was that of the Elizabethan costume, with bits of fancy and fantasy added to give a particular flavor. This style of costuming was prominant for a great many years. The clothes of the performers were based primarily on the daily attire worn at the time and place of the production, and only slight additions or subtractions were made to give a feeling of the character, situation, or location of the play. With few exceptions presentations were staged in this manner until the nineteenth century. Thus a Scottish thane killing his king, a Greek maid frolicking on a midsummer night, a goddess blessing a wedding, and a Roman orator could have many costume pieces in common.

Ballet and opera costumes evolved along more opulent lines, while those used in the theatre tended to less extravagance, though still given to much excess. Many of the costumes of a theatrical company were actually hand-me-downs, acquired from patrons who would bestow discarded garments on the group or give an outfit to a favored performer. It was also common practice for leading actors and actresses to select their own costumes, basing their choice on the accepted conventions of the times, which certainly did dictate an imposing look for the primary characters. Joseph Addison (1672–1719) described the traditional heroic costume in an issue of *The Spectator* of 1711:

The ordinary method of making a hero is to clap a huge plume of feathers on his head which rises so very high that there is often a greater length from his chin to the top of his head than to the sole of his foot. One would believe that we thought a great man and a tall man the same thing. This very much embarrasses the actor, who is forced to hold his neck extremely stiff and steady all the while he speaks; and not withstanding any anxieties which he pretends for his mistress, his country, or his friends, one may see by his action that his greatest care and concern is to keep the plume of feathers from falling off his head. . . . As these superfluous ornaments upon the head make a great man, a princess generally receives her grandeur from those additional encumbrances that fall into her tail: I mean the broad sweeping train that follows her in all her motions and finds constant employment for a boy who stands behind her to open and spread it to advantage. . . . It is, in my opinion, a very odd spectacle to see a queen venting her passion in a disordered motion, and a little boy taking care all the while that they do not ruffle the tail of her gown.

Figure 1-4 Spectacle was a primary function of the court masque costumes designed by Inigo Jones in Elizabethan England. This sketch is for Tethys or a Nymph in Daniel's *Tethys Festival*, 1610. Devonshire Collection, Chatsworth Library, Derbyshire, England.

Figure 1-5   Macbeth appears much more the Restoration gentleman than an early Scots thane in this eighteenth-century production. Engraving from Nicholas Rowe's edition of Shakespeare, 1709. Courtesy Billy Rose Theater Collection, New York Public Library at Lincoln Center.

Historical accuracy or careful delineation of character was given little thought when costuming productions during the seventeenth and early eighteenth centuries, so some steps taken toward more realism in selecting costumes caused particular comment in the mid-eighteenth century. In his *Source Book in Theatrical History* A. M. Nagler refers to a noted French actress of the time, Mlle Clairon. Performing in a small theatre in the 1750s, she was thought quite daring when she presented her role of a sultana without hoops and also toned down her declamatory acting style to fit the acting space. The effect was received enthusiastically by the audience. Diderot exclaimed "A courageous actress,

Figure 1-6 The celebrated Mrs. Sarah Siddons' hairstyle as The Grecian Daughter (right) is very 1782 English.

Figure 1-7 Hairstyle and dress shape place Mrs. Bunn's Queen Elizabeth (above) squarely in the early 1820s.

Publish'd for Bell's Brit:sh Theatre June 24.th 1776.

Figure 1-8 Mr. and Mrs. Berry (left) appeared in traditional heroic costumes as Bajazet and Selima in Nicholas Rowe's *Tamerlane* in June 1776. He wore a high plume of feathers and she a broad, sweeping train. His line: "Now, now thou Traitress."

Mlle Clairon, has just discarded her hoops, and no one thinks it wrong. She will go even further, I say. Ah! what if she dared, one day, to appear on the stage in all the nobility and simplicity of dress that her parts demand!"

Realizing that her change in acting style required a change in her

Figure 1-9 In an eighteenth-century production Mlle Clairon played Medea in contemporary dress while her Jason, Henri Louis Lekain, wore the *habit à la romaine,* an adaptation of Roman armor topped off with a plumed helmet. Bibliothèque Nationale, Paris.

Figure 1-10 Costume sketch by James Robinson Planché for Charles Kemble's much-publicized "historically accurate" revival of Shakespeare's *King John* in 1823. Courtesy Stark Collection, University of Texas Library, Austin.

entire presentation, Clairon complained to a friend: "Ah! . . . Don't you see that it ruins me? In all my characters, the costume must now be observed; the truth of declamation requires that of dress; all my rich stage wardrobe is from this moment rejected; I lose twelve hundred guineas worth of dresses; but the sacrifice is made." She went on to perform Electra "in the simple habit of a slave, dishevelled, her arms loaded with chains" and was declared admirable in the role. This "simple habit" was still relatively elaborate, but it seemed quite innovative at the time.

The cry to let the character dictate the costume also came from others in this era, including John Hill. In his treatise *The Actor,* written in 1750, he indicated that he did not expect unnecessary extremes:

One great source of these abuses in the parts of the waiting maids is that the authors of our farces in general have made persons of that rank the principal characters of the piece, while their mistresses have been little better than cyphers. But we are apt to believe that the authors of those pieces intended that the superiority of character in the servant should be discovered in the course of performance, not by the habit; and that the whole would have somewhat more the air of nature, if when they are both to appear often together upon the stage, the maid were at least not better dress'd than the mistress. . . . We would not desire things to be carry'd so far indeed on this occasion, as to expect a beau to enter in dirty boots, because he is to mention his having come a journey, but then we would not have an Orestes return from the temple, where at the instigation of Hermione, he has been causing Pyrrhus to be assassinated, without one curl of his peruke out of order. Let the look of reality be kept up; and when the actor tells us of some dreadful bustle he has been in, we would have him shew some marks of it by the disorder of his person.

Desire for historical accuracy began to grow in the nineteenth century. The first notable production of this movement was a revival of Shakespeare's *King John* by Charles Kemble in 1823. It was designed by J. R. Planché, a man who was both designer and historian and the author of *A History of British Costume.* Playbills proclaimed that the production was to be done "with an attention to Costume never equalled on the English Stage. Every Character will appear in the precise HABIT OF THE PERIOD, the whole of the Dresses and Decorations being executed from undisputable Authorities." Allardyce Nicoll points out in *The Development of the Theatre* that "Planché put on what was undoubtedly the first completely 'historical' production of Shakespeare's drama, for he paid attention not only to the hero's costume but to those of the meanest underling." Coordinating the costumes of the complete production was an entirely new idea. The lead costumes had often received special attention, but costumes for the extras were usually anything that happened to be handy at the time.

The urge toward more historical accuracy and character meaning in costumes continued throughout the nineteenth century. One company, The Meiningen Players, working out of the small German principality of Saxe-Meiningen in the last quarter of the century, was particularly noted for historical presentation of both sets and costumes and the ensemble work of the company. This group greatly influenced both André Antoine (1858–1943), who proclaimed a doctrine of stage realism at his Théâtre Libre in Paris, and Konstantin Stanislavski (1863–1938) and his work at the Moscow Art Theatre. Stanislavski's

Figure 1-11   Antony speaks over the body of Caesar in the Meiningen Players' production of *Julius Caesar* in London in 1881. The German company was noted for historical accuracy of both sets and costumes as well as for ensemble acting. From *The Illustrated London News.* Courtesy Theatre Museum, Victoria & Albert Museum, London (Crown Copyright).

Figure 1-12 Gordon Craig, a leader in the movement against realism in both costume and stage setting, wanted to transform theatre into "a place for visions." Craig's set and costumes for *Hamlet* at the Moscow Art Theatre in 1911.

reforms toward naturalism and ensemble acting are milestones, even though he tended to extremes at times. Theodore Komisarjevsky reports in *The Costume of the Theatre:*

On the opening night, in the production of the poetical and historical Russian play *Tzar Fyodor Ivanovitch,* the costumes of the Tzar, of the boyars, and of the Moscow people were exact replicas of historical documents and made as far as possible of the genuine old materials. The long bejeweled brocade coats of the boyars had fur collars and were lined throughout with fur, which made them so heavy that it seemed almost impossible for the actors to breathe, let alone move in them. . . . In the production of *Julius Caesar* the stage was so filled with brass armor, helmets, weapons, ample togas, and various minute details of costume and properties that Shakespeare's play was completely drowned.

A reaction against such slavish attention to historical detail arose by the end of the nineteenth century. The cry was for scenery and costumes that were evocative rather than descriptive, a simplicity that would suggest rather than reproduce. Both Adolphe Appia (1862–1928) and Gordon Craig (1872–1966) were leaders in this movement against realism. In Germany Max Reinhardt (1873–1943) became a primary influence with his desire for a visual interpretation that would reinforce the main themes present in the play and thus add an accent or viewpoint to the dominant flavor without slavish devotion to historical accuracy. This type of approach is still prevalent in our theatre. The costume designer can be an artist of the theatre by specifically planning costumes to heighten the visual impact of the play and reinforce the flavor established for the production. Costume design is an important part of the whole presentation. It should not be an afterthought left to the whims of the actors, director, wardrobe mistress, or someone who happens to cross the auditorium at the wrong time.

The visual impact of the play

As the lights come up on the stage, impressions are created before a word is said. The visual impact of a play or character is the first influence on the audience. This impact should be well planned to reinforce the action in the most suitable manner. It is the responsibility of the costume and set designers to provide the proper atmosphere for the play. The scenery must create an appropriate setting and allow the right movement and visual groupings; the costumes present the character and give information that may not be explicit in the text.

Figure 1-13 Costume and set affect the audience before a word has been spoken. The opening picture of Haydn's opera *House Afire,* produced at Yale University in 1963. Costume design by Barbara Anderson. Set design by Lewis A. Crickard.

Figure 1-14   A costume can be layers of clothing, with very little of the body showing. Nun's costume for *The Devils,* produced at Carnegie-Mellon University, 1970. Acrylic sketch by Cletus Anderson.

Figure 1-15   A costume can be nothing at all — or almost nothing, as in the case of these designed by Cletus Anderson for George Romero's film *Knightriders.* Photo by James Hamilton. Courtesy Laurel-Knights, Inc., New York.

What is a costume?

Anything worn onstage is a costume, whether it be layers of clothing or nothing at all. A costume is technically defined as dress in general, including underpinnings, accessories, hairdressing, and makeup. It can be the distinctive style of a people, class, locality, or period. There is no such thing as doing a show without costumes, despite the fact that the desire to do so is often proclaimed. A production to be done "in rehearsal clothes" is a production costumed as though the actors were rehearsing. A scene certainly can be presented in whatever the actors happen to be wearing at the time, but these clothes then become costumes and will have an influence on the audience. Obviously a woman portraying a young girl full of innocence and purity will have trouble convincing the audience of her sincerity if she is clad in a short-skirted, low-cut red knit dress and red patent sandals that lace to the knee. An actor in bare feet, fringed Levis, bare chest, and a headband can probably not overcome the obstacles in his way to be believed as an establishment businessman. Denying costumes by having the actors wear leotards and tights is not eliminating the costume effect at all; the uniformity itself makes a strong statement, as does the shape of the body revealed by these garments. While these are some obvious examples, there are also many subtle ways visual impact can influence the audience, ways that reinforce the need for visual control. The audience sees — and reacts, consciously or subconsciously. There is no such thing as "no costume." Anything worn onstage is a costume, and should be as appropriate and meaningful as possible.

The psychology of clothing

Any study of costume design entails a basic understanding of the psychology of clothing and how styles develop through various periods. The logical question that arises is "Why do styles develop as they do?" There are no definite, logical answers. Quentin Bell has written an excellent book on the subject, *On Human Finery.* He bases much of his work on *The Theory of the Leisure Class* by Thorstein Veblen. According to Bell, Veblen found the study of clothes to be the study of monstrosities and absurdities, and Bell himself says "We are dealing here not with abnormal, but with normal behavior, and when we begin to reflect upon it we discover our normal behavior is crazy."

In his book *Clothes*, James Laver postulates the idea that clothes are worn for three main reasons. The least important of these is the Utility Principle: garments are selected to counteract the effects of the cold or damp. Stronger motivation is found in the Hierarchical Principle, in which clothes are selected because they lend social status to the wearers and display their importance to the world. The third motivation cited by Laver is the Seduction Principle; clothes are donned to make the wearer look as attractive as possible, within the framework of what is considered attractive at any particular time in history. Laver applies the Hierarchical Principle more to men and the Seduction Principle more to women, though a combination of the two often comes into play. The Utility Principle is equally important to both sexes, but "The question of modesty hardly enters into the matter at all."

Figure 1-16 This 1914 Paris fashion could have been the sort of high style that led clothing theorist Quentin Bell to conclude "our normal behavior is crazy."

Figure 1-17 James Laver's Seduction Principle could very possibly lurk behind this advertisement for Arrow collars in a 1910 issue of *The Review of Reviews*.

Figure 1-18 This elegant *toilette de ville* would have cost a great deal of money in 1875. Conspicuous Consumption?

Bell and Veblen agree that styles of clothes are not really determined by such logical factors as climate and comfort. They feel that change in fashion is the result of the struggle of the classes, a way in which the aristocracy can declare its superiority. Social pressures can be very strong influences on behavior and a way to remain socially superior is to dress properly according to the unwritten rules of society. For many years what was considered "socially proper" would keep the members of society in their appropriate niches independent of laws. Governments, in fact, attempted to legislate social status by means of sumptuary laws, which regulated dress by specifically stating who could wear what. Many such laws existed because they were not effective — the old law didn't work, a new law was passed, it in turn proved ineffective, and another took its place. Where laws were ineffective, social pressure held sway. To maintain one's proper place in society, one must dress correctly. A woman once commented to Ralph Waldo Emerson that "a sense of being perfectly well dressed gives a feeling of inward tranquility religion is powerless to bestow." Lord Chesterfield observed "Dress is a very foolish thing, yet it is foolish for man not to be well dressed, in accordance with his rank and way of life."

Humans use clothing to express social superiority in a number of ways. Some of the categories posited by Bell and Veblen are:

Figure 1-19 Fox hunting — elitist, expensive, and useless — qualifies for Quentin Bell's category of Conspicuous Waste. Queen Alexandra, Queen Mary, and the Queen of Norway at a foggy meet of the West Norfolk Foxhounds.

Figure 1-20 The old-fashioned military officer has been characterized as the epitome of waste — glorious but useless. This splendidly mustachioed specimen was posted to the Bombay Lancers. Musée de l'Armée, Parigi.

1. *Conspicuous Consumption.* We adorn ourselves with clothes that cost a great deal of money. Because we can afford to do this and others cannot, we are therefore better than they.

2. *Conspicuous Leisure.* We dress in clothes that make it impossible to do practical work. For hundreds of years this was a sign of the nobility who could hire others to toil for them.

3. *Conspicuous Waste.* Based on the theory that practical things are not beautiful, we show our superiority by indulging in pastimes that have no useful purpose but are expensive to maintain. The most elite sports are polo, fox hunting, and yachting. Football is much too plebeian to be a style-setter. The military officer of the old-fashioned war was the epitome of waste — glorious to see but useless in battle.

4. *Vicarious Consumption.* This method of exhibiting supremacy developed with the Industrial Revolution. The merchant barons were not like the aristocrats who were born to money, and had neither the time nor the inclination to participate in the first three categories. They could express their superiority, however, by ensuring that those connected to their households — their wives, children, and servants — were presented to the world in the most costly way possible.

Figure 1-21   Brill Brothers offered a large helping of Vicarious Consumption in the April 1920 *Harper's Bazar.*

Alison Lurie agrees with the Bell–Veblen theories and expands on them in her *The Language of Clothes.* Conspicuous consumption implies not only expensive clothes but also more of them. While the actual working peasants and servants require few garments, the person of status will often wear many layers. In addition to those layers, the wealthy male might be physically larger, for a man's girth could be associated with wealth, status, and power. This was particularly true in the latter part of the nineteenth century. Lurie speculates that when the world is hungry the physical ideal tends toward fat, and when food is more plentiful the physical ideal is thin. A quantity of clothes worn consecutively rather then simultaneously can also attest to the social importance of the wearer. For example, a Savile Row tailor in 1908 displayed a poster that depicts the sixteen different costumes needed for an Edwardian gentleman to be correctly attired for every high-status activity. And just to get through the day his wife might need a morning costume, afternoon costume, tea gown, motoring outfit, and evening dress. Today this type of consumption is evident in the sports specialties, for in certain levels of society one must have the proper togs for tennis, hiking, golf, exercise, skiing, bicycling, swimming, scuba diving, and so forth — correct in both brand and model names. Conspicuous labeling has also become a status factor, in case the observer should miss the value of the garment. Actually, the garment is valuable because of the label, not necessarily because of any better quality in material or workmanship.

Lurie adds the category of theatrical consumption, which she terms the triumph of extravagance. Theatrical extravagance has a long history. Louis XIV of France, for example, did not stint at his festivities at Versailles, and fifteenth- and sixteenth-century masques were often quite sumptuous although performance times were relatively brief. Today, however, stage costumes are made to be worn many times and, if the play is successful, can be used more vigorously than actual garments. Film costume, on the other hand, continues the tradition of extravagance, for months of work and thousands of dollars can be expended on garments that will be seen for only a few moments.

It is the nature of fashion to evolve from one form to another, seldom taking any drastic new departures, often retaining atrophied parts. For example, the codpiece developed in the late fourteenth century to cover the opening in the front of men's hose when they changed from being separate pieces for each leg to one whole unit. For years it was a practical flap that untied, but when the styles of trunk and leg covering changed this was no longer necessary. Rather than disappearing, the codpiece remained for more than fifty years as a padded-out and embroidered decorative element. In the eighteenth century buttons were used to fasten up the large cuffs of the coat sleeves and one was sewn on the backside of the coat to control the heavy pleats that sprang from the hip. To this day buttons can be found on men's coat sleeves, and one is still placed at the waist of the side back seam of the formal tailcoat, though the pleat has diminished to no more than a slight fold in the fabric. No proper gentleman would consider wearing an outfit without these details, though he probably has no idea why they are there.

Fashion dictates with no regard for the individual and no concern for how the style will look on many who copy it. It declares what will be considered beautiful and therefore what will be thought ugly by reason of no longer being fashionable. The immediate past is often thought the most ugly, for time usually softens what is considered unacceptable.

Figure 1-22 A man's girth might be thought to reflect his wealth at certain periods, according to Alison Lurie. Above is James Buchanan ("Diamond Jim") Brady about 1913. (Compare Figure 1-27.)

Figure 1-23 Fashion is slow to discard atrophied parts. The codpiece, a practical clothing element when it developed in the late fourteenth century, stayed on as a decorative focus long after it was functional. Titian's portrait of Carlos V, painted about 1530, is in the Prado, Madrid.

Today the styles of the early 1960s and 1970s look quite unattractive, the fifties are almost quaint, and the thirties seem rather elegant. James Laver set forth in *Taste and Fashion* a timetable for the way a single costume might be perceived as it moves in and out of fashionable acceptability.

Indecent	10 years before its time
Shameless	5 years before its time
Daring	1 year before its time
Smart	————————————
Dowdy	1 year after its time
Hideous	10 years after its time
Ridiculous	20 years after its time
Amusing	30 years after its time
Quaint	50 years after its time
Charming	70 years after its time
Romantic	100 years after its time
Beautiful	150 years after its time

The past is always seen through the eyes of the present, and the appreciation of the styles of the past is influenced by the style currently in vogue. This is often quite evident in "historical" productions, which can reflect more of the current period of the production than the period being reproduced. Nowhere is this more easily observed than in historical cinema created during this century: a Roman orgy filmed in the

Figure 1-24 We see the past through the eyes of the present. Roman bath in Cecil B. DeMille's 1932 epic *The Sign of the Cross*.

Figure I-25   Katharine Hepburn was a lovely queen in RKO's 1936 *Mary of Scotland,* but her silhouette has little in common with that of the real sixteenth-century Mary, Queen of Scots, shown here in a portrait now in the Uffizi Gallery, Florence. Photograph of Miss Hepburn by Bruehl-Bourges. Courtesy *Vogue.* Copyright © 1936 (renewed 1964) by The Condé Nast Publications Inc.

Figure I-26   Henry VIII's girth probably influenced the styles of men's clothing in his time. The portrait is by Hans Holbein.

Figure I-27   Marie Antoinette, at home in the extreme styles of the 1770s, may have encouraged greater excesses. Portrait by Marie Vigée-Lebrun.

1930s certainly has a different flavor than one done in the forties, fifties, or sixties. The closer the historical line is to that of the present period, the more it will be thought acceptable and attractive.

Since the thirteenth century the West has had an ever-changing concept of beauty. What is considered beautiful shifts as the fashion shifts and the fashion dictates the taste of the society. Many elements influence fashion, and it is probably not possible to pinpoint the absolute prime factor in every change. Prominent individuals, designers or lay people, may have a strong influence on a style, though many in the society may actually be already heading in the direction they take. As Henry VIII got wider he greatly influenced the bulky, horizontal, aggressively masculine style of his times. Marie Antoinette's love of extravagance certainly encouraged some of the extremes of the 1770s. Jacqueline Kennedy Onassis did more for the pillbox hat and the A-line dress than any ad campaign could have. Human nature, with its desire for change and its boredom with current styles, can give impetus to these ever-changing modes. A country that is politically strong and expanding will export its styles to others and will pick up fashions from other nations as trade and influences are exchanged. Political and spiritual events often influence fashion: wars in particular affect the modes of a country. Religion, nationalism, and climate may also leave their mark on what is worn and why it continually changes.

One of the strongest determinants in the ever-changing face of fashion, and possibly that which is the most consistent throughout history, is class struggle: the fight of the upper class to maintain its place. This struggle to uphold status and to keep one step ahead of those considered socially inferior causes an incessant fluctuation, a perpetual striving for improvement. Quentin Bell says that this can only happen in a society in which status has the possibility to change, where a middle class is always nipping at the heals of the upper, seeking to take that last step to the high plateau of fashion. When too many arrive, the plateau is moved, for fashion exists when it consists of a select number and is destroyed when too many are part of its elite world. In his *On Fashion* (1818), William Hazlitt explains "[Fashion] exists only by its being participated among a certain number of persons, and its essence is destroyed by being communicated to a greater number. It is a continual struggle between 'the great vulgar and the small' to get the start of or keep up with each other in the race of appearances. . . ." Hazlitt describes how a style is adopted by the great, copied by "the slavish herd of imitators," then allowed to "sink without any further notice into disrepute and contempt. Thus fashion lives only in a perpetual round of giddy innovation and restless variety."

There are no easy explanations of what fashion is and why it does what it does. The costume designer must nevertheless be aware of some of these various general theories of dress and must also understand all the things the garments may more specifically reveal about the people they adorn.

The challenge of costume design

Costume design is a fascinating world; it must deal with all the vagaries of fashion, take a firm grasp on the "normal behavior that is crazy" and the "perpetual round of giddy innovation and restless variety," and make it meaningful to an audience. It must interpret an area that often defies explanation, distill it so a few strokes say a great deal, blend it with the innovative ideas of many others, and produce a result that is at once individually creative and integrated so firmly into a whole that it cannot be extracted as a separate entity. Costume design is a world of challenges, and these challenges make it a stimulating, ever-changing, often difficult, but seldom boring field of endeavor.

The meaning of clothes

There may be no overall logic to the way fashion moves through history, but clothes worn within any specific time period can reveal a great deal about the wearer. Whether modern or period, garments make a statement that is perceived and interpreted by an audience. Objectively, clothing can easily convey information about sex, age, occupation, social status, geography, season, time of day, action, and period. On a more subjective level the personality and attitudes of the wearer may be indicated by his or her garments. Since anything the actor wears is a costume that will communicate information to the audience, the designer should consider all these variables in order to select the correct message.

What the costume may reveal

SEX

For the most part, clothing indicates sex immediately and obviously. One exception might be those young people of the late 1960s and early 1970s who used clothing and hairstyle to make the sexes look alike. This phenomenon was particularly interesting because it happened in a different manner on two levels of the social scale. The flower children of the sixties took an eclectic view of fashion, with both sexes choosing from rather styleless, earthy, "I-can't-be-bothered-with-society" garments; a few years later the "in" set opted for a high-tech, sleek look that had an almost androgynous air. The manner in which clothing emphasizes or deemphasizes the sex of the wearer can be very telling. A woman in a man-tailored suit with her hair in a bun affects others differently than one with long curls wearing a low-cut, frilly dress.

AGE

Each era has its own symbols for youth and age. In general and logically, young people tend to reveal their figures because they are usually in better shape, while older people tend to cover them up — though the dictates of fashion in certain periods may negate this. Clothing in the twelfth century was bulky, loose, and flowing, good for the older figure but not particularly advantageous to the youthful one. In the fourteenth century clothing became extremely tight-fitting; youth was in its prime and age could look somewhat uncomfortable. The miniskirt favors youth; the sack dress, age. But in any period color, cut, and fit can be great clues to the age of the wearer. In addition to giving information about the wearer's actual age, they may give clues to

Figure 1-28 Fashion designer Rudi Gernreich promoted the unisex look at the beginning of the 1970s. Here his models Tom and Renée wear caftans.

Figure 1-29 Every era has its own symbols for youth and age. Fashion kept Victorian children very much in their place until they were considered old enough to assume adult apparel. An illustration from *La Mode Illustrée*, Paris, 1881.

how he or she feels about age and what other age might be preferred, for he or she might wear clothes that are more suitable to either a younger or an older person.

OCCUPATION

Workers in many occupations can be instantly categorized by what they wear, and this recognition can cause an emotional response. The uniforms of the military and the police are easily recognized and act as symbols of the authority behind them. The costume of the priest and nun elicit a reaction to the church hierarchy they represent. The mailman, nurse, bellboy, chef, and many others proclaim a specific manner of making a living in their garb. Some clothes only give an indication of occupation. A man in jeans and a T-shirt does different work than a man in a business suit. Coveralls could indicate a mechanic, painter, or someone cleaning his garage, but probably not a bank teller or shoe salesman. Time can also vary the occupational meaning. A man in elaborate, particolored clothes in the fourteenth century is probably a noble; in the fifteenth century he would be the court jester.

SOCIAL STATUS

For many years, a primary means of indicating social status was the practicality (or more specifically, impracticality) of the garments worn. The upper classes tended to wear clothes that made it impossible for them to do any work. Combinations of corsets, voluminous gowns, and hoops kept the noblewomen isolated and aloof from the workaday world. A fashion source of the eighteenth century indicates that "a

Figure 1-30 Members of the medical profession can often be recognized by their garments, no matter what the period. Nurses in training at Bellevue Hospital, New York, about 1900.

Figure 1-31 The large gap in social status between these two groups is immediately evident in their attire. Etching in *Harper's Weekly* for February 1, 1873.

slovenly fellow might hustle into his clothes in an hour, but a gentleman could scarcely dress in less than two." The result of this careful dressing could not be soiled by menial labor. The cost of the garment is also commensurate with social status. The lower class has garments with fabric of lower quality, and in earlier periods with less decoration, fewer accessories, and simpler colors, since the cost of dye was prohibitive. While there are some general rules to be made about clothes and status, much depends upon the period in which the fashion functions. In the 1770s the woman of fashion had a high, elaborate coiffure and gown with much color, fullness, ruffles and bows; her maid was drabber in color, plainer in fabric and style, and coiffed simply. In the 1950s the lower-class girl might have worn a beehive, bouffant hairdo with full, ruffly, colorful clothes, while the society matron wore a basic black dress, simply but beautifully cut of fine fabric, adorned only with a gold circle pin or a string of pearls.

Figure 1-32 There can be no visual question that these are members of a Scots regiment, the 42nd Highlanders. Musée de l'Armée, Parigi.

GEOGRAPHIC AREA

The country in which a person lives always affects the way he or she dresses, but in the modern world the variations may not be strong. Small differences can be very significant, however, in creating a special effect. A woman's kerchief tied under the chin might seem European. Tied behind the neck it might be American suburban. Reversed to tie on top of the head it appears West Indian. Historically the costumes of the last six centuries in the Western world might differ more between classes than countries, though some national characteristics and climatic influences may be present. Specific national costumes, or elements of them, have strong recognition value, and the costumes of the Eastern world are very different from those of the West.

SEASON AND WEATHER

Clothing usually changes with the seasons in a very logical way. Hot weather brings out fewer garments of lighter fabrics; cold weather means more and heavier clothing. Historically the difference tended to be more in the weight of the fabric than in the shapes or number of garments. Women could be encased in layers of corsets, hoops, petticoats, and gowns in summer as well as winter. Logic is not always king in the fashion world, even in our enlightened modern age. The miniskirt in midwinter left little to the imagination and much to medication.

Figure 1-33 Although the shapes of the gowns are quite similar, it is easy to see which ladies are strolling in winter and which are about to embark on a spring walk. From *La Mode Illustrée,* 1880 and 1881.

TIME OF DAY

A bathrobe, housedress, cocktail dress, evening gown, or nightgown might be worn at any time of the day, but each tends to suggest a specific time. If a garment is worn at a time other than that usually accepted by society as "proper," an even stronger statement is made. Any garment worn at an inappropriate time calls attention to itself. A person entering in pajamas when everyone else is dressed for a cocktail party must have a very specific reason for the incongruity.

ACTIVITY

Wearing certain clothes may imply that a specific activity is connected with the wearer, whether it has happened, is going on at the moment, or will happen in the future. A nightgown could lead to bed; a white sweater, shorts, socks, and rubber-soled sneakers may indicate a tennis game is in the offing. Enveloping black capes may imply a secretive meeting, and the buckling on of armor connotes an impending battle. In Shakespeare's *The Tempest* Prospero dons his magic robes when he is about to call forth his mystical powers, and Ariel assumes many different shapes for the tasks he must perform.

HISTORICAL PERIOD

The shape of the clothes provides the first identification of a historical period for each era casts its own shadow and has its own ideals of beauty. Historical costumes may not be exact replicas of what was actually worn. History may be the base, with a theatrical reality created that is more meaningful to the staged situation in which the costume will be presented. Clothes lend a great deal to personal identification, and the study of how clothes are worn in modern society can be a clue to how clothes have been worn historically. Use of the historical period to produce meaningful costumes is discussed more fully in Chapter 3.

PSYCHOLOGICAL FACTORS

In the areas discussed above, fairly objective decisions about wearing apparel can be made. There are specific clothes a middle-aged, lower-class scrubwoman would have worn on her way to work in England on a snowy winter morning in 1870. She would most likely have worn heavy, practical skirts and petticoats with a slight fullness to the back, sturdy shoes, a loose top, and a large, shapeless shawl. But if she tried to pretend to her neighbors that she were really a lady's maid a new world of possibilities would have opened up. She might have gone to work and come back home in something with much more style — garments that were more fitted, a real bustle, and better shoes, to give the

Figure 1-34   Rebellion has its own strict dress conformity. Hell's Angels, 1982. Wide World Photo.

impression that her work gave her some status and let her mingle with a better class of people. Then when she got to her place of business and could no longer be seen by those who lived near her, she would have changed into the more practical garments.

Clothes express people's attitudes toward themselves and their society, both what they wear and how they wear it. A certain type of clothing can be worn to conform to a particular society or to rebel against it. If enough people rebel in the same direction, a new society is formed—with rules of conformity as strong as those of the old, but along slightly different lines. Should a person rebel only slightly, he or she may have the "proper" garments but wear them differently; absolute conformists would wear only those articles that would ensure their blending into the crowd at all times.

Clothes can be used to try to change an existing condition. Those who wish to move up the social ladder might dress not as their peers but as those in the group to which they aspire. On the emotional level, a person in a gloomy state of mind might deliberately choose clothes that appear more cheerful, while another might select clothes that reinforce the gloom and broadcast it to the world. The extrovert may wear something outlandish for the pure joy of causing a stir; the introvert may wear only what others are wearing for the security of being part of the crowd.

Figure 1-35   Modart's ad in the November 1, 1921, *Vogue* appeals to the desire to be attractive, claiming the credit can go to the corset "when your appearance is admired."

Clothes can be selected to fulfill the desire to be attractive to the opposite sex. Items can be chosen because they are thought to have sex appeal, though this may be an illusion perpetrated by the advertising firms of the world. The desire to be considered attractive is present in all age groups, and the parts of the body thought to be most alluring vary considerably during history. What was once considered attractive in a specific historical setting must be considered along with the standards of beauty accepted by a contemporary audience.

Objective and subjective factors work together to determine why people clothe themselves as they do. Without an understanding on both levels a costume designer cannot fully develop the possibilities presented by the characters in a given situation. This understanding comes from extensive observation and research.

Interpreting the script and enhancing the characterization

The beginning of a theatrical presentation is a dramatic idea that may take the form of a script or merely a scenario. From this either the producer or director establishes the major focus of the interpretation. The actors and designers help fill out this concept. Designers function as part of a team. Their duty is to work within an established framework and add as much as they can to produce a specific dramatic result without placing undue emphasis on their areas of endeavor. As mentioned, theatre is a collaborative art. One cannot strive to achieve certain effects for selfish reasons; the effect might be grand, but the quality of the total production will suffer unless everyone works toward a common goal. As part of the team, the costume designer should know as much as possible about what is going on in all areas, as should everyone else involved with the production. Unity is best achieved through knowledge, understanding, and good communication.

Costume interpretation draws both from the written material and from the directorial approach. The costume designer studies the script thoroughly to understand both its emotional tone and its physical requirements. The designer must look for the primary and secondary themes of the play and develop an understanding of the characters and their interrelationships. By carefully reading and rereading the script the designer should see how the plot of the play flows, where the important moments are, which characters hold the primary focus, which are minor but with important input, and which merely fill out the scene. He or she can discern what changes occur in them as the story progresses. When the designer is quite familiar with the script, the time has come to discuss the production with the director. The director will probably offer an interpretation of the script to the designers. The ideal interaction occurs when the director and designers exchange ideas, discuss possible objectives, and together evolve the goals for the production. The director should be the focal point of these discussions: it is usually the directorial approach that balances all the elements and acts as the guide for the working relationship. From these discussions the costume designer can then develop an approach that considers both the impact of each individual costume and all the costumes seen as a whole, maintaining a balance between the two. If a costume works only on one level, it does not work for the production. The problems that arise from this lack of integration may be most evident in the "star" costume, which can be designed with the wishes of one person in mind, often with no thought to the total concept.

It is possible for the costumes in a production to be simply decorative or symbolic, but the character costume is more common and contributes more to the total impact of the play. The character costume grows out of the interpretation of the dramatic elements present in a certain role, while the decorative costume is often no more than an extension of the scenic elements. The coronation robes of Richard III are not just typical symbols of a king but special garments selected because of a unique dramatic situation; the pages who stand behind his throne may be necessary only to fill out the scenic picture.

MOTHER COURAGE

PREGNANT PEASANT AND CHILD

Figure 1-36 A great many dramatic possibilities have been explored to produce these character costumes for peasants in Brecht's *Mother Courage.* Design by Ainslie Bruneau. Swatches (below), which have been enlarged to show more clearly the types of textures to be used, were attached to the rendering.

Figure 1-37   The costume for Saint Michael was more a decorative symbol than based on character. His wings were part of the set and not attached to his body at all. Design by Frank Bevan for a production of *Faust* at Yale University in 1949. Beinecke Rare Book and Manuscript Library, Yale.

Script influence on the character costume

The character costume develops from what the characters say and do and what others say about them. It may or may not deal with what the playwright has indicated in the stage directions, depending upon the specific director's approach. Just as people dress according to the many influences on them in daily life, so does the dress of the actor reflect the

Figure I-38   A "small-town boy goes to the big city" cliché costume was just what was needed for the title character in a Carnegie-Mellon University production of *Merton of the Movies* in 1982. Pencil sketch by Cletus Anderson.

influences of the script. Sometimes the character is not well delineated and remains two-dimensional and obvious. The characters in the musicals *L'il Abner* and *Superman* are never any deeper than the two-dimensional comic-strip characters on which they are based. A clichéd villain may very well wear a black hat. An ingenue might be costumed in a dress with frothy yellow ruffles, conforming to stereotyped audience expectations; but if she is trying too hard to make an impression her character takes on another dimension, and too many ruffles or too much jewelry may help to show this.

As the character progresses through a play, so can the costumes progress to underline the change. Costumes can be used to indicate differences of location or time, emotional modifications within the character, or mood variations of the script. When Blanche first appears in Tennessee Williams' *A Streetcar Named Desire* she is a strong figure trying to maintain a foothold on reality. As the play progresses this foothold weakens and the strength crumbles. All of this should be evident in what she wears and how she wears it. For her entrance she would wear her clothes correctly and with confidence; as she leaves she appears lost and uncertain. While the costume can be a great aid in underscoring character development, the design must be carefully considered so that it will not anticipate an action. It must show what the actor is when he begins the scene, not predetermine the outcome of an interchange that will take place. Regina in Lillian Hellman's *Another Part of the Forest* must seem a lovely, charming, dutiful daughter. The audience must not immediately recognize her as the cold, hard, calculating woman the play reveals her to be.

Symbolizing the role

The costume should give as much meaning to the character as possible, but this does not necessarily mean it should symbolize the role. There may be good reasons not to dress a woman of ill repute in a tight-fitting, leg-revealing red satin dress. A jealous wife need not necessarily wear green; nor should young lovers both appear clad in pale blue so the audience knows at once that they will end up together. The actor, not the costume, is the primary means of communication to the audience. The costume designer should not try to do it all. There are, of course, occasions when blatant symbols are just right. This usually happens when the character itself is not too well defined and the action requires instant, two-dimensional recognition. In Jean Giraudoux's *The Madwoman of Chaillot* the costume designer has a wonderful opportunity to go into careful, individualized character delineation in the costumes of the four elderly women since the lines of the script tell a great deal about each one of them, but the presidents, prospectors, and press agents sent to oblivion are presented by the playwright only as symbols and must be easily identified by the audience.

Subjective character indications

Even the more subtle, subjective indications of character must be carefully worked out to be effective on two levels. They can enrich the costume by a careful attention to detail that expands the understanding of the character, but the costume must seem appropriate to the situation whether the subjective indications come across to the audience or not. The audience must accept the costume as appropriate to the scene, even though it may not comprehend the background reasons for the choice of any particular garments. The designer might decide an actor playing a conservative part should wear a dark blue suit and lighter blue shirt; the addition of a red paisley tie and handkerchief can indicate that he secretly wishes to break out of the boring mold that confines him, adding subtle dimension to the effect. If this works within the context of the scene, so much the better. If, however, the tie and handkerchief become the misplaced focus of attention, they must change no matter how strongly the designer and actor feel about the innermost desires of the character. There can be a tendency for the designer, actor, or even director to become more subjective than the play can stand by bringing too many subtle nuances to a character through what he wears and how he wears it. This could prove quite confusing to the audience, which is guided solely by what is presented on stage at any given moment. If the extras reinforce the primary interpretation, fine; if they start off in a direction of their own, they must go.

Figure 1-39   At the beginning of Lillian Hellman's *Another Part of the Forest* Regina's costume must not give away her true character. Design by Bob Perdziola.

The world of the play

The costume in a theatrical production is used to help create a reality for a specific situation. This reality is removed from the everyday world because it is by nature theatrical and intended for presentation to an audience. All costumes must reflect and reinforce the reality framed within the theatrical event. The degree of difference from the real world varies immensely with the type of play and the manner in which it will be presented, and the costume style should reflect this. The script will give the first indication of the world to be created. Both the subject matter and style of language can guide the designer to an effective approach. Costumes for Shakespeare's *Hamlet* differ from those of Arthur Miller's *Death of a Salesman,* though both plays are tragedies.

Elsinore is peopled with characters who speak in iambic pentameter, are confronted with monumental problems, and must fill the vast spaces that suggest the castle around them. Willy Loman lives in a small, middle-class world full of the problems that could beset almost any man, though even here the designer must search for those things that make Willy special and help the audience want to cry out with his wife "So attention must be paid!"

A comic world is not like a tragic one and neither would be the same as the environment required for a melodrama. Greek tragedy has a much different format than Elizabethan tragedy, just as Greek tragedy done in a more classical translation will require a milieu different from one transposed into modern vernacular. Every play needs a world of its own and costumes that will accent its uniqueness.

Figure 1-40   The world of *Hamlet* suggests heightened feelings; sketches can be made with a broad stroke. Costume for Claudius. Watercolor by Cletus Anderson.

Figure 1-41   Willy Loman's *Death of a Salesman* world is small; his costume should reflect attention to small details. Pencil sketch by Cletus Anderson.

The type of physical presentation the play will have can also greatly affect the style of costumes that will best fit into this world. Costumes designed for a production of *Hamlet* to be presented in a 2000-seat auditorium with a proscenium stage would be different than those created for an arena that seats 200. In the large proscenium house most of the audience will be at a distance from the actors and the impact of the costumes must carry to them, while most in the smaller arena will be near enough to the actors to see even delicate detailing. More scenery can work as a background to the costumes on the proscenium stage; an arena eliminates many background pieces and focuses more on the actors themselves.

The amount of money available to mount a production also greatly affects the type of world that can be created on stage. As nice as it would be to consider art only for art's sake, ten costumes that can be made with a $200 budget will differ greatly from ten that can cost $2000. This does not mean the former will necessarily be of poorer quality than the latter, but they will be different. Limitations can be parlayed into ways of exploring new possibilities and discovering new and exciting solutions.

Figure 1-42   Time and money must be considered when designing. The single costume for Beulah will take more than twice as much of both than the costumes for all four bathing beauties. Designs in pencil by Cletus Anderson for *Merton of the Movies.*

The actor and the costume

The costume and the actor should be two inseparable components of a single visual effect. Unfortunately, this is not always the case. If the two cannot work together, the desired visual effect will not be perceived. For actors the costume is an externalization of the character and an extension of their interpretation of the role. As a mask it can free them from their own problems and help them become completely absorbed in the part they play. For this reason some actors may find it difficult to use their own clothes in a contemporary production; too familiar, they may recall too much of an actor's real-life role to allow the proper release. This is not to say that the costume should remain an unfamiliar object to the actor. By the time the play opens the actor should feel that the costume is the real clothing of the character.

The actor is not usually directly involved in designing costumes but must never be far out of the designer's mind. The final section of Chapter 2 discusses the designer's physical and psychological approach to the actor in greater detail.

Costumed groups and movement

Many theatrical productions use the costume as a decorative element not based on character development, but still founded in the basic interpretation or approach to the piece. Even many serious dramas have scenes based on spectacle where some of the actors are really part of the scenery and basically help create an appropriate environment in which the action takes place. Unlike the set, which is more stationary, here the concern is with a moving visual impact that may shift many times during the scene. The character of the individual actor does not concern the designer in this case; what is important is the character of the scene and the total feeling all the costumes must produce to convey the right atmosphere for both the scene and the whole play. A thorough discussion must take place with the director to clarify the blocking and determine what the exact effect of the color and mass of the costumed actors will be.

There are many different instances where groups of costumed actors add to the overall atmosphere of the play, though the individuals within the groups may not be well delineated. The crippled masses of Bertolt Brecht's *Mother Courage* create a specific visual effect, as do the nymphs and reapers in the masque scene of Shakespeare's *The Tempest*. The "tramps and able bodied paupers" in Act 3 of George Bernard Shaw's *Man and Superman* are not individually defined, but the group-character feeling is very strong. The courtiers Saint Joan finds as she

searches out the Dauphin are stage-dressing, but very different from
those who people the court of Richard III as he takes power. The
inherent characterization the chorus line of a 1950s musical may be
only skin-deep, but some sort of group characteristic does define its
presence. In *Guys and Dolls* the Hot Box girls differ from the Salvation
Army team, who in turn are different from the boys of Nathan Detroit's
floating crap game, yet the costume scheme must encompass all three
groups so they hold together and present a unified production along
with the more specifically characterized principals. Designing a group
of costumes for a specific total effect often takes a very special approach. The group characteristic must be clearly defined, and within
this approach the costumes that make up the group should be designed
for very specific people. These may not be differentiated at all by the
script, but the designer can give to each person certain attributes that
make him or her unique within the framework of the whole group.
Given a "crowd of townspeople" the result can be bland and uninter-
esting for both the designer and the audience if a group of miscella-
neous clothes are assembled and distributed merely to cover bodies. If
the designer sees the crowd as an assembly of individuals — the town
drunk, the busybody, the shoe salesman, the piano teacher, the mailman — these people are more real and make up a crowd with more
vitality, enriching the play.

   Costumes create a constantly shifting pattern of colors, textures, and
shapes, and the visual impact of a group of costumes must be effective
in numerous compositions. Each costume should be planned with the

Figure 1-43   A group will be
much more interesting if each
member is given individual
characteristics. Pencil sketch by
Cletus Anderson for the
Simsbury Gents in *Merton of the
Movies.*

total effect in mind, so that as the stage picture shifts the focus remains constant. A certain idea might be perfect for a particular moment, but unless it also works with the prior and following action, it can't be used. One example might be found in *Macbeth*. Lady Macbeth is at home, reading her husband's letter telling her of the witches, their prophecy, and the promotion he has already received. A messenger comes, Macbeth enters, and they are reunited. A designer might wish to costume Lady Macbeth in something casual and intimate to accentuate the sexual bond between her and her husband. In just a few moments, however, she must return to greet Duncan and his retinue and take center stage amid a group of nobles. Her costume, with only minor changes, must then accommodate both situations.

Costume design and fashion design

Costume design is quite different from fashion design and experience in one area may be of little help in the other. Costume design concerns itself with dramatic interpretation and character; it deals with the overall production concept first, the costumes as a whole, then the individual costume. Fashion design need not be collaborative, nor is it concerned with character relationships. Certain trends are set that may or may not be followed; a unity may be established for a particular show but it is not governed by the thoughts and actions of others; a reaction is sought from the finished garment, but a reaction based solely on the garment and not on its relationship to the wearer. Even the method of presentation of the idea differs greatly. The fashion plate is elegant, characterless, often deemphasizing sex. The costume plate strives for character, life, and a flavor of the production.

Figure 1-44 The fashion plate can be quite elegant but does not necessarily deal with character or dramatic interpretation. Figure from a Bergdorf-Goodman ad in *Vogue*, October 1976.

Theatre, a collaborative art

Theatre is a collaborative art. Costume design is only one element of the whole, and blends with the actors, sets, and lights to fill out a director's interpretation of a playwright's idea. But within these confines costume design can be an art in itself, given the right preparation and execution. Costumes that "just happen" might not actually detract from the

Figure 1-45 This simple costume, portrayed interestingly and thoughtfully, was one element in the visual atmosphere of the production of *Faust* designed by Frank Bevan at Yale in 1949. Beinecke Rare Book and Manuscript Library, Yale.

performance, but an opportunity would have been missed to enrich the production. More than ever before the production tendency is to more selective scenery and prop pieces, letting the costumes carry a greater responsibility for creating the visual atmosphere. By their very nature thrust and arena stages are quite costume- and property-oriented. As the emphasis on the costume grows, so does the responsibility of the costume designer, but it is a responsibility with very specific limitations. Once the script or scenario is selected and the direction for the interpretation chosen, everything used to realize the theatrical goal must work for a unified production.

2

The costume approach

The beginning of a project can be a
very exciting time for a designer. A new
challenge is present; a new world waits to
be researched, probed, and developed.
Even if the designer is working on a
familiar script, this is a fresh approach
involving different people and another
opportunity for the exchange of ideas.
The process of designing for the stage is
especially stimulating because it incorporates
this interchange of ideas and encourages

communication between a number of people. This give and take among diverse, creative, energetic men and women provides an opportunity for growth as all seek to bring the play to life before an audience. The costume designer should be eager to develop sketches that will reinforce the interpretation that has grown from this collaboration, and from these sketches build costumes that will enhance the actors' characterizations. The creative urge should remain strong even though there are many steps that must be taken before pencil is set to paper to draw a costume.

First impressions

The costume designer's first concern is to read the script and become thoroughly familiar with the problems and challenges at hand. The initial readthrough should determine the emotional impact of the script; dealing with specific costume problems will come later. The readthrough should develop a sympathy for the aesthetic needs of the play. The overall mood may suggest colors, textures, fabrics, silhouette, and detail treatment. Within the overall feeling specific scenes will have their own emotional requirements, as will specific characters. Thoughts should be jotted down during this initial reading. Additional questions and observations, noted during a second or third time through the script to become more familiar with its ideas, will be added to the first impressions and all taken to the director, with whom they can be discussed to clarify the interpretation that will be used for the entire production.

Take, for example, Molière's *Le Bourgeois Gentilhomme.* The immediate impact is one of bright frivolity and surface plushness, color at fairly high intensity, crisp rather than heavy fabrics. Monsieur Jourdain, the would-be gentleman, is the broadest character in a broadly treated comedy. There are three sets of lovers who must reflect differences in their ages and stations. A number of visual aspects can be considered to advance the spectacle, climaxing with the Turkish scene, in which Jourdain is gulled by his disguised friends as they perform a ridiculous ceremony to make him a *"mamamouchie."* Many of the extremes of the period can be used; the historical setting of the comedy is the French Baroque, a period in which excess was admired and—to modern sensibilities—carried to an extreme. The play was written in reaction to such frivolity and the fun Molière is having at the expense of the

Preceding page: Mr. Henderson's Hamlet with poor Yorick's skull looks much more at home in the eighteenth century than in Gothic Denmark.

"stylish" element of his society should not be overlooked. The designer should record any and all ideas that come to mind and should review these ideas frequently to keep the creative process in motion. These ideas need not be just words; pictures, fabrics, rough sketches, and any other visual aids should be gathered together. An impression of a design concept is not merely an intellectual exercise; words conjure up different images to different people. Anything that actually can be seen and discussed will help establish a more solid common ground for the entire production staff. The designer will also be better prepared for an intelligent interchange of ideas if he or she is knowledgeable about the playwright, understands something of the cultural milieu in which the playwright wrote, and is familiar with the social history behind the play.

Determining the basic interpretation

After the designer is familiar with the script, a discussion with the director will clarify the basic concepts and settle the interpretation to be used. In most theatrical productions the director establishes the guiding concept and sets the lead to be followed by all others working on the show. Theatre is a collaborative art, but it needs one guiding hand. The director should function as a leader, however, not as an absolute dictator. All the designers should bring ideas that might enrich the production.

This preliminary meeting should include the director and all the designers; the success of the visual aspects of the production depends upon good coordination between the sets, lights, and costumes. The shapes and colors to be used to establish specific moods must be agreed upon by all, for each visual element must interact with the others to enhance the total effect. The designers work to create a unique world for a particular production and the better their understanding and the more clearly the ideas are defined at this point, the more valid and convincing this world will be.

The director may have one central theme that will stand as the key to the production. From this will come a choice of period. The degree of reality to be used is established although it may not be maintained at the same level for all the different design elements. For example, a production of *The Seagull* done on an arena stage would most probably use costumes influenced strongly by the actual clothes of the time, but the set could give just a suggestion of the architecture and grounds of the prerevolutionary Russian country estate. The properties, on the other hand, might be quite authentic, perhaps even real furniture of the period. Variations in approach can mesh together well if those involved clearly understand the aims set forth and why they are best fulfilled by a certain style. Scenery involves more than recreating a specific place; it requires a selection of elements that define a point of view, all the while considering the limitations of the theatre and its stage space. This can lead to a degree of stylization. The costume, based on the human figure, is more limited, but rarely must it be absolutely authentic or realistic. A stylized set can lead to arbitrary lighting, in which light is used to its best dramatic advantage without the need for a motivating source of illumination (such as the moon, a chandelier, or an incandescent bulb).

Figure 2-1 These costumes for Chekhov's *The Sea Gull*, designed for a production at Brandeis University in 1966, are based on actual clothes worn at the period of the play. Watercolor sketches by Cletus Anderson.

Coordinating sets and costumes

Ideas for either costumes or sets can come first. There is no rule that one has to follow the other. If the dramatic values of one are more important to the production, then they may receive first consideration.

Some of the areas that need a common understanding are:

Period and source material. One design element may need to be more realistic than another, but both should be based upon the same background material. Often specific painters or books can be used as a key reference. Such visual inspiration can vary widely, from the paintings of Michaelangelo to the drawings of Aubrey Beardsley to the Sears, Roebuck catalogue. The best feeling for a period often comes from sources contemporary to the play's period: statues, illustrated manuscripts, paintings, photographs, etchings, catalogues, magazines, and so on. The basic guide to a color scheme can often be found in a painting. *A Midsummer Night's Dream* might be staged basing sets and costumes on a pastoral scene by Fragonard or the shadowy atmosphere of *Hamlet* on a painting by Rembrandt.

Color and contrast. A limited palette can produce a specific dramatic effect. An entire production could be based on one color, or specific colors could be assigned to various scenes. There are three choices to consider in terms of contrast. The contrast of all the elements can be kept close: the set can be darker with lighter costumes, or the set lighter with darker costumes. If the light-to-dark ratio is close, color can be used to separate the actors from the sets. Light will usually mold the actor, but if the costume and set colors are too similar the actor will tend to blend into the background. There are instances, of course, where this is desirable. If the set is dark and light costumes are used, the lighting can easily highlight the figure. Light sets with dark costumes present certain problems, however, for the details of the face and figure tend to blur and a high light level may accent the set too strongly.

Type of detail. The approach to the detailing of the set and properties might well influence the costumes, and vice versa. If one is scaled up and the other kept at a realistic level, the realistic element will lose importance. When the set is to be quite detailed and busy, the costume approach must separate the actors from the active background. If one element approaches the detailing as a means to comment on the period, this will influence the audience and the way it perceives the other elements.

Movement and stage space. Any potential movement and blocking problems should be considered and a feeling for the stage pictures

Figure 2-2 The scale of the detail is heightened in this costume for one former wife in Béla Bartók's one-act opera *Bluebeard's Castle,* produced at Carnegie-Mellon University in 1976. Design by Cletus Anderson.

desired should be explored. The set and costume designers and director must deal with such questions as: How will the movement of the actors be affected by the space on stage? How must the costume be designed to permit easy movement? Must the costumes be scaled to work within space determined by the sets, or will the costumes determine the scale of the sets?

Textures and fabrics. A realistic production may dictate the types of textures and fabrics that will be used, but designers often deliberately decide to let a specific style predominate. The choice could be for heavy, nubby textures; deep, rich piles; shiny, reflective fabrics; or a light, airy, floating treatment. If the designers' ideas about textures and fabrics are not well coordinated an imbalance could result. *A Midsummer Night's Dream* done in heavily encrusted, realistic Elizabethan costumes against a chiffon-swagged forest will never mesh properly. Similarly, a heavy, textural Elsinore surrounding lightweight cotton costumes will not create a unified visual world for *Hamlet.* Different types of textures and fabrics can be deliberately mixed, but this should be done for a specific result, not just by accident.

Figure 2-3   Coarse textures are indicated in this sketch for the Parade Master in the film *Knightriders,* directed by George Romero. Design by Cletus Anderson.

Establishing needs

Once the general trends have been set, the costume designer can get down to specifics with the director. Both must establish a clear understanding of what is to happen. Quick sketches or pictures from source books provide a concrete reference that will minimize the possible confusion of mere verbal description. The designer should find out how the director wishes to use the costumes, make sure the director knows how they will work on the actors, and explain the limitations the costumes may impose on the production. The director should provide a scene breakdown that details who will be onstage, and when. The two should also settle the time sequences involved and what costume changes might be necessary to indicate them. If the sequencing of the script is to be changed, this should be discussed. Moving scenes around or eliminating intermissions can affect the costume treatment. Taking as much information as possible from the director, the designer can now go back to the script and organize his or her work.

The costume lists

The preliminary approach to the play has been set by the director and designers and the costume designer can now sit down to define the task at hand as concretely as possible and determine the actual physical needs of the play. It should now be possible systematically to lay the groundwork that will enable the designer to express ideas artistically and develop a costume sketch that will satisfy both the aesthetic and the practical needs of the production.

The preliminary costume tally for a play should include every costume or part of costume that will be needed. The designer must go through the script, listing every character in each scene with an indication of what he or she is wearing, even if it is a repeat of something worn before. If a coat is added or a garment taken off, this must be noted. Any extras, crowds, servants, armies, or the like must be tallied. On the same list any action that will affect the costumes should be included, plus any color or costume prop references in the script, annotated to indicate whether these are necessary to the action or can be changed to accommodate a different scheme. Notes should be made where any costume changes occur to anticipate any possible problems involved. Routine information is not the only objective at this time, and clues to the characterizations and imagery found in the script can also be assembled. This is often a long list, unwieldy in its original form, but a necessary step on the path to the actual working outlines.

From these preliminary notations come two essential charts: the costume list (page 61) and the costume scene breakdown (page 62). These may need to be established simultaneously since decisions made about one may affect the other. The costume scene breakdown lists each character and each scene in chart form, as shown in the example following the scenario. A check is placed in each scene in which a character appears, with an indication of what he or she will be wearing. The costume list indicates each character and each different costume he or she will wear. Each costume is numbered consecutively so at the end of the list the total number of costumes in the show is easily seen, and each costume for a particular character is numbered so that the quantity of costumes for any given character is readily available. The list is broken down into Men's Costumes and Women's Costumes, or in larger productions Principal Men, Principal Women, Chorus Men, Chorus Women, and/or Extra Men and Extra Women.

The following scenario is taken from Tennessee Williams' *Summer and Smoke,* Part One of the original Broadway version. This extremely brief indication of the plot may help explain how the costume lists are compiled, but this example will be more useful to the designer who reads the actual script.

Figure 2-4   Quick sketches can be used to suggest ideas to the director. These were done for Molière's *Le Bourgeois Gentilhomme,* produced at the Great Lakes Shakespeare Festival, Lakewood, Ohio, 1969. Designs by Cletus Anderson.

The scene for *Summer and Smoke* is a simultaneous setting, showing a fountain and angel in the town park or square, the parlor of the Episcopal rectory, and the office in the neighboring doctor's home. The action is continuous.

Prologue   *Dusk, an evening in May in the first few years of this century.* John Buchanan and Alma Winemiller, ten-year-old children, are playing near the fountain. Alma already has "the dignity of an adult; there is a quality of extraordinary tenderness or spirituality in her."

Scene 1   *July 4th, shortly before the First World War.* The scene moves from fading sunlight to dusk at the fountain and town square. The Reverend and Mrs. Winemiller, Alma's parents, sit on the bench. Mrs. Winemiller has "slipped into a state of perverse childishness. She is known as Mr. Winemiller's 'cross.'" Alma sings offstage as John enters. He is "brilliantly and restlessly alive in a stagnant society." A couple, Dusty and Pearl, stroll by. Dr. Buchanan, John's father, confronts him, then leaves. Alma enters, flustered after her song, now "prematurely spinsterish," "dressed in pale yellow and carrying a yellow silk parasol." She asks her father to open her bag for her to get her handkerchief. The others leave and Alma and John talk. Rosa Gonzales crosses to the fountain, dressed "in almost outrageous finery, with lustrous feathers on her hat, greenish blue, a cascade of them, also diamond-and-emerald earrings." Nellie Ewell, a girl of sixteen, stops to chat with John and Alma. John leaves and Roger Doremus, "a small man, somewhat like a sparrow," comes to walk Alma home.

Scene 2   *Inside the Rectory.* It is obviously some time later. Mrs. Winemiller has a white plumed hat she has stolen from a shop in the town, concealing it in her parasol. Later in the scene this hat gets torn in a fight with Alma. Mr. Winemiller passes through the room, concerned about the cost of the hat and the embarrassing situation in which his wife has placed them. Alma is getting ready for her group meeting, to be held that evening. She invites John, who is seen in his house. Nellie comes by for her singing lesson.

Scene 3   *Inside the Rectory.* The meeting is in progress, attended by Roger; Vernon, "a willowy younger man with an open collar and Byronic locks"; Mrs. Basset; and Rosemary, "a wistful older girl with a long neck and thick-lensed glasses." John enters, "immaculately groomed and shining," carrying a jacket he leaves behind when he hastily departs.

Scene 4   *Inside the Doctor's Office.* John's arm is wounded and he and Rosa are bandaging it. Alma enters, ostensibly to ask old Dr. Buchanan to give her something to calm her nerves. John loans her his handkerchief, takes her pulse using his pocketwatch, then unbuttons and speaks of the "little pearl buttons" on her blouse when he listens to her heart. He also comments on her topaz ring.

Scene 5   *Inside the Rectory.* A few days later; Alma and her parents are in the parlor. Alma is going out with John and before she leaves picks up a hat, gloves, and veil.

Scene 6   *An arbor at the Moon Lake Casino, a few moments later.* John, in a white suit, and Alma stand in the arbor because Alma refuses to enter the Casino. A waiter, Dusty, brings some wine. John lifts her veil to kiss her, then offends her and leaves to call a taxi.

The scenario for Part Two is not included here, but two important costume references in the second half of the play should be mentioned. In Scene 7, John is "dressed, as always, in a white linen suit." In the following scene John says ". . . every evening I put on a clean white suit. I have a dozen. Six in the closet and six in the wash."

The preliminary list for a production of this play might read as follows:

Prologue.   Early twentieth century, town square and fountain.

ALMA WINEMILLER, age 10. Adult dignity, tenderness, spirituality.

JOHN BUCHANAN, age 10.

} Both in school clothes.

I.1.   Just before World War I, town square and fountain.

REV. WINEMILLER Episcopalian.

MRS. WINEMILLER Childish and stubborn.

JOHN Brilliant and restlessly alive.

DUSTY

PEARL

} Strolling couple.

DR. BUCHANAN

ALMA Prematurely spinsterish. Pale yellow dress and yellow silk parasol. Bag and handkerchief.

ROSA GONZALES Outrageous finery, hat with greenish-blue lustrous feathers, diamond-and-emerald earrings.

NELLIE EWELL Age 16.

ROGER DOREMUS Small, like a sparrow.

All rather dressed up for the Fourth of July.

I.2.   Some time later, Rectory and Doctor's house.

MRS. WINEMILLER White plumed hat and parasol.

REV. WINEMILLER As before.

ALMA Preparing for company. QUICK CHANGE.

JOHN At home.

NELLIE Regular everyday wear.

I.3. That evening, the Rectory.

ROGER Dressed for meeting.

VERNON Willowy, open collar, Byronic locks.

MRS. BASSETT Dressed for meeting, widow.

ROSEMARY Wistful, long-necked, thick-lensed glasses.

ALMA Dressed for meeting. Small buttons on blouse. QUICK CHANGE.

JOHN Immaculately groomed and shining. Carrying jacket and hat.

I.4. Later that evening, Doctor's office.

JOHN Wounded arm, bandage. Shirt and trousers rather messed up. Handkerchief and pocketwatch. MEDIUM-QUICK CHANGE.

ROSA Has come from Casino.

ALMA As before. Blouse unbuttons, line "little pearl buttons." Topaz ring referred to by line.

I.5. A few days later, the Rectory.

ALMA Dressed to go out, picks up hat, gloves, veil. QUICK CHANGE.

REV. WINEMILLER As before, perhaps sweater instead of suitcoat.

MRS. WINEMILLER At-home dress.

I.6. A few minutes later, the arbor outside the Moon Lake Casino.

JOHN White suit.

ALMA As before, hat, veil, and gloves on.

DUSTY Waiter.

From this preliminary list can come the Costume Scene Breakdown (page 62) and the Costume List on page 61. Not every item of the costume needs to be listed at this time, for until the actual designing is done, all the parts may not be known. Color indications and costume pieces specified in the script should be considered carefully to discern if they are necessary or merely a suggestion of the playwright. In this case John's white suits are quite important in delineating his character, but Alma's yellow dress could possibly be a different color if that seems more appropriate to the production. Williams' description of Rosa's costume helps the reader understand his intentions, but her actual costume could vary from those indications if the spirit of Williams' description is retained. On the other hand, Alma's blouse should have the little buttons John refers to as he listens to her heart. Any specific mention of costumes in the script should be noted so it can be discussed by designer and director.

COSTUME LIST

PRINCIPAL MEN

1. JOHN, age 10 school clothes
2. JOHN I white suit
3. JOHN II at home casual
4. JOHN III dirty shirt and pants. MEDIUM-QUICK CHANGE
5. REV. WINEMILLER Clerical suit, add sweater
6. ROGER DOREMUS I summer dressy suit
7. ROGER II medium dressy
8. DR. BUCHANAN good work suit

PRINCIPAL WOMEN

9. ALMA, age 10 school clothes
10. ALMA I good dress (yellow?), purse, parasol
11. ALMA II day skirt and blouse. QUICK CHANGE
12. ALMA III meeting outfit. QUICK CHANGE
13. ALMA IV dressy dress, hat with veil, gloves QUICK CHANGE
14. MRS. WINEMILLER I good dress
15. MRS. WINEMILLER II day dress, parasol, plumed hat (breakaway)
16. MRS. WINEMILLER III day dress
17. ROSA I very dressy, plumed hat
18. ROSA II medium dressy
19. NELLIE I dressy, young
20. NELLIE II everyday dress
21. MRS. BASSETT medium dress, widow

EXTRA MEN

22. VERNON medium dressy
23. DUSTY I working class dressy
24. DUSTY II waiter

EXTRA WOMEN

25. ROSEMARY medium dressy
26. PEARL working-class dressy

The discussion should also clarify when costume changes occur, any quick-change problems that are inherent in the script or may be caused by the way the production is being staged, and any extras that might be needed but are not mentioned in the script. For example, in *Summer and Smoke* the director might find it unnecessary for Mrs. Winemiller to have two different day dresses and at the same time decide that there should be ten extra townspeople onstage in Scene 1. The costume count has just changed from twenty-five to thirty-four: one costume cut and ten added. Problems that might spring from this change in numbers will become evident as the designer continues preparations. An unanticipated advantage could come from the added people. The director could use them to dress the stage atmospherically for a few moments after Alma and Roger leave, thus allowing Alma a bit more time for her quick change.

Time considerations and changes

The director may not wish to have intermissions where they are indicated in the script. A play written in four or five acts is now often done with only one or two intermissions, the other breaks being dealt with as though they were pauses between scenes. This may create a

COSTUME SCENE BREAKDOWN

	PROLOGUE	PT. I, SC. 1	PT. I, SC. 2	PT. I, SC. 3	PT. I, SC. 4	PT. I, SC. 5	PT. I, SC. 6
Alma, age 10	School clothes						
John, age 10	School clothes						
Alma		Good dress: I	Day skirt and blouse: II QUICK CHANGE	Meeting outfit: III QUICK CHANGE	Repeat III	Dressy: IV QUICK CHANGE	Repeat IV
John		White Suit: I	Casual: II	Repeat I	Dirty shirt & pants: III MED.- QUICK CHANGE		Repeat I
Rev. Winemiller		Clerical suit: I	Repeat I			Repeat I, add sweater	
Mrs. Winemiller		Good dress: I	Day dress, plumed hat: II			Day dress: III	
Rosa		Very dressy: I			Medium dressy: II		
Nellie		Good dress: I	Everyday dress: II				
Dr. Buchanan		Good worn suit					
Roger		Summer dressy: I		Medium dressy: II			
Mrs. Bassett				Medium dressy			
Vernon				Medium dressy			
Rosemary				Medium dressy			
Dusty		Working-class dressy: I					Waiter: II
Pearl		Working-class dressy					

situation in which only a few moments are available for a costume change. Double-casting may also pose time problems. If an actor is playing more than one role, special attention must be paid to the time between his exit as one character and his entrance as another, particularly if there is a desire to disguise the actor so the audience will not be aware of the double casting (which may well involve time-consuming makeup and hair changes).

Figure 2-5 Original ideas for the costume of Bedelia in the film *Creepshow* led to the sketch at left, above. But the costume often changes as character develops through conferences and casting. The photograph shows Bedelia as played by Viveca Lindfors. Design by Barbara Anderson. Photo courtesy Laurel-Show, Inc., New York.

The flexible, confident designer

The numbers are now set, or at least as much as they can be at this point in the production. A designer must bear in mind that producing a play is always work in progress. Seldom, if ever, are things finalized in the preliminary stages. As a play progresses from beginning ideas to opening night, many changes take place. Good designers know when it is necessary to compromise and when they must be firm. All the while, the attitude must remain cooperative. The designer must feel confident in what he or she is doing and relay that confidence to the director so that a good exchange of ideas can continue to take place. Nothing can be more debilitating to creative energies than the feeling that a battle must be fought with every new decision. Few problems should arise if a director is truly prepared to do a play and has carefully thought through the guiding concepts of the production. Often, however, work begins on a show before much of the true groundwork has been laid. The director's preliminary ideas may change significantly as work on the production progresses. As a partner in a collaborative venture, the designer should have a feeling for the director's method of working and must prepare for whatever will come. Practically any problem can be solved with enough time and enough money. Difficulties arise when both or either is in short supply, as is too often the case in theatre.

Assessing the work

The number of costumes in a show may be quite easy to determine, but the number alone does not indicate the scope of the challenge facing the designer. Four other elements are equally important. The five critical questions that must be answered are:

1. How many costumes are there?
2. How complex are they?
3. How much time is there to build them?
4. How much help is available to build them?
5. How much money can be spent on them?

1. When arriving at the final costume tally, be sure to consider every possibility. It is always much easier to cut than to add when time and cash budgets have already been set. Consider overcoats and large capes as a second costume, for they cost money and take time to build. Consider underclothes that are seen onstage as a separate costume for the same reason: they require more time and money than undergarments that are not seen, which may be pulled from stock or the actor's private wardrobe. Check carefully for second costumes that may be needed because the actor appears first neat and all together and later, in ostensibly the same costume, in a distressed condition. Kate appears in her wedding dress at the time of the ceremony (Figure 2-6, left). A short time later she is seen after Petruchio has dragged her through the mud and mire (Figure 2-6, right). The same costume could not be used, for it could never be sufficiently cleaned for the next night's performance. A duplicate that is always in the wretched condition must be made.

2. Consider carefully the period to be used and the social class revealed by the costumes. Two Elizabethan court costumes may be much more difficult to build and more expensive than costumes for a dozen medieval peasants. Ball gowns are more of a problem than bathing suits. It is often useful to break down the costume list in terms

of classes of costumes: Type A for those most expensive in terms of time and money (e.g., formal ladies and liveried servants); Type B, which are middle-of-the-road (rented men's formal attire, spinster aunts, and the upstairs maid); and Type C for those easily acquired or made (a chimney sweep, grape pickers, and participants in a girls' pajama party). See examples, Figures 2-7 and 2-8, pages 72 and 73.

3. The time available to build the show can have a great influence on how it is designed. A production to be done in two weeks with forty costumes presents one problem. One to be mounted in three weeks with ten costumes presents problems that are entirely different.

4. The amount of help available must be considered concurrently with the allotted time. The amount of help involves not only the numbers of bodies available in the costume shop; the level of skill of those working is also of utmost importance.

5. The money available for the costumes may be last on the list, but this is not because it is of least importance. It weighs heavily on what can be done in all the other areas. And although money can't buy more time, it can pay for more people to make the time more productive.

All of these elements must be considered together if the designer is to develop a valid, integrated concept for the show.

Figure 2-6 In *Kiss Me Kate*, when Kate is married her dress is in good condition (above left), but soon after the ceremony the wedding gown is much the worse for wear. Double costumes are a must in such situations. Design by Cletus Anderson for the Carnegie-Mellon University production, 1977. Set design by Ed Castro.

Budgeting

Budgeting a production is not an easy matter, for there are no absolute rules one can go by. The first step is to know how many costumes of what type will be needed and then to establish an average cost for each type of costume. This cost will depend largely on the circumstances involved in acquiring the costume and the economy of the area in which the production is being mounted. If built today in a New York costume house, the cost of a Type A costume might be $2000, a Type B $1000, and a Type C $500. Since most costumes are not built in the New York houses, a more accurate budgeting assessment can be reached by considering a typical costume in each grouping and assessing a probable materials cost to each costume element. Consider the following:

Type A Costume   Lady of 1895 (Afternoon Suit)

Suit	12 yd. wool @ $10/yd.	$120
Jacket lining	3 yd. @ $3/yd.	9
Patterning fabric	10 yd. @ $1/yd.	10
Blouse	3 yd. @ $5/yd.	15
3 petticoats	15 yd. @ $2/yd.	30
Corset	fabric, bones, fastening	10
Shoes		25
Hose (5 pair)		10
Hat	fabric, feathers, flowers	15
Braid	skirt and jacket 12 yd @ $1.50/yd.	18
Buttons		4
Parasol	fabric and frame	15
Gloves		5
Notions	thread, fastenings, etc.	3
	TOTAL	$289

An idea of the potential cost of the costume is now established. If part of the costume is available from stock (usually such items as shoes, petticoats, corset, gloves are) the cost is lowered, in this case by $68. This cost breakdown can be done for each costume if individual items vary a great deal and this seems necessary, or one representative costume from each grouping can be examined and the budget determined by multiplying this costume cost by the number of similar costumes. The development and maintenance of a good stock will be discussed later in this chapter.

The cost and availability of different types of fabric vary widely throughout the country. Costume designers should thoroughly explore the areas in which they are working, locate all possible sources, find the best suppliers, and get a feeling for the prices of various types of items that will be used. A shop foreman or buyer can be very helpful in laying this basic groundwork. A comprehensive stock of up-to-date catalogues of items that are not available in many areas or items that are more easily and less expensively purchased in quantity is another important resource.

YARDAGE ESTIMATES

While the actual dollar value of the different elements of a costume can vary too widely to be listed, a chart giving the approximate yardages used should be helpful. The following chart lists these yardages using a fabric width that is common for a fabric typically used for the garment. Following the chart is a conversion list for fabric widths.

GARMENT	YARDAGE NEEDED	FABRIC WIDTH (IN INCHES)
WOMEN		
Blouses and bodices		
Tight fitting, sleeveless	1½	45
Full bodied, sleeveless	1½	45
Fully pleated, sleeveless	3	45
Sleeves		
Long, tight	1	45
Long, full	1¾	45
Short	½	45
Very full, leg-o-mutton	2¼	45
Funnel to knee	2¼	45
Funnel to floor	3½	45
Hanging straight to floor	3	45
Skirts		
Below knee, straight	1	54
Below knee, moderate A-line (2-yd. hem)	1, 1¾*	54
Below knee, full (5-yd. hem)	3, 4*	54
Floor length, fairly straight (2-yd. hem)	1¾	54
Floor length, medium full, general fullness (5 yd. hem)	4½, 5¾*	54
Floor length, medium full, shaped gores (5-yd. hem)	5¾, 6¾*	54
Floor length, full, general fullness (7-yd. hem)	5¾ 7*	54
Floor length, full, shaped gores (7-yd. hem)	7½, 8½*	54
	(For moderate trains add ⅔ yd.)	
Jackets		
Fitted to hip, sleeveless (8 piece)	2½	45
Full to hip, sleeveless	3½	45

* Indicates yardage needed if fabric has a nap or pattern that can only be cut one way.

GARMENT	YARDAGE NEEDED	FABRIC WIDTH (IN INCHES)

Gowns—combine amounts for bodice style, skirt style, and sleeve style, subtracting yardage if it will be possible to cut the smaller bodice and sleeve pieces from the areas left after cutting the skirt gores.

Ruffles and flounces—These can add a great deal of yardage, particularly if they are fairly wide. For example, 2⅔ yards of fabric are needed for a 10-inch finished ruffle with 200% fullness on the hem of a 5-yard skirt (360 inches of ruffle needed, 8 widths of 45-inch fabric, each 12 inches wide = 2⅔ yards).

MEN

Shirts and bodices		
Tight fitting, sleeveless	2	45
Full bodied, sleeveless	2	45
Fully pleated, sleeveless	4	45
Sleeves		
Short	½	45
Long, tight	1	45
Long, full	2	45
Medium leg-o-mutton	2	45
Bagpipe	2	54
Funnel, to knee	2	54
Funnel, to floor	3½	54
Hanging straight, to floor	3	54
Tunics and robes		
To thigh, fairly straight	2½	54
To thigh, pleated	3¾	54
To knee, fairly straight	3	54
To knee, pleated	4½	54
To floor, fairly straight	4	54
To floor, pleated	6	54

MEN AND WOMEN

Capes		
To waist, circle cut	1½	45
To hip, ½ circle (2¾-yd. hem)	2, 2½*	45
To hip, ¾ circle (4-yd. hem)	3, 3¾*	45
To calf, ½ circle (4½-yd. hem)	3, 4½*	54
To calf, ¾ circle (7-yd. hem)	4½, 6*	54
To floor, medium fullness (gored, 5-yd. hem)	4, 7*	54
To floor, full (gored, 8-yd. hem)	6, 10½*	54

* Indicates yardage needed if fabric has a nap or pattern that can only be cut one way.

FABRIC CONVERSION CHART

This chart uses the equivalent fabric area at each width, rounded to the nearest yard or fraction of a yard that is commonly sold in fabric stores. In converting from one width to another consider the number of large pieces that must be cut. Often a certain length of fabric is needed to accommodate these pieces and a few extra inches of width make no difference.

FABRIC REQUIRED	YARDAGE NEEDED IN OTHER WIDTHS					
	36"	42"	45"	48"	54"	60"
½ yard × 36 inches	½	½	½	½	⅓	⅓
× 42 inches	⅝	½	½	½	½	⅜
× 45 inches	⅔	⅝	½	½	½	½
× 48 inches	⅔	⅝	½	½	½	½
× 54 inches	¾	⅔	⅝	⅝	½	½
× 60 inches	⅞	¾	⅔	⅔	⅝	½
1 yard × 36 inches	1	⅞	⅞	¾	⅔	⅝
× 42 inches	1¼	1	1	⅞	⅞	⅔
× 45 inches	1¼	1⅛	1	1	⅞	¾
× 48 inches	1⅓	1¼	1⅛	1	⅞	⅞
× 54 inches	1½	1⅓	1¼	1⅛	1	1
× 60 inches	1⅔	1½	1⅓	1¼	1⅛	1
2 yards × 36 inches	2	1¾	1⅝	1½	1⅓	1¼
× 42 inches	2⅓	2	1⅞	1¾	1⅝	1½
× 45 inches	2½	2¼	2	1⅞	1⅔	1½
× 48 inches	2⅔	2⅓	2¼	2	1⅞	1⅝
× 54 inches	3	2⅝	2½	2⅓	2	1⅞
× 60 inches	3⅓	2⅞	2⅔	2½	2¼	2

FABRIC REQUIRED	YARDAGE NEEDED IN OTHER WIDTHS					
	36″	42″	45″	48″	54″	60″
3 yards × 36 inches	3	2⅝	2⅜	2¼	2	1¾
× 42 inches	3½	3	2⅞	2⅔	2⅓	2⅛
× 45 inches	3¾	3¼	3	2⅞	2½	2¼
× 48 inches	4	3½	3¼	3	2⅔	2⅜
× 54 inches	4½	3⅞	3⅝	3½	3	2¾
× 60 inches	5	4⅓	4	3¾	3⅓	3
4 yards × 36 inches	4	3½	3¼	3	2⅔	2½
× 42 inches	4⅔	4	3¾	3½	3⅛	2⅞
× 45 inches	5	4⅓	4	3¾	3⅓	3
× 48 inches	5⅓	4⅝	4⅓	4	3⅝	3¼
× 54 inches	6	5¼	4⅞	4½	4	3⅝
× 60 inches	6⅔	5¾	5⅓	5	4½	4
5 yards × 36 inches	5	4⅓	4	3¾	3⅓	3
× 42 inches	5⅞	5	4⅔	4½	4	3½
× 45 inches	6¼	5⅜	5	4¾	4¼	3¾
× 48 inches	6⅔	5¾	5⅓	5	4½	4
× 54 inches	7½	6½	6	5⅔	5	4½
× 60 inches	8⅓	7⅛	6⅔	6¼	5⅝	5

COSTUME STOCK

A good costume stock is an invaluable asset to a designer and a theatre company. It should be built carefully, organized well, and guarded religiously. Items should be made with enough seam allowance for later alteration, as long as this can be done without affecting the fit of the costumes in the production for which they are constructed. Items that are pulled from stock and reused should be handled sensibly to prolong their longevity and continued usefulness. For example, it is not sensible to pull a full-length skirt from stock and cut it down to make a short skirt; the cost of the fabric alone in the full-length skirt might have been $100, and the short skirt might be made for $10. Retrimming a garment is often desirable, although this is impossible if glue has been used. Taking a costume apart merely to reuse the fabric may be foolish. The time involved may offset any money saved and a stock item has been lost. In accumulating a costume stock, concentrate on those garments that can be used over and over again, saving everyone much time and money. The integrity of these costumes should be maintained if at all possible so they will continue to be available when they are needed. The time may come when an item is truly needed for a show and must be used in such a way that it can never be reclaimed. Bid it a fond farewell and hope that the stock is now extensive enough for another garment to take its place.

Stock shrinks not just because items are used badly. If a stock is not well organized, items often cannot be used because they cannot be found. Space is always limited, but careful planning should make the best possible use of available space. A good costume stock must also be guarded jealously. Too often, "souveniritis" causes valuable pieces to disappear. This problem cannot be completely solved, but the security of the costumes must be considered carefully in both the storage areas and the dressing rooms.

Labor. Thus far, discussion of budgeting the show has involved only the cost of the costume materials. When labor costs are included in the budget the total amount needed will increase considerably. Much depends on the style and complexity of the production, but labor costs can often account for one-half to two-thirds of the total budget. For example, a show that budgets $2000 for fabrics and the like may add an additional $2000 to $4000 for labor costs.

An accurate knowledge of the production budget may not be possible at the early stages in the development of the designs for a play. Running through preliminary ideas is important as the designer begins to develop the basic concept within a reasonable budget.

The design interpretation and the actor

While the designer is determining the basic interpretation of the script and assessing the work to be done, he or she must always keep in mind the relationship of the actor to the costume. The job of setting the style of the production belongs first to the director, then to the designers. The actors ultimately present the playwright's work to the audience, but they do so following the lead of the script and the interpretation the director has chosen.

Part of this interpretation is the visual aspect provided by the designers, who are responsible for both the overall feeling of the

Figure 2-7   The complex trims and shapes of this costume for Petrucchio in *Kiss Me Kate* make it a Type-A costume (page 65). Design by Cletus Anderson.

production and the individual elements of which it is composed. Many of these ideas may be well underway before the actors are involved in the production. The actors are also most immediately involved with the problems of the characters they are playing, and while they may often want to be involved in developing costume ideas for those characters, they cannot be fully aware of the overall picture and how their costumes must fit into it. The designer must have ultimate control over the costumes to be used and needs as much cooperation and understanding from the actors as possible.

At the beginning of the rehearsal period the designer should present the sketches to the cast, explain the ideas that led to this approach, and clarify the effect the costumes are intended to create in the production.

Some form of work must be shown at this point, even if the finished renderings are not available. The designer should clearly explain the choices that were made for each character, and why. If it is a period show, some historical background would be helpful: Why did people wear the clothes common in a particular period? How did they feel about them? What bearing does this have on this particular production? The designer should explain shapes, fabrics, and any necessary underpinnings. Any changes that are to be made, on- or offstage, should be discussed, focusing the discussion on why they are to occur.

If there is not sufficient time at the first presentation to communicate with each actor individually, this can be done when measurements are taken or at the first fitting. Each piece should be explained: how it can be used; what restrictions or freedoms it will allow; what is practical in terms of pockets, buttons, and so on; what accessories are included; and any special problems that might arise. The total costume should be discussed in terms of the effect it will have on the character. If some of the garments are unfamiliar to the actors, they should be taught how to dress, sit, stand, and move in their costumes. The actors should understand their costumes well enough to "wear" them mentally in re-

Figure 2-8   Gremio's *Kiss Me Kate* costume (left), easier to pattern and executed in less expensive fabric than Petrucchio's, is a Type-B costume (see page 65). The Servant's costume, which has simple pieces and does not require much fabric, is Type C. Designs by Cletus Anderson.

hearsal. It might be very useful to both the actors and the director if copies of the costume designs were displayed at the rehearsal area to serve as a reminder of what will actually be worn onstage. The actors must be thoroughly familiar with the costume-design process in order to better understand the aims of the designer and director and to develop their roles along these lines.

The rehearsal costume

Mentally donning the costume is a great aid to rehearsal and to preparation for the first costume runthrough. So is the proper rehearsal costume. The designer must talk with the actors about what they should wear for rehearsal, provide garments they may need, and explain the type of movement their garments will require.

It is extremely important that the actors rehearse in the same type of footwear they will wear in performance. The footwear is the basis for the stance and movement; a woman wearing heels has a completely different bearing from a woman wearing flats; a man in boots moves quite differently from a man in loafers. Men's period shoes with high heels present a particularly difficult problem because the proper way to wear them is not familiar to many actors, yet the shoes form the basis for the mannerisms so essential to the seventeenth-century plays in which they are used. The well-turned ankle and properly placed leg were the mark of a gentleman, and the proper effect can only be achieved with ease if an actor is thoroughly accustomed to the shoes.

Any actor or actress who will wear a long gown in performance needs a rehearsal skirt of comparable length and weight. If the actual garment is to be made of heavy brocade, then flimsy muslin is not satisfactory during rehearsal for the quality of movement is entirely different. Any hoops or trains to be used should be simulated for rehearsal so the blocking can account for the actual space an actor will need onstage. A designer knows from experience that a woman of 1860 wearing a large hoop cannot move between a chair and settee placed two feet apart, nor can a woman wearing a train back up easily. The earlier these problems are faced and solved, the more comfortable the actor will be in the final costume. The ultimate goal is to help actors wear their costumes as though they had never worn anything else.

Corsets and padding should also be provided early in the rehearsal phase. A corset is used not so much to create a tiny waist, although this illusion may be achieved, as to give the torso the shape of the period and to give the actress a feeling of the restriction that was so much a part of the time. Modern woman is not subjected to rigid figure control and must become accustomed to the restrictions inherent in a corset that greatly influence movement. For years women did not slouch or bend at the waist; the torso moved as a unit and many mannerisms grew out of this constraint. Padding, too, may place restrictions on movement by adding bulk in places strange to the actor. This added bulk must be incorporated into the actor's whole movement pattern so it becomes a part of the characterization.

Rehearsal pieces should be available for any costumes that are removed or put on onstage to enable the actor to become quite familiar with the necessary action. Quick changes offstage should be thoroughly rehearsed as soon as all the garments are ready so that both the actor and the crew will know exactly what is to happen and can approach the moment with confidence and ease.

Everything that can be done before the dress rehearsals begin to help the actors prepare will be an asset to the outcome of the production. The greatest costume in the world can be totally ineffective if it is not worn properly. The designer should follow the rehearsals periodically and help the director and actors arrive at the fullest possible understanding of the costumes and their use.

Reducing actor-designer conflicts

It is often true that there are conflicts between actors and costume designers; good costume designers do everything possible to reduce them. Letting the actor in on preliminary design plans is the best way to begin. The actor is ultimately onstage before the audience and is rightfully concerned about the image he will project. The designer must be always ready to reassure him and must ensure that the costume provides the proper image for the play. The greatest costume sketch in the world is useless if it cannot be turned into an actual costume on an actor in performance — and if the actor doesn't feel comfortable in what he is wearing, it may never be fully effective.

There are many ways to help an actor understand the costume. An actor may wish to wear a costume in a particular color or style because he feels more comfortable in it. The designer should try not to react negatively to the suggestion. After consideration, if the suggestion proves unsuitable the designer should explain carefully why it does not fit into the scheme being used. If the actor's ideas are ineffective because they are outside the line of the period, do not work well with the set, or perhaps will not show up properly in the lighting that will be used, this can be explained in a way that will help the actor see the overall planning of the show. He will realize that design decisions are the result of a serious consideration of many elements and any changes must take into account a number of factors. The actor may indeed have some costume ideas that the designer finds quite acceptable. If the actor really understands his costume he will be able to relay information about business that is established during rehearsal: "I have to hide a notebook on my person, but I don't think I have a pocket"; "The director has decided he wants me to do a somersault here—do you think I can, wearing a bustle?"

There are situations in which a conflict between actor and designer cannot be resolved without conferring with the director, and the designer may not always be happy with the outcome. The designer must be able to take the new information and work it into the scheme in the best possible way. If an established star is involved in the production, a preliminary meeting during the design period might be desirable. There are actors who have very specific ideas about what they wish to look like and if their position in the company is such that they are going to have a great deal to say about what happens, this should be considered at the very beginning.

The actor's actual input into the designing of the costumes is not usually extensive, but the influence of the actor on the costume cannot be underestimated. Fitting the actor in the costume is discussed in Chapter 8.

3

Developing the basic concept

The process of designing costumes for a play can be extremely rewarding if the designer has firm goals. The costumes grow out of a basic concept that is developed from a thorough understanding of the objectives of the play, the director, and the other designers. A knowledgeable collaboration will lead to a performance in which all contributions work together harmoniously. There is seldom enough time to develop a production to everyone's satisfaction, and deadline pressures are always present. But if the work progresses from a solid understanding of what is to be done and why it is to be done in a certain way, decisions at every step will be easier and surer. A carefully considered, well-planned basic concept is invaluable. It permits the designer to exchange ideas confidently with the director and the scene and lighting designers and to present sound ideas to the cast and to the crew.

Developing the character costume

At some point in the process of designing the production the designer must establish a clear understanding of the characters for whom costumes will be created. The timing of this character exploration varies from production to production and from designer to designer.

Theatre is a wonderfully vital, flexible art form. There are no exclusively "right" ways to get things done. People working in theatre must be knowledgeable enough to be able to adapt their creativity to a particular situation and confident enough in their skills to deal with changes, revisions, and refinements of their ideas. Like any other facet of theatre, costume design does not always progress smoothly from one step to another. Many times more than one stage of the process is going on at the same time. Careful character delineation may develop simultaneously with other more general aspects of the production. There must nevertheless come a time when the designer is able to make intelligent decisions about the costumes based upon an understanding of character (Figure 3-1).

The designer does not interpret the script alone. The playwright has given the groundwork, the designer and director have discussed this particular production. The interpretation continues to grow as the actors bring their skill to the roles. Director, actors, and designer all help the character evolve during the rehearsal period.

Many of the details that establish a firm visual reflection of a character's personality should not be discounted because they seem too obvious. On the contrary, the most obvious indications of character — age, physical stature, occupation, social position, and the like — are often excellent ways to enhance a memorable and accurate depiction of

Preceding page: Social level is conveyed by costumes. Sketch for a female character from a low stratum of the society by Frank Bevan for a production of *Faust* at Yale University in 1949. (See also page 89.) Beinicke Rare Book and Manuscript Library, Yale.

Figure 3-1 Sagramore's character called for a costume that would make him large and menacing but not totally evil. Pencil sketch; design by Barbara Anderson for *A Connecticut Yankee in King Arthur's Court,* one of the Once Upon a Classic series produced by WQED, Pittsburgh.

character. The designer should not be reluctant to reinforce visually information the audience receives from the script.

Revealing the character's psychological state and relationship to his or her world and the others in it is a bit more tricky. Here the designer is working more with interpretation than with given facts. There is a chance the audience won't actually understand the designer's motiva-

Figure 3-2   Andrew Aguecheek interpreted for a production of Shakespeare's *Twelfth Night* set in the 1920s at Carnegie-Mellon University, 1981. Design by Ainslie Bruneau in watercolor and colored pencils.

tion for a particular costume, yet the costume must still seem valid and perfectly acceptable for the dramatic moment. And there is also the possibility that the audience will understand too much and the designer will give away the plot. If a boy and girl come onstage both clothed in the same shade of powder blue, even if they don't know each other at first and spend most of the act fighting, chances are awfully good they will kiss and go off into the sunset together before the final curtain.

The designer should read the script again and again to extract as much information from it as possible. Although the relative importance of each of these concerns will change from production to production, a careful reading of the play will enable the designer to answer the following questions effectively: When do the crucial moments occur in the play, and how should they be staged? What type of line, color, and texture will best express these moments? What is the motivation of each character in the play? How does each character fit into the framework of the entire production? Does the character go through changes as the action progresses, and if so, how should this evolution be staged? What did the character do before the action of the play begins, and what will he or she do after the action ends?

The type of visualization that will most effectively achieve the desired outcome will be a result of ideas shared with the director, actors, and other designers. But the designer will find that there is no substitute for a close, personal reading of the script to understand the character well. And, logically enough, the costume designer will find it easier to design a good costume for a well-defined and well-understood character. This is true no matter what period is used for the play (Figure 3-2). If the designer has thoroughly researched both the character and the period, he or she will know those elements that can be used to best help bring this person alive for the audience. The audience does not need to know the reasons behind each costume piece chosen; it simply needs to perceive that this person looks exactly right in a particular situation. It is through this attention to detail and development that the costume designer makes a strong contribution to the production. The actor, the costume, and the situation all fit together to tell the story.

Figures 3-3 through 3-6 (page 82) are examples of how costumes help delineate the character. These four costumes were created for characters in The Leatherstocking Tales, dramatized on the Once Upon a Classic series produced by the Public Broadcasting System. These characters lived in the wilderness of northern New York in the mid-eighteenth century. James Fenimore Cooper's novel *The Deerslayer* inspired the television scripts and was valuable background material for the designer. Since she could not assume that the audience would be familiar with Cooper's novel, costume designs were based on the presentation of the characters in the shooting script. Hawkeye (Figure 3-3), is the young hero. He has lived with the Delaware Indians for years, is very knowledgeable in their ways and is accepted by them. He is also readily accepted by the white men, so he must relate to both worlds. Hawkeye presents an ideal image of a resourceful and honest woodsman. His costume consists of a handmade linen hunting shirt and rough cotton shirt, fringed leather breeches and Indian moccasins, and the powder horn, bag, knife, belt, and gun that were necessities in the wilderness. Lines were kept simple and the garments made of homespun fabrics and leathers. The color scheme used tones in warm off-whites, tans, and medium browns.

Harry March (Figure 3-4) is a different case entirely. A blustering braggart, he connives his way through life, taking advantage of any person or situation he can to turn an easy buck. He is flamboyant, careless, and lazy, always looking out for himself. His clothes must reflect his life in the woods, hence the handmade boots and Indian

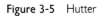

Figure 3-4 Harry March

Figure 3-3 Hawkeye, the young hero of James Fenimore Cooper's Leatherstocking Tales. Designed by Barbara Anderson for the Once Upon a Classic television series. As presentation pieces, the pencil sketches reproduced as Figures 3-3 through 3-6 had smaller color renderings attached.

Figure 3-5 Hutter

Figure 3-6 Rivenoak

leggings, heavy belt, pouches, powder horn, and rifle. His shirt is homespun, but with a ruffle and more flair than Hawkeye's, and somewhere he has acquired an Indian armband. His breeches and vest look very much lived in, and his hat is made dashing with an Indian feather trim. Harry's hair is somewhat unkempt, his face whiskery, and the actor who plays him would ideally have a hairy chest. The colors of his clothes are darker and dirtier than Hawkeye's, in shades of greens and green-browns.

Hutter (Figure 3-5) is an old pirate who lives on a barge with his daughter. An unpleasant man with an unsavory background, Hutter is a complement to the irascible Harry, and his greed soon leads to his death at the hands of the Indians. Though it has been a long time since he has really been at sea, he retains a bit of the flavor of the sailor, and so wears the jacket and scarf commonly worn by sailors. His clothes are worn but not torn; although he doesn't care what he looks like, he does have a daughter to look after him. His beard is scraggly and his hair is very casually tied back. The colors of his costume, grayed blues and browns, tie in with his maritime background.

Rivenoak (Figure 3-6) is a proud and vengeful Huron warrior chief. He is Hawkeye's enemy, but they oppose each other honorably according to the Indian code. His demeanor must reflect his heritage and the contact he has had with the French. He wears Huron moccasins, leggings, breechcloth, bead-and-feather decorations and pouches, but he also wears a shirt of finer fabric and a double gorget that he has received from his benefactors. His Indian blanket is deep red to help give him stature and set him off from the rest of his warriors. Rivenoak's shirt is off-white, and the tones of his leather garments range from medium brown to muted orange. He is thus contrasted with Hawkeye, who wears more yellowish browns.

In each of these costumes, every element was selected because it seemed psychologically right for the character and because it helped create a physical look that enhanced audience understanding of these people and their situations.

The Way of the World by William Congreve is a Restoration comedy that provides a more decorative means of presenting the characters. Lady Wishfort is an overripe grande dame, a foolish woman easily flattered and easily angered (Figure 3-7, page 85). She considers herself the center of a very stylish set and presents herself as an attractive coquette, though she is much past her prime. Lady Wishfort's costume shows her fondness for excess, her delight in surface extravagance, and her true lack of taste. All her choices are amusingly wrong for her age and figure: her overcurled hair, the bows and pearls worn at her neck, her extravagant ribbons and skirt trim all emphasize the width of her overabundant figure. She wears more ruffles than anyone needs at the elbow . . . and all is carried out in reds and oranges.

Lady Wishfort is attracted to Sir Rowland, who is really the servant Waitwell in disguise (Figure 3-8). His costume is also overdone, but in a more elegant way, for he has been created by Mirabell, the hero of the play. Sir Rowland wears a rich, warm rust suit, a color Lady Wishfort obviously would find attractive, trimmed with a great deal of gold braid and accented with a very decoratively beribboned baldrick. His crowning glory is a strawberry-blond wig. Lady Wishfort cannot help but find him enticing.

Petulant is a fop, typical in Restoration comedy (Figure 3-9). He considers himself a man of much wit, learning, and good breeding. In reality he is a coward and a fool. The color of his costume is a delicate beige trimmed in gold and accented with precious lavender bows at the neck, shoulders, and knees. The sash at his waist accents the overly genteel feeling, as does his carefully curled wig and his hat, decorated with very curly ostrich feathers.

Sir Wilfull Witwoud is fresh from the country and shows it in everything he wears (Figure 3-10). The fabric of his costume is coarser, the trim simpler, the cut less fashionable than the clothes of the other characters. He wears boots and even spurs, something no true city gentleman would ever consider, for the proper turn of the calf was very important in polite society. Witwoud's linen is not refined, his wig hasn't been set in years, and the feathers on his hat were more than likely plucked from a bird he himself shot. But because he is coming to the city and wants to show that he is as much a gentlemen as his hosts, he has added a couple of bows to his costume. The colors of his costume reflect the earth tones of his country surroundings.

Notice that the personality of each character is also expressed in the figure's attitude and posture. Lady Wishfort is overly coy, Sir Rowland is manly and elegant, Petulant is too, too genteel, and Sir Wilfull is planted firmly on his heels as he surveys the unfamiliar territory.

Once the designer begins to understand the person to be clothed in the play, the character delineation will be a consideration in each choice that is made. This process of developing the character costume continues throughout the design process, from setting the limitations that will define the world of the play to the choice of line and color that will be used and even to the presentation style of the costume plate.

Setting the limitations

To establish limitations in a production, the designers and director must consider the historical period, geographic area, season and weather, and time of day of the production; and the social status, age, and sex of the characters. In Chapter 1, these categories were discussed in relation to the general meaning of clothes. They will now be reexamined to determine how they can be used for a specific play and cast.

Figure 3-7 Lady Wishfort, like the other three figures, is a character in Congreve's Restoration comedy *The Way of the World.* Designs executed in pencil by Cletus Anderson, 1972.

Figure 3-8 Sir Rowland

Figure 3-10 Sir Wilful Witwoud

Figure 3-9 Petulant

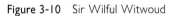

HISTORICAL PERIOD

Many plays have a very definite time set by the playwright (for example, the summer of 1865 in Eugene O'Neill's *Mourning Becomes Electra*). The director may decide to comply with the playwright's timeframe. The designer must then determine the period of time to be researched. Confinement in a narrow period of time often limits the research material available to the designer; it is important to maintain the silhouette of a particular historical period, not to precisely reproduce the clothes worn with painstaking accuracy (Figure 3-11). The designer should feel comfortable enough with the style of a period to design a costume as if he or she were actually living in that period. In some cases, of course, a character must appear deliberately old-fashioned. This must be dealt with carefully, for the audience may not know enough about the costumes of a period to pick up on what is old-fashioned and what is merely strange.

In a play set in 1895, for example, the women's costumes cannot be designed from sources of the entire 1890s, for there were three differ-

Figure 3-11   A costume based on a historical source can be reworked by the designer to make it more suitable to the character. This costume for DeConde in John Whiting's *The Devils* for a 1976 production at Carnegie-Mellon University was based on Anthony Van Dyck's portrait of Viscount Grandison. Acrylic; design by Cletus Anderson.

Figure 3-12 The costumes of these movie prospectors from a production of *Merton of the Movies* at Carnegie-Mellon University suggest the early rural West of the United States. Design by Cletus Anderson.

ent silhouettes in style during this decade. The style in women's fashions dominant in 1895 was in vogue from 1894 to 1896. For men's costumes, which were not as subject to the vagaries of fashion as women's, the period can be broader, encompassing the whole decade and perhaps a bit more. Generally, the farther back in history a play is set, the wider the span of years available to use and still keep within the desired silhouette, for styles did not change as rapidly, source material is not as abundant, and the audience is not as familiar with the fashions. A play set in the fifteenth century whose action takes place in one afternoon can easily be designed with a good feeling for the unity of style using sources from 1425 to 1475. This would be impossible for a more recent fifty-year span—from 1900 to 1950, for example.

GEOGRAPHIC AREA

The script may specify a geographic locale for the play; the geographic setting can also be surmised by the playwright's nationality. At times a specific country is not as important as a feeling for the general area, such as Scandinavia, Middle Europe, or the Mediterranean. At other times the perception of an area within a country must be more specific: New England, the South, or even the backwoods South or West (Figure 3-12). The amount of research material available varies greatly, so the designer must know how widely to range in search of inspiration and

Figure 3-13 No description is needed to suggest weather conditions in Act 2, Scene 2 of *Twelfth Night*. Watercolor and colored pencil design by Ainslie Bruneau, 1981, for a production at Carnegie-Mellon University.

still capture the characteristics of the locale. The plays of Chekhov need the ambiance of nineteenth-century Russia, but sufficient source material might not be available. Since French and English fashions greatly influenced the styles adopted by upper-class Russians in the late nineteenth century, the designer might go to the original sources for basic silhouette ideas, but with enough of an understanding of Russian fashions to keep that flavor dominant. The United States has also looked to Western Europe for many of its styles, but the different social climate of a younger, brasher country often changed the flavor of the fashion when it crossed the Atlantic. At times a play should not be identified with any specific country, and the designer must search for shapes that are universal and do not suggest a specific locale.

SEASON AND WEATHER

In the most practical sense, the time of year must be established simply to ascertain if the actors need overcoats for entrances and exits. A show that takes place in winter can be much more expensive to mount simply because more garments are needed to reveal this fact. Weather conditions can also be indicated by the costume (Figure 3-13). The actual time of year may be very important to the plot or may be quite incidental. The general mood of the play may suggest a season without actually specifying one; a designer may decide to reflect this mood in the colors chosen for the costumes.

TIME OF DAY

This information is usually given in the stage directions, but might not be specifically mentioned in dialogue. If it is important that the audience know the time of day, the designer must select appropriate costumes. Nightgowns, pajamas, and robes are logical choices for early morning and night. Formal wear usually suggests an evening function. In the Victorian era a fashionable woman might have changed often — a housedress for morning, a promenade costume for the midday walk or shopping, a tea dress for late-afternoon receiving, and an evening gown for dinner.

SOCIAL STATUS

The world of the play may be peopled by those in the same social stratum, but often two or three class levels are present (Figure 3-14). Class differences should be clearly defined so that the proper contrast

Figure 3-14 Different social levels are suggested by the costumes in these sketches by Frank Bevan for the 1949 production of *Faust* at Yale University. The two figures at left are upper-class, the one directly below is definitely a peasant. (See also the sketch on page 77). Beinecke Rare Book and Manuscript Library, Yale.

in clothing reflects differences in social status for the audience. For example, the characters in a play might include a well-to-do family, its servants, the poor relations living in the household, and the tradesmen who perform services for them. The dress of the upper-class family members will obviously be more stylish than that of their poor relatives. The servants fall into two distinct levels as well: footmen, butlers, and chauffeurs, all of whom are meant to be seen, are clothed differently from cooks, kitchen maids, and gardeners. The tradesmen would probably dress as "downstairs" domestics do. Another element of society would be introduced with the arrival of a group of afternoon visitors who come from a background of recently acquired wealth. Here the designer has the opportunity to show the age-old struggle between the establishment and the *nouveaux riches.*

AGE

The script usually establishes a specific or general age for a character. How the age of the character is approached can often be influenced by the age of the actor who will play the role (Figure 3-15). Disguising the actual age may be an important part of the design if, as is sometimes the case, an actor is older than the part he will play. For example, telltale signs of age in an actress often appear in the upper arms and neck; a

Figure 3-15   This costume for Gashweiler in *Merton of the Movies* was designed by Cletus Anderson to help a young actor appear believable as the older general-store owner.

costume that does not expose these will greatly aid the illusion of youth. On the other hand, if a young actor is portraying an older role these same body areas may need to be covered because they would reveal the actor's youth. A child's part may be cast with someone who is older and better able to fulfill the acting requirements of the role. The actual age of the actor may be more effectively disguised by selecting garments that seem more youthful than those worn by a real ten- or eleven-year-old. A young woman may be cast as a child because she is ideally short, slight, and ethereal, but her well-developed bustline will not disappear easily. She may be bound down to a degree and her costume should be designed to take the attention away from her chest. A looser fit may also disguise what might seem a lumpy and deep-chested boy.

SEX

Gender is one area where the designer may have little creative leeway. The sex of the character is usually clearly determined by the author, and while it is not unheard of for the gender to be changed, this is usually done by the producer or director and may involve considerable rewriting of the script. One notable exception is Ariel in *The Tempest,* whose gender is often in question, but the director will probably decide if the character will seem more masculine, feminine, or neuter. The amount of "sexiness" that needs to be exhibited by a character may be of primary concern to the designer (Figure 3-16). How this is solved can be influenced by a number of factors, including what was considered sexy in the period in which the play is set and how this will be perceived by a modern audience. The actual appeal of the performer can be a strong factor, for the costume can enhance what he or she already has and try to provide what is missing.

Figure 3-16 Sexiness is the aim of this costume design, with a bit of whimsy thrown in. Watercolor sketch by Cletus Anderson, 1965.

Design guidelines for costume unity

REALISM VERSUS STYLIZATION

The basic concept for the approach to the costumes for a play is partially established when the areas discussed above have been de-cided upon. The designer knows some of the things that must be achieved, and now can begin to establish guidelines for attaining these goals. At this point, the most important question is: What factors will affect my contribution to this production?

A primary decision involves the degree of realism or stylization to be used. In some plays the costumes may need to present realistic clothes of the period, such as those purchased at the corner store today or faithfully reproduced from the Sears, Roebuck catalogue for a story set in the 1920s. This is, however, not random realism, for the designer makes choices in colors and textures that influence the interpretation of the play.

The degree of realism to be used may well be indicated in the language of the play as well as in its subject matter. The very nature of a play written in verse makes its characters different from those who inhabit our workaday world. This mode of expression may lead the designer away from a costume style that would seem mundane and ordinary. In other cases, a more prosaic costume line is ideally suited to

Figure 3-17 The costume at the left for the Ghost of Hamlet's Father grew from the eloquence of Shakespeare's language. Watercolor design by Cletus Anderson, 1966.

Figure 3-18 Small, realistic touches are appropriate for Eva in Neil Simon's *Absurd Person Singular,* produced by the Carnegie-Mellon Theatre Company in 1978. Design by Barbara Anderson.

the play. Consider, for example, the different costume approaches that would be taken for Joseph A. Walker's forthright protest drama *The River Niger,* set in the turbulence of the 1960s, and Maxwell Anderson's *Winterset,* a drama concerned with social unrest in the 1930s but written in eloquent verse.

Shakespeare's language creates an extraordinary world and presents an exciting opportunity for the designer to complement the eloquence in the design concept. Words so carefully selected do not bring to mind the undisciplined clutter of reality but a clarity of line, careful attention to detail, and a control of color that will help create a visual world as rich in meaning. *Hamlet* presented in a historical period can evoke images of lines and textures that make the figure of the actor seem heroic; detail can be suppressed in quantity but rich in the elements that are used; and colors can range from vibrant jewel tones to the shadowy darkness of Elsinore (Figure 3-17). *Hamlet* done in modern dress might still tend toward these elements translated into modern garments. But a modern rewrite of *Hamlet* — such as Elmer Rice's *Cue for Passion,* set in southern California in the 1960s and told in modern prose — does not evoke the same images. The clothes would reflect contemporary reality, since the characters are as unassuming as their prosaic language.

The subject matter of the play can also help the designer set the degree of realism or stylization to be used. A kitchen drama filled with life's little moments of pathos and joy needs costumes detailed with the same attention to the little realities of life (Figure 3-18). A story of the struggle of man against the universe is concerned not with minutiae but with broad, sweeping issues and requires a similar costume idea. Molière's comedies satirize the foibles of his times and are best presented when these elements are carefully considered and the foolishness he is ridiculing is accentuated in the design concept. Using every excess recorded in the fashions and manners of mid-seventeenth-century France would present the audience with nothing but a meaningless jumble. The designer must underline the words of the playwright with careful selection and control.

UNITY THROUGH LINE AND DETAIL

As the designer develops ideas for a play he or she is simultaneously working for a scheme that will hold the costume aspects of a production together and create a world that enriches both the language and content of the script and the other visual elements onstage. The goal is for costume unity, and all decisions about the clothes worn during a performance must consider this. A feeling for the degree of realism or stylization is established, the historical period to be used is set. The

Figure 3-19 Above: A bustle gown of the 1870s, designed by Gustave Janes to be worn in public during the daytime — *toilette de ville* or town dress.

Figure 3-20 Right: Mrs. Alving in Henrik Ibsen's *Ghosts*. Pencil sketch by Cletus Anderson.

period must be more specifically defined so the designer can use only those elements that reinforce the feelings that are right for the play. Any historical period, whether today, five years ago, or the Middle Ages, has many, many nuances. Compared with the multitude of variations in dress during any period, the designer has only a few opportunities to show the audience what this world is like. The feeling of the period must be captured by selecting its most typical and representative lines, not by introducing all the eccentric elements that are the exception rather than the rule. If a character needs to seem eccentric this can only be done in contrast to the other costumes. There can be no variations from the norm if the norm is not understood.

Establishing the period and the most useful elements in it is one step toward a unified costume approach. The designer still has many ways to develop this foundation. The basic line of the chosen era may seem quite suitable as it is, but often an interpretation of the line may better reinforce the mood of the play. In some cases the silhouette may need simplification. The bustle gowns of the 1870s and 1880s can be quite complex, with many puffs and swags (Figure 3-19). A costume for Mrs.

Alving in Ibsen's *Ghosts* could come from this era with the bustle intact but with many of the overlays eliminated to give her an appearance of resolve and control (Figure 3-20). The women in Shaw's *Arms and the Man,* although contemporaries of Mrs. Alving, might be costumed using all the intricacies available. Through an exaggeration of the line and detail, the designer reinforces the personalities of these women, who wish to be considered extremely smart by contemporary Bulgarian standards.

The way the detailing is handled on the silhouette can make a strong statement in unifying the costume effect. Again, the approach is contingent on the period and the importance and quantity of detail used. Costumes of the early Middle Ages are typified by a long, flowing line with very little trim. The emphasis is on mass and texture and the few details that are used then make a strong statement (Figure 3-21). If a great deal of ornamentation is added to the silhouette a definite style has been set (Figure 3-22). The period approach to Elizabethan detail is quite a contrast to that of the Middle Ages. The mass of the costume is still present, but a proliferation of detail is found in almost all areas. So

Figure 3-21   Below, left: This Gothic costume has a long, flowing line and very little trim, typical of the period of its source. Design for Judith in Bartók's *Bluebeard's Castle,* produced at Carnegie-Mellon University in 1976; watercolor sketch by Cletus Anderson.

Figure 3-22   Both fabric and trim are atypical of the Gothic in the costume (below) for Morning from *Bluebeard's Castle.* The choices nevertheless heightened the unreal quality needed for this character. Watercolor design by Cletus Anderson.

much can be happening on one costume that no particular area or type of treatment may dominate; an overall exceedingly decorative effect is achieved (Figure 3-23). Here the designer might stylize by suppressing some of this detail so that what is used is more significant and helps focus the costume (Figure 3-24).

COLOR AND FABRIC CONTROL

An audience first reacts to the color revealed as the lights come up on a scene. Perception of forms and textures follows. This makes color control a primary tool available to the designer, for through the relationships of the colors within a costume and among costumes onstage a

Figure 3-23 This etching of Louise of Lorraine shows the period approach to Elizabethan detail.

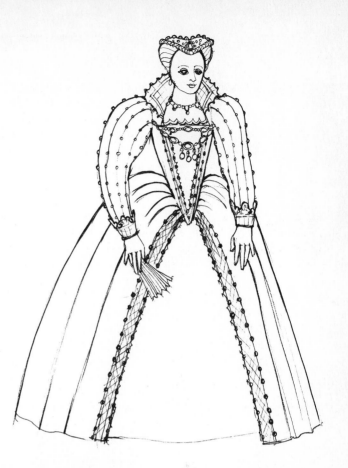

Figure 3-24 The detailing of a period costume might be suppressed for a particular effect. Pencil sketch by Cletus Anderson.

strong unified feeling can be achieved and the individual character development reinforced. Obviously a visual unification will be present if all the characters are clothed in the same color, but this seldom serves the best interest of the characters and the plot, for unity without variation can be monotonous. The designer can creatively incorporate the element of color into the scheme of production by selecting a range that seems most suitable to the mood of the play, then developing variations within the range to delineate the characters. Color should be considered in terms of the actual hues to be used; the chroma or purity of the hue in relation to the neutralized tone that is achieved when the hue is mixed with its compliment; and the value or degree of lightness or darkness of the hue on the scale of white to black. *Hamlet* might be conceived with hues in the jewel tones, with medium to low values at full or three-quarter intensity, producing a deep and rich color effect. Brecht's *Mother Courage,* on the other hand, might be designed in predominant earth tones, neutralized to half intensity or less with medium to low values, creating a result that conveys a sense of affinity with the earth and a struggle for survival. Hues can also be used to clarify different factions in the play. In *Romeo and Juliet,* the Montagues

Figure 3-25 Realistic fabrics were used for this gown for *The Duel,* adapted from a short story by Chekhov. Design by Barbara Anderson.

might be clad in blue, green, and purple shades and the Capulets in reds, oranges, and yellows. Though the hues are in high contrast, the value and intensity levels may be used to unify the total color effect. The designer must keep in mind that hue cannot be divorced from texture or the way the light is reflected off of or absorbed by the colored surface.

The types of fabrics selected for the costume are an integral part of the overall design scheme. If the fabrics chosen are typical of those that might have been used in the period, a degree of naturalism is achieved (Figures 3-25, 3-26); if the fabrics were not common in the era being used, a step toward stylization has been taken. Costumes of the thirteenth century done in wools will seem more authentic to the audience, even if the line has been altered, than the same designs executed in chiffon. English Renaissance costumes constructed in shiny cottons create a world that would not have been familiar in Elizabeth's court. Fabric selection can be crucial to the success of a costume design, for proper tailoring and draping qualities must be present. The designer must know the fabrics that will best fulfill the design ideas and select a range varied enough to meet the needs of the play, but with limitations that will add to the unity of the costumes (Figure 3-27). In a show that seems to express itself best with light, perky cottons, a gown made of

Figure 3-26 These tailored suits seem quite at home in the early nineteenth century because they are made of the same types of wools that would have been used then. From the John Marshall series sponsored by the U.S. Judicial Commission. Design by Barbara Anderson. Photo by Norris Brock. © Metropolitan Pittsburgh Public Television, Inc., 1976.

cut velvet will stick out like a sore thumb. A robe made of lining taffeta will never mesh in a scene where the other costumes are made of heavy satin and peau de soie. The designer may also decide to use plain fabrics instead of patterned ones; low, smooth surfaces instead of course textures; or a controlled combination of these treatments. A combination of plain and patterned fabric distributed throughout the costumes can be quite effective. The designer must always be concerned with visual balance, however. If all characters on stage are costumed in plain fabrics except one extra in a busy print dress, much more attention will fall on this single variation than should for the focus of the scene.

Costume unity, which is established with carefully conceived decisions, must take one more step before it can be given the final stamp of approval. It must also coordinate with the scenery and lights. Before the costume designer develops a basic concept, preliminary discussions take place with the other designers, as described in Chapter 2. Certain guidelines are set at that time for the general approach, but as each designer delves more deeply into the work, new ideas arise and solutions appear that were not evident before. Close communication must be maintained during the design period so ideas can be discussed as they develop. While all the treatments are considered, the color decisions may be particularly crucial. The first dress rehearsal is not the time to discover that the leading lady disappears as she sits in her favorite chair, for it may well be too late to construct a new gown or do reupholstering.

Figure 3-27   An element of humor is added to this costume for *Kiss Me Kate* by the use of nonrealistic fabric. Design by Cletus Anderson.

Considering practical limitations

Up to this point the designer has been making artistic and creative decisions about his or her approach to the play. Before going too far in developing the actual costume designs, the designer should take one more look at the limitations that were discussed in Chapter 2 and evaluate them against the direction the production should now take. The number of costumes needed, their complexity and the amount of time it will take to construct them, and the crew and money available to build them can seriously affect design decisions. It is the responsibility of the designer to create sketches for costumes that can be realized. Costume unity cannot be achieved if three costumes are made of fine fabrics and exquisitely detailed while seven more are thrown together using unbleached muslin and ball fringe. Fabric and trim choices must be made to fall within both the scheme and the budget. If there is not enough time and skilled labor to achieve ten intricately cut and detailed costumes, then an approach suitable for both the characters and the shop time available should be determined. If a number of costumes must be pulled from stock because of time and money constraints, the designer should look through the stock to determine what might be useful and how it can best be integrated into the production. It is irresponsible to develop a concept that can only be realized for part of the costumes when more careful planning would result in a unified production.

RESTRICTIONS CAUSED BY SET OR AUDITORIUM

Any restrictions that might be caused by the blocking or elements of the set should be considered as the costumes are designed. The amount of floor space a costume can take up may well depend on how many people need to be in a limited space. If a four-by-six-foot platform must hold three women, they cannot wear hoops that are four feet in diameter. The length of a train may need to be shortened if the stage space is small and there are many actors onstage in the scene. The rake of stairs or ramps may also influence the amount of fabric that can be effectively used at the back of a costume. A long, gradual incline allows a train to flow gracefully behind the actor, while a steep rake will not hold the fabric, causing the train to bunch in awkward piles.

The physical size of the auditorium can also influence the design concept. In an intimate arena theatre most of the audience is within a few feet of the actor and a subtle approach to detail may project the design quite effectively. In a 3000-seat proscenium theatre only a small percentage of the audience will be close enough to the actors to appreciate subtly detailed costumes, so a broader treatment would be needed to match the scale of the house. In the opposite vein, overscaling the detail for a small performing area can produce an effect that is contrary to the objectives of the production.

COSTUMES AND THE BODY

Costume design has one general limitation: it must relate to the body of the actor. To a certain degree, the costume can be used to change the way the body is perceived by the audience. Creative costumes can enhance an actor's physical stature or modify the body's appearance for a specific character. In either case the basic shape of the actor usually sets the limits on what can be achieved. Corseting can be used to give a slimmer, more controlled figure, but there is a limit past which breathing and movement become impossible. For the most part, the corset molds the waist to a better shape but cannot really take many inches off the figure. Realistic padding can be added to a figure only to the degree that it will blend into the body behind it. A huge tummy that slopes up to a very thin neck or down to very small thighs can be humorous, but cannot be taken seriously. An ample bosom in a low-cut gown looks right only if the actress can blossom out the top of the bodice, which can usually be achieved with careful engineering (see Chapter 8). Padding can only go so far; it is impossible believeably to create an extremely buxom woman from a flat-chested actress in a very low-cut dress.

Basic design lines can also be used to reinforce an emphasis on certain body areas. Shoulders can be broadened by the treatment of the sleevehead and by diagonal body lines (Figure 3-28), which also diminish the waist by stressing the V shape of the torso. A small waist can be emphasized by flairing the hip (Figure 3-29); large hips can be deemphasized by stressing the vertical line. The mass of the costume itself can heighten the visual impact of the actor. But if the mass becomes too great it takes over; rather than making the actor seem bigger, it makes him appear small, insignificant, and lost within the bulk of the costume.

Figure 3-28 The lapel on the overrobe for a town singer in *Kiss Me Kate* (left) accents a very broad shoulder. Design by Cletus Anderson.

Figure 3-29 The small waist is stressed by the pleats that flair the skirt and the stomacher that vees to the waistline in this costume for a town dancer in *Kiss Me Kate*, below. Design by Cletus Anderson.

The actor's experience with costumes

If the designer is familiar with the actors who are cast in the production, it may be helpful to consider the experience they have had with costumes and how easily they are able to cope with them. Some costumes are quite difficult to wear, and some actors do not deal easily with unfamiliar garments. The combination of the two can prove unhappy for all concerned: no matter how right the costume may seem for the character, if it cannot be worn properly it will not be effective. The only message that may come across to the audience is that the actor is fighting his clothes. The designer should try to choose costumes that can be worn confidently by the actors. In turn, the designer should be able to expect cooperation from the cast, for most actors realize that developing a skill in wearing period costumes is one of the tools of their trade.

Researching the production

The designer is now ready for the final step before sketching ideas. At this point, the designer will probably have collected notes outlining feelings to be captured, meaningful details, and lines that will express the mood of the production. Once the approach is clear, thorough research is needed to give substance and authenticity to the ideas.

There are many, many sources to draw from for research, and not all involve time spent in a library. For some plays the best material might be found while hanging out at the local all-night diner, or on the streets near a steel mill as the shifts change. The more common sources, however, are found in printed materials. Social histories and biographies can give the flavor of a period. Anything written about the playwright may help the designer understand how the author felt about the period and characters of the play. Accounts of past productions of the play may expand the designer's thinking by presenting different viewpoints and different solutions. These should be approached as interesting background pieces that can increase awareness and not used as actual sources, for seldom are two approaches identical, and studying solutions found by someone else could stifle original ideas. For example, a designer charged with creating the costumes for *My Fair Lady* should be familiar with the original production designed by Cecil Beaton, but surely there is at least one other way to stage the Ascot scene without using only a black, white, and gray color scheme.

Books on costume history furnish information that has been gathered from many areas, condensed and presented in an easily used fashion. Although important sources, these books have limitations that must be recognized. No one book can ever give a designer enough

Figure 3-30   The Renaissance dress on the right — for a Spanish noblewoman at a fiesta — drawn by Vecellio in the sixteenth century shows how the garments were perceived during the period in which they were worn. The mid-nineteenth-century copy at the left shows a definite Victorian influence on the costume.

information; the field is just too large for any survey to be able to spend enough time on one period. The designer must draw from a number of sources to get a more rounded viewpoint. It is also true that the quality of the drawings and the accuracy of the information can vary greatly. Even in the best of the costume books the information presented is the author's interpretation of the primary sources, or sources that actually come from the period. Costume history books should be used only as a starting point to assist the designer in understanding the period. Primary sources should be consulted as frequently as possible to view the material firsthand and not rely on secondary information. A good line drawing can be very useful in clarifying the different elements of a costume, but it may not give the true flavor of the period. A line drawing that wrongly interprets the source or imposes the period feeling of the time of the author back on the period being presented could seriously mislead the designer (see Figure 3-30). Unfortunately there are many books that err in this direction, but the designer who is thoroughly familiar with the primary sources should be able to recognize these inconsistencies.

The best primary sources vary with the historical period being researched. Good information can be found in statuary, wall paintings, illuminated manuscripts, stained glass windows, tapestries, paintings, fashion plates, etchings, photographs, catalogues, magazines, pictorial histories, medals, dolls: there are as many sources of information as there are means to record human history and culture visually. A guide to the basic shapes of the fashions predominant in the Western world is provided at the end of this book and includes for each period a list of some of the better sources of research material for the era. This is not intended as a miniature costume-history book, however, or as a source to use when designing a production. It is included because the designer needs a starting point to begin researching a show. It is a guide to the basic shapes of historical periods and provides a groundwork that can be used as the designer moves on to more detailed sources.

4

Developing the line

The time has come for the designer
actually to start sketching the costume ideas for the show. Once
the practical groundwork has
been laid, the more artistic
endeavors can begin. This step in
the design process can be accom-
panied by conflicting emotions. The
designer may be eager to give expression
to all the ideas that have grown since work

Figure 4-1 The figure established quickly with just a few strokes of the pencil.

on the play began, yet reluctant to make a definite commitment on paper. This reluctance could arise from a simple lack of confidence: What if I can't create a costume that is just right for this production and what if I can't draw what I mean? It might stem from an imprecise notion of the characters: Are my ideas about the characters sufficiently well formulated to design their costumes? In any event, neither problem can be solved by staring at a blank piece of paper. The best approach is to understand how the figure goes together and to draw it often. As the pencil moves on the paper and the designer experiments with different figures and lines, a feeling for each character grows and costume ideas begin to coalesce.

The quick sketch

The first step in drawing the costume is usually the quick sketch. This is just a rough expression of the designer's initial thoughts, something that can be put down rapidly to start ideas flowing. These sketches should be done freely and quickly; they are not born out of agony. If an idea doesn't seem to be working, start again.

One of the most practical ways to start the quick sketch is to envision both the physical and psychological attributes of the characters. How

Preceding page: This figure seems to be held in position by muscular control. Design for a player in *Hamlet* by Cletus Anderson.

Figure 4-2   Development of a costume for Lady Bracknell.

do they present themselves to the world? What do their bodies look like? How do they stand? Are they introspective or extroverted? Are they beginning to sag, or bulge, or bend? Move your pencil on paper until you begin to develop an awareness of the body of a particular character. An excellent exercise that will help establish the desired figure is to draw the entire figure without lifting your pencil from the paper. Explore the mass, outline, and movement of the character as the pencil goes from one area to another (Figure 4-1). Once you begin to develop an awareness of the character's figure, you will begin to understand the lines that will express the characters in your sketches. Take, for example, the character of Lady Bracknell in Oscar Wilde's *The Importance of Being Earnest.* Lady Bracknell is a very secure, forthright, outspoken woman. As the sketch of her figure begins to develop, the head is up, the chest is out, the stance is firm, the arms open out, the parasol is firmly planted (Figure 4-2a). Her physical characteristics are established in a few quick strokes. In the next step, the lines that reinforce these characteristics are added (Figure 4-2b). Lady Bracknell's torso would be controlled by a corset, which defines the waist, flares the hips, and thrusts the bosom up and out. The corset also provides an excellent psychological base for Lady Bracknell, for it is very much a symbol of the straitlaced, proper world that is the bulwark of her existence. The designer might wish to reinforce what the authors like to call her "forthrighteousness" by adding ruffles or frills on her bodice. The skirt springs smartly at the hip and falls to make a fairly firm outline. The shoulders should be those of a woman who takes command; consider the effectiveness of a slight kick upward before moving into a fairly full puff. The forearms are fitted to reveal the strength of her gestures. The hat wants to go upward and out to crown her domineering air. The parasol is fairly tailored. The general aura of Lady Bracknell has been established.

Reexamining the figure will help the designer clarify the best choices for the character (Figure 4-2c). The hat might be more solid; piling up Lady Bracknell's hair helps give her authority. A high-standing collar adds more rigidity, and the bodice treatment may benefit from more controlled ruffles. Perhaps a suit jacket would give her a more tailored, older appearance; trim on the skirt may add a firmer base. A bit of trim could be added to the parasol, as would befit her station. There are, of course, many decisions still to be made, but the quick impression of the character has been created. The elements should not be chosen at random, however. This Lady Bracknell is being designed for a production set in 1895 and from extensive research the designer would know the lines suitable to the silhouette of that period.

Very early in the designing process the designer should have a good idea of the fabric he or she will want to use. Lady Bracknell's suit, for example, should not be soft and draping. Her costume should be firm but flowing, with crisp sleeves and made of a somewhat stiff fabric without much shine. A faille would be a logical and workable choice of fabric for this costume.

Figure 4-3 shows the development of another costume idea, this time for Polonius in *Hamlet*. The first sketch shows the stance with just a few strokes — head down, shoulders sloping, belly sagging (Figure 4-3a). The next sketch begins to define specific characteristics: the costume becomes simple and bulky, tending to roundness. The neckline of the robe helps accentuate the droop of Polonius' belly and the slope of his shoulders (Figure 4-3b). In the third sketch ideas begin to clarify (Figure 4-3c). The robe is full, pleated at the waist to emphasize roundness, and sits slightly away from the neck so it will not seem to suit Polonius too perfectly. The collar of the jerkin underneath might also be low. The fit of the robe and jerkin makes Polonius' head and neck seem smaller and a bit lost. The sleeves are ample and give more roundness to the figure. Sleeves, collar, and skirt hem are banded in a darker material to break up the areas but are not so wide or heavy that they would add undue importance. He needs a neckchain because of his social position, but the chain must not be too large or important. The

Figure 4-3 Development of a costume for Polonius.

hair tends to be wispy, and might be thin on top. In this case the fabric is soft, heavy, and drapable; a heavy wool with a plush banding that is not too rich would work well.

When working out the quick sketch, jot down your ideas about color or texture or pin appropriate swatches of fabric to the sketch to give added dimension to the costume idea. The more you work with costumes and fabrics, the more you will find that, as you draw, the texture and drape of the cloth will be strongly in your mind. Knowledge of different fabrics will guide the pencil and help create the shape and the drape. Fabric and line constantly reinforce each other.

Laying out the figure

As a designer, you must be able to sketch the figure easily and quickly in order to begin the actual work of developing the character and designing the costume. Whether you are executing a quick sketch or starting a finished rendering, always draw the figure first. The costume is developed using this form as its foundation. Once you have a good understanding of the figure, it may take but a few lines to place the body on the page, but these will be enough to keep the drawing in proportion. If the body is not plotted out first, the pieces of the costume

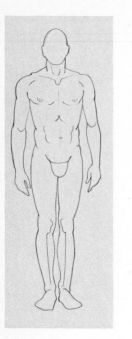

Figure 4-4 The male figure.

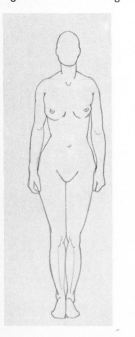

Figure 4-5 The female figure.

may not clothe well-proportioned figures. Too often a sketch gives the viewer a feeling of discomfort—that little nagging sense in the back of the mind that something is wrong. The reason for this is that deep down inside, under the full-length skirt, there is just not enough space allowed for the bottom of the torso and the legs, or perhaps the arm stops before it should—or extends to the knees, giving the figure an apelike quality. A properly proportioned outline of the figure keeps these problems from arising.

The basic figure is about eight heads high (Figure 4-4). This is slightly elongated in relation to the norm, but gives a well-proportioned body that is easy to use. The middle of the figure is the bottom of the torso. The knees come at the midpoint between torso and sole. The head is the top eighth of the body, the area from the shoulders to the waist occupies the next two-eighths, and the area from the waist to the crotch is the final segment of the figure's top half. The pit of the neck is one-third of the way into the second head; the bustline falls at the bottom of this section. The elbow comes to the waist, the wrist to the bottom of the torso, and the hand about one-third of the way to the knee. The male figure has more breadth to the shoulder and chest, about two heads wide, and slimmer hips; the female has narrow shoulders, about one and one-half heads, that are the same width as the pelvic area (Figure 4-5).

As the figure moves, the relationships among body parts must stay the same. An arc extending from the waist with the shoulder as the pivot point will keep the elbow in the correct proportion, as will an arc at the knee pivoting from the hip. The figure must be kept in balance. It must have a firm stance and a feeling for the distribution of body weight. The figure's center of gravity drops from the pit of the neck. If the weight is distributed equally this line of gravity drops to a point between the feet (Figures 4-4 and 4-5). If the body weight shifts, this line falls from the pit of the neck to the support foot (Figure 4-6). When the weight goes to one leg the pelvis shifts, rising over the balance point and dropping the other leg, creating the illusion that the non-weight-bearing leg is longer. As the pelvis shifts, the shoulders may stay square or may counter the move by tilting in the opposite direction. A figure may also be supported by an object such as a cane, table, or stool (Figure 4-7). It is generally better to allow well-proportioned figures to be able to stand alone without the need for props to keep them from toppling over. Supporting objects should be carefully planned if they are used in a costume plate. A figure in action may not have the point of gravity supported in the usual fashion, but may seem to be held in position through muscle control (see p. 105). For a more detailed look at the balance of the body, refer to the source books mentioned in the next section.

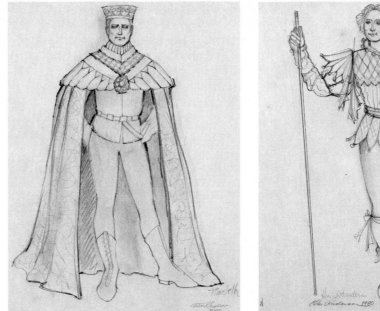

THE HINGE POINTS

The natural reference points of the body are the hinge points, those points that give the body its articulation. In designing the different areas of the costume are scaled in relation to the spaces between these points. The basic layout of the figure must be carefully established in reference to these hinge points and how the hinges connect one part of the body to the next must be understood. One body area does not just sit on another; it grows out of it.

The following discussion gives a very simplified view of how the body goes together as a rudimentary beginning point. For more in-depth information on the figure, see Stephen Rogers Peck's *Atlas of Human Anatomy for the Artist, Drawing from Life* by George B. Bridgeman, and *Drawing the Human Form* by William A. Berry.

THE HEAD, NECK, AND SHOULDERS

Viewed from the front the head appears to be an oval, drawn in a ratio of about 6 to 8, with the ears extending out at the sides in the second quarter. The neck supports the head from slightly inside the jawline. The contours of the neck are formed by the sternomastoid, the muscle that extends from behind the ear to the collarbone. The back of the neck

Figure 4-6   Left: Body weight on the right foot. Costume for *Macbeth* designed by Cletus Anderson for a production at the Pittsburgh Public Theatre, 1980.

Figure 4-7   Right: The staff helps support the figure. Costume for Punch in the film *Knightriders*, 1982. Design by Cletus Anderson.

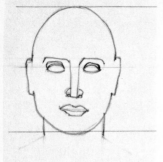

Figure 4-8 The head from the front.

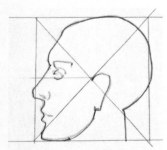

Figure 4-9 The head from the side.

is joined to the shoulder by the trapezius muscle (Figure 4-8). Thus, the neck joins the body on two levels: the pit of the neck at the center front is much lower than the connection at the shoulder. From the side, the angle at which the head sits on the neck and the neck on the torso is more evident (Figure 4-9). The side view of the head is based on a square, for the head is about as deep as it is long. The top front of the ear is located at the center of the square.

SHOULDER AND ARM

The arm is connected to the shoulder by the deltoid muscle, which extends from the trapezius to the muscles of the upper arm. The smallest part of the upper arm occurs just above the elbow, where the upper arm muscles taper into the lower arm muscles. The widest part of the lower arm occurs just below the elbow (Figure 4-10). As the arm bends, the back of the arm from the shoulder to the elbow joint lengthens, and the front of the arm from the shoulder to the bend decreases (Figure 4-11).

THE WRIST AND HAND

The hand joins the wrist at a slight angle that seems to reverse as the hand turns. From the back of the hand the thumb appears to start out higher on the arm. From the palm side, the bulge that leads to the little

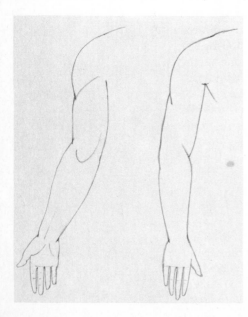

Figure 4-10 The arm, palm out and turned to show the back of the hand.

Figure 4-11 The bent arm.

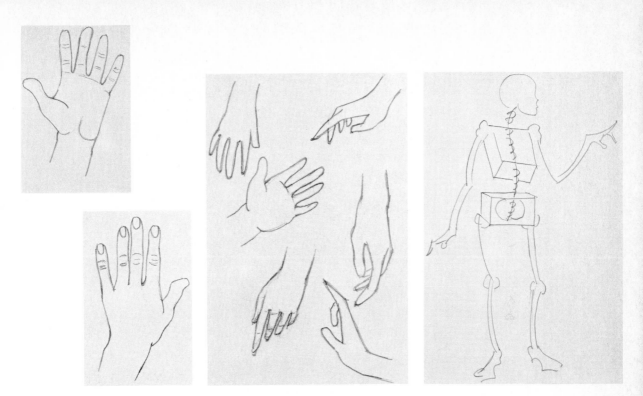

Figure 4-12   The hand.

Figure 4-13   Various hand positions.

Figure 4-14   Block figure.

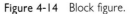

Figure 4-15   Male and female torsos.

finger begins first (Figure 4-12). The palm and fingers, which are about equal in length to the span from the tip of the chin to the hairline, seem to be more of a continuation of the arm, with the thumb growing from one side of the palm. From the back of the hand the fingers can make up slightly more than half the length of the hand; from the palm side the fingers are less than half the length of the hand. It may be difficult to achieve a well-articulated hand, and often a feeling for the gesture of the hand may be quite sufficient to complete the figure. Figure 4-13 shows a number of ways the hand may be indicated with a few lines.

THE WAIST

The torso can be thought of as two blocks connected by a flexible pipe or spine; the top block is the ribcage, the bottom is the pelvis (Figure 4-14). The greater the span between the blocks, the better the possibility to reshape the waistline with some form of corseting. The female waistline curves in, then springs out to the hip; the male waistline is less indented and the hips are narrower (Figure 4-15).

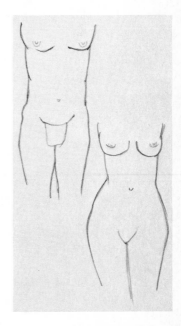

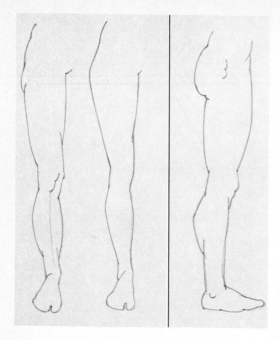

Figure 4-16   Above: Male and female legs.

Figure 4-17   Right: The leg from the side.

Figure 4-18   The foot.

Figure 4-19   The planes of the face.

THE HIP, LEG, AND KNEE

The leg sets into the torso at an angle, forming the hip. This angle is repeated down the leg by the opposing muscles and the indentations of the knee until the ankle bones reverse the direction (Figure 4-16). The curve of a woman's upper thigh is more prominent than a man's; other muscle masses are more obvious in the man's leg. As the knee bends it appears to lengthen the upper leg. From the side the back curve of the buttock goes to the bottom of the torso. The curve of the front thigh muscle starts higher and seems to swing right to the curve of the back calf muscle (Figure 4-17).

THE FOOT

The foot hinges on to the ankle and forms the foundation for the stance. It grows wider from ankle to toes and the weight of the leg sits slightly to the inside so the midpoint of the ankle lines up with the second toe, which is usually the longest one (Figure 4-18). The foot is longer than one head and articulates in three parts: the heel, the arch, and the toes. The foot must be placed so it firmly supports the figure.

DETAILING THE FACE

The figure will not seem complete unless a certain amount of detail is included on the face. A blank oval at the top of the neck calls too much attention to itself. The features can be either indicated sketchily or completely drawn, depending on the ability of the designer. If the features cannot be drawn to add to the character, then a stylized indication that will not distract from the whole should be used. The face may be the first part of the sketch the director notices. It must lead him or her in the right direction to understand the costume for the character.

The basic shape of the head is an oval, almost three-quarters as wide as it is long. A horizontal line through the middle gives the placement of the eyes; a horizontal line bisecting the lower half locates the bottom of the nose. The mouth is about a third of the way down the bottom quarter and the beginning of the chin pad is about a third of the way up from the bottom of the chin. The basic outline of the face goes from the forehead out to the cheekbones, located slightly below the eyes, down and in slightly to the jawbone, a bit below the mouth, then in to the chin (see Figure 4-8, page 112). The planes of the face give three-dimensionality to the drawing, though the actual lines would not be used. The front plane of the forehead is established by a line from the outside of the eyes that slopes up and slightly outward. The side planes end with a line extending from the eye socket. The front of the cheek is established by a line that comes from the corner of the eye and then turns down to the pad of the chin, which also forms the front boundary for the side of the cheek. The other planes indicated are those of the eye socket and eyeball, nose, and upper lip (Figure 4-19). The eyes are placed about the width of one eye apart from each other. The inner edge forms a small loop and the top outer lid overlaps the under lid. The eyelid should ride just at the top of the pupil; a higher placement produces a staring effect (Figure 4-20). The mouth can be established by drawing in the line between the lower lip and the upper lip, which may be in shadow, then indicating the bottom of the lower lip with a line that disappears before it reaches the corners. A shadow under the lower lip gives it dimension (Figure 4-21). A carefully detailed face is

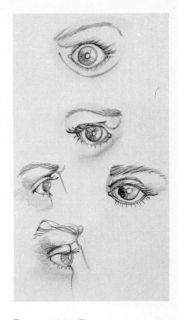

Figure 4-20 The eye.

Figure 4-21 The lips.

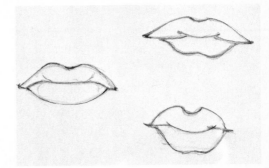

Figure 4-22   Detailed face.

Figure 4-23   Various styles of indicated faces.

shown in Figure 4-22, while Figure 4-23 gives examples of faces indicated by a few lines.

AGE AND BODY SHAPE

The age of a character can definitely be reflected by his or her body. At birth the body is only about four heads high, with the center near the navel. By age two the body is about four and a half heads high; by eight, about six and a half heads; at puberty or fourteen years, about seven heads; and by eighteen, a full seven and a half to eight heads tall. In old age the body tends to sag and shrink though the head remains the same size, so the figure may again be seven to seven and a half heads tall (Figure 4-24). With old age, the body begins to succumb to the force of gravity it has withstood for so many years. The head sags forward, the spine curves, the shoulders droop, the stomach muscles give out, and the whole body is pulled downward (Figure 4-25). Extra weight can also bring a curve to the back as it tries to compensate for the bulk in front, although a young heavy person will seem to be able to carry the fat rather than let it pull the body down (Figure 4-26).

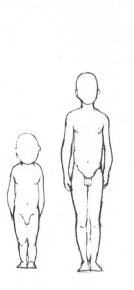

Young | Boy | Young man | Old man
child

Figure 4-24 The proportions of the body change as it ages.

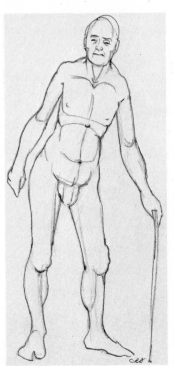
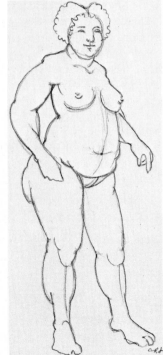

Figure 4-25 Far left: The old body.

Figure 4-26 Left: The heavy body.

Finding the best medium for sketching

There are many types of pencils and paper available for sketching. As you develop your style and undertake different projects, you should experiment with different pencils and paper to see how they work for you. Basically, the paper should not be too smooth. It needs to have some tooth (surface texture) so it can interact with the pencil. Similarly, the pencil should not be too hard. It must be soft enough to allow variation in line. Of course, these are not absolute rules. So much can vary in the way each individual likes to draw and the effect that is desired for a particular project. Judgment and creativity are equally important, but an understanding of your basic tools is a prerequisite.

A hard pencil can give a uniform line that stays quite crisp and distinct, but this type of line is often not very interesting, nor does it convey much movement or help create a three-dimensional quality. A harder pencil seems to move more quickly and produce a surface line. A softer pencil, on the other hand, can work its way around the figure more slowly and give the feeling of moving in and out with the contours. Figure 4-27 shows the types of line that can be produced by pencils of various degrees of hardness and softness. A pencil that works well for a particular designer does not need to be a "drawing" pencil; an ordinary, good-quality writing pencil can be quite effective. An inexpensive pencil, however, can have inconsistencies in the lead that make it more difficult to use.

Just as a soft pencil interacts more with the paper, a paper surface that has some tooth seems to become more a part of the drawing process. Very smooth paper offers too little resistance to the pencil, and paper that has quite a bit of tooth can impose its surface on the drawing style. Figures 4-28 and 4-29 illustrate how different papers and pencils affect the quality of the line. The first is done on smooth paper with a hard pencil and the second on paper with some tooth and a softer pencil.

Figure 4-27   Types of lines produced by hard and softer pencils.

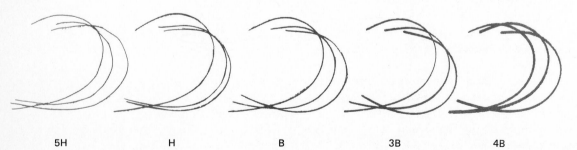

5H   H   B   3B   4B

Figure 4-28 Above left: Figure on smooth paper with a hard pencil.

Figure 4-29 Above: Figure on rough paper with a soft pencil.

Inexpensive newsprint is often used for quick sketches in the early stages of a design. It is quite rough and not very sturdy, so it may not be suitable for a more finished sketch. The type of paper and pencils used need not be the same for every project. Ideas for heavy costumes with little detail may come more easily if worked up on a paper with more tooth and drawn with a soft pencil. Costumes that will be refined, elegant, and highly detailed may develop with more facility on a smoother paper using a pencil with slightly harder lead.

The importance of line quality

A line can be thought of as a path that expresses the action it took to create it. Line used to reveal the costume should be reminiscent or descriptive of the fabric, giving a sense of its quality and weight, the way it hangs on the frame, and how it falls or flows. Line can portray both silhouette and movement. A line showing chiffon is not the same

Figure 4-30   Above: A chiffon costume.

Figure 4-31   Above right: A costume of smoothly flowing fabric.

as the type used to depict a heavy wool. The motion of a crisp taffeta is not presented in the same way the drape of a jersey is. In Figure 4-30 the dancer is costumed in a light, flowing chiffon that catches the air. The line is light and loose and does not completely surround the area it defines, but suggests it. The contour of the figure is still visible through the fabric. The pencil catches the page, then lifts and floats. In Figure 4-31 the fabric is a wool jersey that falls softly into folds. The line flows smoothly as the fabric would; it is more continuous top to bottom without a great deal of variation. Figure 4-32 shows a woman of 1835 in a taffeta ball gown. The fabric is crisp and light, and the line is shorter and varies in intensity to show the movement that would be present in this type of costume. The man in Figure 4-33 is clothed in a heavy wool robe and hood. The line is correspondingly heavy, feeling its way around the thick folds.

The designer must develop the ability to control line quality with ease. The only way to achieve this facility is through practice, constantly using the hand and arm to develop the necessary skill. One useful exercise is to do repeated line variations, containing movement and varying rhythms. The exercise in Figure 4-34 involves establishing a simple figure with a few clear areas, then developing the figure as though it were clothed in fabrics of different weights.

Drawing is a skill designers must master. It is a motor skill that improves the more it is done, but drawing must also be combined with intellect and the power of observation. Drawing is a language for designers. By developing the ability to arrange marks and symbols, designers develop means to record and clarify their thoughts and ideas and to communicate them to others. Sketching combines exploration and investigation. Ideas flow from head to hand to paper. The result should look effortless (though of course it may not be), not tortured and labored. This is not an impossible task; it merely requires repeated drawing. Designers who do not work to develop this facility do themselves a disservice. They will then find they must spend time on simple drawing problems that could be better used in refining the design. Designers are seldom satisfied with the way they draw. Even those with many years of experience still strive to better their skills. So draw whenever and wherever possible. Attend life-drawing classes if they are available and study anatomy books such as those mentioned earlier

Figure 4-32 A ball gown of crisp, light taffeta.

Figure 4-33 A robe of heavy wool.

Figure 4-34 Left: Quickly drawn figures clothed in fabrics of different weight.

in this chapter. Keep a sketchbook handy and when a few spare minutes crop up draw people who happen to be around. If no one happens to be handy, use a mirror. Draw anything that catches your eye. Your subject need not be a person. Control of your arm and pencil comes from constant practice. And the more you draw, the more you will be able to think visually and explore, record, and interpret the world around you.

The elements of design

A knowledge of the basic terminology of design is one more useful tool for the costume designer. The same elements and principles that are used effectively in any form of design can be controlled to produce a desired result in costume design. The following discussion is brief but provides a general familiarity with the elements you will be using as you arrange the lines and shapes you wish to use in your costumes.

LINE

Figure 4-35 Many of the strong lines of the sketch will not be present when the costume is built. Watercolor design for *Pierre Patelin* by Barbara Anderson.

Line has been discussed a great deal without actually defining it. Line can be thought of as a point extended in any direction. It can be drawn in any tone, value, color, or color intensity. It can be long or short, broad or narrow. A line can be drawn in only one direction and is then straight. If it changes direction abruptly it forms an angle. If it changes direction gradually it is curved.

When putting costume ideas on paper a combination of lines is used to express form. These lines may or may not be present or have the same impact in the real costume. Lines that indicate edges of fabric or folds of cloth will not be as evident on the three-dimensional figure as those that indicate bands of trim. While the study of pure line is useful, a line in a sketch should not create an effect that will not be present when the costume is constructed. Figure 4-35 shows a sketch with a strong linear feeling that gives it interest and life, but it is more an illustration than a costume rendering. Most of those lines would not be present in the actual costume, so it might very well lose the punch it seems to have in the drawing.

A line attracts attention according to the amount of contrast it makes with the ground on which it is drawn. In a costume sketch a line may appear quite strong because the dark gray line of the pencil is seen against the light background of the paper. If the line depicts a linear trim that will not be in high contrast with its background in the finished costume, this should influence the way the sketch is drawn or the rendering painted.

A line also attracts attention according to its length. If the tone contrast is the same, a longer line will attract the eye more than a shorter line. Given lines of the same length, a curved line will attract more attention than a straight one because it is more concentrated (Figure 4-36).

Linear harmonies can be created in a number of ways. A straight line has a harmony of direction; the direction of the line does not change. A line that changes direction in a regular fashion produces a harmony of angles (Figure 4-37). If the degree of the angles remains constant but the length of the lines varies, then there is a harmony of angles but no harmony of measure. In Figure 4-38 the angles are all 90 degrees. If the length of the line is constant but the angle changes, there is a harmony of measure but no harmony of angle (Figure 4-39). Curved lines may produce similar harmonies if the curves are based on the same radius.

A line that creates a shape and repeats it produces a linear progression. The repetitions make up a harmony of shape. If the repetitions are exactly the same, there is a harmony of measure and shape in the progression (Figure 4-40). If the size of the shapes varies, then there

Figure 4-36   A curved line is more eye-catching than a straight line of the same length.

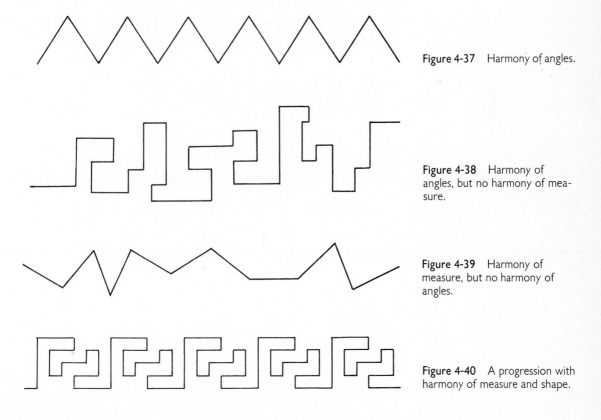

Figure 4-37   Harmony of angles.

Figure 4-38   Harmony of angles, but no harmony of measure.

Figure 4-39   Harmony of measure, but no harmony of angles.

Figure 4-40   A progression with harmony of measure and shape.

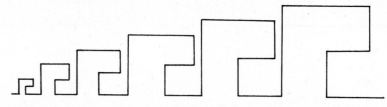

Figure 4-41   A gradation.

exists a harmony of shape without a harmony of measure (Figure 4-41). A progression in which the size of the shapes increases or decreases in a regular fashion creates a gradation, which is also illustrated in Figure 4-41. A gradation is not perceived unless there are at least three elements that progress in a regular fashion, drawing the eye along. If the intervals between the elements are too great, the gradation will not be perceived.

The types of lines and harmonies used can greatly change the effect of a costume. Figures 4-42 and 4-43 show two costumes based on the same simple shape: one is executed in curved harmonies, the other in straight line and angle harmonies. In each there are harmonies based on a certain type of line with variations in measure and gradation. Two very different types of character grow out of the same basic garments by emphasizing a different type of harmony. The actual use of linear harmonies is seldom this blatant, but exercises in excess often help clarify an idea that can then be incorporated with a bit more finesse.

Figure 4-42   Left: A costume with curved harmonies.

Figure 4-43   Right: A costume with straight-line and angle harmonies.

Figure 4-44 Line direction can influence the audience. Above: the dominant vertical line.

Figure 4-45 Above: The dominant horizontal line.

Figure 4-46 Above right: The dominant diagonal line.

The direction of the line can elicit certain reactions in an audience. Vertical lines emphasize height and can produce a feeling of uprightness and grandeur. The vertical follows the line of growth, which lends itself naturally to the body (Figure 4-44). The horizontal line is not as fundamentally suited to the human figure because it goes across the natural line. The horizontal feeling tends to be more inactive and solid and adds bulk to the figure (Figure 4-45). The diagonal line may give the costume more activity and flow, for it implies action and dynamic movement (Figure 4-46).

SHAPE

Shapes are formed when a line returns to itself and creates the outline of an area. In a costume drawing this may be actual or implied. A line may clearly define the edges of a shape or the shape may be visible even when every segment of the line is not present. The eye of the viewer will complete the picture that is implied by the lines that are drawn (Figure 4-47). The harmonies and variations that are found in lines are also present in shapes.

Figure 4-47 Above: The outline of a figure may be clearly defined or implied.

ORDER

Design can be thought of as a means of creating order, and order in design terms is revealed in repetition, sequence, and balance. While these are more easily controlled by the easel painter, a knowledge of the manner in which these elements are used is also good background for the costume designer.

REPETITION

Repetition is the simplest form of order. The most basic repetition might be illustrated by a plain sheet of paper, for no matter where the eye looks on that paper the same tone is repeated. A straight line produces a repetition in one direction and can also have a repetition of tone if the line remains constant. A certain shape may be repeated and creates a repetition even if the size (measure), tone, and attitude vary (Figure 4-48). Here a single element, the triangle, is repeated, bringing a certain sense of order. The sense of order is increased as the number of elements that are repeated is increased. The order is considered perfect if all the elements repeat; that is, shape, measure, tone, attitude, and interval (the space between shapes) (Figure 4-49).

REPETITION FOR HARMONY

Harmony is produced by repetition. To create a harmony at least one element must occur two or more times. The greater the number of repetitions and the more strongly they are felt, the greater the harmony. Wide intervals between elements or a strong contrast that will catch the eye may break the flow of the repetition and weaken its strength and the strength of the harmony it produces.

Figure 4-48   A repetition of shape with variance in size, tone, and attitude.

Figure 4-49   A perfect repetition.

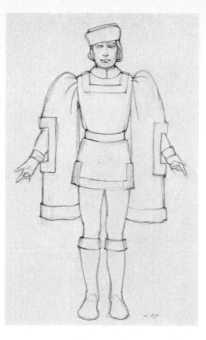

Figure 4-50 A close harmony can make a boring costume.

If harmony brings order into a composition, then variety could be thought to bring disorder, for it breaks the flow. But it is through the control of variety that interest and focus can be added to the design. A close harmony can make a boring costume (Figure 4-50). Variety must be present to add interest and focus. A great deal of variety can be interesting, but it is often confusing and muddles the figure.

Harmony can be established in measure by the repetition or recurrence of a certain size and in shape with the repetition or recurrence of a certain shape. There are three ways of bringing harmony into tone: first, by value harmony, in which the values, or amount of lightness or darkness in the tones all occur near the level of the one value that is to predominate; second, by having little contrast between colors or hues and producing harmony of color; and third, by keeping the amount of neutralization in each color about the same to create harmony of intensity. Any of these harmonies may be used together or separately.

SEQUENCE

The order of sequence in design becomes apparent when the eye is drawn from one element to another in a systematic way. Like harmony, sequences can be perceived in positions, measures, shapes, attitudes, intervals, and any of the components of tone: hue, value, and intensity.

The types of sequence are: sequence of continuation or repetition, sequence of alternation, and sequence of graduation or progression.

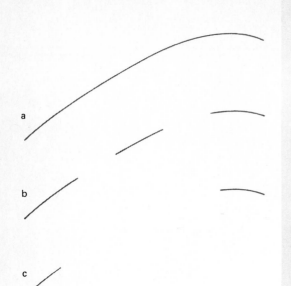

a

b

c

Figure 4-51 (a) The sequence of the line is easily followed. (b) A broken line with the sequence still felt. (c) A large interval that interrupts the sequence.

Figure 4-52 Above right: A costume with a sequence of repetition and a sequence of alternation used as trim.

The simplest form of the sequence of continuation or repetition is the line, which the eye can follow easily from beginning to end. In Figure 4-51a the sequence of the line is easily followed. In Figure 4-51b the line is broken, but the sequence is still perceived, for the eye is able to connect one segment to the next. In Figure 4-51c the feeling of the sequence is broken, for the interval is large and the eye may not be able to make the connection. A row of buttons down the front of a costume creates a sequence of shapes and tones. If the buttons are too far apart, the feeling of sequence is broken and they become isolated spots.

The sequence of alternation is produced when any sequence is broken repeatedly and at equal intervals. This continuation of regularly recurring breaks or accents creates a feeling of rhythm. The rhythm can be produced by the regular alternation of any of the elements mentioned before; position, tone, shape, measure, or attitude, or by the alternation of any combination of these elements. Figure 4-52 shows a costume in which a sequence of repetition and a sequence of alternation are used for the trim. The repetition moves continuously around the figure. The alternation also moves but does so in a more interesting fashion, incorporating a regular rhythm with the movement.

In design the sequence of progression takes the form of a gradation of one tone, position, measure, shape, or attitude to another, always by degrees. The change that occurs is both gradual and uniform. A smooth wash from white to black through the range of grays is a gradation of value. Figure 4-53 shows a costume that uses a number of gradations. There is a gradation of curved shapes on the arms and a more linear gradation trimming the skirt opening, then reversing up the center front of the bodice. The chain of the pomander hanging down from the belt has a gradation of measure. The beads are all the same size (except, of course, for the large one at the end, introducing variety and focus), but the spaces between the beads form the progression.

BALANCE

The simplest form of balance is symmetrical balance, in which the shapes or lines on one side of a vertical axis are mirrored on the opposite side. Since the human body is relatively symmetrical, a symmetrical balance is often the starting point for a costume design. But symmetry alone does not mean the design has a sense of balance, for the elements used may not hold together well. They may cause the focus to split and keep the eye moving when it should be able to achieve a sense of equilibrium (Figure 4-54). Figure 4-55 shows a costume with good symmetrical balance: the elements are in control and well focused.

In asymmetrical balance the same feeling of control and focus must be present, but the elements used are not an exact inversion on the vertical axis. Balance is achieved by some form of opposing or contrasting elements that still bring a sense of equilibrium to the composition. In this case the eye of the designer is of utmost importance. He or she

Figure 4-53 Left: A costume using a number of gradations.

Figure 4-54 Center: A symmetrical costume that does not balance well.

Figure 4-55 Below: Good symmetrical balance. Claudius from *Hamlet*. Watercolor design by Cletus Anderson.

Figure 4-56 An asymmetrical costume. Dancer in the *Carousel* ballet. Watercolor design by Robert Perdziola, 1982.

must be able to feel the balance and cannot simply calculate it. Figure 4-56 is an example of asymmetrical balance on a costumed figure.

Two more design elements have a very strong effect on a costume: color and texture. Texture will be considered in more detail later in this chapter; color is discussed in Chapter 5. Control of the line and the shape can be considered separately as an exercise on the way to a design. Line and shape combine with color and texture to produce the final result. As line and shape are developed, the designer must always be aware of the ultimate contribution of the other two design elements to the finished product.

Developing the costume line for the production

Part of setting the style for a production is deciding upon the period in which it will be done. This could mean England in the 1780s, medieval Scotland, the Belle Epoque, a world set centuries in the future — practically anything. But whatever it is, the time in which the play takes place will give to the body a certain silhouette, a basic line that defines the period. The period should be selected because its silhouette enhances the play, delineates the characters, and helps the audience better understand the ideas being presented. If the silhouette doesn't do this, perhaps it is time to go back to the drawing board and rethink the period to be used. A play presented in the period for which it was intended, either because it was written during that era or because that was the specific historical time the author selected for the action, usually settles itself into the given silhouette quite easily. When the period is changed, problems can develop because the line may run contrary to the characters and situations. A good, hardy farce like *The Menaechmi* by Plautus may not work well in a period that stresses a long, elegant line. A sophisticated drama such as Ibsen's *Hedda Gabler* may not be effective in a period based on quick, short lines. A serious play of the late 1960s may very well be more effective to a modern audience if either updated or predated, for the miniskirt can be a difficult line to take seriously. As the designer works out the silhouette of the costume, further discussions with the director may be needed to clarify what both want the effect to be. If the designer feels a change in period would be beneficial, he or she should be able to explain why the silhouette is not as effective as it could be and have some well-considered alternatives to present.

A costume can be defined by the shape it makes in space. It is a form that must be understood from the front, side, and back. This understanding begins with an in-depth investigation of the period in which the play is set. Even if changes will be made in the historical silhouette the designer must be knowledgeable about the era that is the basis for the designs. An understanding of the foundation under the costumes, the shapes that are used for the different body areas, and the type of seaming that constructs those shapes are all indispensable. The designer must be able to see the whole picture, know how it goes together, and not get sidetracked by historical detail. The details can be fascinating and certainly eye-catching, but they are not the starting point. In architecture the adage may be that "form follows function"; in costuming, "frill follows form." (And certainly "form follows function" has not been a guiding motto for clothes, for too often form inhibits function.) The designer must know the shape of the period and also must comprehend some of the philosophy behind it and discover the ideals of the period. The details of history should not be slavishly reproduced, but adapted as needed for particular requirements without losing the flavor, sense, or integrity of the period. It is certainly a useless exercise to go to the trouble to pick a specific moment in time and then abandon those elements that make the era unique.

THE SILHOUETTE AND ITS RELATION TO THE HINGE POINTS

The silhouette to be used for a production needs to be specifically defined in its relationship to the hinge points, or articulation points, which are the body's major reference areas. The silhouette is established by the way it relates to these points. It is not helpful to say that women's sleeves during a certain period were ten inches long. What is important to know is how that sleeve relates to the elbow and shoulder. The proportions of the costume must be considered in relation to the proportions of the body. The size of that sleeve will vary greatly if the bodies it adorns vary by just a few inches. The hinge points define the proportions of the body and the specific period silhouette is created by the way it relates to these body units. Consider each area to clarify the way the line should be placed.

Neck. The neckline of the period costume can vary greatly, sometimes relating more to the shoulder treatment, sometimes confining the neck tightly and restricting movement. Some periods have one style that is most typical; others incorporate many styles, several of which may be equally right for the same character. A proper Victorian woman may wear a bodice with a high, tight-fitting boned collar for afternoon tea and a ball gown with an extremely low neckline that evening.

Shoulders. The manner in which the sleeve joins the body will often determine the type of shoulder emphasis the figure will have. The

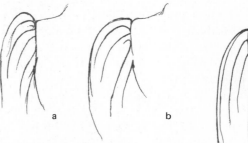

Figure 4-57 The type of sleeve can vary the line of the shoulder.

sleeve is most often set into the body of the garment at the top of the arm, though there are occasions where the armhole cuts farther into the shoulder line, extends from it, or begins to curve down the upper arm. A broad shoulder might be enhanced by the fullness of the sleeve, padding in the sleeve or shoulder, or a costume piece that extends the shoulder line, such as a wing or a roll. The amount of fullness on the top of the sleeve and the manner in which it is controlled are both important to the line, for the shoulder gives a different appearance if the fabric "kicks" up, extends out, or droops (Figure 4-57). There is usually a certain range of shoulder variation within one period, and within the range are many choices that can assist the visual characterization.

Bust. The one major reference area on the body that is not a hinge point, the location of the bust relates closely to the neckline treatment and to seam and trim placement on the front of the bodice.

Elbow and wrist. The articulation points of the arm are used to determine both the length of the sleeve and the proportion of the sleeve elements. Many long sleeves are broken up or trimmed in relation to the elbow.

Waist. The waistline of a garment can vary anywhere from under the bust to the hipline. It can be actually delineated by a seam if the top and skirt are cut separately, by a belt that creates a definite line, or by separately constructed garments such as a skirt and blouse. The waistline might be simply implied by the way the garment fits and falls in fullness when vertical seams go from shoulder to hem. The placement of the waist is crucial and must be specific. It should definitely separate the upper and lower body areas and not wander haphazardly around the middle of the body. The waist can be a straight line around the body or may point downward at the center front, which appears to lengthen the upper torso.

Hip, knee, and ankle. These hinge points most often relate to the length of the body garments or to the manner in which the main trim areas break up the garments. The latter is particularly true with women's clothes, for in proper society a woman's legs were kept hidden by her clothes until this century.

Specific decisions must be made about the way the costume relates to the body. This relationship helps create the style of the production. The influence of costume on the human figure begins with the underpinnings, such as corsets or padding that may reshape the human form, and continues through all the outer layers of clothing that are seen by

Figure 4-58   The basic Mrs. Malaprop.

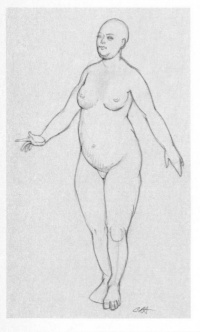

the audience. A specific look is established that says "This is what is important about these clothes in relation to these characters in this play." Good design does not happen by accident. It must be carefully planned and thought through.

Individual costume characterization

Once the basic line for the show is selected and the proportions of the costumes established, each character must be individually considered in terms of the stylistic elements of the period that best support his or her role. Think first of the dominant silhouette; then concentrate on the major areas of variation within the basic look. After these are determined the details within the areas can be developed. This does not mean that the details are less important than the general shapes. When planning the costume of a specific character, a designer may start with the idea of a certain type of detail. For example, a design might be based

Figure 4-59   Below left: Mrs. Malaprop as she assumes the silhouette of the period.

Figure 4-60   Center: Mrs. Malaprop with the extravagant details that would please her.

Figure 4-61   Right: The simpler Julia.

on dainty, frilly ruffles; a very wide belt to give a strong, solid waistline; or a narrow tie knotted very precisely and held down with a tie bar. These are valuable images that should always be kept in mind, although they are usually not the starting point in the development of a design idea. As a designer, you must know what the line is before you know where to put the ruffles and where the waistline is before you know what kind of belt to use. These images grow out of an overall feeling for the character. Be sure to find that feeling and capture it in the general line. The details will then seem absolutely right when added to the basic concept.

Take, for example, Mrs. Malaprop in Richard Brinsley Sheridan's *The Rivals.* She is a woman a bit past her prime, although she would never admit it. Mrs. Malaprop is self-indulgent and pretentious, rich and fashion-conscious, but her idea of what is fashionable does not coincide with the opinion of the world in general. Although she is a very foolish woman, Mrs. Malaprop is an endearing character. Deep inside she might well look like Figure 4-58, a forthright but rather matronly woman. If she is to be dressed in the styles of 1775 her silhouette would adjust to the fashionable look of the day, as in Figure 4-59. In this sketch, the corset binds Mrs. Malaprop and serves to pull her together tightly. Although not small, her waist is precisely confined, and her skirt springs out in a full silhouette. Her bosom blossoms up and out of the top of the corset (those excess pounds have to go somewhere). Costumes of this period often are soft, with ruffles at the neckline and the sleeves, and Mrs. Malaprop would certainly want to incorporate this in her outfit to enhance what she would consider her youthful qualities. Hairstyles of the period were high; and Mrs. Malaprop, always seeking the height of fashion, would wear high hairstyles. The skirt could be closed in front, but given a choice of showing two skirts or one, Mrs. Malaprop would probably opt for two. Her basic period silhouette is established. Now the details that will help fill out her character can be added. In Mrs. Malaprop's case this can be a great deal of fun, for given a lady prone to such extravagance in language, it is hard to imagine she would try to contain herself in her dress. The result might be similar to the costume shown in Figure 4-60. In the same play the initial ideas for Julia's costume could be quite different, though based on the same silhouette. She has youth, beauty, simplicity, and taste. Figure 4-61 shows an approach to her silhouette.

Consider the character of Hamlet as he might be costumed in two different periods. He is a young man of royal birth mourning the death of his father and confronted with the probability that his uncle is a murderer and his mother an accomplice. Surrounded by the opulent court, he is alone in his internal and external search for truth and justice. One design approach might include the use of rich fabrics in a simple, youthful, and somber line. Figure 4-62 gives this basic feeling in a late-fifteenth-century costume. The jerkin is slightly V-pleated to emphasize the wide chest and narrow waist, the sleeves are full to stress broad shoulders. The simple, short skirt accents the long leg. The total effect is attractive, masculine, and subdued. Figure 4-63 is an Elizabethan costume, which can be much more complex than a costume from the fifteenth century. Here elements that will stress the same effect are chosen—broad shoulders, wide chest, narrow waist, long legs. The padding that could have been used in the pumpkin hose and peascod belly is minimized. The effect is quite similar, though the period feeling is totally different.

There is a great deal of useful variation within the styles of any period. The designer clarifies the world he or she wishes to create for the play by selecting those elements that best present both the period and the mood desired for a particular production. Within set limitations, the designer must find the variety needed to best delineate the different characters. And the elements that are selected must be controlled to be effective artistically, balanced in line and shape, and expressive in color and texture.

Figure 4-62   Left: Hamlet in the late fifteenth century.

Figure 4-63   Right: An Elizabethan Hamlet.

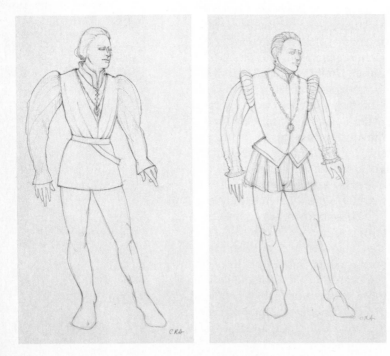

Research to understand line

Determining the proper proportions for a costume is not a simple matter, for each era has its own idea of beauty and fashion. A skirt that might seem too voluminous in one setting might be just right in another. A sleeve could be too full for one silhouette, too skimpy for another, and ideal for a third. Thorough research in a period will help the designer understand how the different elements were used at a particular time. These elements must then be interpreted to bring out what will best illuminate the particular production for the modern audience. The guide at the end of this book gives the designer a means to approach this research. It provides a delineation of the shapes of each period, describes the underpinnings needed to create the shape, tells what was considered fashionable in a particular era, and explains how the fashionable look was achieved. Also included are lists of other sources for further exploration.

Detailing within the basic costume areas

While the basic line gives structure to the production, costume details can greatly contribute to character interpretation and add flavor, zest, and a feeling of completeness. A costume detail is any addition to the primary structure. It can be extremely simple, such as a small piping to reinforce the construction lines, or a narrow edging to accent a collar or cuff; or as complex as a textural surface, perhaps of lace overlays, or braid and jewels. Details also include costume accessories such as hair styles and ornaments, shoes, handkerchiefs, purses, canes, etc. — anything needed to complete the picture. Good costume design is based on character interpretation and much can be said about a character in the costume details that are used. A designer must develop an eye for detail, for using detail effectively is an essential skill. Small additions can make an amazing difference in a costume. At first glance the gentleman in Figure 4-64a seems properly dressed, but he somehow does not seem to be complete. Compare him with Figure 4-64b. While essentially the same costume, the added details create the impression of a gentleman who is unquestionably all put together.

As discussed earlier, it is the designer's responsibility to set the style of the show and the manner in which the costumes are detailed is a primary part of that style. When planning detail the designer should begin with the historical period, then translate elements found in the research into details that best delineate the play and its characters. The silhouette should be understood first, then the detail examined to see how it affects the overall feeling of the period and how it relates to the various areas of the costume.

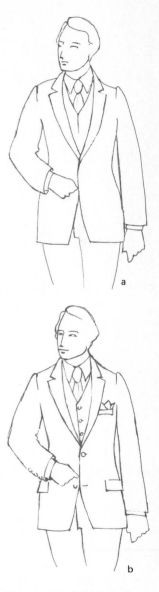

Figure 4-64   (a) A lack of finishing details makes a sketch seem incomplete. (b) With all the elements included, the suit seems much more finished.

Figure 4-65   Left: The early medieval costume relied more on line than on detail. From a medieval illuminated manuscript of Pliny's *Natural History*. Laurentian Library, Florence.

Figure 4-66   Right: Elizabethans used a great deal of decorative detail. Queen Elizabeth I, the "Armada" portrait. Collection of the Duke of Bedford.

Detailing can vary greatly from period to period. For example, the early medieval period relied mostly on line, with an occasional belt, border treatment, or brooch (Figure 4-65). The Elizabethans, however, used a great deal of decorative detail; their fabrics might have been covered with braid, jewels, and puffs of cloth (Figure 4-66). A gentleman of the early eighteenth century felt properly dressed with elaborate embroideries banding his coat front, pocket flaps, cuffs, and vest, all of which were accented by very decorative buttons (Figure 4-67). By the end of the eighteenth century a proper gentleman wore well-tailored wools with subtle detailing. The highlight of his costume was concentrated around the collars and scarves worn at the upper chest and neck (Figure 4-68). The historical guide in the appendix describes the type of detailing found in each period and the general way in which it can be used. This discussion will provide a clear idea of what is important to look for in primary sources, and how the differences between costumes of different nationalities within the same time reference might be noted. In the same period of time, the silhouette is often quite similar from country to country, but the type of detail may more clearly define the geographic area of the costume. Figures 4-69 and 4-70 show two women painted just one year apart. Jane Seymour's

Figure 4-67 Above left: The early-eighteenth-century gentleman enjoyed elaborate embroideries. Etching of the Count Struense, physician to the King of Denmark.

Figure 4-68 Above right: The late-eighteenth-century gentleman approved of subtle detailing. Etching of Goya's portrait of Don Manuel Garcia de la Prada.

Figure 4-69 Below left: Titian's portrait of Isabella of Portugal, wife of Carlos V of Spain, about 1535, reveals a southern approach to costume detail. Prado, Madrid.

Figure 4-70 Below right: Jane Seymour's costume is rigid and enclosed, typical of the northern countries. Portrait by Hans Holbein, 1536. Mauritshuis, Amsterdam.

details show the rigid, enclosed feeling of sixteenth-century England, a treatment more typical of the northern European countries. The portrait of Isabella of Portugal reveals the same line, but the hair is looser, the sleeves more open, and soft gathering is used in her dress; this painting evinces a more southern approach to costume detail.

Costume focus

A performer's costume should draw the attention of the audience to one particular body area. This concentration of the attention of the viewer is known as costume focus. The choice of details is one of the

Figure 4-71 Trim must balance so the eye will move to the top of the figure. Victoria in *The White Devil.* Watercolor. Design by Howard Kaplan, 1982.

principal means the designer has to control the focus of the costume. The primary focus of any costume is usually around the shoulder and head area. If the detail draws the attention of the audience to the foot or left thigh, there must be a good reason for it. For the most part, actors like to use their faces as a prime means of communicating, and if the eye of the audience is drawn to another area some important aspects of the character may be missed. Given a simple costume, the eye tends to go to the face as the most animated part of the body.

As trim is added it needs to balance so the eye will still move to the top of the figure (Figure 4-71). A great deal of detail can be used without creating a lack of focus on the figure, but it must be carefully controlled. The costume can have many interesting things for the eye to look at as long as the eye finally ends up where it should (Figure 4-72).

Figure 4-72 A costume with a great deal of detail, but the eye still goes to the face. Costume for Birdie in *Another Part of the Forest.* Design by Robert Perdziola, 1982.

Figure 4-73 Above: Woman in American day dress with pleated trim, 1863.

Figure 4-74 Right: A "merveilleuse" of about 1798. Engraving by Horace Vernet. Cooper-Hewitt Museum, New York.

Detail on a costume must relate to the body area it adorns. There are no absolute rules on how to do this, for much depends on the period used as a source and the degree of realism or stylization set for the production. Perhaps some examples of details that do *not* work well will make it easier to understand the way detail relates to an area. These examples come from primary sources. Just because something was really used in a period does not necessarily mean it was artistically wonderful. Bad design has existed as long as clothes have.

Figure 4-73 shows a lady of the 1880s in a light gray gown with pleated trim. The activity and contrast of the banding keep the eye on the thickened waist and broad skirt and away from the demure face. The detail in Figure 4-74 almost swallows up the French miss out for a stroll. The hat overwhelms her head and the ruffles on her arms and bodice defy anyone to concentrate on her face. The woman in Figure 4-75 may not be happy with her reception at the ball. The trim on her skirt will attract and hold the eye more than any other part of her costume.

Costume detail can be either a readily evident addition or a subtle reinforcement of the line of the costume. The direction it takes will be an important aspect of the style of the show. The detail may be quite austere, perhaps only used to emphasize the silhouette. Piping and buttons in the same color as the costume will give a sense of finish but

Figure 4-75   1824 ball dress.

will not impose a decorative element (Figure 4-76a and b). These same items done in a contrasting color make a much stronger statement (Figure 4-76c). If the scale of the detail is increased it may become more important than the silhouette and make the first impression on the audience. In Figure 4-77a the trim on the coat accents the shape of the period. In Figure 4-77b the overscaled trim takes the focus and makes the shape of the garment secondary.

Figure 4-76   (a) Plain bodice. (b) Piped bodice. (c) Bodice with contrasting trim.

Figure 4-77   (a) Trim that accents the shape of the period. (b) Overscaled trim that takes focus.

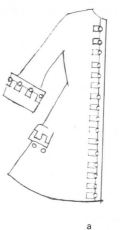

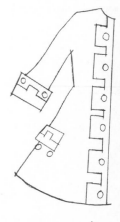

Figure 4-78   Left: Historical source that might be suitable for a high comedy. An early-twentieth-century illustration from *L'Art de la Mode,* New York.

Figure 4-79   Below left: The source adapted for a serious play.

Figure 4-80   Below: The source as it might appear in a musical or a farce.

An exercise that may help you understand detail better is illustrated in Figures 4-78 through 4-80. For this exercise select a historic source and use it as the basis for a costume in a serious play, a high comedy, and a broad farce or musical extravaganza. The source will probably be fairly suitable for one of these. In this case, Figure 4-78 might be fine for a high comedy just as it is. Figure 4-79 takes the source and adapts it so it seems more appropriate for a serious play: the trim is somewhat simplified and the line is more dominant. In Figure 4-80 the effect is broader and more suitable for a farce or musical. The decorative elements have been emphasized to make a strong statement. This example employs a surface approach to the use of detail. The decisions on the changes are arbitrary and stereotypical because there is no written character to delineate, but the tone of the costume has clearly been changed by the use of accents and trims.

A designer must have a good understanding of the use of detail, but well-organized elements have no meaning if they do not grow out of the character. Since the basic costume line of the show may be quite similar for many of the roles in it, it is through the use of detail that each becomes differentiated and the true flavor of the character shows. The designer who knows the psychology and motivation of each character will know how to approach the costume details. When a group of sketches is presented each character, of course, should be clearly labeled. But even if the drawings are not named, the director should be able to recognize each character because of the details the designer has selected that help personify the people they have been discussing since the preliminary stages.

Returning to *The Importance of Being Earnest,* there should be no doubt who is Lady Bracknell and who is Gwendolyn, though both have the same social background. Lady Bracknell is forthright and commandeering, and expects to be obeyed. Gwendolyn will be very much like her mother when she gets older, for she is a female who knows her own mind, but now she enjoys playing the role of the young coquette. Lady Bracknell's details might present the straightforward dominance of the more matronly figure. Gwendolyn's details will tend more toward youth and frivolity, but with a hint of the iron maiden underneath. When Gwendolyn travels to the country she comes face to face with Cecily. Here are two young women of quite different backgrounds, who, beneath it all, are really very similar. The details for Cecily should present her as more of a country girl, but with the finish and strong-mindedness to match Gwendolyn tit for tat. Gwendolyn, of course, would make sure she was "London perfect" before venturing off to the hinterlands.

Attention to little touches of detail can bring just the right quality to a character. Consider, in William Inge's *Picnic,* the characters of Rosemary and Howard as they finally go off to get married. Rosemary is a spinster schoolteacher who has wanted desperately to get married for a long time. It's a goal she has dreamed of and prepared for. She probably has everything she would need packed neatly in a box in her closet so when she leaves she has with her all those things she thinks a bride should have — matching shoes, gloves, purse, hat, and probably a nice lace handkerchief. Howard, on the other hand, really had no intention of being caught in marriage and has to make do as best he can. He has pulled a suit, shirt, and tie out of the closet; they probably are not recently pressed. His shoes haven't been polished lately and show the ravages of the Kansas dust. His belt doesn't match his suit very well — it was the first one he found — and he never even thought about a handkerchief. He is dressed, he is there, but his heart is not really in it. The picture Howard creates on his wedding day leads to one final thought about costume detail.

The way in which clothes are worn can reveal as much about characters as the clothes themselves. The dressing of the garments, or the way they are arranged on the body, is an important character detail that should not be overlooked. A white shirt carefully buttoned at the neck with necktie snugly in place suggests a much different attitude than a shirt with the top button undone and the tie slightly loosened. Belt and pants encircling the waist squarely present a man who is not the same as one who wears his trousers sagging slightly below the belly. The designer thinks not only about the clothes, but also about how the performer wears them at various times throughout the play. The sketch will present the costume at one particular moment. It may remain this way during the entire performance. But characters' situations may change: they may get more tired, or drunker, or receive some unexpected guests. The designer should provide a guideline to the alterations that could take place and know what impact the variations in detail will have on the total costume.

Movement and the costume

No matter how much the designer wants to let flights of fancy soar through a continuing swell of unencumbered creativity, certain practicalities will continually intrude. The actor or actress must be able to move in the costume. This should always be in the back of the designer's mind. At some point it becomes a primary consideration, and the designer must make sure that the action required by the play is possible in the clothes he or she has in mind for the characters. When the line that will give the production the right artistic feeling is established, the physical action that will take place must be considered. To

Figure 4-81   (a) The extended point of the bodice would greatly restrict the mobility of the wearer. (b) The padding of the peascod belly can limit a man's ability to bend. (c) Metal body armor can be extremely confining.

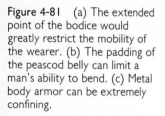

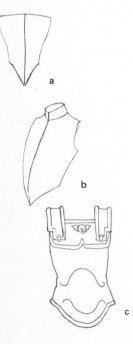

some extent, all costumes must accommodate movement, and some periods are particularly restricting. The modern actor often needs a mobility that just doesn't exist in certain period costumes. The movement must be directly related to the manner in which the costume fits or restricts the hinge points.

The waist. Any type of bending is restricted by corseting or padding. Strong boning that extends past the waistline will begin to immobilize the torso. The body can still move from the hip, but a very long point in front can make bending and even sitting difficult, for the point can poke into the thigh in a very uncomfortable manner (Figure 4-81a). The Elizabethan man's peascod belly, which does not confine the waist like a corset, still keeps the actor from bending forward, for it must be set on a stiffened piece to hold its shape (Figure 4-81b). Most metal body armor is extremely confining. Take, for example, the Roman molded cuirass, or *lorica* (Figure 4-81c). Made of bronze, it often extended from chest to thigh. It made the Roman officer look quite impressive but was not too practical. He could stand around and give orders, but it was up to his less encumbered underlings to carry on the real business of war.

The shoulder and arm. Of course, actors must be free to move their arms on stage; the costumes of many periods, however, constrict arm movement severely. A tight sleeve attached to a tight bodice may well keep the actor from reaching very far up or forward. The constriction is caused because the length of the arm seems to change as it rotates in its socket. The distance from waist to underarm to wrist as the arm hangs might be 28 inches (Figure 4-82a). When the arm is raised, this could change to 33 inches (Figure 4-82b). If the sleeve is tight and can't ride down the arm, and the bodice is tight and can't ride up the body, the arm cannot be fully extended. In addition, if the armseye of the bodice is cut low, both the bodice underarm and the inside sleeve are shorter, restricting movement even more. Fitting the armseye of the bodice high under the arm will allow more movement. Adding a gusset to the sleeve will also improve the movement of a constricting costume. A gusset at the underarm adds a bias insert that can stretch and give more length ot the sleeve.

If the armseye is placed at the end of the shoulder, just above the arm joint or slightly inside it, the arm should be able to raise easily. The more the armseye extends past the shoulder and fits down on the arm, the less the arm can move upward, for this seam, in effect, ties the arm down to the body.

A sleeve that fits the arm tightly can restrict bending if the sleeve is not cut to allow more space for the bent elbow. This is discussed more fully in Chapter 8.

Figure 4-82 The distance from waist to wrist is much longer when the arm is raised than when it hangs at the side.

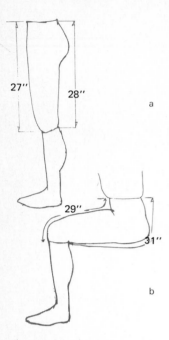

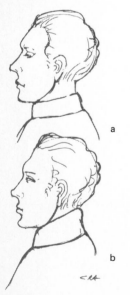

Figure 4-83 Both front and back measurements of waist to below knee are longer on the seated figure.

Figure 4-84 The rigidity of the high, tight collar may be relieved if the front is lowered.

The legs. The problems that can arise with leg movement are often similar to those of the arms. Trousers that are cut high in the crotch will allow for more extension of the leg. Knee breeches, which fasten under the knee, must have extra length in front and back for sitting and bending, for both areas get longer as the leg bends (Figure 4-83). The full-length skirt should present few obstacles to regular movement if care is taken with the cut and fit (see Chapters 7 and 8).

The neck. A high, tight, stiffened collar can definitely immobilize the neck and head (Figure 4-84a). This rigidity can be quite appropriate to some characters and some periods, but the actor must realize what restrictions it will place on him. If the feeling of the high collar is desirable but more movement is necessary, sloping the collar so that it is lower in front allows the chin to drop without losing the line (Figure 4-84b). A very low neckline may cause some difficulties for an actress. If the bust is to stay in the dress there must be tension on the neckline. While problems may arise as she bends over, the most crucial movement occurs as she leans back and raises her arm. A nice tight fit should keep all elements in their proper areas.

These are the most common movement problems that arise. Should the actor need to do a somersault or scale a fence, even more careful attention should be paid to the design.

The quick change

One more practical area should be given consideration after the basic line has been established — the quick change. All kinds of miraculous transformations can take place in less than a minute if they are carefully conceived, but a quick change not thoughtfully planned can be a nightmare for all involved and break the flow of the show. It is also irresponsible for a designer to create a costume change that is physically difficult and mentally straining. Changes that cannot be easily completed in the available time force the actor to expend more energy backstage than onstage.

All possible quick changes are noted from the beginning of the work on a play and recorded in the costume list and scene breakdown. These change requirements should be in the back of the designer's mind. The designer wants to create a costume that is right for the character and that also can be changed quickly. The quick change is not the first goal, with peripheral considerations about the individual character added on. Some compromises with what might be the ideal costume may be necessary, but these changes will have a better chance of capturing the right character feeling if the designer has first clearly established what is necessary to create the character.

Figure 4-85　*Left:* Hanswurst as the Gossip in *House Afire,* presented at Yale University, 1963. Design by Barbara Anderson.

Figure 4-86　*Center:* Hanswurst as Leander.

Figure 4-87　*Right:* Hanswurst as the Old Hag.

Keep three primary points in mind when planning a quick change.

1. *As much of the costume should come off and go on in a unit as possible.* For example, a shirt, vest, and coat can be preset to be entered as one unit. A skirt, bodice, and petticoats can be tacked together so they are stepped into as one garment. (And stepping into a costume is usually faster and easier on the hairstyle than slipping it over the head.)

2. *Fastenings should be simple and easy to find.* A long row of buttons or hooks and eyes are not easily or quickly negotiated. Velcro is excellent for getting *out* of a garment quickly, although it is not as satisfactory for getting *into* one, for it can be difficult to line up properly and needs firm pressure to make it stay securely. If a zipper is used it should be heavy-duty, because it will receive a lot of wear and tear. Buttons or hooks on cuffs can be set on a small piece of elastic that will stretch to allow the hand or foot to slip through without undoing the fastenings.

3. *The actor should have to do as little as possible.* The most efficient changes happen when the actor can come off and stand in the wings, moving his hands and feet when necessary to get in and out of the garments as the changers take care of all the fastening and unfastening. Actors tend to get nervous, and if they grab something upside down or backward a well-timed change may not succeed at all.

An example of quick-change costumes done for a Haydn comic opera is shown in Figures 4-85, 4-86, and 4-87. The actor began one scene as a village gossip (Figure 4-85), had forty-five seconds to become a lord (Figure 4-86), and a short time later turned into an old hag in thirty seconds (Figure 4-87). Two dressers were used for the changes. The actor started the scene wearing the shoes, hose, and breeches for the second costume under the first. All the pieces of the village-gossip dress were sewn together as a unit. The little shawl was tacked to the dress as far as the back opening, then snapped in place as it continued to wrap around the body. As the actor came offstage, Dresser A unsnapped the shawl, then took off the hat and glasses as Dresser B unzipped the dress. Dresser A pulled the sleeves over the hands and dropped the dress down. The actor turned while stepping out of the dress and put his arms in the shirt that Dresser B was holding. Dresser A fastened the shirt at the neck with one large hook, Dresser B grabbed the coat and vest (preset together), and the actor made sure he was holding the shirt ruffles in each hand so the sleeves would stay down. Dresser B helped the actor into the coat and vest, Dresser A pulled the vest together in front, carefully lined up the closing, and pressed the Velcro together. (The vest was fastened with Velcro because the actor had to get out of it even faster than he had to get into it.) Meanwhile, Dresser B got the wig positioned on the actor's head, checking to make sure it covered his hairline. Dresser A handed him his handkerchief and he was ready.

The change to Figure 4-87 was done in a similar fashion. Dresser A opened the vest and Dresser B took off the coat and vest while A took off the wig. Dresser A unhooked the shirt; B pulled it off from the front. Dresser A held the dress as the actor stepped into it, B pulled it into position from the back and zipped it up as A put on the wig, which had the hat already pinned to it. Dresser A checked the position of the wig and hooked the hat tie on the side as B stuck on the nose, which had been prepared with double-sided adhesive. The breeches, shoes, and hose stayed on under the costume. And again the actor was ready to go with very little effort on his part, though the crew needed a rest. Actually, it takes good discipline on the part of the actor to stand in the right place, do those moves that are necessary, and not try to help, which would only confuse things.

Fabric, texture, and the basic design

The effect of the fabric chosen for a costume must always be a part of the overall design idea. Developing the design on paper is a fascinating part of the work, but it is the fabric that really brings the design to life—and the texture of the fabric is an important component of the total effect. As the design begins to take shape, ideas about the fabric should also take shape. By the time the sketch is completed the designer must know the type of fabric that will be used and its texture (Figure 4-88). A good costume designer has a definite feel for fabric and for the three-dimensional effect of the costume. The costume is not merely an

MOTHER COURAGE   CHAPLIN in DISGUISE

CLOAK - CASSOCK - HAT added AS
DISGUISE TO COVER PASTOR CLOTHES

Figure 4-88 The type of fabrics and textures that will be right for the costume should be known by the time the sketch is completed. This costume calls for heavy, rough wool-type fabrics. The Chaplain from *Mother Courage.* Design by Howard Kaplan, 1981.

illustration on a piece of paper; the designer must conceptualize the actual costume that will appear onstage. Specifically, it must be determined what space it will take up and how it will move, which cannot be done without a good idea of the fabric of which the costume will be made. Designers who are not familiar with a great variety of types of fabric lack a fundamental knowledge of a basic concern in their work. Chapter 7 discusses most of the fabrics available, but words are not adequate when exploring this field. Designers must feel their way through fabric stores and racks of clothes and costume storage areas. They must physically accumulate boxes of fabric swatches and mentally store away images of plush and nubby and shiny and sheer.

Figure 4-89   The fabric for Merlin's robe was an unknown quantity until a bolt of blue-violet velvet shot with silver was spied during a shopping trip. Design by Barbara Anderson for *A Connecticut Yankee in King Arthur's Court* for the Once Upon a Classic series. © Metropolitan Pittsburgh Public Broadcasting, Inc., 1977.

When doing a sketch they may not realize that a costume specifically calls for silk moirée taffeta, but they should realize the fabric must be light, crisp, and shiny, with a water-marked shimmer.

Ideas for fabric and texture do not necessarily follow after the line has been begun; they may be the first ideas that occur to the designer. While thinking about the style of a show or a particular character, first impressions may well be those of texture and the flow of the fabric. On reading *Macbeth,* for example, the images might be those of something heavy, thick, and rough, maybe even furred. The fairies in *A Midsummer Night's Dream* might evoke thoughts of shimmery sheers. Lady Sneerwell's social set in Sheridan's *The School for Scandal* could seem ideally suited to shiny, slick surfaces.

A designer who doesn't find delight in fabric is perhaps in the wrong business. Sometimes when designing a show a particular costume or even a set of costumes seems quite elusive. Shadowy ideas may be drifting around in the designer's mind, but nothing flows off the tip of the pencil. Then one day a piece of fabric surfaces that almost seems to jump up and say "Here I am—I'm just what you need to give shape to those vague forms that won't come out of the back of your head." The allure of fabric can also be dangerous. Costume designers who really like what they do soon discover one of the most serious drawbacks in this business: They can't move home base easily, for they quickly acquire drawers and trunks full of pieces of cloth they just couldn't resist.

5

Designing the costume: color control

Color is a very powerful component
of costume design; it makes
the strongest initial visual
impact and will register on
the eye of the audience
before the line or the detail. Careful
color control provides a strong influence that will lead the audience toward
a desired emotional response.

Color should not be an afterthought applied as though one were finishing up a set of paper dolls. Ideas about color begin to grow with the preliminary reading of the play, and the color concept is often one of the very first areas the designer and director explore together. The color idea develops in conjunction with all the elements that will be used to present the production. Since color is such an integral part of designing costumes and presenting a play as well as an important factor in our daily lives, careful thought must be given to what color is and what it does.

What is color?

Colors result from light waves, which are a particular kind of electromagnetic energy. Visible light is a very small part of the electromagnetic spectrum, which includes radio rays, infrared rays, ultraviolet rays, x-rays, gamma rays, and cosmic rays. All these rays travel through space at the same speed in the form of waves, which are measured from crest to crest. Radio waves are the longest, several thousand feet across; gamma and cosmic waves are at the short-wave end of the spectrum. Light waves fall somewhat in the middle range, between infrared and ultraviolet rays, and these visible rays measure about 1/33,000th of an inch at the red end and 1/67,000th of an inch at the violet end. White light includes all the colors of the visible wavelengths. If a beam of white light is sent through a prism the light is dispersed or broken into bands of different wavelengths, which produce the colors of the spectrum (Figure 5-1, p. 165). The rays of light that make up the spectrum can be gathered by a converging lens and white light would once again be produced.

SUBTRACTIVE COLOR MIXING: THE PIGMENT COLOR WHEEL

What we know as color is a phenomenon that actually happens within the eye itself. Certain wavelengths of light are perceived as certain hues. We recognize a specific color in an object because of the wavelength of light reflected from the object to the eye. An object does not actually have an intrinsic color. Its molecular structure is such that it absorbs certain wavelengths and reflects others, a phenomenon known as selective reflection. The eye then interprets these reflected wavelengths into various hues. As a ray of white light hits something that

Preceding page: The field of costume design can range from clothes that are historically based to something as abstract as this dance costume. Design by Cletus Anderson, 1965.

appears red, all the colors of the spectrum but red are absorbed and the red light is reflected. The colors that result from this absorption are known as subtractive colors. If the wavelength is not present in the light source the color that is produced by that wavelength cannot be reflected and thus perceived. When a green light is directed on a red object the object will appear black, for there is no red light. A white object, while it absorbs some light, reflects all colors equally. A black object absorbs all light rays, subtracting all colors.

Pigment refers to the color agent or colorant in objects, whether the green glaze of a ceramic vase or a tube of red paint. The three primary pigments in the subtractive color wheel are red, yellow, and blue. These three colors, when mixed, will absorb all the light rays projected on them, with a dark, neutral tone as the result. Combinations of these colors also produce the subtractive color wheel. The twelve-part color wheel (Figure 5-2, p. 165) is a useful tool that shows twelve distinct hues that can be easily identified and used as a basis for any of the infinite color variations possible. A combination of two primary colors produces a secondary color, which is located halfway between each primary.

Red   + yellow = orange
Yellow + blue   = green
Blue   + red   = violet

A combination of a primary and its adjoining secondary results in a tertiary color.

Red   + orange = red-orange   Green + blue   = blue-green
Orange + yellow = yellow-orange   Blue + violet = blue-violet
Yellow + green = yellow-green   Violet + red   = red-violet

The red-violet or purple tones might be considered artificial, for they do not appear in the spectrum (which is a linear band running from red to violet), but they are certainly present in the color wheel and complete the circle. The twelve-tone color wheel is standard, but it can be expanded by combining adjoining colors. The step between red and orange could go from red to red-orange-red to red-orange to orange-red-orange to orange and so on.

ADDITIVE COLOR MIXING: THE LIGHT COLOR WHEEL

Adding colored light differs from mixing colored pigments. The three primary colors of light are red, green, and blue. When mixed equally these colors produce white light. In combinations of varying proportions, the primary colors can produce all other colors of light. The most common example of this is found in the color television set, which has only red, blue, and green screens yet shows the viewer an entire range of colored images. Since colored light rays are added to each other on the same surface, this is called *additive mixing*. Figure 5-3 (p. 165) shows the light color wheel created by this additive mixing. Red and green produce the yellow tones, red and blue the violet tones, and blue and green provide the blue-green tones. Any two complementary light colors (those that are opposite on the color wheel) combine to produce white light, since all three primaries are then present: red and blue-green, blue and yellow (red and green) and green and violet (blue and red).

BASIC COLOR VOCABULARY

While the use of color and its interpretations can be very subjective, a designer should be familiar with the basic color theories and vocabulary. The exact terms may vary slightly with different color systems, but the designer who understands the underlying concepts should be able to adjust to variations.

The term *color* is a general classification often used to refer to a number of qualities of the tone that is perceived. Color is more specifically defined by its three primary qualities — hue, value, and intensity — which are explained in the following paragraphs.

Hue. The term *hue* specifically defines the unmodified colors found in the spectrum. Figure 5-2 (p. 165) shows the twelve-hue color wheel. The hues opposite each other on the wheel are known as complementary hues. They are considered complementary because their combination is a mixture of the three primary hues. For example, blue and orange are complements. Orange is made of yellow and red; when blue is added, the primary triad is present. Red and green are complements, since green is made of yellow and blue and the red-green combination creates the red-yellow-blue primary triad. Blue-green and red-orange might be thought of as blue- (blue + yellow) and red- (red + yellow). The primary triad is complete. This completion occurs with other groups of colors that can be thought of as *color chords*. These color chords result from complementary pairs, triads from equilateral and isosceles triangles, and tetrads formed from squares and rectangles. The diagram on page 157 shows the color wheel with a group of chords all of which contain the three primaries. Shown are the pair formed by blue and orange; the triads combining blue, yellow-orange, and red-orange and blue, red, and yellow; and the tetrads combining blue, red-violet, orange, and yellow-green and blue-green, blue-violet, yellow-orange, and red-orange. Color schemes can be developed based on

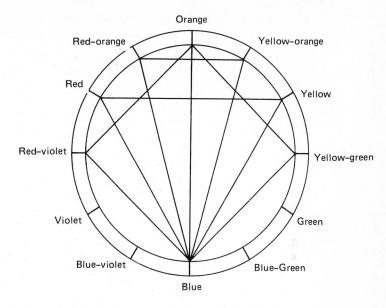

Color chords

the hues contained in color chords. Remember that in subtractive color, any of these combinations that make up the chords when mixed together will form a dark neutral tone because the light is absorbed and no specific hue is reflected back to the eye.

Combinations of hues are sometimes considered that do not combine to incorporate all the primary colors, but instead relate to only one section of the color wheel. The hues adjacent to each other on the wheel are known as analogous hues. Yellow, yellow-orange, and orange are analogous, as are red, red-violet, and violet.

Color intensity, or chroma. The color wheel presents the hues at their full intensity, or chroma. They are the pure hues, uncontaminated by combination with other hues, black, or white. As a hue is mixed with its complement the purity of the colors, or the intensity or chroma, lessens. The hue becomes neutralized. As equal parts of the complementary hues are mixed, the result is a gray tone. Figure 5-4 (p. 166) shows the combinations of the complements blue and orange. The blue moves from full intensity to one-quarter neutralized to one-half neutralized to three-quarters neutralized to the neutral gray that is halfway between the blue and orange. Past the gray the orange tones take over as they move from three-quarters neutralized to one-half neutralized to one-quarter neutralized to the pure hue. The formulas below the chart give an idea of how the mixing is achieved, though when actually working with paints it is never quite so easy to accomplish.

Color values. The scale that indicates the light-to-dark relativity of the tones between white and black is called the value scale. The value scale is often considered in nine steps from white to high light, light, low light, medium, high dark, dark, low dark, and black. The hues fall at various levels on this scale. Yellow is a bit below high light, violet is about at low dark and red and green just below medium (Figure 5-5, p. 166). While each hue has its own level, it can be moved up or down the scale by adding white or black. Tones produced by adding white are called tints; those that result from adding black are called shades. There are relatively few tints of yellow, for it begins close to white on the scale, but there are many shades of yellow as it moves toward black. Similarly, only a few shades take blue down to black, but many tints of blue are available.

TONAL VARIATIONS AND THE COLOR SPHERE

While there is only one true hue of any color, its variations in terms of intensity and value are myriad (Figure 5-6, p. 166). Except for red and green, which are complements at the same value, mixing to neutralize a color will change the value as the darker and lighter hues are combined. But no matter what the intensity, the value can change, and no matter what the value, the intensity can change. Noted colorist Johannes Itten, in his book *The Elements of Color*, presents the color sphere, which is based on the work of Philipp Otto Runge. This is fascinating to study, for in one geometric figure he encompasses the idea of all the color variations. The north pole is white, the south is black, the central core consists of the achromatic or gray scale. The perimeter at the equator is divided into twelve equal sections, presenting the hues of the color wheel. On the surface of the sphere tints of the hues move toward the white pole and shades move toward the black. Figures 5-7a and b (p. 167) show the two halves of the color sphere. A plane bisecting the sphere at the equator displays the hues as they are neutralized toward gray (Figure 5-8, p. 167). A plane bisecting the sphere through the poles reveals two complements on each side of the gray core and the tints, shades, and neutralized tones of both hues (Figure 5-9, p. 167). By use of the sphere one can easily visualize the three most common ways of defining colors: by hue, value, and intensity or chroma.

COLOR CONTRAST

When color is used in theatre or in any other endeavor, one tone does not make a statement in itself. The interaction of colors must always be considered. Itten refers to seven different types of color contrast, which are interesting to consider because they can increase color awareness. His seven contrasts are:

1. Contrast of hue
2. Contrast of value, or light-dark contrast
3. Cold-warm contrast
4. Complementary contrast
5. Simultaneous contrast
6. Contrast of intensity or saturation
7. Contrast of extension

By understanding these contrasts the designer can begin to see the effects of color use in a production. Control of these variables is another means to create an effective design.

Contrast of hue. The most intense contrast of hue employs the three primaries—red, yellow, and blue. These three clearly differentiated hues can be used to produce a vigorous effect. The intensity of the contrast of hues is diminished as the hues are removed from the three primaries (Figure 5-10, p. 168). Orange, green, and violet are not as vibrant a combination, and yellow, yellow-green, and green are even less so. Black and white might be included with any pure hue in experiments with this form of contrast. Contrast of hue is found in the folk art of peoples everywhere and in illuminated manuscripts, testifying to the pleasure inherent in creating colorful effects. A red dress with green trim could be visually too active on stage because the contrast of hue is too strong. Yellow or violet trim might be much more suitable.

Value or light-dark contrast. Value contrast deals with those variations displayed in the value scale. The ultimate contrast is white and black, with an indefinably large number of grays possible between them limited only by the eye's ability to perceive the variations. Light-dark contrasts can also be present with all the hues, but the true hue hits only one place on the value scale. A dark yellow is no longer truly yellow, but has been combined with a tone of a lower value, for pure yellow can only appear at high light on the value scale. Similarly, true red can only lie below the middle of the light-dark scale, since a light red or pink tone will be closer to white on the scale; a lighter tone will have been combined with red to change the value. A color grouping in which all tones are at the level of yellow will present quite a brilliant yellow, while other tones will be more washed out, for no other color is at the value of yellow unless some white has been added to it (Figure 5-11, p. 168). The two hues with the strongest light-dark contrast are yellow and violet; on the value scale, yellow falls in naturally high light and violet in low dark. Value contrast is often particularly strong in the light shirts and dark suits of men's costumes.

Cold-warm contrast. The two poles of the cold-warm contrast are blue-green and red-orange (Figure 5-12, p. 168), the two colors that are at right angles to the light-dark axis drawn between yellow and violet. Experiments have shown that people definitely associate warmth and activity with the red-orange side of the spectrum and coolness and quietness with the blue-green. For example, in one instance workers did not feel a chill in a red-orange room until it was six or seven degrees colder than the temperature that chilled workers in a blue-green room. In general, the warm tones are considered to be yellow, yellow-orange, orange, red-orange, red, and red-violet, while the cool tones are yellow-green, green, blue-green, blue, blue-violet, and violet. Itten lists a number of contrasting terms that can be thought of in the same vein as warm and cold, which might prove useful in the color interpretation of a play:

Cold	*Warm*
Shadow	Sun
Transparent	Opaque
Sedative	Stimulant
Rare	Dense
Airy	Earthy
Far	Near
Light	Heavy
Wet	Dry

Complementary contrast. Complementary colors have been discussed earlier in this chapter. Complementary pairs have interesting properties. Put side by side, they incite each other to maximum vividness; mixed together, they neutralize each other to gray-black. The mixing of complements to form the grayed tones can produce many more interesting variations than possible with the black-white scale (see Figure 5-6, p. 166). Pointillists, who created their paintings by placing hundreds of tiny dots of color on the canvas, found grays much more vibrant when dots of the complements were placed side by side and the mixing was done in the eye. This same effect is sometimes found in fabric. If thin blue and orange threads are closely woven together, the fabric will appear gray at a distance, but a vibrant gray with both blue and orange overtones.

Simultaneous contrast. Simultaneous contrast occurs in the eye, for when a color is perceived the eye requires the complementary color and will generate it simultaneously if it is not present. An experiment that clearly shows this phenomenon can be performed by taking sheets of the six pure hues and placing on each a gray square of the same value (Figure 5-13, p. 169). The gray on the yellow will have a violet cast; on the violet it will seem yellowish. The gray on the orange hue will tend toward blue; on the blue it will tend toward orange. The gray on the red will take on a green feeling, while the gray on the green will go more to red. If a strip of the same gray is placed near each color but is slightly separate and surrounded by white, it will not appear to be the same tone at all, for the eye will not alter it.

A similar phenomenon is called successive contrast. When the eye stares at a colored square, such as red, and then closes or looks away, an afterimage of the complement (green in this case) appears. In both cases the eye is completing the spectrum and providing the hues that are missing. Brightly lit, intense hues in costumes on stage could cause the eye to distort the color or detect an afterimage when the costume moves.

This phenomenon that causes the eye to seek to complete the spectrum should be considered when developing color schemes. To many, a harmonious color scheme would seem to be an analogous one, where the hues are quite similar. Because the eye always tries to balance out the color and harmony, however, a harmonious color scheme might be based on complementary colors, or any of the color chords that combine to include the three primaries and complete the spectrum.

Contrast of intensity or saturation. As explained earlier, intensity relates to the degree of purity of a color. The contrast of intensity or saturation is the contrast between the pure, uncontaminated hue and its dull, diluted variations (Figure 5-14, p. 169). Colors can be diluted in four ways:

1. *By adding white.* This produces tints and renders the character of the color somewhat cooler.
2. *By adding black.* Black in general seems to deprive colors of their quality of light and eventually takes over and deadens them.
3. *By adding gray.* As gray is added to the pure color it moves it toward a duller or more neutral tone.
4. *By adding the complement.* The pure color begins to be neutralized, but usually in a much more interesting fashion than when gray is added.

A costume can easily jump out of a group because it seems intense and pure compared to the grayed or diluted shades around it. A red dress will take focus when surrounded by tones of pink.

Contrast of extension. Contrast of extension deals with the relative areas of two color patches or the contrast between a larger area and a smaller one. Color areas can of course be brought together in any size, but there are proportions of one color to another that seem to put the hues in balance. Hues that are higher on the value scale seem to have more brilliance and require less area to balance with hues of a darker value. Goethe, though better known for his literary endeavors, experimented with light and color and set up numerical ratios for different hues. Although only approximate, they give a good idea of the way colors balance against each other. The values are:

Yellow	Orange	Red	Green	Blue	Violet
9	8	6	6	4	3

Using this, the proportions of the complementary pairs are:

$$\text{Yellow} : \text{Violet} = 9:3 = 3:1$$
$$\text{Orange} : \text{Blue} = 8:4 = 2:1$$
$$\text{Red} : \text{Green} = 6:6 = 1:1$$

A color bar of violet and yellow would then be in balance if the ratio were inverted and there were three parts violet to one part yellow. The orange-and-blue bar would balance if the blue area was twice the size of the orange. And the red-and-green bar balances when the areas are of equal size. Inverting the values on all the complements gives the harmonious areas for all the primary and secondary colors:

Yellow	Orange	Red	Green	Blue	Violet
3	4	6	6	8	9

From this it is easy to see that yellow balances with orange in a $3:4$ ratio, with red in a $3:6$ $(1:2)$ ratio, with green $3:6$ $(1:2)$, with blue $3:8$, and with violet $3:9$ $(1:3)$. The proportion of yellow to red to blue would be $3:6:8$, and for orange, green, and violet $4:6:9$. Other ratios can be discovered on the same basis. A color wheel that shows the harmonious relative areas of the hues can be constructed. There are a total of 36 units assigned to the six hues and the wheel is made up of 360 degrees. Ten degrees of the arc can be allotted for each unit, so the wheel would have 30° yellow, 40° orange, 60° red, 60° green, 80° blue, and 90° violet (Figure 5-15, p. 169). The proportions given relate only to the balance of the pure hues. As the color changes in intensity and value its relationships to other colors also change.

COLOR RELATIONSHIPS

One fact is absolutely certain about color: Color is never absolute. Color perception varies with circumstances, which can involve the surrounding objects, the available light, the type of color surface, or the frame of reference of the viewer.

Variations in color relationships occur in all the different ways color is perceived and are present in all the types of color contrasts. The six basic spectrum hues—red, blue, yellow, orange, green, and violet—easily bring to mind specific colors. Yet these six hues present a decidedly different color feeling when seen before a white, medium gray, or black background. A blue square on a yellow ground has a vibrancy that will not be present if the same square is placed on violet (Figure 5-16, p. 170). The same yellow that may seem lifeless against beige could be too active when paired with a bright green.

The value of either hues or gray tones is quite relative. Green might appear quite dark in a grouping of yellows and oranges, but quite light if the other tones are blue-violets and violets (Figure 5-17, p. 170). Medium gray is very dark surrounded by white and light gray, quite light in the midst of black and dark gray.

As with value contrast, cold-warm contrast can vary as the tones that are used vary. Blue-green and red-orange are always cold and warm, respectively, but the other colors can take on different meanings. A red-violet may seem quite cool when grouped with orange hues and very warm when shown with cool ones (Figure 5-18, p. 170).

The effect of changing the intensity of a color is again relative. The same color can appear dull when placed next to a more vivid tone, and vivid if paired with a duller one. Green at half intensity will seem quite subdued next to pure green, but very colorful if combined with a green that has been almost completely neutralized to gray (Figure 5-19, p. 170).

The contrast of extension illustrates clearly how color areas can be balanced by considering the effect of the color and the size of the area. An understanding of this can lead the designer to interesting effects that are achieved by offsetting this balance.

It is extremely important that the designer have a well-founded understanding of color and what it does under different circumstances. The best way to achieve this is to experiment with color combinations to increase awareness of what is possible. The most effective way to explore color is with paintbox and brush in hand. Making up color charts can be a bit tedious, but the experience is invaluable. The most encompassing exercise would be to create a color sphere, illustrating the vertical section of each complementary pair, which involves producing the basic hues and varying both value and intensity. This is not easy, for any set of paints has variations in pigment that can produce unlikely tones, according to the rules. Don't throw away the mistakes. They may not fit into the well-organized color chart, but they can be wonderful ideas for useful color schemes you would never think of yourself with this sort of experimentation.

Work with colored papers can also help to develop an awareness of color relationships, for they can be mixed and matched easily and quickly to create an interaction among tones. Color-Aid papers come in small sets (either 3 inches by 5 inches or 5 inches by 7 inches) of over 200 tones plus black, white, and grays, and Pantone color-swatch books provide more than 500 tones. These are wonderful as a starting point, but it is amazing how quickly one realizes just how limiting this number of colors can be. Basic relationships can be explored, but the minute one tries to set up a specific scheme for a costume the right tone is nowhere to be found.

Color computers offer another extreme. A computer is able to show more than 6,000,000 different tones. Though color computers are not now widely used in theatre design, their importance could grow dramatically in the near future.

When working on color exercises, pick a neutral shape to use for your examples. A square or rectangle works quite well and is easily produced. Varying the shapes can give connotations to the color that makes appreciation of tone alone more difficult. Colored fabrics can also be very useful for exploring color combinations, though they add the element of texture to the color feeling. They therefore provide a less accurate exploration of color theory, but do show colors more as the costume designer usually sees them.

COLOR SYMBOLISM

Thus far, an attempt has been made to remain very objective about colors, judging them purely on their physical properties. Color, however, causes definite subjective reactions in the beholder. The subjective response is not easily specified, for the psychological reaction to color is a very personal thing, conditioned by experience and environment. Some color responses are generally accepted as relating to a majority of people, and these should be considered.

Nature is a constant that influences everyone's color sensibilities. The tones of the outside world are always there, familiar and therefore comfortable, and anything that falls within these guidelines is readily accepted by the audience. Grass is green. If it is red it is unnatural. Mashed potatoes are white. If they are blue they are unpalatable. The seasons of the year are known by the colors they present. Spring gives the yellow-greens and pastels of new growth, summer is full of deep green foliage against bright blue skies, autumn brings rusts, reds, and oranges, and winter closes the year with its whites, grays, and gray-blues. The designer should realize that variations to the colors of nature may startle the audience. This technique could be very effective in certain instances. No one will believe an ingenue with a pale green face, but if she has just returned from the grave this odd complexion may be just perfect.

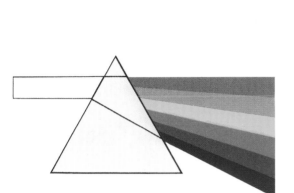

Figure 5-1 White light sent through a prism is dispersed into bands of different wave lengths.

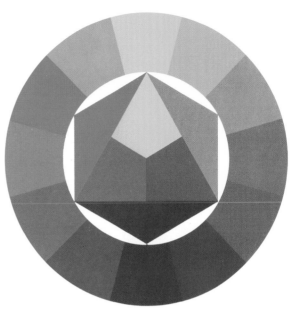

Figure 5-2 The twelve-part color wheel. From Joseph Itten, *Elements of Color* (New York: Van Nostrand Reinhold, 1970).

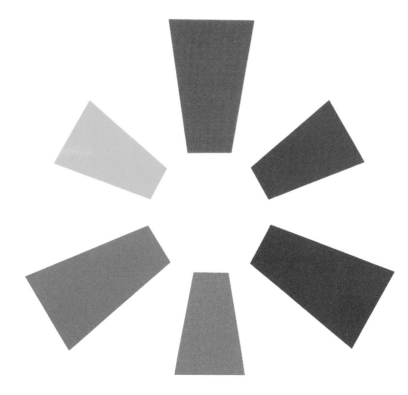

Figure 5-3 The additive color wheel.

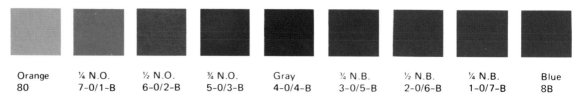

| Orange
80 | ¼ N.O.
7-0/1-B | ½ N.O.
6-0/2-B | ¾ N.O.
5-0/3-B | Gray
4-0/4-B | ¼ N.B.
3-0/5-B | ½ N.B.
2-0/6-B | ¼ N.B.
1-0/7-B | Blue
8B |

Figure 5-4   Blue and orange and their degrees of neutralization.

Figure 5-5   The value chart.

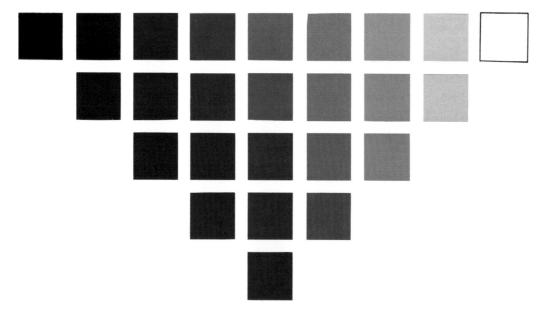

Figure 5-6   The value and intensity chart, hue red.

Figure 5-7 The two halves of the color sphere. From Itten, *Elements of Color.*

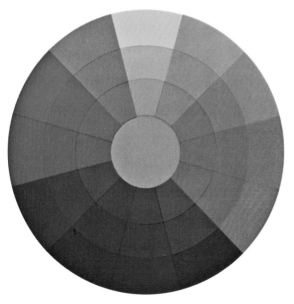

Figure 5-8 The sphere seen as if bisected by a plane at the equator. From Itten, *Elements of Color.*

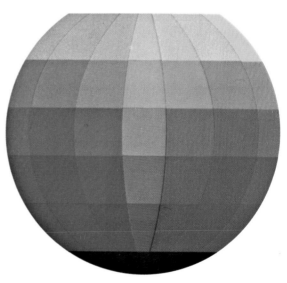

Figure 5-9 The sphere bisected by a plane through the poles. From Itten, *Elements of Color.*

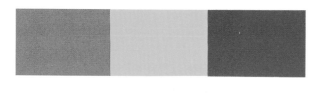

Figure 5-10   The contrast of the three primary hues is more intense than that of the secondary hues.

Figure 5-11   A color grouping with all tones at the value of yellow.

Figure 5-12   Red-orange and blue-green are the two poles of warm – cold contrast.

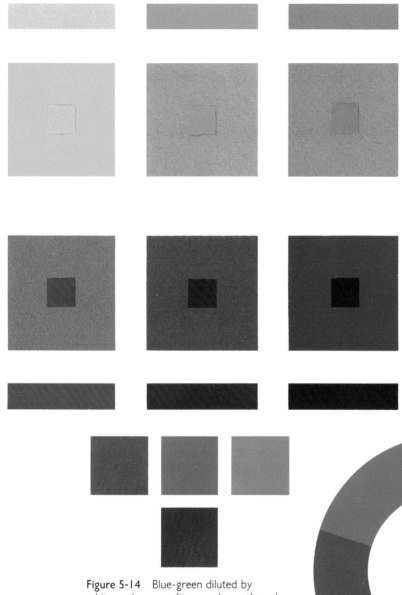

Figure 5-13   The three primary and three secondary hues with gray.

Figure 5-14   Blue-green diluted by white, red-orange (its complement), and black.

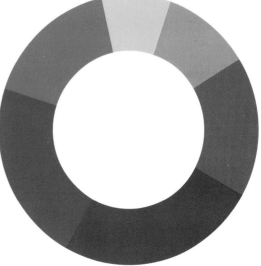

Figure 5-15   The color wheel showing the harmonious relative areas of the hues. From Itten, *Elements of Color*.

Figure 5-16 The same blue on yellow and lavender backgrounds.

Figure 5-17 The same green appears darker with light tones and lighter with dark ones (left).

Figure 5-18 Red-violet seems cooler with orange tones, warmer with cool ones (below left).

Figure 5-19 The same green on a colorful and a more neutralized background (below right).

Figure 5-20　A costume collage can express the color feeling along with the textures for the production.

Figure 5-21   The stronger colors at neckline and hair pull the focus of these costumes to the face. Designs by Ainslie Bruneau for guests in bathing suits in *The Merry Widow.*

Figure 5-22   The color scheme used for Alonzo in *The Tempest* shows him to be more outgoing and powerful than the more restrained, less flamboyant concept for Gonzolo in the same play reproduced on page 241. Design by Bob Perdziola.

Nature and conditioning provide colors with meanings that may hold true for a number of people. The following emotional responses to the six basic colors are not written in granite, but they should be considered because of the types of reactions that may be found in the audience:

Red Warmth, activity, power, passion, strength. Red variations can run quite a gamut, from satanic, bloody, warlike deep tones to cherubic pinks.

Orange Festivity, active energy, earthy vibrance. Variations to orange can go from warm, restful beiges to dull, withered browns.

Yellow Brightness, knowledge, youth, radiance. Pure yellows seem to tend toward truth and understanding while neutralized yellows move more to distrust and decay.

Green Fruitfulness, lush nature, contentment. Greens reflect the growth in the world, but when grayed can become sinister or when mixed with blue take on a colder, more aggressive tone.

Blue Coldness, passivity, spiritualism, faith, introversion. Light blue has a transparent quality. Blue becomes more vibrant as it moves to black, and grayed tones seem suitable for superstition and the supernatural.

Violet Piety, mastery, menace, chaos, solitude, royalty, terror. Violets can cover a great range from the lilac of lovely spring flowers to the terrifying purples that may inhabit a nightmare.

Color symbols. In any society certain color symbols are used so often they are readily accepted as the way things ought to be. A variety of conditioned responses may be triggered in the audience when a certain tone is presented on stage. Red is associated with fire trucks, flashing alarms, stop signs, and the garments of high church officials. Yellow is the color on caution signs; a lighter association is implied by the slogan "blonds have more fun." Green means go, and a shade of green is used for "Mr. Yuk" on poison labels. The Virgin Mary always wears blue, as do policemen. Brides wear white; priests, nuns, and mourners wear black. The color of the military uniforms of a country can evoke a response. Certain colors are expected in certain situations. If they are not used, the reason should be clear.

Color symbolism can be quite helpful, but if not used carefully it can get in the way of the story line, for it could tell too much or move in a direction that goes against the plot. For example, a vibrant red is often associated with a lady of ill repute and in some situations could be used quite effectively as such. If, however, the audience isn't to know immediately about the lady's moral shortcomings it would be better not to clothe her in such a blatant symbol. If a character seems about to lose touch with reality, misty blues and lavenders might seem ideal. But if the character is a waitress in a hash joint these tones are quite inappropriate for her uniform and confusing to the audience. It is often wise to avoid the temptation to make the costumes of lovers match. What's the use of going through the whole plot if the audience knows instantly by his pink shirt and her pink dress that they will end up together? In many cases color symbolism can be helpful, but the colors must hold effectively within the scene even if the symbol is not read by the audience, and they must not tell too much about the character too early in the story.

Color approach to a production

SPECIFIC COLOR NEEDS DEFINED IN THE SCRIPT

A play may have specific color needs written into the script. The designer notes color indications when reading the script and includes them in the complete costume lists needed to begin work on a production. It is important to decide if a color mentioned in the script is essential to the play or if it can be exchanged for another equally appropriate color. For example, Cyrano refers to his white plume, and that symbolic plume is quite central to the play. George Bernard Shaw was very fond of specifying the settings and costumes of his plays in great detail; in *Candida* he describes Marchbanks as wearing "an old blue serge jacket, unbuttoned, over a woollen lawn tennis shirt, with a silk handkerchief for a cravat, trousers matching the jacket, and brown canvas shoes." From this we can get a good idea of how Shaw saw the character, but there is no reason that this must be followed to the letter. However, in *The Devil's Disciple* the Presbyterian minister, Anderson, must have a black coat as Shaw suggests, for a black coat is an easily recognized symbol for a minister and by donning Anderson's coat Dick Dudgeon assumes the other's identity to fool the arresting officer.

The situation of a play may require costumes that automatically make a strong statement in the color scheme. If the scene is a formal ball, the men will be in black and white, properly attired in tuxedos or tails. If the British are invading the American colonies the Redcoats will make a strong color impact. Should the scene open in a convent, black and white are once again important. When a group of Keystone Kops chases a villain down the street a large block of blue can't be avoided. Uniforms, church costumes, and formal wear produce a strong color direction and the color helps produce an expected emotional response in the audience.

In the same vein, the setting of the play may strongly point to the use of certain colors and establish color limits for the costumes. A scene in a forest could provide an environment of dominant green tones, just as one in a castle may tend to stone gray. Black velour curtains or a blue cyclorama are stage elements often used for either practical or artistic reasons, and either sets a strong color direction.

COLOR IDEAS FROM THE DIRECTOR

Just as a guide to the color scheme can come from the script, so can it come from the director. The director may want a certain color feeling in a certain scene. It is then important for the designer to make sure the colors of the rest of the play revolve around that scene properly. For example, if the final scene of Shakespeare's *A Midsummer Night's Dream* were to be done as a sumptuous masque, with the wedding party and courtiers all in golds and whites, the designer would not want to use those tones in the earlier scenes but would save them for the visual impact at the end.

It is possible for a director to have some color ideas for a play that the designer does not agree with and vice versa. When this happens it is usually more efficient to work up color ideas around both suggestions and see which seems best for the play. In most cases, satisfactory solutions can be found through intelligent discussion. Color ideas can come on quite strongly, but there is seldom only one color solution to any problem. Don't get so tied to one scheme that other possibilities can't be considered. The other ideas may or may not work, but if they are disregarded without a chance it doesn't do much for the feeling of friendly cooperation that is best for this kind of work.

COLOR FOR CHARACTER IDENTIFICATION

Color can be a valuable tool to help the audience keep track of character relationships, particularly in plays with large casts where individuals may not be clearly defined but group identity is important. In Shakespeare's *Romeo and Juliet* the Montagues must be different from the Capulets. In *Richard III*, Richard's supporters must be distinguished from Richmond's. In *Macbeth* one army must differ from another, and when nobles change sides the audience needs to know whom they are fighting for when. Good color control helps the audience identify any opposing forces, whether armies, cheerleaders, or good and evil.

Planning the color

Color should be discussed not in general terms but with a color layout at hand that all can view and comment on. The designer may have a well-developed sense of color, but it may not be at all like that of the director. Something that seems quite charming as it is talked about may not be at all effective when actually looked at. It may be even more often true that certain color schemes may not sound like they will work, but when actual tones are arranged effectively before the eye the possibilities become much more clear.

The first color indications may come from a photograph, painting, or collage that says something about the show to either the designer or the director. It need not be totally right, but it is a conversation starter for preliminary discussions. It shows a direction. Given this, the designer can work on a more specific color presentation, one that more carefully applies itself to the emotional color feeling of the show. This could also take the form of a preexisting photograph or painting, or a color collage made specifically to portray the colors that will be seen on stage.

Any color guide the costume designer uses is a tool that helps develop the color scheme and should incorporate enough variety to suggest all the costume effects that will be needed. It should also contain some of the colors that will be used in the scenery, for this provides the setting in which the costumes will be seen. A layout for Shakespeare's *As You Like It* is incomplete if it concentrates only on woodsy, pastoral tones since it ignores the beginning court scene, which should have a very different color feeling. If a production of *Hamlet* is to be done with a set featuring the gray walls of Elsinore, the costume colors should be presented as they will appear in gray surroundings.

While a color layout presents the hues, values, and intensities that will be emotionally right for the show, color should not be completely divorced from texture. A photograph or painting may be chosen because it contains implied textures that are right for the desired effect. A photograph of a decaying or weathered piece of wood might contain the same shades of browns and grays as a photo of a modern office building. If the costumes were to be done with textured, painted, aged fabrics the former would be more appropriate; if they were to be clean, crisp, stylish clothes, the latter would be better.

A costume collage can give the designer a wonderful opportunity to express both the color feeling and the texture of the show, for anything might be incorporated (Figure 5-20, p. 171). Actual fabric swatches are excellent for this purpose. Of course one does not necessarily already have the fabric that will be used in the show; the designer will use the fabric swatches that have accumulated in his or her collection. To this can be added anything that will enhance the feeling—metallic bits, pieces of beading, old sticks, torn-up doilies, spatters of paint, a leaf or flower—anything that opens up possibilities and sparks the imagination to use color.

Colored papers are probably least successful when used in a collage, for while they provide various tones, they are flat and relatively lifeless. If the show is to be costumed in flat cottons they may be perfectly suited to the presentation. If not, they can be a bit stifling.

SETTING COLOR LIMITATIONS

Color control can be used to produce a unified visual effect in a production, one that is appropriate to the emotional content of the play as a whole and to the individual characters. Colors picked at random with no consideration of their influence on the audience may add nothing and could produce a jarring reaction. Combinations may occur that disturb the audience and break the concentration on the scene or misplace the focus, so a scheme or plan for the color should be established.

Various types of color schemes can be set up based on the three main properties of color. The hues that are to be used could be limited. In *As You Like It,* maroons, blues, and purples could be designated for the court scene, with browns, oranges, greens, and yellows reserved for the forest. The tonal values to be used could be defined. In Sheridan's *The Rivals* the color tones could all range from medium to white, giving a bright, airy, pastel feeling. Lowering the intensity of colors can help bring a unified quality to the picture. Brecht's somber *Mother Courage* could well be done with the colors one-half to three-quarters neutralized.

Never think that limitations have to produce a dull theatrical picture. There are so many variations available that almost any type of scheme can be exciting if you allow your imagination to roam and use what you know about all the properties of color. A production done only in shades of brown could be quite breathtaking and give a very colorful effect, for there are light browns, dark browns, warm browns, cool browns, intense browns, grayed browns . . . one could give the feeling of having a whole color riot of browns alone. In addition to the variations possible within the most limited palette there are also variations provided by the textures of the fabrics. Even a production done only in black with white accents could be fascinating and have a great deal of variety. The only true black will be a velvet with the pile running up. All others will appear a degree or so lighter, depending upon the textures of the fabrics used.

COLOR PROGRESSION

A color progression can easily be established for some productions. The colors used in a staging of *Mother Courage* could become less intense as the war continues and drains the life and color from the landscape and its inhabitants. The townspeople in Durrenmatt's *The Visit* might be quite drab as the play starts, then gain in color as they draw nearer and nearer to accepting the bribe offered them. Ibsen's *Peer Gynt* might be defined effectively by the colors Peer encounters on his odyssey.

COLOR COORDINATION OF SCENERY AND COSTUMES

No costume color scheme can be completely successful on its own. The costumes are always seen in relation to the surrounding space, which is usually the scenery, and the color of one element will influence the other. This does not mean that the colors should always match. It *does* mean that the designers should know how they will go together and what effect they will produce. If the ingenue is to stand out like a jewel she might be costumed in a bright, crisp yellow. But if the set is yellow, perhaps she should appear in a white dress. If some characters need to look uncomfortable and out of place in a situation, their costume colors should not seem at home in the surrounding setting. Once the color progression is established for the show, the steps it makes and where they occur should be clear to both the scenic and the costume designer. Tones that are very similar should retain a degree of differentiation. Colored stage light can make some hues blend together. It is always discomfiting to design a costume that looks on stage as if it were made from the fabric left over after covering the sofa.

Friendly cooperation should also be the keystone of the relationship between the scene designer and the costume designer. There are no rules about whose ideas are more important and which area should get first consideration. This will depend entirely on the production and the circumstances. The scheme should develop because all involved are exchanging ideas and trying to find the best possible way to present the play. It may soon become obvious that either the scenery or the costumes will make the strongest visual statement, so decisions could be made in one area that will facilitate the effectiveness of the other. Thorough discussion allows both designers to work on their color ideas separately and come up with schemes that will work beautifully together with only slight adjustments. As discussed earlier, certain color requirements may be specifically stipulated in the script. It is highly likely that the Forest of Arden in *As You Like It* will be done in green tones; the costume designer should consider this from the beginning. It is equally probable that a scene in a nunnery will require many black costumes; the scene designer should always keep this in mind. But some color decisions are more arbitrary and deal with the designer's individual vision of the production. If the set designer is determined to use red wallpaper and the costume designer is just as set on a red gown for the leading lady, compromise will obviously be necessary.

Realism and stylization in the color scheme

Costumes that must give a strongly realistic effect need a color scheme drawn from colors that were popular and commonly used in the period and locale in which the play is set, or at least those generally accepted as the ones most prevalent in that particular time and place. For more recent periods, colored photographs are good reference materials; for earlier times, paintings give the flavor of an era, though it may well be idealized by the artist. From paintings it becomes quite apparent that the tonality of an Elizabethan tragedy is quite different from that of an eighteenth-century pastoral play. The former seems more often depicted in deeper, richer colors; the latter in lighter, frothier ones. The basic guidelines are given by the period. Limitations to define a more specific color scheme may be set within these guidelines.

A very stylized look can be given to a production by nonrealistic use of color. An Elizabethan tragedy done in pastels will instantly be a step removed from the dark intrigues commonly associated with this type of drama. A Molière piece done in black, white, and gray immediately lets the audience know that this production takes an unconventional point of view. Color stylization nevertheless does not have to be so blatant. Subtle variations can be used to create an effect that gives a slight twist that adds interest without calling attention to itself.

The individual costume within the color scheme

The color scheme provides the plan for the entire play. From this scheme the tones that will be used in each scene are selected; then those that will give the main thrust to each costume are chosen.

A scene breakdown color plot can be quite useful in laying out the show. With it the designer can project how each scene will look and judge the effectiveness of the color control. This color breakdown can be laid out in the same form as the scene breakdown in Chapter 2, or it could be done as illustrated in the chart on page 180. The format here is perhaps easier to read for this purpose since the colors in each scene go across the page, forming a line similar to the position of the actors on the stage. Only the predominant costume colors need be included, in approximately the same proportion they will be seen in the costumes. For example, with a red costume trimmed in black, a much larger area of red than of black is represented graphically.

The color computer could be invaluable at this step when the cost comes down to a range where it fits into a theatre budget. The tones could be selected for each costume, laid out in proportional blocks, and stored. The basic planes of the stage space could be defined, characters called up and placed for any desired moment, and even the background tones laid in. The important scenes for the entire show could be created, called up at will, and adjusted easily to try out the most effective combinations. What a great toy, or tool, for the designer to be able to play with!

As a designer looks at the colors that will be used in a scene, the action of that scene must be carefully considered. The colors must

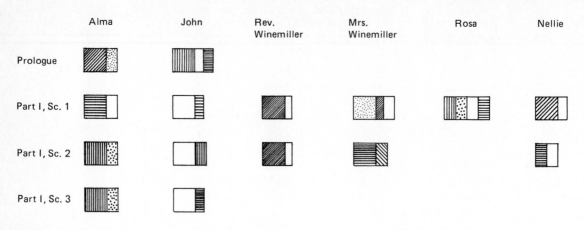

	Alma	John	Rev. Winemiller	Mrs. Winemiller	Rosa	Nellie
Prologue	▨	▥				
Part I, Sc. 1	▤	▥	▨	▨	▥	▨
Part I, Sc. 2	▥	▥	▨	▥		▤
Part I, Sc. 3	▥	▥				

Scene breakdown color plot
for *Summer and Smoke*

reinforce the dramatic focus. For example, if the scene is a coronation, there can be little doubt that the colors worn by the king should be emphasized and highlighted over all other costumes on stage. As Hamlet watches the play within a play the stage will be filled with many courtiers, plus the players, yet Hamlet must retain the dramatic focus of the scene. A color plot should be established as soon as possible, using the fabrics chosen for the production and viewed under the stage lighting worked out for each scene, for the colors may react differently with different lighting effects.

One word of warning: Many costume shops are equipped with fluorescent lights, most of which illuminate with a spectrum not very close to that of incandescent stage lighting; the red areas are particularly bad. A fabric that seems like a pleasant maroon in the shop might on stage appear closer to fire-engine red. It is very important to have some form of incandescent light available, even if it is only one spot that can be turned on to check tones. If the spot is equipped to take various colors, it would be even better. The warning must go one step further, for many fabric departments are also illuminated by fluorescent lighting. Sometimes it seems as if most of the world is against revealing the true colors of fabrics. When shopping, particularly for red tones, use either an incandescent light or daylight from an outside window to check the color of a fabric before making a commitment.

COLOR WITHIN THE INDIVIDUAL COSTUME

Abstract discussion about the proper way to set up the color schemes for the individual costumes can be a bit difficult, but when the designer is in the midst of a project, actually deciding which colors are best for which characters will not seem such an elusive task. Equipped with a clear idea of basic color theory, a knowledge of the play and an understanding of the characters, and a thoughtful consideration of the overall color scheme, the designer's task is far less formidable. A costume will often have one or two main colors and accent colors, though in some schemes any number of tones can be used on one character. If only one or two main colors are used, the amount of contrast in the accents can depend on the types of characters and the type of color scheme. An approach to the color accents that is consistent throughout the play must be established. This does not mean that the accents must all be the same, but they must seem related and appear to belong to the same world. If a great many hues are used in one costume, they must be balanced by means of values and/or intensity so the costume will maintain itself on the same plane.

Color harmonies are created in a costume through the control of hue, value, and intensity, but total harmony can become total monotony. Every costume needs focus, and the focus is usually aimed more toward the speaking part of the body. The arrangement of color as well as of line can lead the eye to the face (Figure 5-21, p. 172). In a simple peasant frock, only one tone may be used and the color accent will be the face and hair. As more tones enter the picture more care must be taken so the attention of the audience will not be misplaced. If a man wears a black suit with white shirt and blue-striped tie, the shirt and tie will help focus attention to the top of his body. If he wears yellow shoes they had better be important to the scene, because that's where the audience will be looking.

The basic approach to the harmonies and contrasts to be used in the costumes is established in the overall color scheme. The choices that are made for each individual are influenced by the characterization presented in the script (Figure 5-22, p. 172).

In Sheridan's *The Rivals,* Mrs. Malaprop is much too outrageous to clothe herself in a quiet color scheme, while the more demure Julia would probably not have nearly as much contrast in her ensemble. In Molière's *Le Bourgeois Gentilhomme,* Monsieur Jourdain is terribly eager to join the world of the elite and embarks on this mission with full force and no noticeable taste; his colors would reflect this approach to life. Cléante, the young suitor for Jourdain's daughter, is much more straightforward and honest, and the colors of his clothes should reflect this.

Ideas about colors should never really be separated from ideas about textures. The types of fabric used greatly influence how the color is perceived. Kelly-green cotton, satin, and velvet can produce three completely different color feelings under stage light. Texture variations could provide the variety and focus needed for an effective costume. Traditionally a bride is dressed only in white, but a bridal outfit usually does not seem monotonous, for contrast and focus are provided by veilings, laces, and trims. And, also traditionally, the highlight of the outfit is the bride's shining face, with the glow of victory in her eyes.

Certain color combinations make some tones seem to advance and others recede, just as some tones will seem of lighter weight and others heavier. These effects depend very much upon the way the tones are put together; the designer must be able to judge the effect against the intent. As a general rule, lighter tones advance from a dark background while darker tones recede into it; darker shades advance from a light background while light ones recede. Warm tones advance while cool ones retreat. Lighter tones seem to have less weight than darker ones. All this is nevertheless quite relative, resulting from the types of tones used and the way they are assembled.

The spatial qualities of color can be useful when the designer wishes to minimize some figure problems. For (as the ad agencies put it) a full-figured woman, a lighter panel for the front of the gown and darker shades to the side will help achieve a slimming effect. Darker hose are more attractive on heavy legs for the same reason, for the mesh is lighter as the eye sees it straight on and shades as it wraps around the leg. As lighter, brighter tones tend to advance they may not work well for slacks on a hippy figure. Which brings up an important question: When a set of chorus costumes is rented, why does the size 48 always come in bright orange?

The swatches or color chips used to do the color layouts for the individual costumes should always be arranged in the proportions seen in the costume, relative to the way they will appear on the body. This makes them more helpful to the designer, who can begin to visualize how the completed costume will look. As a result, the designer will be able to give a more accurate impression to the director of what is to come.

The effect of colored light on fabric

Costumes and scenery are revealed to the audience by the stage lighting used for the production. Stage lighting employs color mediums to help mold the picture, add interest to the composition, and heighten the emotional impact of the scene. The color mediums in the light can greatly influence the color effect of the costumes and scenery. Thus far, we have discussed the coordination of the sets and costumes. The tie-in with the lighting designer is equally important, although it may happen later in the process of developing ideas. Much of the work of the lighting designer cannot begin until the stage areas have been set and the color feeling established.

The costume designer and lighting designer can discuss the basic color feeling early in the design process. Once the costume designer has selected most of the fabrics that will be used in the production, a practical session with the lighting designer can be arranged. If they can set up a couple of spotlights and lay out the fabrics by scenes, viewing each set in the main colors to be used, they will both have a much better idea of what they are going to achieve. The costume designer may need to adjust the tonal values of some of the fabrics and may also need to know how bright the light tones will be compared to the darker ones. Very light tones can in some circumstances seem too bright onstage; when darkened slightly by dyeing, they can remain more within the overall picture while still appearing white or very light. The lighting designer can at this time see if the colors he or she wishes to use will best enhance the fabric or if another combination will produce the desired effect.

It is usually quite true that if, at dress rehearsal, the lighting and the costumes are not working well together, it is easier to change the color in the light than to construct new costumes. Of course, everyone involved will be much happier if the elements can be tested together before the last minute with a sense of mutual cooperation. Dress rehearsals are tense times at best. Everyone is working very hard to get everything to coalesce for the opening, which always seems to be coming too soon. Everything that can be tested ahead of time should be; there is no surer way to fix all those unforeseen bobbles in the master plan.

Many of the effects of colored light on fabric can be anticipated by merely thinking through the effect that a certain colored light will have on the colored fabric, or considering how selective reflection works. Red fabric in blue light will not seem red. It will be a nondescript dark tone, for the blue light has no red rays to be reflected. Orange fabric in red light will appear red. The orange fabric reflects red and yellow rays, the red light provides only red rays. If green light is added, the orange fabric will appear orange, for the green light with the red mixes to create yellow.

Much color theory is easy to understand if you logically anticipate how one element will affect another. In practice it may not work out as cleanly as one might think. Color elements, whether dye, paint, fabric, light mediums, or the like, are rarely pure, and unforeseen variations always pop up. Accept this as a given fact and be prepared to cope when necessary. For example, even so-called primary blue stage color filters have some red in them. These will distort but not completely destroy the appearance of red fabric. Maintaining a good balance can be tricky.

The pure primary or even secondary light colors are seldom used on acting areas; they are much too intense and transmit little light. They may be employed for a special effect or to tone the scenery, but even in

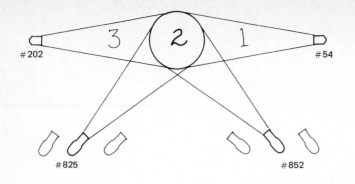

Light plot for one area, showing possible color distribution

these cases a tint of the color is usually used because it transmits more light and delivers more illumination to the stage.

Many tones are available in the color media used for stage lights. One of the best-known companies is Rosco, which has three lines of color media that combine to provide more than 200 different possibilities. Even those with the same name in all three sets do not produce quite the same color light, so it is always best to check the fabric with the actual media to be used. Take, for example, Bastard Amber, numbers 02, 202, and 802. Bastard Amber is a very pleasant color that mixes pinks and yellows and as such might be expected to fade out the blues a bit while enriching the other tones. Bastard Amber 02 and 202 do this; 802, which has more pink in it, is much better in the blue range while maintaining the interest of the other colors.

The stage is seldom illuminated with only one color. It is generally divided into acting areas and each area is lit with at least two instruments, usually more. An excellent location for the primary instruments is at an angle 45 degrees up and 45 degrees to the side of the center of the area. The instrument on the right has a color different than that on the left, so the actors on stage appear molded by light. Another set of instruments could be used from each side to help mold the figure even more. In this case the lights from the front might use the lighter tones, with slightly more intense tones coming from the side so the three-dimensional quality is heightened and more color interest created. Back light could also be added.

Since more than one color is used in an area, a deficiency in one tone can be compensated for by another. If Bastard Amber is used in one front light, the other might use Special Lavender, number 54, which brings life back to the blues without killing anything else. A four-color combination might use the Bastard Amber and Special Lavender from the side and lighter tones such as No-Color Pink (number 825) and Smokey Blue (number 852) from the front. No-Color Pink enhances all but the blue tones, which are picked up by the Smokey Blue.

So many variations are available that it is difficult to say what a specific color will do on a specific fabric. There are too many Bastard Ambers and too many blue-green cottons. The chart on page 185 is meant only to suggest what might be expected in some circumstances. The designers need to experiment and see what would actually happen when a certain color is used on a particular fabric.

Rosco Color Media	General effect on color wheel	Good uses and combinations
Bastard Amber 02, 202, 802	Fades blue	Good warm tones Pleasant warm effect with Surprise Pink Good balance with Special Lavender
Pale Gold 803	Deadens blues; can give a rather grimy feeling	Balances with Smokey Blue for clear light effect; colors fairly true but not lush
No-Color Straw 804	Almost clear; deepens yellows	Balances well for clear effect with light Steel Blue
Light Straw 805	Quite yellow	Better for side than front
Golden Amber 815	Very strong; distorts most of the spectrum. Kills blues; violets go brown, red and orange blend	
No-Color Pink 825	Grays blues considerably	Very warm feeling with Bastard Amber
Flesh Pink 826	Strong pink	Balances well with blues Good balance and warm overall tone with lavender tones Very warm feeling with Violet
Bright Rose 829	Kills green; yellows and violets change considerably	
Surprise Pink 841	Reds and oranges jump	Strong color effect with Bastard Amber Balances well with Daylight Blue
Pale Lavender 53	Colors fairly true	Good cool whites
Special Lavender 842, 54	Spectrum holds pretty well, reds may jump slightly	Cool color effect
Violet 844	Strong color, can gray yellows	Good balance with Bastard Amber Very warm effect with Flesh Pink
Pale Blue 849	Blue-green tint tends to subdue reds	For light, cool effect; balances with Daylight Blue
Daylight Blue 851	Blue with red in it so reds tend to jump	For light, cool effect; balances with Pale Blue
Smokey Blue 852	Tends to dull reds	With Pale Gold produces white light that presents colors clearly but not lushly
Steel Blue 854	More a blue-green; dulls reds	
Pale Yellow Green 869	Colors fairly true	Good early-morning feeling
Chocolate 882	May dull cool tones	Gives a murky, warm feeling

Scenes that need strongly colored lighting effects should be given particular attention when thinking through costume colors. If strong sunlight is called for, the blues that can be used should be checked carefully. In night scenes red fabrics might either be dulled down or jump. A dulled red effect probably won't bother the audience much, for it expects a certain dimness at night. But if a red costume starts to glow and take on a life of its own, there had better be a pretty important person inside it who should monopolize the focus of the scene. The ability of a strong light color to change the color of a costume is not necessarily bad, and some very interesting effects can be achieved. But they should not be a surprise. Try things out and know ahead of time what the lights and costumes will do together. A "happy accident" can be very pleasant, but a minor catastrophe that can be expensive and wearing on the nerves can happen just as easily.

Color is the first scenic element to hit the audience and the one that is the most difficult to control because so much can influence it and affect the way it is perceived. An A-line skirt is always an A-line skirt, but a yellow skirt can be changed in a number of directions. Good color control requires a great many decisions of judgment. The designer must absorb as much as possible about the use of color and realize that there are new things to learn with every new show.

6

Costume presentation: rendering or final sketch

The costume is designed. The decisions have been made about the line and the color. The ideas must now be expressed in final form. It is easy enough to say "And now, on to the final rendering!" But for many designers this can be traumatic, perhaps because it seems like the ultimate commitment. What the show is going to look like is supposed to appear on the page. The drawings will be shown to everyone involved. Suddenly the pencil is too heavy to pick up.

The costume rendering or final sketch is important, but it should be considered a means and not an end in itself. The costume, not the drawing, is the final product, but the drawing is the vehicle that communicates the designer's ideas to everyone involved in the production (Figure 6-1, p. 189). In fact, it provides a means for designers to communicate with themselves. A carefully done sketch brings the costume impressions from the imagination to the paper, where designers can sort out their ideas, judge the effect, and make specific decisions to clarify choices. This is the last private moment to organize thoughts. Once the rendering gets to the shop there will be many demands, often simultaneous, on the designer. He or she should know what is required beforehand so that well-considered judgment will take the place of spur-of-the-moment decisions.

Effective costume renderings or final sketches serve a multiple purpose as the designer presents the work to others (Figure 6-2, p. 189). They certainly help convey ideas to the director, for they clearly display the look and atmosphere of the show. Sketches can inspire the actors by showing them how they will look and by pointing out character nuances that can help them. The sketches can interest the crew members and get them excited about building this show and making costumes that will look just like the drawings.

The costume design presentation

The costume design presentation is not necessarily a work of art; it is a clear indication of what the costume will be, easily read by those who need to see it. It must provide enough information for the costume to be understood; if everything cannot be seen on the main figure, supplemental sketches should be added (Figure 6-3, p. 190). If possible, it should include swatches of the actual materials and trims to be used, or perhaps texture indications, so the designer can present as much information as is needed to clarify his or her ideas (Figure 6-4, p. 190). A sketch should be an honest representation of the costume, something that can actually be built to give the same effect when worn on stage.

Preceding page: The fantasy costume can be a real challenge for a designer. Costume design by Susan Tsu for The Queen of the Netherlands in And the Sea Shall Give Up Its Dead, produced by WHA-TV for PBS. Colored pencil and graphite on drawing paper. A 14-inch figure on an 11.75-by-18-inch sheet of drawing paper.

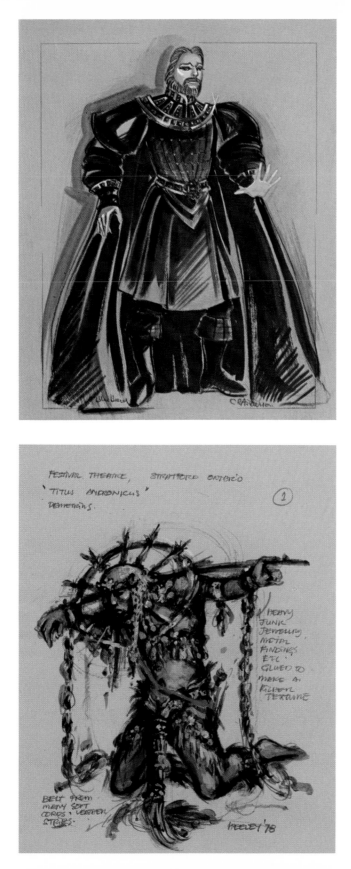

Figure 6-1 The costume sketch is the way the designer communicates ideas. Costume designed by Cletus Anderson for Bluebeard in *Bluebeard's Castle,* produced at Carnegie-Mellon University. Watercolor and charcoal on gray Crescent Charko-board. Figure is 17 inches high on a 16-by-20-inch board.

Figure 6-2 A costume sketch can be an inspiration as well as a description of the costume to be built. Designed 1978 by Desmond Healey for Demetrius in *Titus Andronicus,* produced at the Festival Theatre, Stratford, Ontario. Acrylic on tan paper. Figure is 10.5 inches high on an 11-by-14-inch sheet.

Figure 6-3 Supplemental sketches may provide information not visible on the main figure. Costume designed by Kevin Rupnik for Mrs. Loveit in *The Man of Mode,* produced at the Juilliard School. Done on Strathmore drawing paper with Windsor Newton watercolors and overdrawn with some Prismacolor and pencil. Plate 16.5 by 14 inches. Principal figure 8.5 inches high.

Figure 6-4 Additional sketches may clarify the ideas of the designer. Costume design by Christine Oagley for an English Soldier in *King Lear,* produced at the Utah Shakespeare Festival. Watercolor, Prismacolor, and soft pencil on gray mat board. Plate 11 by 20 inches. Principal figure 13.5 inches high.

Figure 6-5 The costume plate can be done in an illustration style that corresponds to the period to be used for the production. Costume design by Susan Tsu for Emilia in *Othello*, produced by the Intiman Theatre, Seattle. Gouache, graphite, Magic Marker, and gloss medium on gray mat board. Total figure 12 inches high on a 10-by-16-inch board.

Figure 6-6 A certain amount of elongation may be used very effectively in some costume plates. Costume design by Carrie F. Robbins for The Bride in *Frankenstein*, produced at the Palace Theater, New York, 1981. Mixed media.

Figure 6-7 The set of the body and positioning of the limbs should not hide important areas. Costume design by Susan Tsu for Teiresias in *Antigone*, produced at the Intiman Theatre, Seattle. Gouache, graphite and ink with a gouache-and-salt background. The borders were taped and a wash of color was laid in, sprinkled with salt, and left to dry. The figure was drawn and painted over the prepared background. 10.5-inch figure on a 10-by-15-inch plate.

Figure 6-8 The costume rendering should present a clear design. Design by Ainslie Bruneau for Olivia in *Twelfth Night,* produced at Carnegie-Mellon University. Windsor Newton watercolor tubes and pencil on T. H. Saunders watercolor paper. Figure is 14 inches high on a 15-by-21-inch sheet.

Figure 6-9 The figure should have a physical attitude to the body that makes it seem alive. Costume design by Frank Bevan for Egeus in *A Midsummer Night's Dream,* produced at Yale University. Casein on beige Bainbridge Board, Rough. The figure is 14.5 inches high on a 14-by-20-inch board. (Below left)

Figure 6-10 All elements, including hair, headdress, accessories, and footwear must be included on the plate. Costume design by Howard Kaplan for Zanche in *The White Devil.* Designer color and pencil on charcoal paper. 14-inch figure on 13-by-20-inch sheet. (Below right)

MISS JULIE

JULIE - ACT I

CHIFFON RUFFLE FAB.
SHIRRED OVER
BODICE FAB.

CHEVRON
STRIPE ON
BODIC

SATIN PIPING
ON LACE OVERSKIRT
HEM

Figure 6-11 The completed rendering must contain all the elements of the costume. Costume design by Kevin Rupnik for Julie in *Miss Julie*. Windsor Newton watercolors, Prismacolor, and pencil on watercolor paper. Figure is 10 inches high on an 11-by-15-inch sheet.

Figure 6-12 A costume plate should have life, and humor, if appropriate. Costume design by Michael Olich for Dolly in *You Never Can Tell* produced at the Alley Theatre, Houston. Designer color and pencil on mat board. Figure 12 inches high on an 11-by-16-inch board.

Figure 6-13 Swatches and notes may be necessary to give a clear guide to the shop of the way the costume should be constructed. Design by John Conklin for a Gypsy woman in Rossini's *The Turk in Italy*, produced by the New York City Opera, director Tito Capobianco. Acrylic and colored pencil on a smooth sketch paper. Figure 11.5 inches high on a 13-by-18-inch sheet.

Figure 6-14 A symmetrical single figure well placed on the page. Costume design by Cletus Anderson for Little John in the film *Knightriders,* directed by George Romero. Charcoal pencil and oil wash on Fabriani watercolor paper. Figure is 16.5 inches high, matted in to 12 by 18 inches.

Figure 6-15 Single figure balanced by notes and swatches. Costume design by John Sullivan for Rigoletto in a production by the Opera Theatre of St. Louis. Windsor Newton gouache with some charcoal pencil on oil canvas paper for the texture. Painted very broadly to suggest the heavy and coarse fabrics used. Figure is 13 inches high on a 12-by-18-inch sheet. (Above right)

Figure 6-16 Figure, helmet detail, and swatches arranged to balance the plate. Costume designed by Cletus Anderson for Sir William in the film *Knightriders.* Charcoal pencil and oil wash on Fabriani watercolor paper. Figure is 16 inches high on a 13-by-19-inch sheet. (Right)

Figure 6-17   A number of chorus costumes can be presented on one plate to give the same type of group effect that will be seen on stage. Design by William P. Brewer for *See Saw*. Watercolor, pencil, and marker on cold-press paper. Figures are 11.5 inches high on an 18-by-24-inch sheet.

A certain amount of idealization can be included if it will give the flavor desired in the production. For a period production, the costume plates might tend toward the illustration style used at that time (Figure 6-5, p. 191). If the style of a farce is to have a broad, comic-book feeling, the plates could reflect this. A play that incorporates a lot of movement might have renderings that show this activity. But if a costume will not be seen with three wind machines always blowing at it, it should not be illustrated as such. Delicately flying fabric can make an exciting sketch, but yardage hanging limply off the actor will not look particularly fascinating. It is very poetic to think of the costume sketch as showing "five yards of emotion," but a shop cannot build this, nor can an actor maintain the fever pitch of intensity and action needed to duplicate the impression created by the sketch.

No matter how clear and accurate the costume sketch is, it may not be properly understood by someone viewing it. The sketch must be as complete as possible, but it is up to the designer to discuss each sketch, point out the various elements, note how the articles work, what comes off, what has pockets, and so forth. Many people cannot conceptualize a drawing and do not really understand what they are seeing until they have a three-dimensional object before them. Some of these people are directors and it is not uncommon for them to say "I didn't know it would look like that," even though the costume was completed exactly as it was presented on the sketch. This can be devastating, so it is important for the designer to guide others carefully as they view the renderings and help them understand the important elements.

Establishing the figure

The figure on the costume plate should emphasize physical qualities that are important to establish the character. Should the role call for a heroic and elegant personage, some elongation might be used (Figure 6-6, p. 191). A figure of eight to eight-and-one-half heads is well proportioned. It provides a long line that still looks natural. Figures in fashion illustrations are commonly more stylized, often ten to eleven heads high, and so extremely elongated that they are unrealistic and unrealizable. All the figures need not be ideally proportioned; the costume plates should reflect physical differences between characters.

The detail of the costume can be seen more easily on a figure that opens out. The set of the body and the positioning of the limbs should not hide important details (Figure 6-7, p. 191). Arms folded over the chest of a woman wearing an intricately tucked, pleated, and trimmed blouse hide significant information from the viewer. If she is wearing a plain sweater, the position of the arms is far less important. Some costumes cannot be completely seen on one figure, no matter how it is posed. An 1885 bustle gown has as much going on in back as it does in front, and both sides may not be the same. Additional sketches will undoubtedly be needed. If an actress stays curled up in a ball the entire time she is on stage, perhaps the costume plate should show this as the main view. (A supplementary sketch will still be necessary: it's too hard for the shop to build a curled-up ball.)

The aim of the costume rendering is to present a clear design that helps convey and support the character (Figure 6-8, p. 192). The design is developed with careful thought to the overall approach to the production; the lines, colors, and textures are selected because they best delineate the character within the guidelines of this overall approach. The final sketch should present the ideas in a manner that keeps them within the range of this overall production scheme.

Vitality can add a great deal of interest to the sketch. The figure need not be engaged in violent action but should have a sense of movement, a physical attitude to the body that makes it seem alive (Figure 6-9, p. 192). A figure flattened out on the page as if plastered there by a steam roller does little to sell a costume idea. Hand props can often be used effectively to add a bit of spark to the presentation. These props can also be important because they help clarify characters by showing them with objects they will actually use in the play. The Gravedigger in *Hamlet*, for example, looks like just another peasant until a skull or spade is placed in his hand to define his occupation. Sir Toby Belch in *Twelfth Night* could well be depicted raising a tankard of ale, for it certainly would be in character.

The sense of vitality in an effective costume presentation is a function not only of the way the body is placed on the page but also the technique used to draw it. Two different approaches can be used to draw the final figure, each with advantages and disadvantages. The full-sized figure can be drawn on tracing paper or newsprint and traced onto the paper or board. This is perhaps a good approach for the beginning designer, for the figure can be worked through and corrected without unduly smudging the background and spoiling the painting surface. Unfortunately, the traced figure can seem lifeless. If the figure is drawn directly on the paper or board it will usually have a more spontaneous and vital feeling, but the surface may get messy if much redrawing is needed. One fairly effective compromise is to draw the figure on tracing paper, trace just enough on the board to establish a basic outline, then finish it by drawing in the rest on the actual surface; the line can still have some spontaneity without obvious trial-and-error efforts. A costume plate should not look tortured and sloppy. Extraneous fingerprints and smudges can be quite distracting and lead the viewer to question the quality of the designer's craftsmanship.

The figure should be transferred onto a plate with a homemade graphite sheet. This is made by taking a piece of tracing paper and laying on a wash of graphite with a very soft lead. This will transfer the figure with a line that can be easily erased or painted over. Typewriter carbon paper produces a permanent, unattractive line, and commercial pencil carbon does not erase easily. If medium- to light-weight water-color paper is used, transferring could be done on a light table: the drawing is overlaid with the watercolor paper and secured on a piece of glass that is illuminated from below by a bright light. The line thus appears through the heavier paper.

The completed rendering must contain all the elements of the costume, including the hair, headdress, accessories, and footwear (Figures 6-10 and 6-11, pp. 192, 193). All must work together on one actor onstage, so they should all be carefully designed to create the character's proper image and present a complete picture of what is to be. In addition, some suggestion of anatomical details—facial features, fingers, toes—will need to be included if the figure is to look finished.

Media

There are a great variety of color media, boards, and papers to use for costume renderings. No one type is better than any other. The effectiveness of any material depends upon what it is being used for and who is using it. It is quite important for the beginning designer to try a number of media in order to understand how the different materials work and to discover those that are most effective. Materials should vary, depending upon the type of plate that is to be produced. A heavily textured show with a lot of yardage and minimal detail will probably be presented quite differently from one with neatly tailored, smooth fabrics that are delicately trimmed.

When exploring media for costume plates, it is important to keep one thought in mind. The end result resembles a colored drawing rather than a painting. The materials to be used could be the same, but the requirements are a bit different. Because of this the very finest materials are not always required, although it is important to have good tools since they make the work easier and the results better. Materials, whether color media, papers, or brushes, come in student's grade and artist's grade. The former is more suitable while experimenting and learning; the latter will be much more satisfactory to the skilled designer. Producing the costume plate is not always the easiest thing in the world. Fighting inferior materials can make this task much more difficult, while using good equipment can make the experience a delight.

PAPERS AND BOARDS

The papers and boards that can be used for a costume rendering come in a great variety of surface textures, thicknesses, fiber content, and colors. Some are best suited for particular paints; others are more versatile and can adapt to many different techniques.

Watercolor paper, which comes in white or off-white, makes an excellent ground for many types of costume plates. Handmade papers are by far the best because they have a higher linen rag content. The paper is made of a felted mass of interlaced fibers that catch and hold the color medium. The ability of the paper to catch and hold the paint in these interstices is very important. High linen rag content produces an excellent working surface, one that is flexible, takes paint easily, and can be worked on without destroying the surface, since the paint can be blended, blotted, or picked up with a sponge or brush without dissolving the paper. Cotton fibers are not as good, but are found in papers that are quite usable. Wood-pulp papers produce neither a particularly pleasant surface to work on nor one that can be worked over without some disintegration of the surface. Handmade papers are extremely absorbent and thus are sized with a weak gelatin or hide glue solution. Quality papers are watermarked. The watermark is readable on the side of the paper that is most suitable for painting, and can be seen by holding the paper up to a source of light. The surface of handmade paper is much more interesting than paper made by machine, which tends to have a monotonous grain. As might be expected, it is also much more expensive. Good handmade papers are manufactured by Arches, Fabriano, J. B. Green, James Watman and Son, and T. H. Saunders. Usable but less expensive papers are Bockingford (a cellulose-fiber paper) and Strathmore 500 (a cotton-fiber paper).

The finish on the paper can greatly influence the look of the final drawing. The primary finishes applied to papers are cold-pressed (CP), not pressed (NP), rough, and hot-pressed (HP). Cold-pressed and not-pressed finishes provide an open or coarse texture. Rough delivers an even coarser grain. These are all suited to transparent color media, but rough is more difficult to control because of the very high surface texture, or tooth, though it can give an interesting textural feeling when used for a broad style of presentation. A medium tooth can be effectively employed either for a wash or for fine detail and is serviceable for much costume work. Hot-pressed paper has a smooth surface and is thus better suited to line-and-wash work or opaque paints than to transparent watercolors.

Thickness is also an important factor in the behavior of the paper. Watercolor papers are graded by the weight of a ream (variously 472, 480, 500, or 516 sheets). Thin is 72 pounds per ream, intermediate is 90 pounds, and fairly heavy 140 pounds. Very heavy sheets, which are more like boards, can be as heavy as 250 or 400 pounds per ream. Seventy-two-pound paper is quite thin and may corkle, or wrinkle, when worked; 90-pound paper is a good working weight; and 140-pound paper can be used to provide an even sturdier background — though, of course, it is expensive. If thin paper is to be used it can be prestretched to minimize any corkling. To do this the paper is completely saturated, then fastened down with paper tape to a sturdy, flat surface to dry. It may wrinkle a bit in use, but will flatten out again when the moisture evaporates. Some of the better papers come in blocks that have a gummed surface around all the edges, holding the sheets together as a solid mass. The top sheet can be used while it is held in tension, then removed from the block after it is dry. Pre-mounted watercolor papers are already adhered to a board and provide a very sturdy working surface. These are expensive and get quite heavy if a number are needed.

Illustration or art boards can provide an adequate working surface for the costume designer and are sturdier and heavier than watercolor paper. The sturdiness is an advantage, but the heaviness is not. A show with fifty costume plates done on board can be a real strain on the back. Boards provide an interesting surface, however, for some projects.

Boards come in hot-pressed and cold-pressed finishes, although the cold-pressed surface usually has less texture than most watercolor paper. Boards also come in different plies or thicknesses. The thicker board stands up better if a lot of paint is to be used, but for a costume rendering the thinner board is quite satisfactory. Good-quality white boards are manufactured by Crescent, Bainbridge, and Bristol.

A colored background can be provided by using mat boards and papers, Ingres-type papers, or pastel papers such as Krash and Canson Mi-Tientes. The surface varies from fairly smooth to moderately textured and is soft enough to allow the paint to sink in and not blend or move on the paper. These are therefore more suitable for opaque techniques or pastels. Although the surface quality of these boards and papers is not ideal for a watercolor technique, they are usable and come in a range of colors that can lend a specific mood to the presentation. A shade should be selected that reinforces the color scheme used for the play and that does not intrude on the costume sketch. Lighter tints are usually most satisfactory, though a darker, fairly neutral shade can be used effectively. Hot pink or purple may be a bit hard to take and is certainly not easy to work on for any length of time.

As mentioned previously, the rendering is a colored drawing and the surface used should be a pleasant one on which to draw. In addition, if a transparent color medium is used, allowing the paper to show through the paint or leaving holidays (blank spaces), the paper should provide some luminosity and vitality to the painting. With an opaque technique the paper merely needs to hold the paint, and its qualities are obliterated by the color.

COLOR MEDIA

Watercolor. Watercolors are transparent glazes made from finely ground pigments combined with gum arabic. They come in dry cakes, semimoist pans, and tubes. Quality watercolors provide both clarity of color and density of pigment. Among the more reliable manufacturers of watercolor paints are Windsor and Newton, Grumbacher, Pelikan, Rowney, and Reeves.

A watercolor rendering uses the brilliant white of the paper for the white and pale tints of the presentation. Because of this, the quality of the paper plays an important part in the final result. A rough surface adds clarity, sparkle, and luminosity to the work.

Watercolor can be applied with either a dry or a wet technique. The approach to coloring the rendering is quite direct, for the paint is applied in single strokes or washes instead of in built-up densities. The transparent wash is really the basis of this approach. To achieve a smooth wash the desired color should be mixed in sufficient quantity, then applied in slightly overlapping horizontal strokes with a fully loaded brush. The paper should be at a slight angle and the pigment remixed each time the brush is dipped in to keep the color uniform. The brush should go across the area, then back again, then be reloaded for the next stroke. Blotting paper can pick up any excess pigment at the bottom of the wash. To avoid streakiness, some papers should be dampened before the wash is applied. Washes may be overlaid to deepen the color or change the tone, though the first color should be allowed to dry before the second is applied unless a loose, wet effect is desired. More than three layers can give a muddy, unattractive result. It is important to remember that watercolors should not be used so thickly that they fill up or clot the grain, because heavy strokes give a dull, flat effect.

A slightly drier technique uses a fully loaded brush to create a stroke that follows the folds of the fabric, leaving occasional holidays and white lines to accent the dimensional qualities of the costume. Dry-brushing is a third technique that can be used to add detail and interest. The brush is dipped in the dissolved pigment, then wiped on an extra piece of paper so the paint is applied with little water in the brush.

Watercolors are very difficult to change, although some corrections can be made if good paper or board is used, for the paint can be picked up with a wet brush or sponge. This procedure may alter the surface texture, however. Highlights can also be recaptured in this fashion.

They could be preplanned and a masking agent, such as Copydex, painted on before the color is applied. The masking agent is then rolled off the paper when the rendering is completely dry, revealing the white paper.

Gouache. Gouache or designer's colors are opaque watercolors or colors that have white incorporated in them. When applied, gouache forms a solid body of color and creates a thicker layer of paint than watercolors. Unlike watercolor, which is more like a stain, gouache does not rely on the paper to appear through the color. It can be worked from dark shades to light as well as from light to dark. Tinted backgrounds can be used quite successfully with this medium. Because white is contained in every color but black, the dried tones are lighter than the wet color and have a mat, slightly chalky appearance. Gouache can be used with any of the boards and papers mentioned earlier, though the very smooth or very rough are not ideal for most projects.

Designer's colors, which commonly come in tubes, are made by Pelikan, Windsor and Newton, and Grumbacher, among other manufacturers. To apply a wash the paint should be thinned with water to the consistency of very thin cream and either applied from the top downward, like the watercolor wash, or flooded into the areas in pools of color. This medium works better on a flat surface than on a tilted one. A second coat can be applied after the first has been allowed to dry thoroughly. The washes can be overlaid and modeled with a finer brush. The dried paint surface is rather absorbent, so a fairly wet brush should be used if a smooth effect is desired. The dry surface is also easily marked; blotting paper can be placed over previously painted areas to allow freedom to work without fear of spoiling what has already been done. If alterations are necessary, the gouache can be picked up from the paper by soaking the area with a sponge, then blotting it, brushing more water onto the area, and blotting it again until enough paint has come off. Paint can be reapplied to this section. Gouache may be thinned to give a watercolor effect, but the resulting tones will not be as brilliant as with watercolor.

Tempera. Tempera paint was the primary medium used by fine artists before oils became popular in the fifteenth and sixteenth centuries. Originally egg yolk was used as a binder for tempera paints, and pigment and egg yolk are still combined by those who prefer to mix their own paints. Today *tempera* usually refers to any kind of paint that contains oils in emulsion and that can be used with water. Artificial tempera emulsions are available in tubes from such companies as Rowney, Grumbacher, and Windsor and Newton.

Tempera paints are extremely durable and are characterized by a brilliant, luminous crispness. Unglazed, they have a pleasing flat finish; they also can be polished with a soft cloth to a satiny, semigloss appearance. When varnished or glazed they have a great depth of tone.

Tempera is not as well suited to a casual, spontaneous style as some other media are. It dries rapidly, becomes quite insoluble, and cannot be softened for blending. Because of this inflexibility its mastery requires practice and its use in a costume rendering calls for serious consideration. Those accustomed to working with tempera find that it is very hard and strong and easily takes overpainting with more tempera or oils.

Tempera can be used on a number of surfaces but works best on a rigid panel or on a canvas mounted on a panel and primed with gesso. Gesso, the primer, is a base of whiting, chalk, or plaster of Paris mixed with glue, casein, or a gelatin solution. Unprimed papers and boards can be used, but the result is not so permanent. When working in tempera the paint should be built up in washes or glazes of color using fine brushstrokes. It should not be applied thickly, for then the surface will be more likely to crack. This tendency to crack makes tempera less suited to a flexible surface such as canvas and lightweight paper.

Poster and show-card colors are sometimes labeled tempera, but are not. Their use in costume renderings is not advised because they produce a thick, chalky color and are not easily blended.

Acrylics. Acrylics, actually acrylic polymers, are synthetic resins in which pigment is dispersed in an acrylic emulsion. Acrylics can be thinned with water but they dry to a tough, flexible film that is impervious to water. They can be used on a wider variety of surfaces than any other medium. Only an oil-primed surface is unsuitable for use with acrylics. An excellent surface can even be created by using any type of mounting cardboard coated with acrylic primer or emulsion paint with the brushmarks left to give bite to the surface.

Rowney, Liquitex, and Grumbacher all manufacture fine acrylic paints. Acrylics come in tubes or plastic containers and can be worked like watercolor and gouache, but they dry more quickly and become impervious to water. A retarder of glycerine can be added to slow down the drying time. Acrylic washes, which dry fast and have a hard edge, are not as brilliant as those done in watercolor, but a number of layers can be applied without producing a muddy effect. Acrylics do not cover particularly well, and two thin washes are often more effective than one thicker layer.

Acrylics are also suitable for impasto, which is thick, heavy painting done with bristle brushes or a palette knife and more commonly associated with oil paints.

Because the acrylic is insoluble, corrections can be made by painting over the area when it is dry with white acrylic, emulsion paint, or gesso and starting the work again. Regular acrylics dry to a semigloss finish, but a polymer medium added to the wet pigment will produce either a mat or gloss finish. These media can be added to watercolor or gouache to give them an insoluble finish that can be worked over when dry. Mat medium is also often used with watercolors to speed the drying time and extend the pigment.

Casein. Casein actually refers to pigments bound with milk curd. Commercially prepared casein is available in tubes. It is well suited to rigid panels, boards, and heavy paper because it does have a tendency to crack. It can be used with a thick, thin, or smooth application technique and dries to a mat or semimat finish that can be polished to a dull sheen with soft absorbent cotton. Casein is coarser and less sensitive than gouache, though it can produce a gouachelike effect. It can also be diluted and used like watercolor, though it has much less brilliance. It should be applied with plenty of water and a wet brush.

Oils. Oils are wonderfully suited to easel painting; in scope and flexibility they surpass tempera, watercolor, and pastel. They became popular in the fifteenth century, and by the sixteenth century the use of oils supplanted tempera in serious painting. Oils can be easily manipulated to produce a wide range of effects, from transparent to opaque to heavy impasto. Unfortunately, their drawbacks make oil paints ill suited for costume renderings. Oils are most commonly applied to a stretched canvas, a bulky method of presenting the many costumes needed in an entire show. Stretched canvas can also be easily damaged in transit. Other suitable surfaces are wood, hardboard, and heavy cardboard, all of which, in quantity, are bulky and heavy. Oils can take weeks or months to dry properly, a time commitment most designers can't make to their work. With a drying agent added and thinned with turpentine, an oil wash will dry more quickly, and quick-drying oils have also been marketed recently. In any event, since working with oils involves not only the tube paints but media such as linseed oil and turpentine, a project becomes more involved, time-consuming, and odoriferous. Despite these drawbacks, oils are a fascinating medium, and a designer could enjoy experimenting with them even though they may never become the primary means of presenting a project.

Pastel. Pastels can produce good, true colors because not much medium is mixed with the pigment to create the crayons, but the variety of colors available is more limited since they cannot be combined like paint to create new shades. It is also true that the results may not bear up well under wear and tear since the color can smudge and smear. Soft pastels, such as those made by Rowney or Grumbacher, combine the qualities of drawing and painting and work well on almost any type of soft drawing paper with a rough surface that will file off and retain particles of the pastel crayon. Papers most commonly used with pastels are fibrous and include drawing and watercolor papers; pastel papers with soft, fine, sandpaperlike coatings; and flocked papers with velvety finishes. Pastels are best applied with firm strokes using plenty of crayon. If the grain of the paper becomes overloaded with the pastels, subsequent layers will clog and become smeary. The pastels can be manipulated with paper stumps, stiff bristle brushes, and fingers. Pastels can produce wonderfully wispy, soft effects. Because the result is so fragile, the rendering must be sprayed with a clear fixative. This must be done with a carefully applied light mist, for oversaturating the picture causes the color to lose its brilliance and darkens the tone. Excess fixative can also run and cause ridges in the drawing.

Even fixed pastel drawings are not particularly sturdy and are not ideally suited to costume renderings, which can be battered around quite a bit in portfolios or costume shops. In a costume rendering, pastels can be most effectively used to highlight and accent a painted sketch. Pastel pencils, such as those made by Carb-Othello, are especially suited to this use. Oil pastels and crayons, both the artist's grade and the regular children's type, are much sturdier and more resistant to smudging and smearing. They can be blended to a degree on the surface of the paper.

Pencils and markers. Colored pencils and felt- and fiber-tipped markers are excellent to use to explore quick color ideas or bring out details and highlights in a painted rendering. Pencils are available in both waterproof and water-soluble styles and with either thick or thin leads. Water-soluble pencils come in a limited range of colors, while some manufacturers make more than seventy shades in the waterproof style. The markers also come in a wide range of colors. Felt-tips give a much broader line than the fiber-tips, and have a shorter life. The ink in both is spirit-based and tends to evaporate quickly, especially if the cap is left off.

BRUSHES

Good brushes are extremely important. When made by hand from fine materials by skilled craftsmen, they can be expensive. Buying and using cheap brushes can nevertheless be a false economy. With proper care a good brush will last longer and improve the quality of the work.

Since most costume renderings are done with water-based media, the watercolor brushes are the first the designer will need. The best brushes are made of red sable in a style called round, which has a good point, smoothly shapes out to fullness, and comes back in slightly to the handle. There should be no concave droop to the point. These brushes have good resilience and durability. They can be examined by wetting the brush, shaking out the extra water, then molding it gently with the fingers to make sure it forms a good point. The point of the paintbrush is made of the ends of the hair carefully placed to create the brush's shape. It should never be cut or trimmed.

Some less-expensive red sable brushes that also work well are made with shorter hair or a blend of sable and oxhair. Next in quality are the Russian fitch sables and the brown and black sables. Camel's hair brushes are not made of camel's hair at all, but a variety of other types of hair, mostly squirrel. These are usually too soft and do not have good elasticity or life. They tend to be rather floppy and moplike. Oxhair brushes are more rigid and do not work well with watercolor.

Brushes are sized by numbers; a higher number indicates a larger brush. Always use the largest brush possible; don't try to fill in a big area with a little brush. Sizes 2, 4, 8, and 12 will form a good beginning brush collection.

Oils are used with a greater variety of brush types and shapes. The most common types are the red sable oil brushes and bristle brushes made from white hog bristles. The four basic shapes are the rounds, used for the application of thin paints and detail work; brights, which are short with squared ends and used for laying on thick paint; filberts, which are broader than rounds, gently curving to a pointed end and used for drawing strokes; and flats, which are similar to brights but have longer bristles and hold more paint. There are also specialty brushes such as the fan and blender, which are two varieties of the wide, full brushes used to blend wet paint.

Brushes should be cleaned immediately after each use. Those used in water-based media should be washed with soap and water, preferably a yellow bar laundry soap; thoroughly rinsed; gently shaped; and stored upright. Oil brushes should be cleaned first with mineral spirits, then with soap and water. Care must be taken to remove all the pigment from the head of the brush. If pigment begins to accumulate there the brush will be ruined because its shape will be distorted.

Acrylics can be more destructive to brushes than other media be-cause they may begin to dry in the head while the brush is still being used — paint accumulates even if the brush is kept submerged in water. Special polymer or acrylic brushes made with nylon bristles can be used, for they are less expensive and clean more easily. They come in the various shapes already mentioned. Either oil or watercolor brushes can be used with acrylics and if paint begins to build up it can usually be gotten out by using methylated spirits.

COLLAGE

A collage technique can also be used to present costume plates. In a collage a combination of fabrics, papers, trims, laces — anything the designer feels expresses his or her ideas — is glued to a board and combined with paint or other color media to create the costume effect. It is sometimes difficult to find materials that stay in the right scale for the size of the figure, but a collage can produce a fascinating presentation and give a real feeling for the textures of the completed costume.

The layout of the costume plate

Just as the costume needs to be well designed, the costume plate should be laid out with an eye to organization and form. When placed properly in the space the figure will not crowd the sides, seem to float out the top, or fall off the bottom. A certain distance from the lower edge of the paper can be established as the floor line for the series so that when the plates are lined up all the figures appear on the same plane. A child should not be the same size as his father, but he can stand on the same floor and not float somewhere at thigh level. If detail sketches and fabric swatches are to be included, the figure should be placed so the other elements can be included and still present a well-balanced plate. Figures 6-14, 6-15, and 6-16 (page 195) show three different layouts that might be used to incorporate different elements that are to be presented. Figure 6-14 has a fairly symmetrical single figure well placed on the page. Figure 6-15 shows the placement of a single figure and swatches to balance the figure. In Figure 6-16 the figure, detail, and swatches are all arranged attractively, with the focus on the figure.

Placing the fabric swatches can sometimes be a bit tricky. They should be grouped in proportion to the way they will be seen on the costume, attached so the fabric can be felt, and not steal the focus from the figure.

The optimum size of a costume plate is tied directly to the size of the figure the designer wishes to use. The paper should contain the figure easily, not crowd it in or be so large that the amount of space diminishes the costume. As you explore different methods of presenting your work, try different sizes of figure. For some projects you may want to work in a small area; for others a large plate may be more effective. The actual size of each plate reproduced in this chapter is indicated to show the variety that can be used to help the designer visualize how a figure looks on different types of mounting.

The title of the play, the name of the character, and an identification of the costume are shown on each plate. The lettering need not be the ultimate example of the calligrapher's art, but it should be executed neatly and in a consistent style. Lettering that is so extensive or elaborate that it upstages the drawing can be quite pretentious, for the design is the important element being presented and time and space should not be wasted on fancy words. However, the signature of the designer should be included, along with the date, though it should not be tremendously prominent. Although the beginning designer often seems reluctant to sign his or her work, it is important to remember that the designer is not always sitting right beside the plates to claim them. Others viewing the renderings may want to know who did them and when they were done, and credit may inadvertently be given to the wrong person if designs are not properly identified.

Sometimes a designer gets the urge to use an elaborate background in the plates. This urge should usually be suppressed. Unless they are well executed, backgrounds can be distracting and diminish the impact of the presentation. Even if well done they may disturb the focus. A simple wash or tone behind the figure could add interest and a sense of depth to the sketch, but it is not wise to add unnecessary detail. The effort should go into the costume design, not into a glossy job that can mislead the viewer.

Despite this warning an almost uncontrollable urge will probably come over the designer to try some exotic types of background. Somehow it will seem absolutely necessary to use some form of spattering, stenciling, footprints, or foreign newspapers as the ground for the costumed figure. It is probably wise to give in to this desire early so you can see if this is really necessary and get it out of your system. You will probably discover that this gimmick contributes little but distraction and adds a great deal of time to the process. The costume plate is meant to present honest ideas, not become a campaign ad or a poster.

In the same vein, mats or elaborate mountings of various types are also unnecessary and add both time and weight to the work. Costume plates can be mounted for a formal exhibition but not as part of the work in progress. The purpose of the sketch is to aid in creating a set of costumes for a production. When the sketches are given to the shop they may be covered with acetate to help preserve them through the wear and tear of the building process. Photocopies are also very useful at this time for those constructing the costumes to keep handy for easy reference and notes.

A set of plates should be considered as a group with a number of constants that will present a uniform impression when shown together. The same type board and color medium should be used throughout. The size of the figures should remain consistent, as should the type of lettering and the way the fabric swatches are arranged, though the placement of the last two items may vary because of the placement of the figure on the plate. Occasionally the sizes of the plates vary. This could happen if a costume is so big it just won't fit on the standard size being used, or if a number of costumes are to be presented on one plate, which might be desirable with groups of minor characters (Figure 6-17, page 196). Minor characters and chorus costumes are sometimes done in a slightly smaller format, which can be quite acceptable if done consistently. A well-organized set of plates could use 10-by-14-inch paper vertically for the principal players and horizontally for the groups of smaller figures.

The costume plate should be an honest presentation of ideas that are clearly arranged and neatly executed. It is intended to sell the design of the costume and the quality of workmanship of the designer. A brilliant idea on a messy plate may not be deemed acceptable because the director is too distracted by the smudges and paint blobs, or because he or she questions the craftsmanship the designer will use when actually producing the costume. On the other hand, a flashy plate that has little actual substance may sell a badly designed costume the first time a designer works for a director. The designer may never get the chance to try again.

7

Costume construction

Exploring the costume ideas, sketching preliminary drawings, and developing those sketches into finished renderings are very rewarding processes for the designer. Taking the costume plates to the shop and presenting them to the craftspeople who will bring the ideas from paper to stage can also start an exciting phase of the work. Once again the designer is participating in a give-and-take of ideas. The process of distilling ideas and expressing them graphically provides creative satisfaction, but it is a solitary experience. Many people work in theatre because they like the group collaboration, so beginning the actual construction period can be a delight.

Well-prepared costume designers must know how to read a sketch. They do not always have to be brilliant at construction, although that skill can be invaluable at times, but they must know enough about construction to be able to guide the craftspeople who work with them. In many costume shops the foreman and drapers are extremely talented and experienced. They will know instantly what must be done to realize the sketches, and the designer and shop will probably recognize this compatability after a preliminary meeting. Talented craftspeople with this kind of skill can actually enhance the designs with their knowledge and would probably be upset if the designer tried to tell them how to do every little thing.

In many building situations, however, people with this type of knowledge and experience may not be available. It is therefore vital that the designer know how to interpret the sketch as a matter of self-preservation, for a good design can be easily lost in poor construction.

Developing an approach to building

The approach to building a show must be the same as the design approach. The entire production is considered and decisions are made about the fabrics, lines, and yardages that will work best to establish the silhouette and movement. The way the costumes are constructed can be a strong unifying element in the overall look of the production. Certain lines must be set to provide a basis for variation. A skirt with a five-yard hem is a full skirt, but the feeling it gives the character will be different if all the other skirts have eight-yard hems, or perhaps only three-yard hems. A robe of corduroy has a certain weight and depth; it can seem rich next to robes made of cotton, or less elegant if other robes are velvets. Edging an area with gold braid may add richness, but the effect is not as strong if another costume is edged with a band of three different golds appliquéd together.

A careful look at the entire production should reveal the basic lines that are to be used for the show. For women, the number of pieces in the bodice and the size and shape of the skirt may be the place to begin.

Preceding page: The approach to this costume for Molière's *The Imaginary Invalid* is not realistic and will give the production a very stylized look. Design by Cletus Anderson.

Not all the costumes will be built the same; many may be variations on a theme. The seven-piece bodice is a very good approach to the women's costumes from the beginning of the sixteenth century to the end of the eighteenth (see Figures 8-16 and 8-17, page 256) and can be chosen as the line for the middle and upper classes in a play that takes place within this time period. Once the theme is chosen, there may be many variations, for the placement of the neckline, the positioning of the seams on the body, the waist treatment, and the type of closing to be used can shift according to the design and the body of the actress (see Figure 7-1).

Nineteenth-century costumes are more intricately tailored. Women's dresses encase a curved figure created by a corset molded to accent those curves. This means that the basic line of the bodice may need more pieces to shape the body. The seven-piece bodice has three front pieces and four back pieces. It can fit well in the earlier periods because the necklines tend to be low with the bosom pushed up by a flat-center front piece A nine-piece bodice (Figures 8-18 and 8-19, page 257) has five front pieces, with four in back, and can mold much more easily around the curved bustline to the high neck that is a common feature of nineteenth-century day wear (see Figure 7-2). Vertical darts might be incorporated if a seam line needs to be eliminated, though often the seam line reinforces the period feeling. Horizontal darts are usually not suitable for period construction.

Figure 7-1   A seven-piece bodice was used for this costume for *Kiss Me Kate*, produced at Carnegie-Mellon University in 1977 (below left). The desire was was to suggest the Renaissance but keep the more modern overtones of the 1950s musical, so corsets were not used to reinforce the line. Design by Cletus Anderson.

Figure 7-2   Nineteenth-century tailoring was used in creating the realistic costume below for a play based on Chekhov's *The Duel*, produced at Yale University in 1961. The silhouette is definitely molded by the corset. Design by Barbara Anderson.

The line of the woman's bodice can also reveal the class of the character. Variation in social status can be indicated by the intricacies present in the construction.

The size and shape of the woman's skirt can also help establish a unity for the world of the play. Usually one or two distinct styles are needed and should be mocked up or developed in muslin and checked with the proper types of petticoat. Once the basic fall and flow are established variations to accommodate the differences in design and actor size can easily be indicated.

When setting the line of the show it is important that the designer mock up enough forms to be sure the period feeling is correct, but time may be wasted if certain similarities are not recognized in preplanning so that patterns are not unnecessarily duplicated. Sleeves may have a great deal of variety, but each does not need to be tackled as an entirely new problem. A certain sleeve design can be solved, then the next worked on in terms of what has been learned from the first. For example, sleeve B is similar to sleeve A but needs more kick or flair at the top of the cap and is 4 to 5 inches less full. Mockups are most often done in unbleached muslin because it is inexpensive when purchased in bulk, is easy to work with, and can be marked on easily. In some cases, however, the costume itself will be made of a fabric whose qualities are so different from muslin that the mockup will not tell the designer what he or she needs to know. This is particularly true if the real fabric will be very sheer, very drapy, or very heavy. Then a patterning fabric that has more of the qualities that will be present in the actual costume should be used. A shop that has a budget for basic equipment should always keep an eye open for closeouts where bolts of fabric of different weights can be acquired at reasonable prices. Color should make no difference in this type of purchase (though something inoffensive is always preferable), but weave, weight, and texture are of primary importance.

Establishing the line of the men's period costumes before the nineteenth century is very similar to the approach for the women. The bodice generally has no more than three to five pieces. Robe and tunic skirts are seldom shaped to control the fall in the same manner as the women's, so here the question may simply be one of fullness and length.

The line that will keep the men in a play set in the nineteenth and twentieth centuries looking like they all live in the same world can be created in very subtle ways since variations are not great from period to period. The fit at the waist, the width of the lapel, the number of buttons on the front of the coat, and the width of the pants are some of the areas where a style can be set.

Skirt lengths for either men or women require particular consideration. A skirt that appears to be floor length seldom falls to the floor in

front, to enable the actor to move without lifting it. The center front may need to be three-quarters of an inch to an inch off, then taper from the side front to hit the floor at about the side seam. In any skirt of this length, or with a train that is gradually added from the side seams to the center back, the performer must realize that movement is freest when it begins with a forward motion. A direct step to the side or back may cause the actor or actress to tread on the garment. A small step forward followed by turn will help the skirt to follow the actor or actress and stay out from under the feet.

The length of a skirt that does not reach to the floor is usually geared to a certain point on the body. The skirt might fall to the anklebone, the bottom of the calf muscle, above the knee, or perhaps the middle of the thigh. If the costumes are designed for a proscenium house with a raised stage the length may need to be a bit longer than might seem right in the costume shop because a large part of the audience will be lower than the performer's eye level and the perspective on the skirt length makes it seem higher. In some shows, particularly when characters are grouped together in a line (such as a chorus grouping) the skirt length might be set at a particular distance from the floor rather than geared to the individual. Chaos will prevail if ten women are lined up onstage as a group that should have a unified feeling and each hem is an inch or two different from the one beside it (Figure 7-3).

Figure 7-3 These three chorus dancers for *Kiss Me Kate* in a production at Carnegie-Mellon University were different heights, but the consistent skirt length helped them look like a well-organized unit. Design by Cletus Anderson.

In any of these instances, deciding on a line for the show does not mean that everything must conform to a central overview. It is a means of establishing certain guidelines for the look of the play, then filling out the picture in relation to these guidelines. Even in construction there must be a point of reference that can be used as a control. The variations must be carefully worked out in terms of what they will mean to the costumes and the characterizations as they take off from this point of reference.

Translating the sketch to the costume

The designer must develop an eye for translating the costume from a two-dimensional sketch to a three-dimensional form, a crucial skill not easily acquired. It involves being able to read the sketch to determine what body areas are involved, then deciding on what portion of that area the costume piece covers. Essentially, the body breaks up at the hinge points: neck, waist, torso, knees, ankles, shoulders, elbows, and wrists; and the costume must relate to these points in order to give flexibility and movement to the form. The hinge points are the references that can be used to block in the basic design lines. An example of how this is done can be seen in Figure 7-4, a simple chorus costume for a town singer in *Kiss Me Kate*. The body areas are easily defined; the bodice goes to the waist, the skirt to the floor, and the main break up of the sleeve is just below the elbow. With tape measure in hand, these areas are considered in relation to the measurements of the performer who is to be costumed. The neckline of the bodice drops a little over a third of the space from the base of the neck to the waistline at the bottom of the sash. If the neck-to-waist front is 14½ inches, the top neckline is 5 inches down, the underbodice shows for ¾ inch across the bust, 1 inch over the shoulder, and the band of the overbodice is 1 inch. In relation to these, the top of the V-opening is 2½ inches. The bodice trim appears to taper down so it will be half its original width at the waist, or ½ inch, and the V-opening tapers slightly larger, or ¾ inch. The sash is about the same as the bodice opening, or 2½ inches. It hangs down about ⅖ of the length of the skirt, or 18 inches. The shoulder seam covers over half the shoulder measurement, often 5 inches, which would make it 3 inches, probably divided equally between underbodice, bodice trim, and bodice. The puffs of the sleeve come to just below the elbow, 12 inches on a 22-inch arm, the upper puff ending at 5½ inches. There is about 1½ inches extra length at the fullest point on the upper puff, and 2 inches on the lower. (Distribution of sleeve fullness is described in Chapter 8.) The tight sleeve comes to the wrist, the ruffle to the knuckles, and is therefore 3 inches long, slightly longer than the width of the sash.

Figure 7-4 Costume design for a town singer in *Kiss Me Kate*. Design by Cletus Anderson.

Cross-checking some of the measurements to make sure the scaling is consistent must be done regularly. There are three major problems that cause the actual costume to differ from the proportions created in the sketch. First, of course, the dimensions may be wrong and can easily be corrected with a little reassessment. Second, the sketch may create something of an optical illusion so that what seems to be one size at first glance may really be another when carefully considered in relation to the areas around it. The third cause of discrepancy is that the proportions of the sketch do not relate well to those of the actor and must be reinterpreted. If the actor's body and the design are in conflict, the scale may need to change. This may be evident as the pattern is developed, or become more obvious as the mockup is fitted and the three-dimensional garment is viewed on the figure.

The skirt for the town singer is quite full at the hem, about 6 yards, and gored so it is flat in front with some gathering to the sides and back at the waist. The total waistline is no more than two and a half times that of the actor. A more detailed drawing might be needed for the headdress, but the basic size can be ascertained from the sketch. The padded roll is 4 inches high on top, or about the same distance as from the middle of the eye to the top of the forehead. The height of headpieces should be considered carefully, for there is a general tendency to overscale them.

Figure 7-5   Above: Costume design for Bluebeard in Bartók's *Bluebeard's Castle*. Design by Cletus Anderson.

Figure 7-6   Right: Costume design for Witwoud in *The Way of the World*. Design by Cletus Anderson.

Consider now the sketch for Bluebeard in Béla Bartók's one-act opera *Bluebeard's Castle* (Figure 7-5). The costume for the town singer relates closely to the actual physique of the actor. Bluebeard, however, strives to add stature and create a more monumental presence. Actually designed for a baritone standing about six foot three, the scale of the costume could closely resemble that of the sketch. With distance from neck to waist 20 inches, the collar is 7½ inches deep in front, starting ½ inch below the base of the neck. It extends the same width on the shoulders, starting an inch away from the base of the neck. The standing collar is 2¼ inches wide, the jeweled band around the outer edge 2¾ inches, made up of ¾-inch gold bands and ⅝-inch circular jewels. The belt, slightly narrower than the collar trim, is 2½ inches and the buckle 4½ inches across. The side belts are 1½ inches for the wider pieces on a 1-inch backing.

The arm treatment is broken into three sections. If the arm is 24 inches long, the oversleeve appears to be a bit less than half, or 11 inches; the cuff from the top of the gold trim down is less than the collar, or 6 inches; and 7 inches of the undersleeve are showing. Some sort of padding or interlining is needed for the undersleeve to add bulk to the arm. The trim on the cuff is the same width as the belt, or 2½ inches. When considering the arm, always think of what the bent elbow does to the areas. A deep cuff and a short sleeve both may have problems if they conflict with the bending of the arm. The width of the boot cuff, slightly less than that of the arm, is 5¼ inches.

Again, the flair of the skirt—which ends just above the knee—would indicate gores, but here the skirt shapes to the waist with pleats deep enough to hold the fold from the waist to the hem. The hemline is about 100 inches and the waist 74 inches, which allows for a 34-inch waistline and 10 pleats, each taking up 4 inches. The cape is extremely full and gored with a seven- to eight-yard hem, but pleated into the shoulder to give fullness at the top.

The sketch for Witwoud in *The Way of the World* (Figure 7-6) is quite straightforward yet somewhat stylized. The coat fits well to a lowered waist, has three side pleats, and ends at the knee. The trim up the front opening of the coat appears to gradate to the waist, then remain constant over the chest area. The designer might actually intend this or might have been thinking of a uniform band up the front (a more usual way to trim a coat) but unconsciously allowed the width to grow when drawing because the area of the skirt was increasing. The pocket flaps definitely do grade, following the line of the first pleat and getting both wider and deeper as they approach the hem. The jabot covers half the distance to the waist; the cuff is one fourth the length of the arm.

Once the principal areas of the costume are established, the trim is scaled to the space that is actually available. On Witwoud there seem to be twenty-two buttonholes across the coat-front trim. If the actor is 6 feet tall and the coat from knee to neck is 40 inches, the centers would be 1¾ inches apart starting 1½ inches from the bottom. The total width of the buttonhole would be half an inch. If the actor were only 5 feet 6 and the coat front 36 inches long, the number of buttonholes would have to be fewer to give the same effect, and the width of each might be slightly less.

The ability to convert from sketch to costume accurately is an essential skill for designers, whether they are in charge of building their own costumes or simply advising those who will build the show for them. It is a skill that is enhanced by experience and designers who are learning their craft should take every possible opportunity to develop their "eye." An excellent exercise to aid this training can take place in the costume workshop. As costumes designed by others are being built novice designers can pick a sketch and make notes on how they would scale it themselves. They can then go to the rack and find the actual costume, see how their notes compare to what is being done, and see how the sketch compares to the actual costume. The more the eye is tested, the better it will become at visualizing a 12-inch sketch actually constructed for a six-foot actor. The designer must always think in terms of the relationship of the costume elements to the natural body blocks and to each other.

A general guide to the yardage needed for different costume elements is provided in Chapter 2. This can be refined to give a more accurate picture after the actual pattern shapes for the show have been determined, as discussed in Chapter 8. If the budget allows and the fabric is available, err slightly on the side of too much rather than too little. A great deal of time can be wasted if it takes hours to lay out a pattern because it won't quite fit the available fabric, or if work must stop because more fabric must be purchased. And if the cloth has been treated in some way—dyed or painted, for instance—it may be impossible, or at best very time-consuming, to match a second piece to it.

Fabric selection

The importance of selecting the proper fabrics for the costumes cannot be underestimated. Unless a fabric has the right qualities it will never produce the line and movement that can realize the design effectively. The appropriate weave, weight, and texture are actually more important than the color on many occasions because a certain quality of drape must be inherent in the fabric, while the color feeling can be corrected by dying or painting. If this is not possible, color relationships might be shifted slightly to accommodate this color variation.

Fabric selection has been complicated in the past few years with the great number of synthetic fiber varieties on the market, plus many blends of synthetic and natural fibers. For some costumes the new fabrics are even more suitable than the originals they are made to resemble. Often they are not appropriate at all, for the draping quality is entirely different. The following discussion introduces fibers, how they are made, and the qualities that they can usually be expected to have. The more common fabrics are discussed in some detail; those less usual are mentioned briefly to at least familiarize the designer with the term, since one never knows what type of fabric might suit a particular purpose. The list of synthetic fibers is based on their generic names, for each year new variations appear on the market under new trade names registered by specific textile companies. All fabrics are now carefully marked as to their content, but the quality and specific treatment of the fabric can vary so greatly that this marking does not necessarily tell the designer what the fabric will do. It is always best to pull out one or two yards and see how it seems to drape and what movement qualities it has. Designers must constantly feel and test fabrics, even though it may not make them the most popular customers in the fabric department.

NATURAL FIBERS

Wool. One of the oldest and most universally used fibers, wool has a protein base and comes from the fleece of sheep (and sometimes goats). It is made into fabrics that are sold as either woolens or worsteds. Woolen yarns consist of short fibers that are not made to be parallel and tend to be soft and fuzzy. Worsted yarns are smooth and strong, spun from longer wool with the fibers lying parallel to one another, and usually have a high twist. Woolens most often have a rough, textured surface; worsteds have a smooth surface that makes the weave more conspicuous. Wool comes in a wide variety of weaves and weights, from the lightweight worsted challis, which drapes beautifully and can be quite cool to wear, to a heavy woolen broadcloth suitable for a winter coat. Though most wool has good draping qualities, the fabrics with harder threads and tighter weaves are less supple. Wool can be quite flexible and resilient, wrinkling slightly and dropping the wrinkles easily when hung out. It has a high degree of absorbency. Woolen

Figure 7-7   The appropriate weave, weight, and texture are vital to a costume, and good tailoring can be achieved effectively with wools. Costumes for the John Marshall series sponsored by the U.S. Judicial Commission. Photo by Norris Brock. © Metropolitan Pittsburgh Public Broadcasting, Inc., 1976. Design by Barbara Anderson.

yarn is a good insulator: the soft, fuzzy surface traps the air. Worsted can be cool in the summer because it allows for a greater circulation of air while absorbing body moisture. Wool may be attacked by moths unless treated with a mothproofing chemical in the finishing process, and the effectiveness of some of these is diminished by laundering. Some of the types of fabric available in wool are tweed, broadcloth, flannel, challis, crepe, and jersey. Other hair fibers that produce speciality wool fabrics are angora, cashmere, camel, alpaca, llama, and vicuna. Wool fiber has an affinity for dye, though care must be taken in noncommercial dyeing to keep some types of the fabric from shrinking, felting, and fuzzing. Wool blends are becoming more and more common. The dyeing properties of the synthetic fibers that are combined with wool may not be the same. The synthetic also may be one particular thread of the weave, so part of the fabric may dye readily while another part remains untouched. This is often the case in a tweed-type fabric that is a combination of fibers.

One method of judging the quality and usability of wool — or any fabric, for that matter — is referred to as its "hand." Though this may not seem a very scientific term, it is commonly used in reference to fabrics by those who work with them and indicates the quality that can be defined or evaluated by the sense of touch. The more fabrics one handles, the keener the perception of the variations.

Silk. A continuous filament protein fiber, silk may be cultivated either where the silkworm is raised in a carefully controlled atmosphere specifically for the purpose of producing fibers or in the wild, where the silkworm is not controlled but spins a cocoon under natural conditions. Often referred to as the Queen of Fibers and for years a status fabric of the highest social classes, silk is believed to have first been discovered about 2640 B.C. by a Chinese empress. The Chinese guarded the secret of silk production for 3000 years, trading the luxurious fabric but allowing no one to know its source. Gradually the secret spread to Korea and Japan, and by the sixth century A.D. silkworms were known to the Byzantine Empire and a silk culture began to grow in the West. Sericulture, or the production of cultivated silk, is a process not so easily automated as some textile manufacturing, and escalating labor costs have made silk fabric extremely expensive. Probably partly because of its cost and inaccessibility, silk is thought of as a luxury fiber, but it cannot be denied that it is a delight to the eye and the touch. It drapes easily, is pliable, and has good elasticity and ability to retain its shape. Silk made from cultivated cocoons, which are not pierced by the moth's leaving, is unwound or reeled in a continuous filament that may be from 800 to 1300 yards long. A number of cocoons will be reeled together to produce a stronger strand, and 2500 to 3000 may be needed for one yard of fabric. These long fibers make more lustrous yarn than short ones, though any of the silk thread is dull and harsh until it is boiled in soap and water to remove the gum the worm combines with the silk. The filaments from the wild silkworm's cocoon, which are harvested after the moth has left, have thick and thin places and are used for such fabrics as pongee or shantung, which features an uneven appearance. Another source of silk yarn is spun silk, made from silk wastes, which are shorter, broken, or tangled fibers that are processed, combed, and spun and used in pile fabrics, knitted goods, and blends. Silk takes dye well and can have a depth of color or jewel-like tone hard to find in any other fabric. It can be washed and ironed if the yarn is not creped, though it should be checked to make sure the dye is color-fast. Sometimes metallic salts are added to the silk to increase the weight of the fabric, give it a fuller hand, and improve its draping qualities. Natural silk is quite strong; weighting lowers its tensile strength and increases its deterioration. Fabric treated in this manner is also subject to waterspotting because water displaces the weighting substance. Fortunately, most manufacturers now use a waterspot-resistant finish.

The second category of natural fibers is composed of cellulose fibers such as cotton, flax, jute, hemp, and ramie. These are built up naturally during the growth of the plant and come from the seed, stem, or leaves. Rayon is also cellulose but considered manmade because cellulose fibers are not in their natural state; they are regenerated by being dissolved and resolidified. Characteristically, natural cellulose fibers have good absorbancy and conduct heat well. Smooth, open fabrics allow air to circulate for coolness. Fuzzy surfaces provide good insulation for warmth. They can be easily cared for as they thrive on soap-and-water washes and are actually stronger when wet than dry. They can withstand high temperatures, so no special precautions are needed during ironing. Fabrics from cellulose fibers do wrinkle easily unless treated with various resin finishes, which may give a starchless finish, ease of ironing, crease recovery, and permanent pleating. These fabrics are resistant to moths but subject to mildew if stored damp, though a special finish may minimize this. The cloth has a tendency to shrink, but various finishes are now applied that practically eliminate shrinkage.

Cotton. The most widely used fiber in the world, cotton comes from the seed of the cotton plant, which blossoms and produces a bole or pod of cotton fiber. Cotton was well known in both India and Egypt more than 3000 years ago. It was introduced into Italy by the Arabs and to other parts of Europe by the Crusaders. Mentioned in England in the thirteenth century, its use became more general in the sixteenth century and by the eighteenth century England was the center of cotton manufacturing because the improved looms the English had developed made mass production possible. Cotton was first cultivated in the United States in the early seventeenth century and is now grown in the southern half of the country from Virginia to California.

Cotton is classified by its staple, or fiber length, and its grade and fiber character. The staple varies from about half an inch to 2 inches. A longer staple, such as pima, is classified as the finer cotton. The grade is determined by the color, ranging from white to gray, and the amount of extraneous material (dirt, hulls, leaf cuts, and the like) that remain in the cotton. After cotton fiber is separated from the seed in the cotton gin it is carded, or pulled through teeth to clean it further and produce a continuous rope of fiber called sliver. This can be drawn out and twisted to form yarns for weaving or further combed to create a finer fiber. Convolutions or ribbonlike twists characterize cotton fibers. When cotton is mercerized, the yarns or cloth are treated with a caustic soda, which causes the fibers to swell and some of the convolutions to straighten out. This creates a fiber that is more lustrous, absorbent, and receptive to dyes. When mercerized under tension the yarns or cloth are more lustrous, while slack mercerization produces stretch cottons since the yarn crimps as the fibers swell and become shorter. Cotton dyes well, but the color may fade and the fabric weaken with long exposure to the sun. The varieties of cotton fabric are legion: light, heavy, smooth, rough, shiny, dull, pile, or flat. Long known as a fabric for work clothes because of its long life and cleanability, new weaves and finishes have established cotton as a fashion leader acceptable for any occasion.

Linen. Obtained from the stem of the flax plant and the oldest textile fiber known to man, linen fabrics were found in the Swiss lake dwellings of Neolithic man, dating back over 10,000 years. Fine-quality linen used as Egyptian burial wrappings 6000 years ago has been found in good condition and the Old Testament contains references to the use of linen. Belgium, France, Holland, and the Soviet Union are the chief flax producers, and although Ireland no longer grows the fiber, it produces fine-quality linen. More important in the past than it is today, flax fiber represents only 1 percent of the total world production of fiber. Linen tends to be an expensive fabric because the processing of flax is extremely laborious and production costs are high in terms of manpower, even though the fabric mostly comes from areas of cheap labor. Flax also seriously depletes the soil and a field can be sown only about once in seven years. Linen fabric nevertheless has many desirable characteristics. It is stronger than cotton and its tensile strength increases when wet, so it is very washable. The long, hard fibers do not soil easily and give up a stain readily. The fiber has a silky luster that is much more pronounced than that of untreated cotton and is a better conductor of heat, carrying it away from the body faster. It absorbs moisture quickly, dries fast, and is lintfree. While it may be dyed to a degree, linen does not dye easily due to the hardness and lack of penetrability of the fiber. Natural linen is yellowish-buff to gray and heavy bleaching may weaken the fiber. It has very little elasticity and shrinks and creases easily. Dress linens are often treated with crease-resistant chemicals that make them much more usable but less durable. Nontreated linen, used for elegant table linens, has poor flex abrasion and can crack if repeatedly folded in sharp creases, but can last many years if rolled or hung. Linen is made into a variety of fabrics in plain and twill weave, as well as the beautiful damasks familiar in table linens.

LESS COMMON CELLULOSE FIBERS

Ramie. A grass cloth used for several thousand years in China, ramie's fiber is similar to flax, but it is pure white and has a silklike luster. One of the strongest fibers known, it is stiff and has low resiliency, thus wrinkling very easily if not treated, and has a low elasticity and breaks if folded repeatedly in the same place. It is made up into fabrics resembling linen and is used for suitings, shirting, and table linens.

Jute. A stem fiber chiefly exported by India, jute is the cheapest textile fiber. It is used mostly for backings, bagging, and wrapping for it is thick, stiff, and not particularly strong. Jute is naturally a light tan and cannot be bleached. Its most commonly known form is burlap, which can be used as a decorator fabric dyed in dark colors. The dye, however, is not particularly fast. Jute deteriorates fairly rapidly under moist conditions, so burlap does not wash or dry clean successfully.

Hemp. Another bast, or stem, fiber that gives long, strong fibers, hemp is difficult to spin into fine counts, so it is more often utilized in the manufacture of canvas, cordage, ropes, and fishing lines. Sisal is a leaf fiber similar to hemp that is easier to process for cordage and ropes.

MANMADE CELLULOSE FIBERS

Rayon and acetate. Both rayon and acetate fibers come from the same base and are considered manmade, but they can have different properties and do have a basic difference in construction. Rayon is made from regenerated cellulose; the cellulose from cotton linters off the cotton seed or wood pulp is put into a solution and then extruded through spinnerets into fiber, physically changed but chemically the same as cellulose. Acetate is the result of a chemical change, for the cellulose is combined with acetic compounds to form a cellulose derivative, cellulose acetate, before being extruded. There are several differences between rayon and acetate: rayon scorches with too much heat while acetate melts; acetate dissolves in acetone but rayon does not; rayon is more absorbent and has less static than acetate; acetate wrinkles less when dry; and rayon is more versatile and can be made into fabrics similar to any of the natural fabrics, while acetate is usually used for silklike garments.

Early rayons wrinkled very easily and did not wash well because they lost a great deal of strength when wet. Both these problems have been solved by modification in the manufacturing process. Rayon is a very versatile fabric that can be produced at low cost. It is very absorbent, easily dyed, has good creping qualities, and does not pill. Some types are stronger than others. Rayon has fair abrasion resistance, blends well, and can have excellent color fastness. A few of its trademark names are Avril, Avron, Bemberg, Celanese, Cupioni, Enka Rayon, Fortisan, Jetspun, Lirelle, Nupron, and Zantrel.

Acetates have an excellent hand and good draping ability, fair wrinkle resistance, but poor crease retention. They must be ironed at low temperature, are usually low in cost, and have limited strength. Some well-known acetate trade names are Acele, Avisco, Celafil, Celaloft, Chromspun, Estron, and Loftura. Triacetates, a chemical variation of acetates, are less sensitive to heat, have good wash-and-wear properties, wrinkle resistance, pressed-pleat retention, and colorfastness. The best-known triacetate is Arnel. Acetates do not dye easily with household dyes.

SYNTHETIC FIBERS

Nylon. The first truly synthetic fabric, nylon was introduced to the consumer in 1939. It is made of air, water, and coal in a melt-spinning process in which the melted solution is extruded through a spinneret, then drawn or stretched to organize the molecules and add strength. Nylon fibers can be woven into a variety of types of fabrics, such as chiffons, batistes, linen textures, jerseys, shantungs, and velvets. There are some basic qualities that all nylons share, though they vary with the type of yarn and fabric construction. Nylon is a light fiber and one of the strongest, and its strength does not deteriorate with age. It is very resistant to abrasion and is one of the most elastic of fibers. The degree of resiliance is high and wrinkles fall out readily. Nylon fabrics may or may not conduct heat well. Smooth, tightly woven fabric does not permit air to circulate and keeps the body heat and moisture in; it is particularly well suited for winter apparel such as windbreakers, but not suitable for summer garments. Sheer nylons permit more circulation, and spun nylon, made of thousands of short, crimped fibers, acts as an insulator for warmth. Nylon does not absorb moisture. It can drape fairly well if it is soft, sheer, or a medium-to-heavy weight fabric. Many types of nylon will dye well; others will only take a tint. Whites, however, pick up color easily when washed with other fabrics and may become gray. Nylon can be combined with any of the natural or manmade cellulose fibers. Some of the more common nylon tradenames are Antron, Cantrece, Capriolan, Crepeset, Nytelle, and Qiana.

Acrylic fibers. Acrylics are manufactured much like nylon, but their principal raw materials are coal, air, petroleum, limestone, and natural gases. Acrylics are soft and bulky but lightweight. While commercial colors are quite color-fast, acrylics do not dye well with household dyes. They are not as strong or resistant to abrasion as nylon but do have good wrinkle resistance. Acrylics make up well into sweaters, furlike pile fabrics, and blankets, while blends are used for men's suitings, woven dress fabrics, slacks, sportswear, and carpeting. Acrylic holds its shape well, washes easily, dries quickly, and needs little or no ironing. The most common acrylic tradenames are Orlon, Acrilan, Creslan, and Zefran II.

Modacrylics. Modacrylics are modified acrylics, such as Dynel or Verel, that are resistant to flame, water, microorganisms, insects, and sunlight. They have good color-fastness, wash-and-wear properties, and wrinkle resistance. Modacrylics do not dye easily with household dyes and melt unless ironed at low temperatures. They are often used for knitted pile fleece, furlike fabrics, and wigs.

Polyester fibers. Made of a combination of an alcohol obtained from petroleum and an acid, these fibers come in both filament and spun yarns. Polyester fibers truly require little care, possess excellent wrinkle resistance, stand up fairly well to repeated launderings, do not sag, and can be permanently pleated. Color-fast in commercially produced fabric, they do not dye easily in the workshop and require special dyes if a significant color change is desired. Polyester comes in many types of fabric, and when it is blended with natural fiber many easy-care qualities are added. It can be ironed at a moderate setting. It also is made into a fine stuffing that does not mat and is lightweight, comfortable, and nonallergenic. Well-known trademarks for polyester are Dacron, Avlin, Encron, Fortrel, Kodel, Quintess, and Vycron.

Other generic groups of manmade fibers include anidex, an elastic fiber; azlon, produced from protein found in plants such as peanuts and

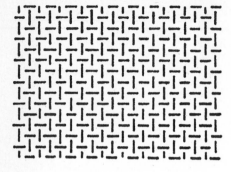

Figure 7-8   Plain weave

Figure 7-9   Basket weave

soya beans; fiberglass, which is strong and wrinklefree but has poor abrasion resistance and is found mostly in draperies; metallics, used as decorative additions for glitter or sheen; nytril, which is furlike; olefin (such as Herculon), popular for seat covers and outdoor furniture; rubber, which has good stretch and recovery and is used for foundation garments and swimwear; saran, which is tough, flexible, stiff, and resistant to stains and weather but can only be ironed at very low temperatures; spandex (such as Lycra or Vyrene), which is lightweight with good elasticity and used in foundation garments, swimwear, support hosiery, and general stretch yarns; vinal, which is strong and abrasive resistant; and vinyon, used as a bonding agent for nonwoven fabric.

These are all the generic classifications for the manmade fibers set forth in the Textile Fiber Product Identifications Act of 1958; the generic term must be included in all labeling. New variations under different trademarks and improvements of the fibers are developed every year.

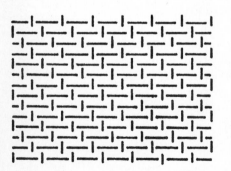

Figure 7-10   Filling faced twill

Figure 7-11   Herringbone weave

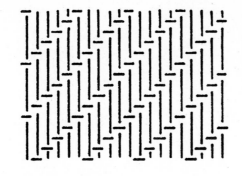
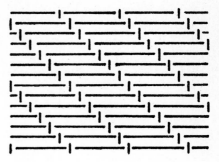

Figure 7-12   Four-float warp satin

Figure 7-13   Five-float filling sateen

WEAVES

Many types of weave are used in making fabrics. The threads that run the length of the piece are called the warp and those that run across the fabric are called the fill. The three basic weaves are plain, twill, and satin. The simplest is the plain weave, which has yarns at right angles passing alternatively over and under each other (Figure 7-8). A variation of this is the basket weave, in which two or more warp or filling yarns are used as one (Figure 7-9). A rib variation is achieved if either the warp or fill yarns are much heavier than the other, or if the weave is unbalanced with more threads woven closer together in one direction.

Twill is the most durable of weaves and is produced when the filling yarns are interlaced with the warps in such a way to form diagonal ridges across the fabric. In an even twill the fill passes over the same number of warps it passes under, while in an uneven twill the fill passes over more warps (but not more than four) than it passes under, making a filling-faced twill. In a warp-faced twill the warp threads are the most prominant. Figure 7-10 shows the fill passing over two warps and under one. The most common twill variation is herringbone, where the diagonal runs one direction for a few rows, then reverses and goes in the opposite direction, with a variation at the apex of the V to reverse the wales (Figure 7-11).

Satin and sateen weaves produce a shiny, smooth fabric because more of either the warp or fill are visible on the right side. In satin, made of silk or rayon, more warp threads are exposed on the right side (Figure 7-12), while sateen, made of cotton, has more fill fibers showing (Figure 7-13). The weave is similar to twill except the top thread does not interlace with the under thread for four to twelve yarns. For example, in satin weave, if the warp skips seven fillings before interlacing it is a seven-float warp satin, while a sateen weave in which the fill skips five warps is a five-float filling sateen. The sheen has a definite direction and

Extra
filling
yarn

Filling

Figure 7-14   Pile weave done with extra filling yarn

patterns should be cut accordingly and not turned so that some run the length of the fabric and some the width. This weave produces smooth, lustrous, rich-looking fabric, but the longer the float, the more potential for snagging and pulling. A variation is satin crepe, in which a smooth yarn is used for the warp and a duller, tightly twisted or creped yarn is used for fill. This easily draped fabric is reversible, giving two very different surface effects.

Fancier weaves include pile, jacquard, dobby, and leno. The pile weaves, such as velvets, velours, and plushes, have soft, sometimes clipped yarns or pile on the right side; the back is smooth, showing the weave. The pile is produced by weaving an additional warp or filling yarn into the basic structure. The additional yarn is drawn away from the surface of the fabric by wires or by extra fill yarns that are later removed. The looped yarn either can be left as a continuous filament or cut. Velvets, terrys, and plush fabrics are made with an extra warp yarn, while velveteens and corduroy are made with an extra filling yarn (Figure 7-14). Velvet is sometimes made by a double-cloth weave, in which two fabrics are woven on the loom at the same time, each with its own set of warp and filling yarns. An extra warp yarn is woven between the two, then cut to produce two separate pile fabrics (Figure 7-15). Most pile fabrics have a definite direction and must be cut with all pattern pieces lying the same way.

Small patterns are made on a loom with a dobby attachment, which makes designs that are simple, limited in size, and usually geometric in form. The dobby or cam raises or lowers twenty to forty harnesses that control the warp threads to form the pattern. One of the most familiar types of dobby weave is bird's-eye, a small diamond pattern with an eye in its center.

More complex patterns are done on the jacquard loom, which has a mechanism that controls thousands of heddles, needlelike wires through which the warp threads pass, which allows them to be lifted

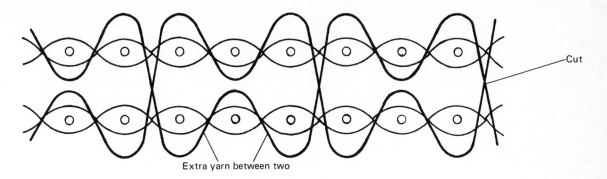

Cut

Extra yarn between two

Figure 7-15 Pile weave with extra warp yarn woven between two fabrics

independently. Cards are punched to the pattern for each fill line of the design. As the cards progress the warp yarns are raised according to the pattern holes. This is the most expensive form of weaving, and setting up the loom may take several weeks or months.

The leno or gauze weave involves two sets of warp threads and one filling thread. The warp threads seem to twist around each other at the interstice of the fill thread. Actually, they are simply moved from side to side with the fill thread holding them in place. The pattern may be that of a figure eight (Figure 7-16) or one thread may be in tension while the other moves about it (Figure 7-17). The weave gives a lacelike effect such as that found in marquisette or casement.

Knitted fabrics make up a large portion of textile goods and can be produced faster than woven fabrics. Knitting is comprised basically of a series of loops dependent on each other. The loops that run the length

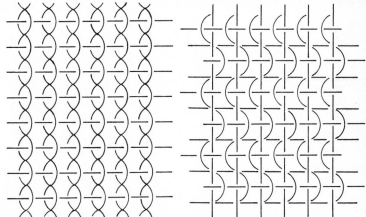

Figure 7-16 Leno weave in figure-8 pattern (right)

Figure 7-17 Leno weave with one thread in tension (far right)

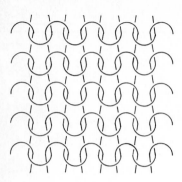

Figure 7-18   Weft knitting

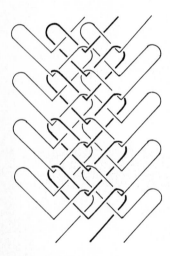

Figure 7-19   Warp knitting

of the piece corresponding to the warp yarn are called the wale, while a row across similar to the filling yarn or weft is a course. Knitting machines produce either warp or weft knitting. Weft knitting, which is most similar to hand knitting, is produced by yarn fed to a series of needles in a crosswise direction (Figure 7-18). In warp knitting many yarns are fed vertically to an equal number of needles and the individual warp yarns are interlooped into the loop of the adjacent warp yarns (Figure 7-19). Doubleknits are made like woven double cloth: two cloths are knitted with an occasional stitch binding them together.

True crepe fabrics are not the result of the weave, which may be plain, but are caused by the yarn, natural fiber or rayon, which is highly twisted. The large number of turns in the yarn make it lively and kinky. It is then moistened and dried in a straightened condition. After weaving the yarns are moistened once more and they again become lively and kinky, producing the crinkle characteristic of true crepe fabrics. One variation is seersucker, in which the warp yarns are regular while the filling yarns are alternating groups of regular and creped yarns. When the fabric is finished, it is wet, causing the creped yarns to shrink and to produce crosswise puckers in regular stripes. Synthetic fibers, which are not affected by water, cannot be used in this manner, but a crepe effect can be achieved by texturing the polyester yarns. A crepe effect can also be achieved by weaving high-twist yarns in irregular interlacings. Slack-tension weave can produce another form of seersucker. Here two warp beams are used, one with the yarns in regular tension, the other with the yarns in slack tension. These are then alternated in groups to form stripes the length of the fabric. The slack-tension yarns are longer and give a crinkled stripe to the finished fabric. Finally, a crepe effect can be added to a fabric with a finish. A chemical can be printed on the woven cloth, causing it to shrink in areas while the untreated fabric crinkles in between.

Nonwoven fabrics come in two categories: felt, whose fibers are interlocked by a combination of chemical action, mechanical work, moisture and heat; and other nonwovens, which use a bonding agent. Felt is made of wool or fur, often blended with other fibers, and comes in a great variety of thicknesses. Wool is the most suitable fiber for felt because the physical properties of the fiber make it snag together and tangle easily. Other nonwovens are made of cellulose fiber and synthetics, held together by a bonding agent or the thermoplastic quality of the fibers in the blends. Many new types and uses for the nonwoven fabrics are developed every year.

CHECKING THE HAND OF THE FABRIC

A general knowledge of the origin and characteristics of different types of fabrics is a good background for designers, but with all the blends and synthetics that are on the market today they must develop a knack for understanding the hand or feel of the goods. They must be able to pull out a length of material to see if it will react properly, then check the contents for any fibers that will fight against the right line or particularly enhance it. Polyester fabrics often drape beautifully, but their resilience can give the folds an undesired roundness. Cotton-and-dacron combinations can give a soft yet crisp look but may not be acceptable if the garments must look old and slept in (Figure 7-20). Dacron chiffons are very soft and drapy but do not hold air and float as well as silk. Linens have a lovely quality but unless treated for wrinkle-resistance may be difficult to maintain if a crisp, neat look must continue through an energetic act. Synthetic fibers may not tailor well; they will not ease and shrink to take a shape.

Designers should always keep their eyes and hands on fabric, both in the store and in the workshop. They should observe everything that is going together, no matter whose show it happens to be. They should notice how the fabric is reacting to the treatment it is getting, then note the fiber content and file away the information. An actual file box with swatches attached to cards and notes of interesting characteristics that have been observed is an excellent source for a designer beginning to explore the world of textiles.

Figure 7-20 Real cottons were used so they would look worn and wrinkled in this costume for The Leatherstocking Tales. Photo by Walt Seng. © Metropolitan Pittsburgh Public Broadcasting, Inc., 1979. Design by Barbara Anderson.

When searching for the best fabrics for a show, designers must not be limited to dressmaker fabric departments. Some of the most suitable fabrics for period productions are found in the drapery and upholstery sections. There are nevertheless some pitfalls to avoid in this area. Drapery fabrics made of fiberglass should not be purchased unless special construction methods can be used. When cut, fiberglass is extremely uncomfortable against the skin. Fiberglass fabrics are also not particularly durable and pull apart at stress seams. Upholstery fabrics backed with a rubber coating should also be avoided. They are uncomfortable to wear, do not drape or mold well, and if dry cleaned may become extremely stiff and rigid.

Dyeing the fabric

While the proper fabric for a costume must have the right body and drape, color is certainly another primary factor in the creation of a costume. The search for just the right shade can keep a designer involved for days or weeks. Sometimes this problem can be solved in the dye area of the costume shop, but before this is tried, two important facts should be ascertained: Will the fabric take the dye? What happens to it during the dyeing process?

TYPES OF DYE

There are many types of dye that can be used, and in general, as discussed previously, the natural fibers, rayon, and many nylons will dye readily with household or union dyes such as Rit or Tintex. Most commonly used because they are readily available, these contain a blend of many different types of dye and therefore dye a wide variety of fabrics and may even work to a degree on some acetates and polyesters. These dyes can produce fairly intense colors if used in increased quantities and processed in near-boiling or boiling water, but the colors tend to fade after repeated washing. When dying plant fibers salt is added to the dye bath, though it may be already present in packaged dyes; with animal fibers, vinegar assists the dyeing process. The life of the color will be prolonged if the garment is washed separately in cool water with a mild detergent. Garments that are dry cleaned maintain their colors quite well. Union dyes are easy to use because they require no special chemicals or procedures.

While union dyes are not especially effective on polyester, acrylics, and some acetates, these fabrics can take a tint, particularly if a mordant such as alum (which makes the fiber more receptive to the dye) is rinsed through the fabric before dyeing, or even added to the dye water itself.

The alum may react with the dye, changing the color, so this must be checked. Alum can also be used with wools to give them a deeper, richer tone. Blends of natural and synthetic fibers may dye to a degree, but will not go to dark shades with union dyes. If a fabric is made up of yarns of different types of fibers, they will not dye uniformly. This can sometimes give a very interesting effect. Patterned fabrics can often be overdyed quite successfully. Cotton drapery fabrics can be very useful for period garments; they are available in period style prints, often on a white or light background that can be dyed down. Of course, the colors of the pattern, particularly the lighter ones, will also be affected by the dye.

Disperse dyes, which are brilliant in color and stay well through both washing and dry cleaning, were especially created to dye acetates and other synthetics such as polyester and nylon. They will dye silk and wool with slightly less intense results. These dyes work best if a mild detergent is included in the dye bath, and the fastness depends on high heat during dyeing, almost to the boiling point, and thorough rinsing.

Basic or cationic dyes provide very brilliant colors but tend to fade when washed. They hold up fairly well when dry cleaned. Basic dyes, which need acetic acid or vinegar added to the dye water, are particularly useful when dying silk, wool, and some acrylics. They will dye cotton, linen, and rayon if the fabric has been mordanted. This mordanting is done by dipping the fabric in a tannic acid bath, heating and cooling it, letting it dry, dipping it in a tartar emetic bath for thirty minutes, then dyeing it. This process can be time-consuming, so a quicker means to almost the same brilliance of color is to dye the fabric with the household or union dyes, then to overdye it with the basic dye. With this process, called topping, the union dye works as a mordant for the basic.

Direct dyes are relatively inexpensive and easy to use. They work in a fashion similar to the union dyes. The colors are not as brilliant as some of the other types, but they do work quite well on cotton, achieving a more intense color than the union dyes. Their major drawbacks are a tendency to fade when washed, though this can be slowed down with the use of cool water and mild detergent, and an inclination toward streaking. Direct dyes are most effective on cotton, linen, and viscose rayon and sometimes work well on silk, wool, and nylon.

Fiber-reactive dyes produce brilliant, quite permanent colors that take well from lukewarm to cold temperatures. This makes them extremely useful for handpainting, silkscreening, or batiking. They work best on cotton, linen, and viscose rayon and can be used on silk and wool, though with less brilliance. Salt and washing soda are added to the dye water.

Acid dyes work particularly well on silk and wool and may be effective on nylon. Sometimes referred to as aniline dyes (though other types of dye also contain aniline), they need acetic acid or vinegar added to the dye bath. They tend to wash out if care is not taken. Acid dyes do dry clean quite satisfactorily.

DYEING TECHNIQUES AND PROBLEMS

Some fabrics take dye well, but wetting them and/or heating them may change certain characteristics. A drapery fabric called antique satin is a good example of this. The fabric right off the bolt has good body and drapes well. It dyes easily, but after it becomes wet it loses all its body and is extremely limp. In this form it might be just right for certain costumes, but it will never make the sweeping ball gown it was so suitable for previously. Many wools dye well, but soft woolen weaves may shrink and become heavier. Washable wools do not do this, but they also do not dye as readily. Shrinking can be somewhat minimized if the fabric is warmed up and cooled gradually during the dyeing process. Wool that might shrink should not be put in a dryer. The surface quality of wool may become rougher during the necessary agitating or stirring to allow the dye to take evenly in the fabric, particularly in the washing machine. Again, this may be quite desirable to give a heavier, more rustic quality. Some synthetics tint, but the dye will migrate to the edges of the folds if spun out, producing a very streaked effect. And some sheers, most specifically crisp ones, may acquire wrinkles in a hot dye solution, particularly during the spin cycle if done in a washing machine. These wrinkles will be heat-set and will never come out. All fabrics should be thoroughly wet before dyeing. Some must be washed to remove sizing or chemicals in the fabric that make the yarns resist the color. All fabrics should be stirred while dyeing to minimize streaking and blotching.

The only safe way to dye fabric is to take a piece and try it to see what will happen. Always check the size of the piece before and after processing it. Some shrinkage may be quite acceptable, but enough fabric must be purchased to allow for it. If the small piece proves difficult to dye and cannot be made to achieve the desired color except by boiling on the stove, don't be fooled into thinking it will work if a large amount is to be used and the only way available to dye it is the washing machine. It will not take on the proper color if the needed heat is not provided.

An excellent book on this subject is *Fabric Painting and Dyeing for the Theatre* by Deborah M. Dryden (New York: Drama Book Specialists, 1981). The author, who is quite experienced in using a variety of techniques, provides a clear guide to many types of fabric treatment.

Fabric painting

Although dyeing is the most practical technique to achieve an overall color change, the color of a fabric also can be changed by painting. Painting a fabric, in addition to providing an alternative to dyeing, can produce unique effects in a costume.

Painting can be used to shade the form of a constructed costume. The sides or folds of a garment can be toned down or sections can be highlighted to add to the costume's three-dimensional quality. A garment that cannot be immersed and maintain its shape might be lightly sprayed to change the color tone, though this is difficult to do successfully if the effect should look smooth. Painting can add a textured look to a fabric, create a pattern, or reinforce an already existing pattern.

Various techniques and materials can be used to achieve the different desired effects. General shading and toning can be done with a brush, aerosol sprays, or an airbrush. An interesting surface texture can be achieved by spattering, often with more than one color. Patterns can be created using a silkscreen process, a simpler stencil technique, batiking, or merely by brush painting or airbrushing the shapes on the

Figure 7-21   Costume for Macbeth (below left) painted to give it dimension and age. Designed for a National Geographic film by Barbara Anderson. Photo courtesy the National Geographic Society.

Figure 7-22   Armor for the film *Knightriders* (below) painted for texture and interest. Photo by James Hamilton. Courtesy Laurel-Knights, Inc., New York. Design by Cletus Anderson.

Figure 7-23   This costume for Richard Basehart as King Arthur masquerading as a peasant (below) was both frayed and painted. Designed for *A Connecticut Yankee in King Arthur's Court* in the Once Upon a Classic series by Barbara Anderson. Photo by Mitchell Greenberg. © Metropolitan Pittsburgh Public Broadcasting, Inc., 1977.

Figure 7-24   Leathers for the Indian costumes in The Leatherstocking Tales (right) were dyed and oiled to give them age and wear. Photo by Walt Seng. © Metropolitan Pittsburgh Public Broadcasting, Inc., 1979. Design by Barbara Anderson.

fabric. An existing pattern can be reinforced by painting in highlights and shadows with a brush or marker. Dimension can be added to the pattern with hot glue and filler compound. Color can be mixed in with the compound before it is applied or painted on after it has set.

Fabric painting can be done with union dyes, fiber-reactive dyes, dyes dissolved in alcohol and combined with shellac (known as FEV or French enamel varnish), water-base or oil-base textile inks, acrylic paint, metallic paint and bronzing powders, shoe or leather paints and dyes, floral sprays, spray enamels, or permanent markers. The union dyes are better for light shading effects, for though they are dissolved in hot water, when brushed or sprayed on they are relatively cool and deep colors will not take and stay. The fiber-reactive dyes produce an intense color when cool and can be effectively set by steaming. Actually, many of the dyes mentioned earlier can be used to paint costumes if they are combined with a dye paste and steamed to set the color. The FEV, or dye dissolved in alcohol with shellac as a binder, can produce deep, transparent tones but may stiffen the garment if used in any quantity. The textile inks, acrylic and metallic paints, and the spray enamels can also stiffen the fabric to a degree, depending on its original

texture and body and the amount of medium used. Floral spray is more flexible. Leather dyes and markers can add fairly intense color when used in small areas that can be easily controlled. They do not stiffen the fabric, but the markers are not particularly permanent and may lose brilliance in either washing or dry cleaning.

Modifying the fabric with some type of painting or dyeing treatment can produce interesting results that are often very effective in the theatre. To get a feeling for what can be done, find some good-sized scraps of various materials and experiment with different media. Actually experimenting with paint and fabric may open avenues that would never have been considered before.

Any spraying, dyeing, or painting done with materials that have potentially toxic fumes must be done in a well-ventilated area and some type of mask or filter should be worn. Many materials used by theatre craftspeople are potentially dangerous if not used properly. Two sources for the safe use of these materials are *Artist Beware* by Michael McCann (New York: Watson-Guptill, 1979) and *Safe Practices in the Arts and Crafts: A Studio Guide* by Gail Coningsby Barazani (College Art Association of America, 1978).

Aging the costume

Most of the techniques mentioned above embellish and enhance the costume to create a particular style. Sometimes the desire is to break down the fabric and the form to give it a well-worn or lived-in look. Aging garments is an art in itself and should be approached with a definite feeling for the ways clothes would break down and disintegrate on their own if they had been in the circumstances prescribed by the play.

A well-worn garment is usually more soiled and frayed around the stress points: the neck, cuffs, hem, elbows, pockets, knees, and seat. These areas can be sanded down or roughened up with a rasp and edges can be torn and snagged. Inner structures, such as shoulder pads and interfacings, can be removed to encourage sagging, and this can be quickly enhanced by weighting down the areas that should be baggy and droopy, then wetting or heavily steaming the garment and letting it dry with the weights in place. Faded areas can be created by carefully scrubbing in bleach or cleanser. Paint can be lightly sprayed or brushed over a roughened surface to highlight it for a faded, dusty quality. Browns and grays can be worked into areas that should be dirty and grimy. Black is more difficult to use effectively since it may produce a harsh, unrealistic appearance. Costumes that have been both worn down and painted down are seen in Figures 7-23 and 7-24.

A costume that needs to be aged down but must be reclaimed after the production can be treated with colored hair sprays. These are a bit more expensive than the other painting and spraying media but usually clean out quite successfully. Real dirt, which can also be used for a moderately smudgy look, is practically always readily available around any theatre.

Keep two things in mind when aging costumes. Know which areas of the garment should logically show the most wear and work them down in gradual steps. It is very easy to age something a bit more if it is needed, but trying to bring it back if it has gone too far can be very difficult.

8

Patterning and building the costume

Developing costume patterns is not difficult but does require a familiarity with fabric shapes and how they work on the body, a willingness to explore and try different approaches to discover the best solution, and a sense of neatness and order so that the end result will be recognizable and usable.

The two primary methods used in creating a costume shape are flat patterning and draping. These are

Figure 8-1 The bustle at left, above, could not be flat-patterned and was first draped in muslin on a form. Costume for the Carnegie-Mellon Theatre Company. Design by Barbara Anderson.

Figure 8-2 Most of the patterning for the turn-of-the century gown at the right was done flat, but the center front of the bodice needed to be draped on a dummy. Costume for the Carnegie-Mellon Theatre Company. Design by Barbara Anderson.

not mutually exclusive systems, though each has its advocates (who are sometimes rabid on the subject). The most sensible solution is to be proficient in both methods and to use whichever will be best to solve a particular problem. Many times techniques from each approach are needed to construct the costume.

In *flat patterning* the shapes of the pieces are drawn up on patterning paper or brown paper, transferred to fabric, then basted together and fitted on the person or dummy. In *draping* the uncut fabric is pinned directly on the person or dummy, with the pin lines creating the potential seams and excess fabric cut away as the shapes begin to approach the final form. Some garments cannot be flat-patterned and must be formed around the body figure (Figure 8-1). Many costume shapes can be drawn up more quickly than draped, then refined when put on the figure (Figure 8-2). This can be an extremely efficient approach, particularly if there is a shortage of dressmaker's dummies, which are expensive and may not be found in quantity in small costume shops. Although a live model can be substituted for a dummy, he or she can't be pinned into and may fidget if required to stand for a long time. And always keep in mind that a body that must just stand there is one that cannot be sewing hems, buttons, or hooks and eyes.

Preceding page: Costume for Gonzalo in Shakespeare's *The Tempest.* Design by Robert Perdziola, 1982. Compare Figure 5-22, page 172.

This chapter deals mainly with flat patterning because it is a concept that can be easily presented on the printed page in a limited space. Once the eye begins to recognize the basic shapes that are used to encase the different body areas, the designer can experiment with different ways to achieve the design. A good patterning imagination is invaluable. A pattern is a work in progress. The basic shape should be quickly achieved, tried and adjusted, considered, ripped apart if an area isn't working, and pinned again. Seams are always flexible and can be changed. If a line isn't right, investigate the cause of the problem, consider its remedy, undo the seam, and try it again. The more a person works with patterns and thinks about what is happening, the easier it is to create different shapes and drape new forms. When working up a pattern always think about what each line is doing; never copy something automatically. Understanding each length and curve leads to understanding how to make necessary changes.

Pattern sources

Costume patterns do not have to be completely created in the shop. A number of sources are available to help the process along, although a preexisting pattern seldom matches the sketch exactly. Through developing patterns the designer understands how shapes work and are adjusted and can then more easily use other patterns as a starting point. Experience will help the designer see where they must be changed.

Historical patterns can be found in some costume history books and patterning books, including *The Cut of Men's Clothes* and *The Cut of Women's Clothes* by Norah Waugh, five volumes by Herbert Norris titled *Costume and Fashion, A History of Costume* by Carl Kohler, *History of Costume* by Blanche Payne, two volumes of *Patterns of Fashion* by Janet Arnold, *The Evolution of Fashion* by Margot Hill and Peter Bucknell, and *The Blue Book of Men's Tailoring* by Frederick Croonberg, as well as some nineteenth- and twentieth-century fashion magazines. Some patterns are merely indications of the way a piece of clothing was cut; others have been drafted from actual garments. Either may be a good source of ideas, but often modern cutting methods give better results. The fitted gowns of the fourteenth century were sometimes cut flat from several narrow lengths of fabric sewed together to make a wide piece. This caused rather awkward seams across the fall of the skirt. Today the gown would be cut with a princess line, which has seams from shoulder to hem. In this manner the seams follow the flow line of the gown and enhance the movement. In the eighteenth century the bodies of men's coats had only center back and side back seams.

When constructed this way, the front of the coat hangs from the body in a rather unattractive manner. This can be alleviated by a dart under the arm or slightly to the front of the coat. The seaming of bodices and jackets in the nineteenth century was often quite interesting and intricate. These patterns will still need to be adapted, for the reshaping of the body with corsets and pads was often more extreme than advisable today, and people were much smaller than they are now.

Commercial patterns can be quite useful when building a fairly contemporary show, but don't assume that just because the pattern is purchased it is always right. For example, the amount of fullness in a skirt may be exaggerated in the drawing. Be sure to check the inches around the hem listed on the back of the pattern packet. Sleeves are sometimes cut with a skimpy cap that may look fine but can really hamper movement. Even though there may be problems, a commercial pattern can save enough time to be valuable if it is carefully checked and adjusted where necessary to relate to the costume sketch. Historic patterns from the commercial pattern companies are not particularly useful for serious stage work. They present a modern impression of a period garment with seaming and control that is a bit too simple to give a true historic feeling.

Measurements

Bringing the design to the stage begins with the sketch in one hand and the measurements of the actor in the other. An accurate set of measurements is essential but not necessarily easy to acquire. The human body is flexible and expands and contracts easily, and the measurer has few specific points to go to and from. There is no absolute way to take measurements, but each shop should establish a system to be used and make sure everyone understands what the numbers stand for. Figure 8-3 illustrates a standard measurement chart and Figure 8-4 indicates the hither and yon of many of the areas. Those not indicated on the chart are explained in the guidelines. A tape tied securely around the waist can help locate some of the areas. The process is often most efficiently done with one person measuring and another writing, but the numbers should not be projected for everyone in the room to hear. An actress will not be pleased if "Weight 210, bust 46, waist 35, hips 48" is announced to the world. And even if it is not announced she will probably inform the person with the tape measure that she is losing weight and will be much smaller by the time the show opens. The standard answer to this stock statement should be "Oh, fine, but we'll just measure you as you are now and be happy to take your costumes in as soon as you drop the weight." More often than not this will not be a problem that really has to be faced. Measure someone with a pleasant expression and no extraneous editorial comments.

Some possible guidelines for taking measurements follow.

NAME_____

CHARACTER_____

Figure 8-3   Costume Measurement Sheet

COSTUME MEASUREMENT SHEET

TELEPHONE NUMBER_____   DATE_____

HEIGHT _____1_____	WAIST TO THIGH___23____
WEIGHT _____1_____	WAIST TO KNEE____24____
CHEST OR BUST___2_____	WAIST TO FLOOR___25____
WAIST____3_____	INSEAM TO FLOOR__26____
HIPS_____4_____	CROTCH_____27_____
WIDTH OF BUST___5____	GIRTH_____28_____
SHOULDER TO BUST__6___	THIGH_____29_____
SHOULDER TO WAIST__7__	KNEE ABOVE____30_____
UNDERBUST_____8_____	KNEE BELOW____31_____
UNDERBUST TO-WAIST__9_	CALF_____32_____
WIDTH OF CHEST - FRONT_10_	ANKLE_____33_____
BACK__10_	NECK - BASE___34_____
SHOULDERS - BOTH__11___	MID___35____
ONE__12___	HEAD_____36_____
NECK TO WAIST-FRONT__13_	HAT_____37_____
BACK__14_	DRESS OR SUIT___38___
ARM LENGTH - OUTSIDE__15_	SHIRT OR BLOUSE__39__
TO ELBOW__16_	TROUSERS - INSEAM__40__
INSIDE__17_	WAIST__40_
AROUND BICEPS____18___	GLOVE_____41_____
AROUND FOREARM____19___	STOCKING/TIGHTS__42__
AROUND WRIST_____20___	SHOE_____43_____
ARMSEYE_____21_____	BALLET SLIPPER__44___
UNDERARM TO WAIST_22_	BRA SIZE_____45_____
	OTHER_____
	_____
	_____

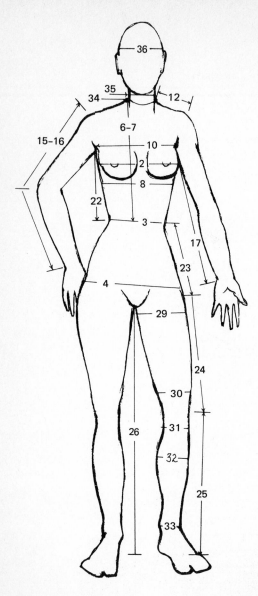

Figure 8-4 Figure guide for measurements

Height and Weight (1) Ask the actor for these, but realize they may be inaccurate. Women often underestimate their weight and men overestimate their height.

Chest or Bust (2) Measure the relaxed chest around the largest area.

Waist (3) Measure just above the hip bone where the body is pliable and can be condensed.

Hips (4) Measure low on the hip at its fullest point. Always find the maximum that will need to be encompassed, but eliminate wallets and keys in pockets.

Width of bust (5) Women only. Take the point-to-point measurement.

Shoulder to bust (6) Women only. Measure the distance from near the neck to the point of the bust. Note if the actress is not wearing a bra, for the point of the bust is usually much lower without a bra than with one.

Shoulder to waist (7) Take the measurement from near the neck straight down to the waist. For women, over the bust to the waist.

Under bust (8) Women only. Measure around the chest right under the bust.

Width of chest front/back (10) Measure across the front or back of the chest from the point where the arms join the body. These two measurements do not add up to the chest measurement, for the depth of the body is not included.

Shoulders - Both (11) Measure across the top back of the shoulders to the ends of the shoulderbone. One (12) Take the measurement from the side of the neck to the end of the shoulderbone. One shoulder is less than half the shoulder measurement because the width of the neck is not included.

Neck to waist - Front (13) Measure from the top of the collarbone to the waist. Back (14) Measure from the last large vertebra to the waist. The neck joins the body on an angle and neck-to-waist back is practically always two to three inches longer than the front.

Arm length - Outside (15) Measure from the shoulderbone to the wrist over the elbow on a slightly bent arm. To elbow (16) Pick this up on the way to the full arm measurement. Inside (17) Measure from the point where the arm joins the body to the wrist.

Around biceps (18) Take the measurement of a relaxed muscle unless the actor has particularly well-developed muscles that will be used extensively during the production. Forearm (19) Measure just below the elbow at largest part. Wrist (20) Measure below the wristbones.

Armseye (21) Take the circumference of the join between the arm and torso.

Underarm to waist (22) Start directly in the armpit.

Waist to Thigh (23) Measure above the hipbone to the bottom of the buttocks, measured on the side. To Knee (24) Take the measurement to midknee. To Floor (25) Take the measurement to the floor if the actor is shoeless, and to the bottom of the body heel if shoes are worn.

Inseam to floor (26) Measure from high in the crotch to the floor or the bottom of heel if shoes are worn. To avoid embarrassment it may be easier to hand the actor one end of the tape and ask him to place it as high as possible at the inside top of his leg with the measurer taking care of the end of the tape at the floor.

Crotch (27) Measure from the center front of the waist through the legs to the center back of the waist.

Girth (28) Measure from the shoulder through the legs and back to the shoulder.

Thigh through Ankle (29-33) Take the measurement of the largest circumference at all these points.

Neck - Base (34) Take the measurement where the neck joins the body at the point where the planes change and a collar would be attached. Mid (35) Measure slightly below the jaw line, at about the top of a standing collar.

Head (36) Measure the circumference around the forehead, just above eyebrows.

Hat (37) The actor or actress may know his or her hat size. Hat size is approximately the head circumference divided by *pi*, which equals the diameter. For example, a 23 inch head is $23 \div 3.14 = 7.3248 = 7\frac{3}{8}$. Hat sizes come in eighths. Conversion charts are available from hat companies.

Dress or Suit (38) An actor may know his suit size. It is based on the chest measurement, but the size of the shoulders can make a difference. Having a few jackets of known sizes handy that can be slipped on the actor is useful. Women's dress sizes can vary considerably. More expensive clothes often carry smaller sizes than cheaper ones. A regular size 10 could be a size 6 in a designer garment.

Shirt or Blouse (39) Blouse sizes may be the same as dress sizes or convert to bust size. A size 10 is a 32, a 12 is a 34, a 13 is a 36, and so on. Men's shirt sizes come in neck and sleeve length; the average is about 15-33, or a 15-inch neck and a 33-inch sleeve. The sleeve length is taken from the center back below the neck base over the extended, bent elbow and back to the wrist.

Trousers (40) Inseam and waist - The size the actor buys and feels most comfortable in may not exactly coincide with the measurements taken. Men seldom wear their trousers at their actual waistline.

Glove (41) Measure around the knuckles, excluding thumb.

Stocking/Tights (42) For dancers, even the brand might be useful.

Shoe (43) Be sure to include width.

Ballet slipper (44) Practically always smaller than shoe size.

Bra (45) Cup size is particularly important. A woman with a 36-inch circumference around her chest could wear a 36A or a 32D. The former will seem somewhat flat chested; the latter will not.

Other. Check the sketch for any additional information that will be needed. It is sometimes useful to know if the actress has pierced ears. Any fabric allergies should be noted. If a wig is to be made the measurement around the hairline and from the forehead to the nape of neck will be needed, as well as the measurement across the top of the head from ear lobe to ear lobe.

All these measurements will not be needed for every show, particularly if it is a modern-dress piece and the garments are to be found or purchased. But if it is possible, take all measurements that might be even vaguely useful, for the measurement not taken is the one needed first. (That seems to be a rule engraved in the secret costume shop in the sky, right next to the one that says the actor in white falls on the floor every night.) If the actor is to be with the company for a while his complete measurements might as well be on file. Be sure to fill in the date and change it if the measurements are updated. Bodies don't always stay the same so it can be useful to know when a set of measurements was taken.

The three-piece bodice

The basic, three-piece bodice may not be used often in intricate period construction, particularly for women, but it is extremely valuable as a handy visual reference for a specific body. A basic bodice, fit carefully and snugly to the body, can be pulled out and used as the starting point for any number of shapes, even if the body is to be changed. The basic body shape is there. If it is to be corseted or padded this can be taken into account. This pattern is usually done in muslin or a fairly thin cotton. When heavier fabric is used for a costume the pattern should be expanded slightly for the thicker the fabric the more distance needed to encase the body.

The patterns in this chapter are drawn to scale and done for a woman wearing a size 10 and a man wearing a size 38. The relationship of the pattern size to the measurement chart is given. The actual size of the piece shown can be taken off the patterns by using the given scale.

The male and female bodice can open either center front or center back. The opening should be a straight line if at all possible. The straight of the fabric, which follows the line of the weave, is indicated on each pattern piece. Any change in the straight can alter the way the garment will fit.

Figure 8-5 shows the pattern for the male bodice. If the shoulders are rounded, a shoulder dart will help the fit. If the waist is quite a bit smaller than the chest a back dart will ensure a good line without diagonal pulls toward the side seam. A back dart should not go higher than the bottom of the shoulderblade. The darts and extensions that will be needed at the shoulder are indicated with a dotted line. Front darts should not be used on the man's bodice because they tend to give the feeling they are shaping the bust. If the front will not fit well in one

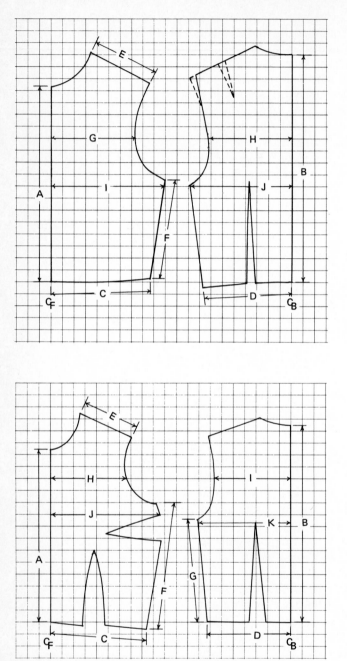

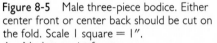

Figure 8-5   Male three-piece bodice. Either center front or center back should be cut on the fold. Scale 1 square = 1″.
A   Neck to waist front
B   Neck to waist back
C and D   Waist plus dart
E   Slightly less than one shoulder
F   Underarm to waist minus 1″ to 1½″
G   Width of chest front
H   Width of chest back

Figure 8-6   Female three-piece bodice. Either center front or center back should be cut on the fold. Scale 1 square = 1″.
A   Neck to waist front
B   Neck to waist back
C and D   Waist plus darts
E   Slightly less than one shoulder
F   Underarm to waist minus 1″ to 1½″ plus dart
G   Underarm to waist minus 1″ to 1½″
H   Width of chest front
I   Width of chest back
J and K   Bust

piece seams should be added rather than darts. This is not often necessary.

The basic female bodice (Figure 8-6) is quite similar to the male, except, as might be expected, bust darts are added to the front. These are placed by locating the point of the bust and placing the ends of the darts no closer than one inch from the point. The darts for an average size bust are about 1½ to 2 inches, deeper for a large bust and less for a smaller one.

The basic bodice gives the costume shop a permanent record of the shape of the actor's body. It should be kept on file and used as a reference whenever a costume is needed for a particular actor.

Creating the proper body shape

The basic bodice provides a record of the body as it is. Often what is needed is the body as it isn't. Rearranging the figure seems to be a favorite pastime of the designer and the costume shop as areas are added to or, hopefully, subtracted from and organized.

Padding

Padding out the figure should be done with careful attention to the way the body grows on its own and how the appearance of extra weight will relate to the body of the actor. Always keep in mind the actual body areas of the actor that will show and let the added poundage grow in a logical manner. If the legs, arms, and neck show, the torso can only be so thick to still seem realistic, or the impression will be that of a small body lost inside a mattress.

Padding should be constructed to hold its shape through heavy use and frequent cleaning. Made of layers of cotton and dacron, the padding can be quite warm because it is worn right next to the body. While the undergarment can be aired out, it will need frequent washing.

Padding that is to add considerable poundage to the figure should be made on some type of full-torso base of light but sturdy wash-and-wear fabric (Figure 8-7). The crotch strap is quite important to keep the tummy in place, but as a kindness should hook toward the front so the actor can undo it himself. The back of the garment may zip or tie. Areas to be padded should be marked and noted where they need to be the thickest. A smaller padding could be made on a T-shirt or leotard. This does not stand up as well, but it is a fast approach to a washable base.

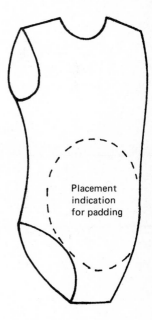

Figure 8-7 Full torso base for padding

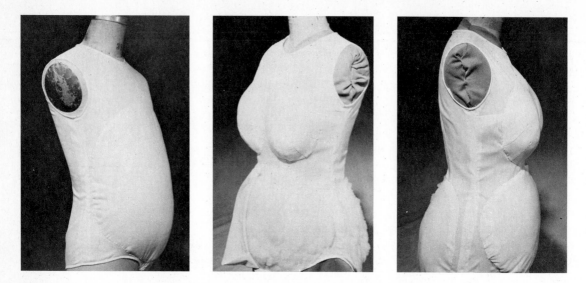

Figure 8-8   Basic belly padding (above)

Figure 8-9   Layers of dacron batting are used to create the padded area for a matronly woman's figure (center).

Figure 8-10   Finished areas covered with a soft jersey (right)

Dacron or polyester batting is the best material to use for the thickness even though it is more expensive than cotton for it is lightweight and washes and dries easily and quickly. This should be applied in flat, smooth layers, each a bit smaller than the one before, until the desired thickness is reached. Long, fairly loose padding stitches should be used to attach the batting to the base all over the area as well as around the edges. This will hold the fluff in place but not tighten it down to distort the shape.

Figure 8-8 shows the basic pot belly, which is constructed as one area since it grows as one area. Figure 8-9 is the body of a matronly woman with five separately padded areas: two breasts sagging with age, a protruding tummy, and two buttocks that should extend a bit to the side to suggest heavy thighs. After the batting is securely tacked so it will not shift when washed the padded areas are covered with a soft stretch fabric such as cotton jersey to smooth the edges and hold it firmly together (Figure 8-10).

Any padding that is to look as though the body has expanded realistically will be more effective if it is done with batting so that many flat layers can be added with control and finesse. Wadding, or fibers that come in a more pillowlike mass, are more suitable for stuffing rather firm, presewn shapes, such as hip rolls, Elizabethan shoulder rolls, and teddy bears.

Corseting

For over four centuries women were tightly confined in some form of boned corset. This had a great influence on the way they moved and the look of their bodices. Some form of corseting is often necessary to achieve the appearance of a period, though the extremes to which corseting may have been carried are neither possible nor necessary. In earlier times girls went into corsets at a very young age and they adapted to wearing them, both physically and mentally. The modern actress is not accustomed to such confinement, nor is she as small to begin with as her earlier counterparts. The 17-inch waist is usually not possible, but a controlled figure with the appearance of a small waist can be achieved. The natural waistline is oval (Figure 8-11). Corseting brings the waist to a circular shape so that from the front the waist appears much narrower, accented by the spring of the hips. Because of this, bringing in the waist just an inch or two can produce a rather striking effect (Figures 8-12 and 8-13). In addition to confining the waist the corset gives a firm line to the torso and controls the bust, but it must not restrict the diaphragm to a degree that will hinder breathing. As the corset is laced on, an actress should keep her ribcage expanded so the space for a breath will be there. When the actress first begins to wear the corset in rehearsal it will probably seem quite tight and uncomfortable because it is so unfamiliar. The more she wears it the more she will become accustomed to it and learn to deal with it, if not love it. But don't try for an unnecessarily tight squeeze. A lovely, small waist is useless if the actress falls over in the middle of a scene from lack of breath.

The best source for corset patterns is Nora Waugh's *Corsets and Crinolines*. The change in women's shape is traced through the centuries and clear layouts are provided for a number of corsets based on surviving examples from various periods.

Figure 8-11   The natural waistline (left) is oval.

Figure 8-12   The eighteenth-century corset pulls in the waist and pushes up the bust (center).

Figure 8-13   The nineteenth-century corset (below) molds more of the torso than the one in Figure 8-12.

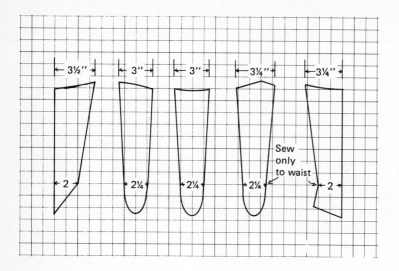

Figure 8-14 Corset suitable for the sixteenth, seventeenth, and eighteenth centuries. Bones on each seam and between each seam. Scale I square = I″.

Figure 8-15 Nineteenth-century corset. Scale I square = I″.

Patterns for the corsets displayed in Figures 8-12 and 8-13 are shown in Figures 8-14 and 8-15. Figure 8-14 is more suitable for the sixteenth, seventeenth, and eighteenth centuries, where the bodice line was quite straight and the bustline was either confined or pushed up. Figure 8-15 shows a corset that might be used in the nineteenth century, in which the curves of the body are more evident. The eighteenth-century corset particularly will need fairly wide shoulder straps to keep the side front line smooth and the bust pushed toward

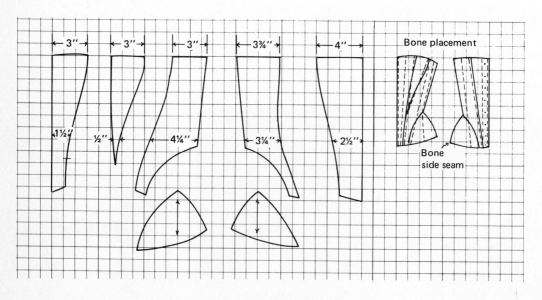

the center to enhance the cleavage. If at any time more emphasis is needed at the bust than the actress is able to provide, bust pads should be added inside the corset but to the outside and slightly under the bust to push what is natural in where it will do the most good.

Corsets should be made of tightly woven, strong fabric that washes easily and does not have much thickness, which would add bulk. An extra layer should interface the area under the grommets. The corset should be completely lined, the lining and outside sewed together along the front, top, and back, then turned. Bone channels are sewed through both layers, the bones slipped in, and the bottom bound off. Both front and back may be grommeted, but the corset will be easier to wear if a corset fastener or heavy-duty zipper is used in front, for it can then be taken off without completely unlacing one side. Grommets with a fairly wide lip, not eyelets, should be used so they will not pull out easily under the strain. A narrow bone between the grommets and the edge of the fabric will strengthen the area under the most stress when the corset is tightly laced. Metal boning in various lengths and widths can be acquired from companies that supply them for therapeutic corsets and trusses.

Though it might seem redundant, there are occasions when it is necessary to both pad and corset the same figure. The well-endowed, well-established matron could need an ample body that is obviously controlled by serious engineering.

Petticoats

The most commonly used underpinnings are petticoats. While identical petticoats may be used for a number of different periods, a petticoat should be chosen because it reinforces the line of the costume. If the fullness of the petticoat does not match that of the skirt it will either be ineffective or fight against the desired line. An empire gown needs petticoats that fall from under the bust, a princess line underskirt must fit smoothly to the hip line. Full skirts will commonly need more than one petticoat, and if the overskirt has a bit more flair at the bottom or heavy trim on the lower portion, the top petticoat could have a deep flounce to add support. While particularly decorative petticoats may be needed for specific costumes, the standard stock of these underskirts should be out of sturdy but easily laundered fabric with a good amount of body. Contrary to the rumor that "anything will do for costumes," old sheets are not sufficient. Save them for Halloween.

Some skirt shapes require padding or boning as well as petticoats to create the proper shape. *Corsets and Crinolines* is again an excellent reference for these undergarments.

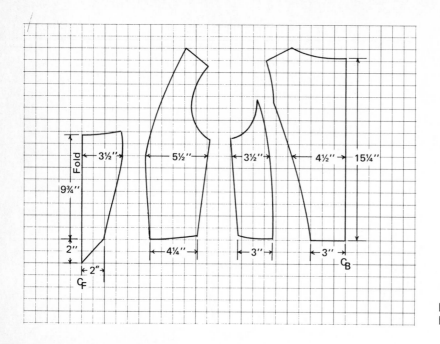

Figure 8-16 Seven-piece bodice. Scale 1 square = 1″.

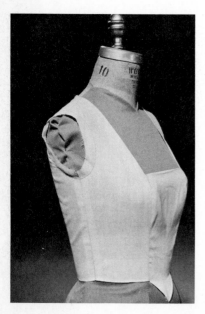

Figure 8-17 Seven-piece bodice in muslin.

The proper petticoats, corsets, and padding must be available when working up patterns because the outer garment is very much dependent on the underpinnings to give it the right line. Time will be wasted and work will need to be redone if the undershape is not correct as the pattern develops.

Period bodices

The cut of a period bodice should reinforce the design line, not fight with it. Except for the neckline, the lines of the bodice usually follow the verticality of the figure, so most seams and darts also follow the vertical. A horizontal seam may add a design line, such as a yoke, but horizontal darts are seldom attractive in period garments, and in most cases can be easily avoided. Vertical or diagonal darts may be quite useful in fitting, but in many cases where a dart is all right a seam might be better, for it extends the line and eliminates the problem of making the dart disappear smoothly.

The seven-piece bodice (Figure 8-16) is quite useful for any period where the body line is fairly straight, the bust is pushed up, and the neckline is not too high. It is particularly common to those periods that would use the earlier corset, such as the sixteenth, seventeenth, and eighteenth centuries. The piece that may be a bit tricky is the side front,

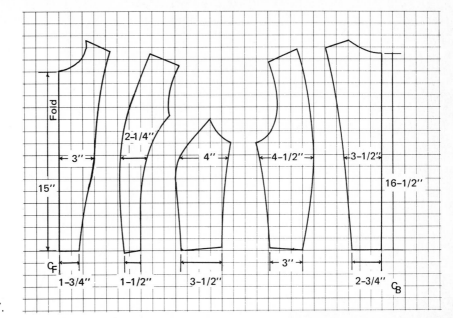

Figure 8-18 Nine-piece bodice. Scale 1 square = 1″.

for the bustier the lady the more the top of that piece must curve away from the neck. This problem shows up as extra fabric around the armhole. Release the shoulder, smooth the side front up, and repin it. Then redraw the neckline, which will be more toward the shoulder. Also be sure that the last inch of the center front curves in slightly to tighten across the bust and keep the lady in place. Figure 8-17 shows the completed bodice pattern.

The nine-piece bodice can be the basis for a costume that has a higher neck and more curves to the bustline, such as those common in the nineteenth century (Figure 8-18). The extra piece in the front allows for more contouring. Again, the side front piece may need to curve more for the fuller figure. If the side front-to-side seam puckers it may well smooth out by taking in the upper part of the side front-to-front seam. To do this, loosen half the shoulder and take out the side front/front seam down to about the bust point, smooth the side front piece up to get rid of the puckers, and repin it. The seam line on the center front will probably remain almost the same; the adjustment is in the side front piece. Figure 8-19 illustrates the assembled nine-piece bodice pattern. The back of the bodice could be as shown or could be constructed like the seven-piece bodice, with the shoulder and center back extended to the neck. In the nineteenth century another piece was sometimes cut into the back to give the effect of many seams converging on a tiny waist.

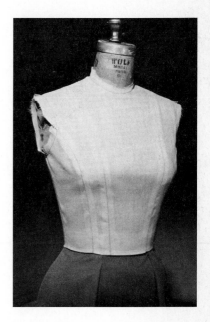

Figure 8-19 Nine-piece bodice in muslin.

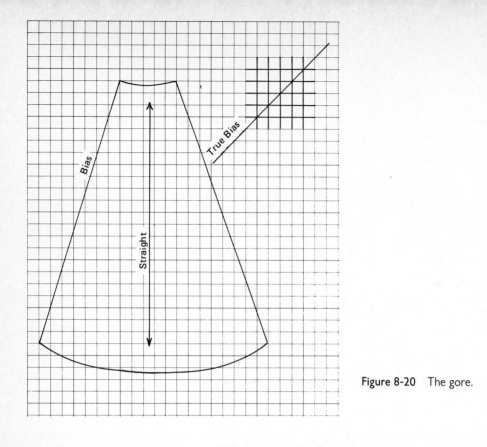

Figure 8-20 The gore.

When patterning it is often wise to cut inch-wide seam allowances on all pieces, with two inches at the opening and waist. This usually provides enough fabric for adjustments when necessary. Very wide seam allowances can hinder the fit, particularly on curves. The pattern should be initially drafted up showing only the seam lines so the eye can see the shapes to be used. Seam allowance should only be considered when the pattern is ready to cut. Much time can be saved if the eye is trained to gauge the one and two inches automatically.

The seams on these bodices are easily adjusted to accommodate variations in the lines of the design, if the shape still allows for the fullness of the body where it is needed. For example, the difference between the bust and waist needs to come in under the bust area. It cannot be taken in at the side without causing the fabric to pull strangely. But the center front piece can widen or narrow at the waist to a degree, provided the side front is altered to add or subtract the same amount of fabric.

Period skirts

A skirt can be a straight piece of fabric bunched in at the waist, but it is more often a garment made up of gores that are narrower at the waist and wider toward the hem. The way these gores are shaped determines

Figure 8-21 Basic full period skirt in muslin.

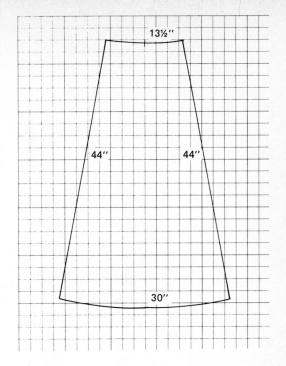

Figure 8-22 Gore pattern for basic skirt.
Scale 1 square = 1".

the fall of the skirt. As fabric is suspended along the straight of the weave it falls close to the body in a very organized fashion. A gore that widens toward the hem cuts across the weave of the fabric diagonally or on the bias (Figure 8-20). True bias is on a 45-degree angle from the straight. The bias will fall into folds and flow more away from the body. Because fabric cut more to the bias will fall more away from the body, gores can be made to give a skirt a very particular drape and flow. Pleats and darts can also be used to control the shape.

Most skirts have more fullness to the sides and back than in the center front, which makes sense since most female bodies have more fullness to the side and back than the front. The degree to which this happens varies considerably from the basic period skirt, which is full all around with just a bit more in back than in front, to some bustle gowns, which are almost straight in front with all the fullness behind.

The skirts in this section are patterned for someone 44 inches from waist to floor and do not have a hem included.

Gores in a basic skirt with general fullness (Figure 8-21) could be symmetrical. A nice fullness for a skirt of this type would allow for three times as much fabric as needed in the waist and about five yards in the hem. If the waist is 27 inches the total size of the waistline would be 81 inches, the hem 180 inches. In a skirt done in six gores, each gore has 13½ inches at the top and 30 inches at the bottom (Figure 8-22). This could be pleated so the fullness is the same all around (8-23a), or so more of the skirt is to the side and back (8-23b). Pleats that fall into general fullness such as these should not be too deep at the waistline.

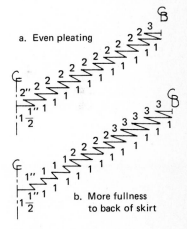

Figure 8-23 Possible pleating diagrams for the basic skirt. Each has 13½" on the outside of the skirt, with 27" used in the pleating.

A full skirt that will have pleats that hold their fold from waist to hem without being pressed will need gores more specifically shaped to do this. The skirt illustrated in Figure 8-24 has a six-yard hem with eight pleats achieved in seven gores. The gores get fuller as they move to the back and are shaped so the front of the gore will fall straighter and the back of the gore will flow out (Figure 8-25). This causes the skirt to flow naturally toward the back of the figure. The offset of the fullness of each gore is indicated by a line dropped from the center of the waistline. The skirt gets slightly longer as the pieces approach the

Figure 8-24 Muslin period skirt with eight deep pleats done with seven gores.

Figure 8-25 Pattern for pleated skirt of Figure 8-24. Scale I square = I".

Figure 8-26 Muslin of full, high-waisted skirt with back pleats.

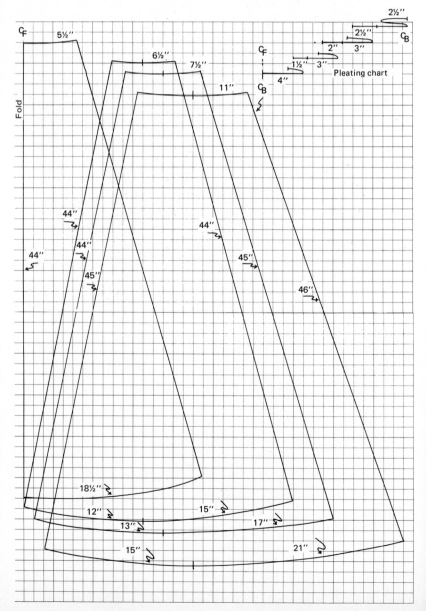

center back because it will be falling out more from the body. Petticoats are, of course, under the skirt.

Figure 8-26 shows a skirt that falls from under the bust, has some fullness in front, and a great deal more in the back controlled by six pleats. Because each pleat is a gore the fall is easily controlled. The skirt has a 6½-yard hem and 6-inch train, and is made for a 30-inch underbust (Figure 8-27).

Deep pleats such as those used in these two skirts need to maintain the fold of the fabric from waist to hem and must be carefully laid in on

Figure 8-27 Pattern for skirt shown in Figure 8-26.

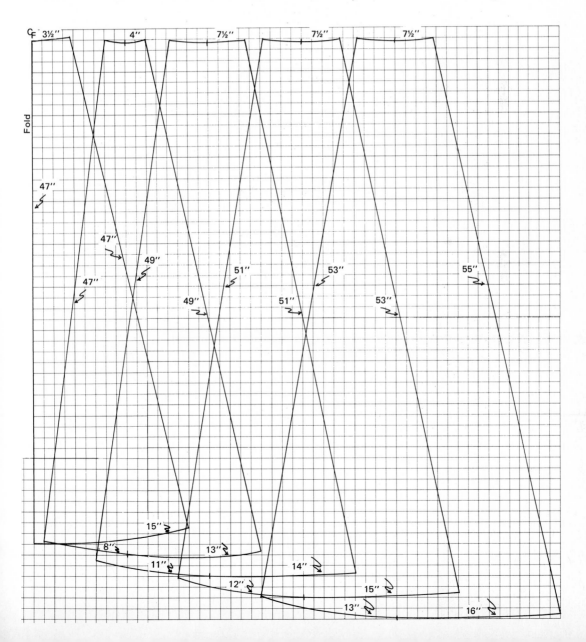

the form with the petticoats in place or they will not fall properly. Often the outside fold of the pleat must be raised so it will fall smoothly from the waist and not pooch out awkwardly. Once the pleat has been arranged the waistline must be remarked and if taken apart would no longer be the smooth curve indicated on the pattern. This cannot be accurately plotted ahead of time and is an adjustment that can be easily made on the form.

A skirt that fits the waist and hipline smoothly is shown in Figure 8-28. In this skirt the front fullness is controlled to the knee, then flairs; the back falls out from just below the hipline and is much fuller. The

Figure 8-28 Muslin of period skirt that fits the hip smoothly.

Figure 8-29 (a; right) Pattern for skirt shown in Figure 8-28. (b; p. 263) Side back and back pieces that can be used with center front and side front pieces of the same skirt. Scale 1 square = 1″.

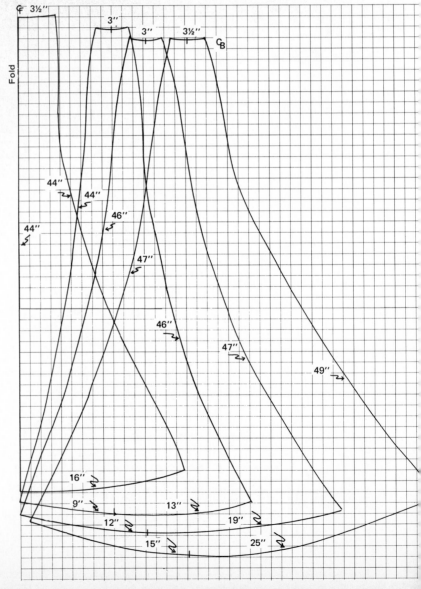

hem is 6 yards. The tops of these pieces must contour the body more than those skirts that have fullness beginning at the waistline (Figure 8-29a). The waist is 27 inches and the hipline 39 inches, a measurement now necessary to consider because of the smooth fit to this point. A skirt with a similar line but not quite as stylish and easier to fit is created by substituting the two back pieces shown in Figure 8-29b. In this skirt, a pleat 2 inches deep that uses 4 inches of fabric is added to each of the back pieces. These can be pleated in on the figure and sewn down to the hipline to maintain the smooth top to the skirt.

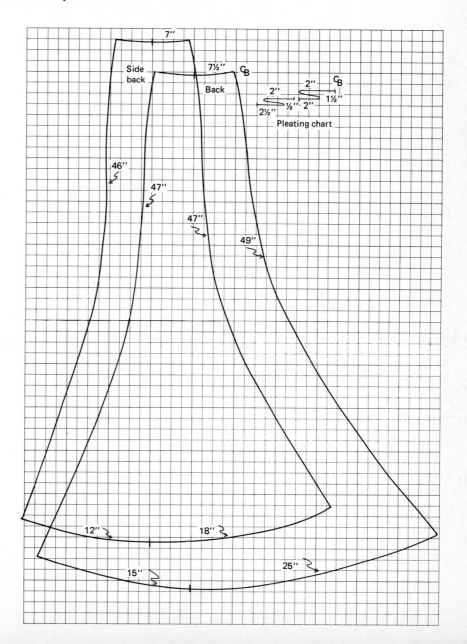

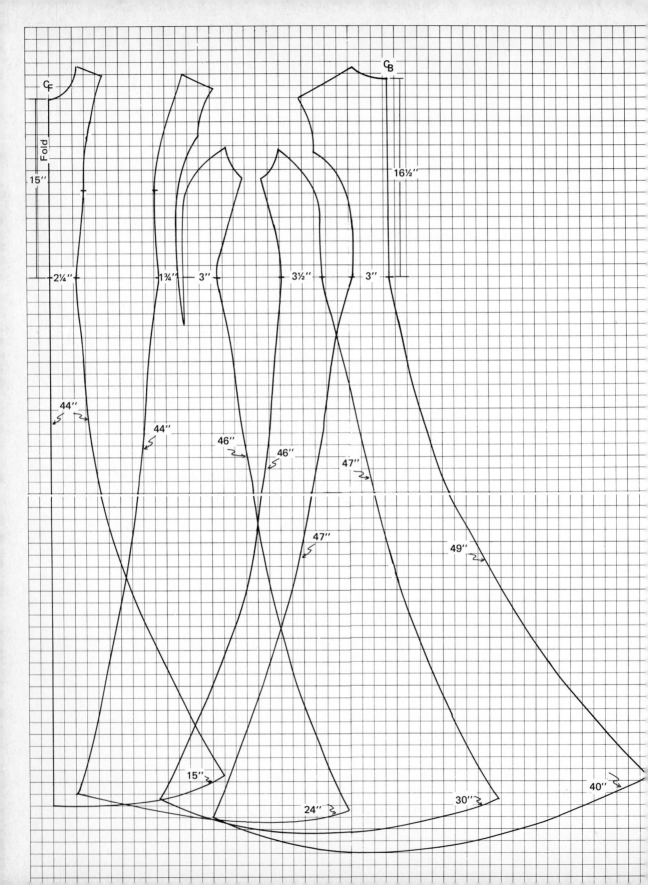

The princess-line gown

A combination of the skirt and bodice that is often used and can be a bit of a challenge to fit is the princess-line gown. A very attractive gown can be done in seven pieces; it uses a skirt similar to the skirt illustrated in Figure 8-25 and a nine-piece bodice rearranged to become seven (Figure 8-30). The side front and the side pieces are joined with a long dart extending into the skirt. This skirt fits smoothly to the flair of the hip, then goes into fullness. The hem is 5½ yards (Figure 8-31).

Figure 8-31   Muslin of princess-line gown

Figure 8-30 (page 264)   Pattern for princess-line gown. Scale 1 square = 1″.

Trousers

A basic trouser pattern is shown in Figure 8-32. Many commercial patterns for trousers are available that show various pockets and the way the belt and fly front are done. These can be easily adjusted to construct most styles of trousers with a fly front or back zipper if the primary way they fit is understood.

The crotch seam is longer in the back than the front because on most people there is more back than front. Tight trousers fit and move better if the crotch seam is toward the front for this causes the upper part of the back inside leg seam to be cut more toward the bias, which will give and mold with movement. The front curve may be about 4 inches

Figure 8-32   Basic trouser pattern. Scale I square = I".

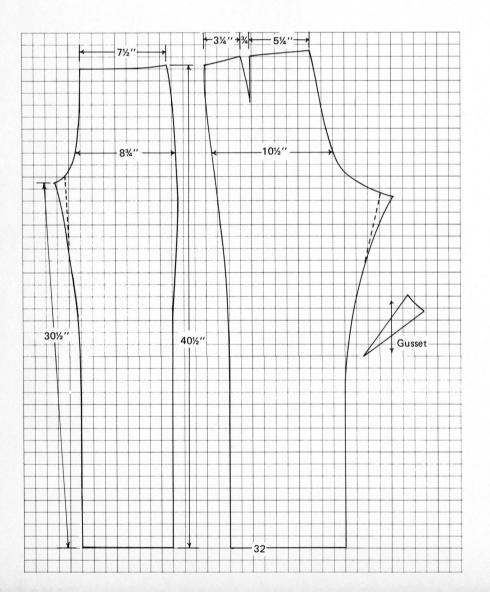

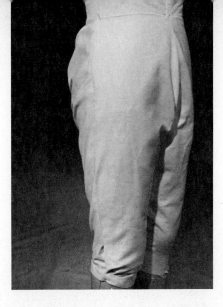

Figure 8-33 Muslin of full fall breeches

shorter than the back. A dart is needed to fit the back of the trousers in to the waist. The side seam may curve in slightly, but not too much because the side of the body does not curve in a great deal. The fullness is more in the center of the buttock; the dart must be placed there. A yoke in back can eliminate the need for a dart, for it is cut on a curve to shape the top into the body. Women sometimes need a front dart as well because they are curvier and have a greater difference between hip and waist. Very tight trousers may need gussets, or triangular bias insets, at the top of the inside leg seams. These will allow for more stretch as the leg moves and extends. They are usually about 2 inches wide and 6 inches long, and are set in to the body of the garment, not added on as extensions (see the dotted line in Figure 8-32). The need for the gusset is not as common now as it used to be, for if the crotch and inside leg seams are sewn with a stretch stitch the trousers may give enough so they will not rip out with every jump. Don't do this, however, until the fit is set. This type of stitch is not easy to remove.

Fitted knee breeches present some interesting problems. Since they are fastened below the knee they cannot give with the leg as it bends. If the breeches must fit absolutely smoothly with no extra length any-where, hope that the actor only stands up in the play for he will not be able to sit down. If he is to move freely the breeches must have a bit more length at the knee in front and at the waist in back for as the leg bends the distance over the knee and around the backside from the waist get longer.

In the eighteenth century and early nineteenth century knee breeches were fastened in front with fall closings. Figure 8-33 shows full fall breeches in which the whole front unbuttons and drops down. The waistband, done in two pieces and left open in the back to lace together, slopes down in front so the third button on the waistband also buttons up the front flap. Underflaps extend from the side to the center

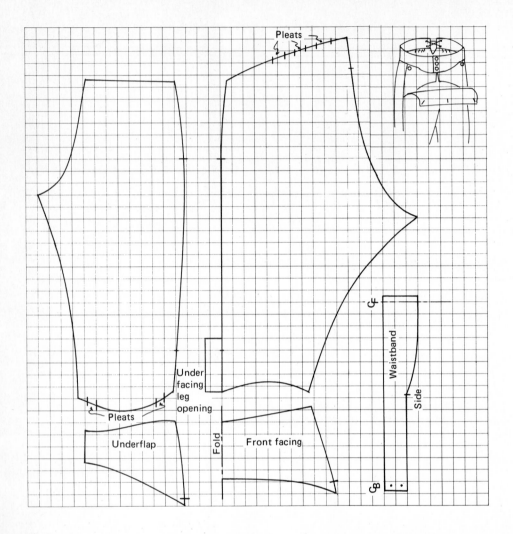

Figure 8-34 Pattern for breeches in Figure 8-33. Scale 1 square = 1".

front, attached to the waistband (Figure 8-34). There are three pleats on each side of the back of the breeches and one pleat on each side of the knee with a narrow band finishing the bottom. The breeches are for a figure with a 32-inch waist, 39-inch hips, and 25 inches waist to knee.

A later version is the small fall breeches (Figure 8-35), in which only part of the front drops down. A half-inch opening on each side provides the seam allowance for the underflap and the fall facing, which is 2 inches longer on each side to form an inch-long extension to cover the slit. The waistband is straight and the fall one inch higher so it can overlap and button up to the waistband (Figure 8-36). The back could be the same as in Figure 8-34. This type of closing can also be used for the full-length trousers of the early nineteenth century.

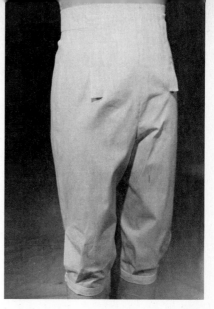

Figure 8-35 Muslin of small fall breeches

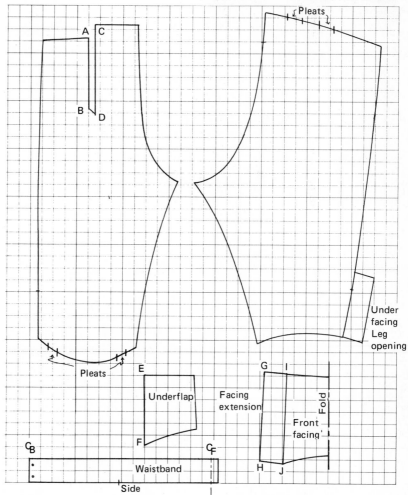

Figure 8-36 Pattern for breeches in Figure 8-35. Scale 1 square = 1″. Fall facing is formed by sewing crotch seam, then stitching CD to GH on both sides. With right sides together the facing extension is folded so GH is over IJ and the top of the fall is stitched, as well as the 1″ seam at the bottom of the extension on each side, from JH to fold. The fall is turned right side out and the bottom of the extension topstitched to the main body to reinforce the end of the opening.

Sleeves

Sleeves bring more variations to costumes than any other single element, and the proper way to construct them is often misunderstood. The top of the sleeve has two parts, the cap and the underarm. BCD is the cap in Figure 8-37 and DEA is the underarm. CD is slightly smaller than CB because more space is needed at the back of the arm to allow for forward movement. ACE is a bit larger than the corresponding area in the body of the garment, about one-and-one-half to two inches, so the sleeve can ease in slightly over the deltoid muscle at the shoulder. The rise in the cap is usually 5 to 6 inches, and the width, just above points B and D, usually needs to be 8 inches or more so the cap over the upper arm muscle does not tie the arm into the body. Fullness can be added to the sleeve by slitting it up the middle and spreading the two pieces the desired amount. The top curve should be adjusted slightly so it remains a curve and does not flatten out.

These patterns are sized for an arm 23 inches long and of medium build.

A tighter one-piece sleeve must be changed to accommodate the bending arm so small darts are put in at the elbow area. This makes a little pocket for the bent elbow, which takes up more space than the

Figure 8-37 Below: One-piece straight sleeve pattern.
Scale 1 square = 1".
ACE   Armseye plus 1½" to 2"
AB and DE   3" to 3½" each
CG   Length of arm
CF   5" to 6"

Figure 8-38 Right: One-piece sleeve with elbow darts.
Scale 1 square = 1".

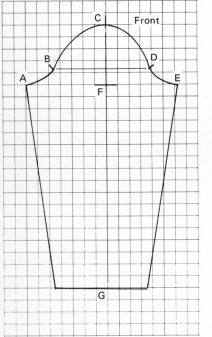

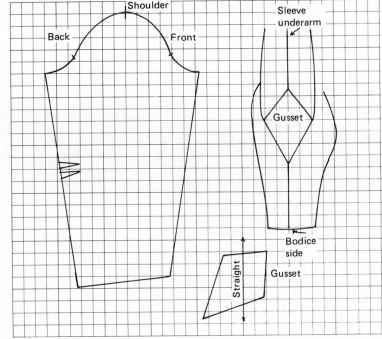

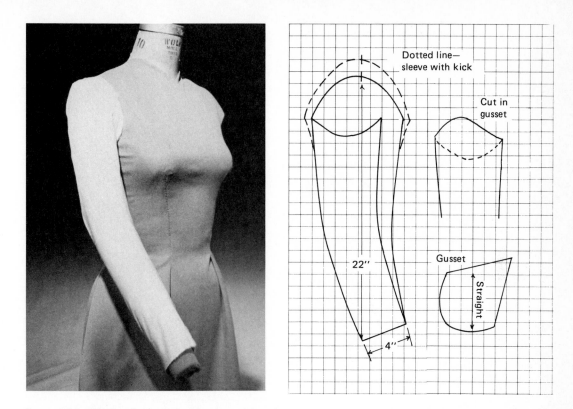

Figure 8-39   Muslin of two-piece tight sleeve (above).

Figure 8-40   Right: Two-piece tight sleeve pattern. Scale 1 square = 1".

straight one (Figure 8-38). Elbow darts are functional, but not too attractive. A tight sleeve with a better line and more of a period look is done in two pieces with the bend of the arm built in (Figure 8-39). The cap of the sleeve is on the upper arm, the underarm curve on the underarm piece, and the seams follow the natural bend of the arm, ending on each side of the wrist (Figure 8-40). This type of seaming is much more useful when developing period sleeve patterns because the seams relate more to where fullness and control are needed. Few exciting things relate to the underarm seam. Any tight sleeve attached to a tight bodice might need a gusset. The gusset is cut on the bias and sewn as indicated in Figure 8-38. It is not sewn directly to the seam lines, but about an inch inside them. The gusset for the two-piece sleeve has a rounded top since there is no underarm seam on the sleeve. Another solution to the movement problem is to cut a gusset right into the sleeve. To do this, added fabric is cut into the underarm piece (Figure 8-40). This is not quite as effective as the added gusset for there is no bias to give, but it is simpler to do.

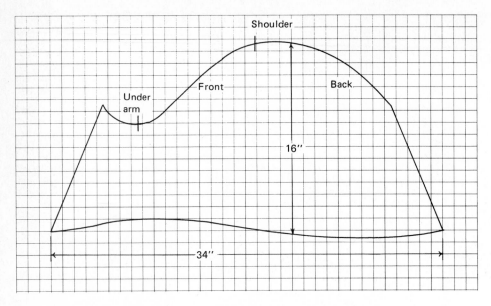

Figure 8-41   Pattern for one-piece upper arm puff. Scale I square = I".

Figure 8-42   Muslin of pattern in Figure 8-41 added to two-piece tight sleeve.

Figure 8-43   Pattern for two-piece upper arm puff. Scale I square = I".

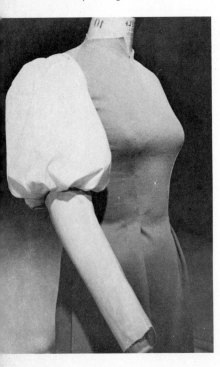

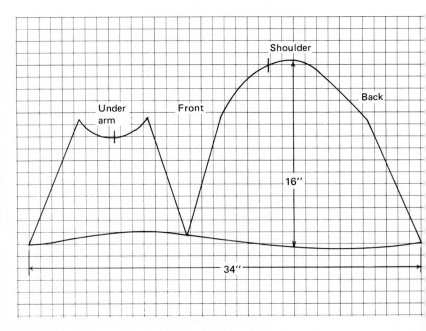

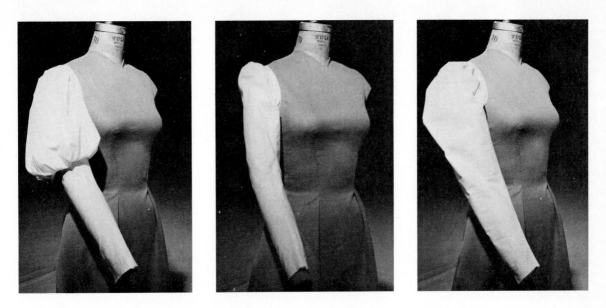

Figure 8-44   Muslin of pattern in Figure 8-43 added to two-piece tight sleeve (left).

Figure 8-45   Muslin of tight sleeve with kick (center).

Figure 8-46   Muslin of moderate leg-of-mutton (right).

Fullness and length are added to a sleeve at the back of the arm, not the underarm. Two styles of puffed sleeves attached to the straight two-piece sleeve are shown in Figures 8-41, 8-42, 8-43, and 8-44. In Figures 8-41 and 8-42 fullness is added by extending the upper part of the sleeve and adding more fullness plus length to the back seam. The shortest part of the puff is the underarm, where extra fabric is awkward and gets in the way. This sleeve is gathered over the cap with more fullness slightly to the back. The sleeve in Figures 8-43 and 8-44 is similar but does not have the extra width in the cap. To make the top smaller but with the same dimension at the bottom the puff is made in two pieces like the undersleeve. Both puffs are attached 8 inches up from the wrist (Figure 8-40). Panes could be added over the puff, each pane varying in length the way the puff does with the longest in back and the shortest under the arm. These must be carefully angled into the armhole to fall properly.

The two-piece straight sleeve can expand into the leg-of-mutton style. If the cap of the sleeve is made slightly higher and the outer sleeve widens a bit (dotted lines in Figure 8-40), the head of the sleeve will have a kick to it (Figure 8-45). If the outer sleeve widens and raises more, a moderate leg-of-mutton will result (Figure 8-46). The pattern

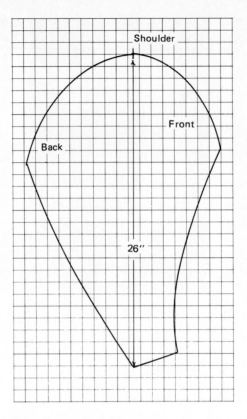

Figure 8-47   Pattern for outer sleeve
piece used for Figure 8-46.
Scale 1 square = 1″.

for this, Figure 8-47, is still used with the undersleeve shown in Figure
8-40. The pattern for the very full leg-of-mutton or gigot sleeve is
shown in Figure 8-48 and still works with the regular undersleeve
shown in Figure 8-40. This sleeve is extremely full at the top but fits the
forearm and wrist (Figure 8-49). If the sleeve is to have a certain
amount of fullness all the way down it may be possible to cut it in one
piece, with the wrist and forearm sections of Figure 8-49 widening.
These sleeves will need crisp interfacing to hold them out. Patterns for
simpler, full sleeves are available with modern patterns.

The funnel sleeve, illustrated in Figure 8-50, is very long on the back
seam, only arm length in front, and quite wide at the opening. The
bottom curve reverses itself so there will not be extreme points at either

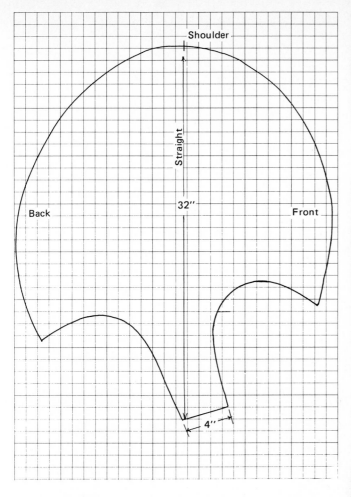

Figure 8-48 Pattern for outer sleeve piece for very full gigot sleeve.
Scale 1 square = 1″.

Back

Shoulder

Straight

32″

Front

4″

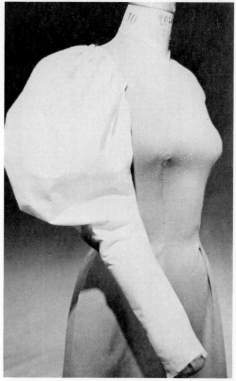

Figure 8-49 Muslin of gigot sleeve.

Figure 8-50 Muslin of funnel sleeve.

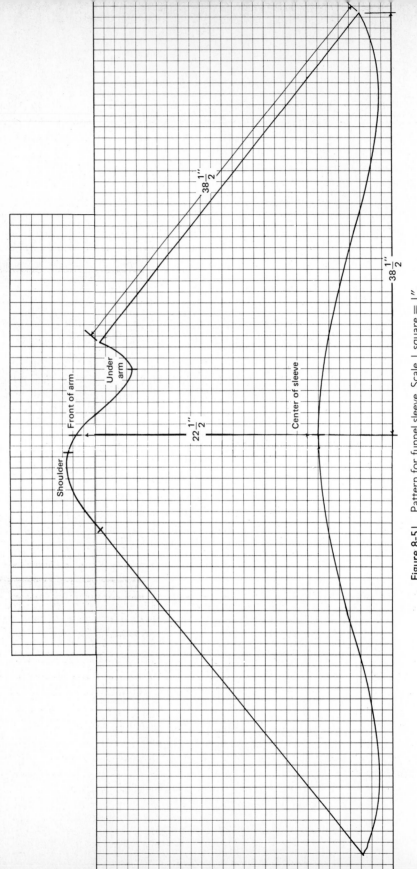

Figure 8-51 Pattern for funnel sleeve. Scale I square = I".

the wrist or back seam (Figure 8-51). The back seam joins the body rather high, more toward the shoulder seam, to position the long point gracefully at the back of the arm. If the sleeve has a front slit it should be cut with a seam on the center line, which indicates the front of the arm, slightly ahead of the top of the shoulder.

The bagpipe sleeve (Figure 8-52) has a top curve like that of the funnel, but the cap is extended and pleats more into the armseye. The back seam curves out, then in toward the wrist, and is pleated into the wristband. The center of the sleeve is slightly longer than the arm to allow a bit of fullness (Figure 8-53).

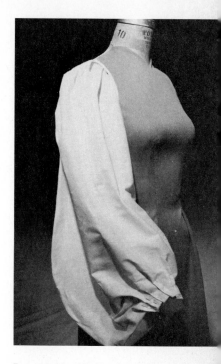

Figure 8-52 Muslin of bagpipe sleeve.

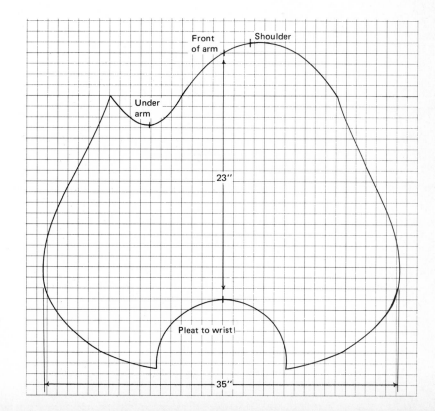

Figure 8-53 Pattern for bag-pipe sleeve. Scale 1 square = 1″.

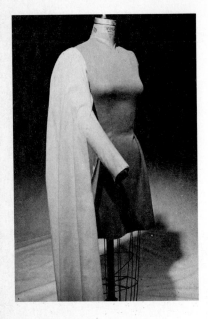

Figure 8-54 Muslin for long slit sleeve.

Figure 8-55 Pattern for long slit sleeve. Scale I square = I".

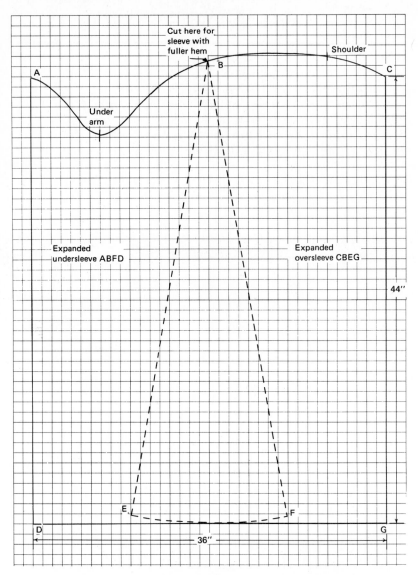

The long slit sleeve (Figure 8-54), could be cut straight with the only seam on the front of the arm if a great deal of fullness is not needed at the bottom. If more fullness is needed a back seam that flairs out could be added. This sleeve is quite full at the cap and pleats into the armseye (Figure 8-55). The pleats in any full sleeve should be carefully angled into the body of the garment or they may poke out quite unattractively.

Men's coats and tailoring

Early men's garments are often simpler to construct than women's. Costumes that require tailoring can be much more difficult. The cotehardie, doublet, and jerkin are easily developed from the basic bodice. The cotehardie is extended to the hip line and will need both a centerfront and center back seam, particularly if the chest has a bit of padding (Figure 8-56). The pleated jerkin uses the flat basic as the body for the costume; the good fabric is pleated over it, attached in place, and the excess fabric trimmed away. The skirt is pleated to match the top from a slightly curved gore to allow it to flair properly over the hip (Figure 8-57).

Figure 8-57   Diagram for pleated bodice and skirt assembly.

Figure 8-56   Cotehardie pattern. Scale 1 square = 1".

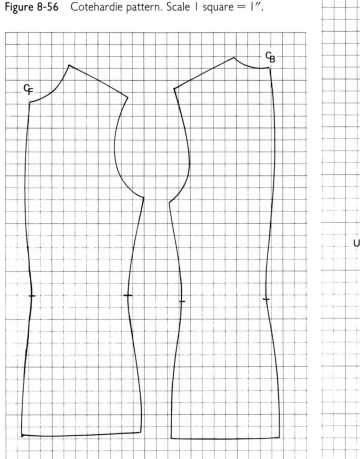

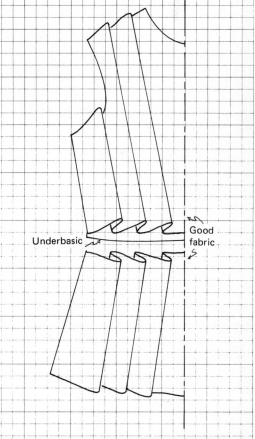

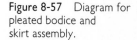

Figure 8-58 Restoration coat.

Men's tailored coats began to appear in the seventeenth century and brought with them more complex sewing techniques. Special interfacing and tacking are necessary to create and hold the proper shape. A thorough explanation of tailoring can be a book in itself, or at least a very long chapter. Figures 8-58 through 8-61 show the basic shapes of a few men's coats from different periods. These shapes can be useful, but the costume will not be effective if it is not tailored properly. Nothing can look more homemade than a man's suit that's tossed together as though it were a cotton blouse. An idea of what is included in tailoring follows, but for in-depth knowledge of the field, refer to sources such as *Basic Tailoring* from the Time-Life series *The Art of Sewing*. A good designer pattern for a man's jacket available from one of the better commercial companies can also be very helpful in explaining the step-by-step approach to such construction. An excellent exercise toward understanding how a coat really goes together is to find a well-tailored jacket at a used clothing store and take it apart, carefully noting down each step that has been done as it is discovered. Two good references for patterns for men's garments are *The Cut of Men's Clothes* and *The Blue Book of Men's Tailoring*, which has some construction techniques included.

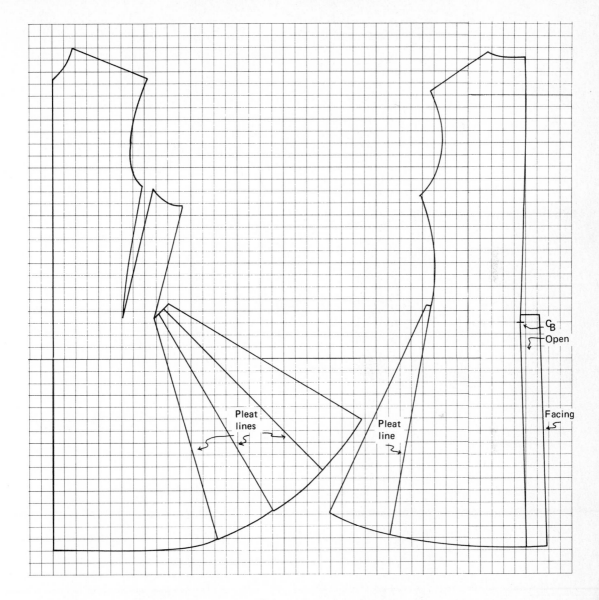

Labels within figure: Pleat lines, Pleat line, C.B., Open, Facing

Figure 8-59 Pattern for Restoration coat.
Scale 1 square = 1".

The Restoration coat of the late-seventeenth-century shapes to the body to a degree and has moderate pleats at the side (Figure 8-58). This is one of the earliest styles of tailored coat (Figure 8-59). It should be interfaced throughout to hold the flair and pleats in place. Coat fronts, which are premade interfacings for the chests of suit coats, can be purchased from a tailors' supply shop and give a good shape to the front of the coat. These are made for the modern suit coat, but can be added to or trimmed away as necessary. Shoulder pads, which help a good shoulder line, are centered over the top of the shoulder and extend ⅝ inch past the seam line, with a long, thin, narrow pad called a sleeve head also attached to the seam line to help shape the top of the sleeve. A narrow twill tape should be sewn around the neckline, which is collarless, before the facing is attached. The twill holds the neck curve so it will not stretch out. If the coat is to button a front overlap should be added, extending about ¾ inch past the center front line. The vest for this period is cut like the body of the coat, with the front overlap, but usually with only one pleat at the side. The back could be shorter and does not have to be interfaced.

Figure 8-60   Muslin of early eighteenth-century coat.

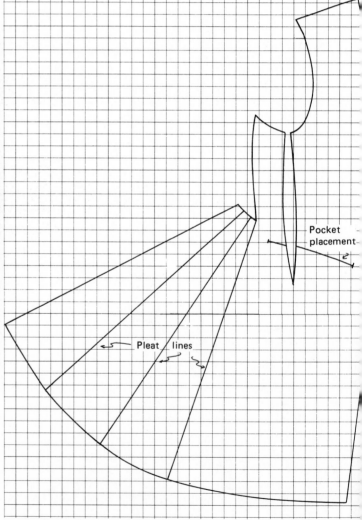

Figure 8-61   Pattern for early eighteenth-century coat. Scale 1 square = 1″

The coat in Figure 8-60, which could come from the second quarter of the eighteenth century, fits more closely to the chest and has a side seam and pleats that are nearer to the side back. Because of this a dart from the armhole to the pocket flap will give a better fit to the front, though this was not done during the period. The coat has three pleats on each side and one on each side of the center back slit (Figure 8-61). Basic construction notes are similar to those for Figure 8-59. The vest has a straight center front that can button closed, is a few inches shorter than the coat, has two side pleats, and is often shorter in the back. The vest front is heavily interfaced to help hold out the coat front.

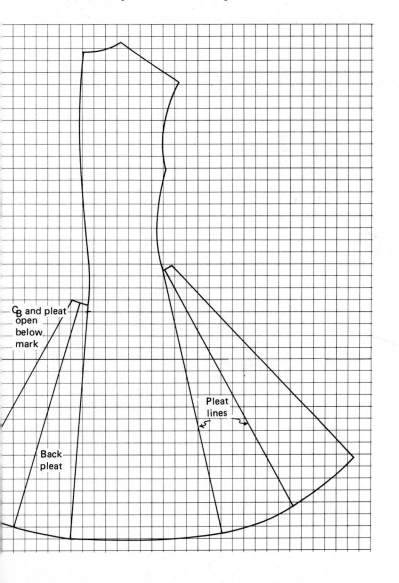

The coat body in Figure 8-62 is somewhat the same, but adapted for later in the century by cutting back the front even more, narrowing the pleats and eliminating one. The side back seam has been moved even more toward the center back and the pleat on each side of the back slit has been eliminated (Figure 8-63). This coat is not as stiff as the earlier ones, and while it should be fully lined it only needs interfacing in the

Figure 8-62 Later-eighteenth-century coat

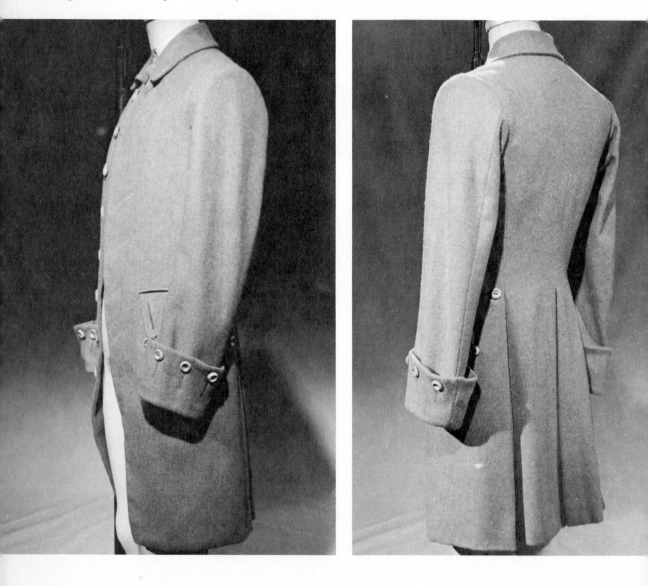

front over the chest and down the opening. A modern coat front can be adapted to this by adding horsehair interfacing 4 to 5 inches wide extending down the front edge. Since the entire armhole is no longer interfaced a twill tape stay should be sewn in to keep it from stretching. This coat could have a standing collar that steps back about an inch from the center front.

Figure 8-63   Pattern for later-eighteenth-century coat. Scale I square = I".

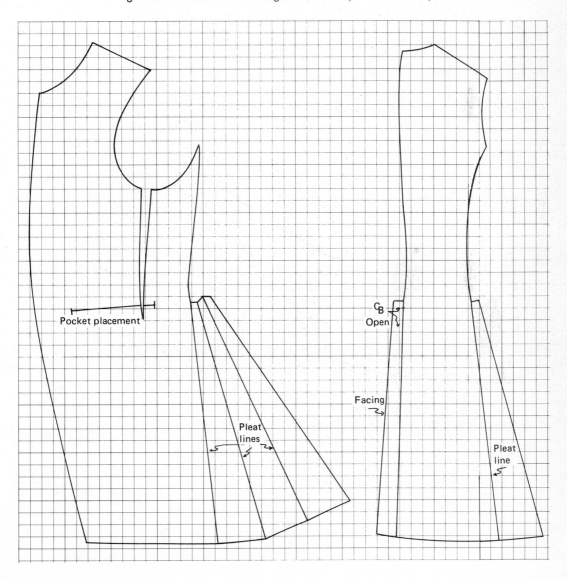

Figure 8-64   Early-nineteenth-century coat

Tailoring men's coats was honed to a fine art in the nineteenth century as the aristocrat turned from the gaudy peacock to the impeccably structured, much more conservative gentleman. Figure 8-64 is an early-nineteenth-century style that shows some of the trends that begin to develop. The front shoulder seam extends past the top of the shoulder into the back of the coat, which lowers accordingly. The body of the coat molds the chest and waist closely. The side back seam curves into the center back even more and the pleat becomes much smaller (Figure 8-65). The lapel develops on the front of the coat and the standing-falling collar is added. The collar and lapel must be handled very carefully to fall correctly on the body. Both have the fabric and interfacing attached together with padding stitches, which are stitches applied while the two parts are curved in the way they will fall. These stitches go over the interfacing, through to barely catch the good fabric and out over the interfacing again in a regular fashion all over the area. A narrow twill tape is also sewed on to define the actual fold line. To thoroughly understand this and the other tricks of the tailoring trade, refer to the tailoring references mentioned earlier.

Men's tailcoats, frock coats, and suit jackets were cut in many interesting ways in the nineteenth century. These are fascinating to explore and can sometimes be combined with a good modern commercial coat pattern to develop the shape more rapidly. Coats can be roughed up in muslin, but it is quite difficult to get some of the steps really to work and to refine the shape until a fairly decent-quality wool is used. Good pressing is often as important as good sewing when tailoring is being done, so never skimp in this area. Pressing may even involve a board or tailor's clapper used to beat the seams or edges. While some shortcuts can be developed for stage purposes, tailoring is a time-consuming process and cannot be rushed through if a professional-looking garment is to be created. It is not really necessary to sit crosslegged on the table, though many still say this is by far the best way to do the handwork, but care, skill, and a lot of practice are needed.

Mocking up the patterns

Enlarging small-scale patterns is a fairly mechanical process and usually done on brown paper because the line can be drawn or erased easily. Brown paper is also relatively inexpensive. Patterning paper with some type of grid marked on it can speed up the process because a scale is already indicated and horizontals and verticals are easily found. This type of paper is much more expensive but sometimes worth it in the time it saves for smaller, more complex patterns. Skirt patterns are drawn as easily on the plain paper.

When drawing a pattern, whether enlarging or creating from

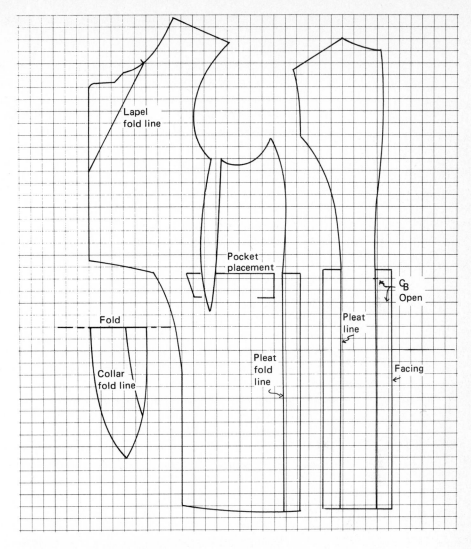

Figure 8-65 Pattern for early-nineteenth-century coat. Scale 1 square = 1″.

scratch, never stop thinking about what the lines mean and how they will go together. Some patterning books—*The Blue Book of Men's Tailoring,* for example—have very carefully listed step-by-step formulas for laying out the shape of the garment. The following is an excerpt from the "Systematical Outline for Sack Coat" to establish various points on the center back line:

Square out and down from A
A to V is ⅓ the breast measure.
V to B is 3 in.
A to C is ¼ of total height plus ½ in.
A to D is ⅓ of height plus 1 in.
A to E is ½ height minus 5 in.

It continues for eighty steps. When all the steps have been completed a pattern for a sack coat is on the page and can be quite accurate even if the pattern maker has not thought at all about what line AV stands for or why VB drops 3 inches. This type of copying is not useful to someone who wants to develop an eye for the way shapes are created. Each step should be considered to know the reason for the direction. Each line should have a meaning so that if a change is needed the direction of the change is immediately clear. The eye must gauge distances and understand outlines and how they will react when draped on the body. If a pattern is tried on the body and altered, take a good look at the alterations and understand what changes they make in the original shapes. Careful understanding is a great boon to the well-developed patterning imagination. Soon a pattern drawing that once took two agonizing hours to create can be done with ease in fifteen minutes. The eye understands, the hand makes the proper moves, and a shape is there to cut and try.

Patterns are usually mocked up in muslin because it is inexpensive if bought in bulk from a wholesaler and is easily marked. If the actual costume is to be made of fabric with drastically different properties than muslin, a patterning fabric that is more similar should be used. Muslin will never float like chiffon, drape like Qiana, or stretch like milliskin. The pattern is marked on the seam lines and cut with a 1-inch seam allowance, except at the waistline and the closing line where 2 inches better allows for adjustments. Extra allowance may or may not be left at the pattern hemline, though it must be on the actual garment. As much of the pattern as seems logical should be machine-basted together to begin the fitting. For example, the body parts should probably be together, and the sleeve, but not attached to each other. After the fit of the chest and shoulder has been set the sleeve can be pinned on. In most cases it is useful to baste the pieces together slightly past the end of the seam, but do not backstitch unless the stitching will be under a great deal of tension. The seam thus can be easily ripped open if necessary without the danger of tearing the fabric.

Fitting the actor

Costume fittings should be well organized and efficiently handled if everyone involved is to remain as happy as possible. The actor should not be called more often than really necessary and his time well used while he is there. If he realizes the shop is functioning smoothly and will not waste his time, he is much more likely to be prompt, cooperative, and make a special trip should an emergency arise. In a professional company an actor is only required to come in for a very short time, usually two hours a week, outside the regular rehearsal-call time. Then efficiency is quite necessary, for it becomes a question of economics.

Before an actor is called all the components of his costume should be checked so that as many different elements as possible can be fitted at the same time. It's depressing to have someone come in and say "I need Joe for ten minutes to check a collar" when Joe just left. If he has been in the shop for an hour he's not going to be happy to return right away, but the crew member who needs him may be stalled until he gets that ten minutes.

For the most efficient use of everyone's time, the patterns and garments that are to be fitted should be assembled—together with all the shoes and underpinnings that might be needed. Ideally the fitting should take place in a separate area large enough for the actor, those who will need to work with him, a mirror, table for equipment, a chair, and hanging area. Unfortunately this lovely little room is often not available and the fitting takes place in the middle of the shop. This is another primary reason to get the fitting done in the most efficient way, for fittings always eat into the time needed to get the costume built. Those people in charge of the costume must stop what they are doing to work with the actor, and others who are working around the area often find the fitting much more interesting than the seam or button they should be sewing.

Creating a good atmosphere

It is almost as important to be able to handle a fitting well from a psychological point of view as it is to be skillful with pins and fabric. The costume is a work in progress. The actor must realize that changes may be necessary and that the alterations being done will present him in the best possible way. The crew member in charge of the costume must also realize that some areas may need to be reworked. This is not necessarily because he or she has not done a good job, but because something else might be more effective. A fitting is not the time to lay blame or make accusations. If a costume doesn't close, accusing the actor of gaining weight or the crew member of sewing the seams together on the wrong lines achieves nothing but ill will. Solve the problem in a pleasant way and find out why it happened later. If the craftsmanship is shoddy, speak to the crew member privately. Don't create a fuss in front of the actor: it will embarrass the crew member and make the actor feel insecure about the final outcome of the costume. If a pattern works well, say so. An encouraging word can work wonders.

Should the actor be concerned about the way something fits, listen to his problem, show interest in solving it, and explain what might be done, even if the change seems quite minor. If nothing can be done, say so, but in such a way that the actor understands and feels you are really trying to be helpful. Don't just rudely dismiss the complaint, no matter how appropriate this might seem. A hostile actor is not a pleasant co-worker.

Another problem is a bit more difficult to solve. Extraneous comments can sometimes create difficult situations. Someone casually looking up from his work and remarking "Gee, Phil, that really makes you look fat" or "What's that funny pucker in the back?" can start the actor worrying about something that might never have occurred to him. It's not considered too democratic to put a muzzle on the crew, and if someone thinks something really looks good it's nice for him or her to say so. It is not out of place, however, to remind the crew that the costumes are still being developed during the fittings and actors are sometimes a bit insecure about their appearance. If anyone spots a problem he or she should quietly mention it to someone in charge and not announce it to the world. This approach will probably work very well with the crew. The remaining fly in the ointment is the friend of the actor who walks into the room and feels obliged to make some sort of crack.

Fitting problems can also arise from simply having too many bodies in the shop at the same time. Know how many people the crew can take at once and schedule no more than that. If three people can be handled efficiently, don't let the stage manager send up eight at once just because there is a rehearsal break. The other five will waste their time and could slow the process by being in the way.

Adjusting the pattern to the body

Set the pattern on the actor as squarely as possible and pin up the closing so the work can be done on a well-situated piece that will not shift. Check the armholes and neckhole to make sure the curved-seam allowance does not catch against the body, keeping the fabric from lying properly. This practically always happens at the front of the base of the neck and where the arm joins the chest and back. The seam allowance must be clipped at these points before any other adjustments can be accurately made; it must be clipped in far enough to release the tension but must not go into the body of the garment. Do not clip extraneously; the seam allowance just cut may be the one needed in the next alteration. If a clip is necessary, do it deep enough to count.

Try to pin fairly symmetrically; variations can be reallocated later on. Do not take in or release indiscriminately. Locate the area that most logically needs the adjustment. If a bodice is too big it could be tightened up by taking in the center back seam, but this might bring the side seams toward the back, create diagonal pulls, and do nothing for the bust area. Another solution could be to take in both side seams or the side front and side back seams. If a seam is replaced or a dart taken, make sure the pin line continues until the line tapers off or goes into the seam allowance.

When a satisfactory fit has been achieved, mark the seam line at the neck, the waist, and both armseyes. One side might do if the pattern has been taken in quite evenly, but if the usual variations occur two will be better. These marks should move continuously around the body, so be particularly attentive where the line crosses a seam. Watch out for ticklish actors. The waist mark in particular can sometimes be a killer. Check the costume design for any particular markings that should be indicated. If lines are drawn for more than one costume, which is entirely possible, do them in different colors and write on the muslin which line corresponds to which drawing.

Sleeves should be pinned in place carefully and checked for movement and length. The cap of the tight sleeve must be wide enough across the upper arm muscle to allow forward and upward movement. The full sleeve is easy to fit because it does not bind the arm or restrict movement, but achieving the right length can be a bit tricky. If the full sleeve is too short the effect of the fullness is lost and it may hinder movement; if it is too long the fabric will droop on itself, cover the cuff and perhaps part of the hand, and look awkward. The fabric should be just long enough to hold out the fullness and slightly longer to the outside and back than under the arm. Soft, heavier fabrics will droop more than crisp ones. If a sleeve is too long in the fitting, pin a tuck in the middle of it until the right length is achieved.

The general length of a skirt can be estimated, but the actual hem usually cannot be taken until the skirt is constructed in the real fabric because the weight of the fabric can cause a variation. The movement capability in tight trousers should be checked as well as the way the seams fall down the leg. Should the seams twist, open them on both sides, allow the fabric to fall straight, and repin. The front length of knee breeches should be marked with the actor seated to allow enough fabric to go over the bent knee and the back length marked when he is standing.

During the fitting process someone should be available to take any necessary notes.

This checklist will be useful as you organize the fittings for a show:

1. Patterns should have as many pieces basted or pinned together as possible, with body pieces and sleeves separate. Seams should be basted past the end, but not backstitched.
2. Everyone who might need to see the actor should be notified that he has been called.
3. All the elements that might be needed for the fitting should be gathered into one space.
4. Someone should be available to take notes as the fitting progresses.
5. The pattern should be set squarely on the body and pinned in place.
6. Any area with a curved seam allowance that may keep the fabric from lying properly on the body, such as arm- and neckholes, should be checked and clipped.
7. The garment should be pinned as evenly as possible from side to side and in logical places to solve the fitting problems.
8. Neck, waist, armholes, lengths, and any design lines should be marked as soon as a good fit has been achieved.
9. The pattern should be checked immediately after the fitting to make sure all areas are clearly marked. It should be organized as soon as possible.

Finishing the pattern

As soon as possible after the fitting the pattern should be finalized. What seems obvious and easy to remember at the time can become quite fuzzy and vague a few more fittings and hundreds of questions later. Each alteration should be carefully marked and each piece labeled with its position, the name of the actor or costume, and the top, bottom, front, or back if there is any chance confusion could arise. Nothing is worse than finding an extraneous costume piece on a table and not knowing to whom or where it goes. The pattern should then be taken apart, pressed if necessary, and organized so cutting can be done easily and accurately.

The best way to organize a pattern in most cases is to "even it up." Though the human body is never actually symmetrical, it is usually wise to pretend that it is and make a costume that is symmetrical. Once a garment starts to go askew all kinds of problems can arise: pulls on one side that aren't on the other, pleats at different intervals from the center front—if the true center front can even be located, trim that is an inch from one shoulder and an inch and a half from the other . . . one variance seems to beget three more, until the only solution seems to be to take the whole thing apart and start over.

No matter how carefully a fitting is done there are usually variations

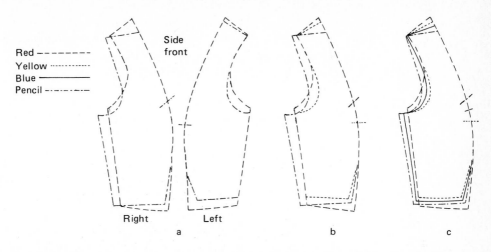

Red — — — —
Yellow ···········
Blue ————
Pencil —·—··—··—

Side front

Right   Left

a   b   c

Figure 8-66 A method for evening pattern pieces after the fitting.

from side to side. These can easily be evened up by using the following method. Matching pieces should be laid on top of each other, seam lines coinciding and on the outsides. If the pieces were cut and marked together, matching the cut edges will also match the seam lines. Any new lines drawn on one piece should be traced to the other so the changes on both sides are now visible on one piece. The final seam line can be marked halfway between what was done on side A and what was done on side B. An example may help clarify this process.

A system for the colors of pattern lines should be established for the shop. A useful code is to mark all the preliminary patterns in red, the intermediate evening-up lines in yellow, and the final seam lines in blue. If a line has not been changed the red will stand; if it has been changed the blue line will supersede it.

Figure 8-66a shows the two side front pieces of a seven-piece bodice with the original pattern lines and the pencil lines drawn in the fitting. In Figure 8-66b the two pieces have been pinned together and the lines from the left side transferred to the right with yellow tracing paper. In Figure 8-66c the blue line is located halfway between each correction. Note the underarm seam. Since this was not changed on the left side the final blue line is located halfway between the pencil correction on the right and the red line, which was the good line on the left. Most of the front seam was not changed so the red line remains. The mark on the front seam indicates where the center front piece joins on. This too is evened up. Darts are done in the same way. Perhaps it should be noted that the blue line is actually created by placing the blue tracing paper under the pieces as they are seen in Figure 8-66b and the tracing wheel is used to draw in the line, which will appear on the left side. The piece can then be flipped and the blue copied to the right so the final lines will appear on all the pattern pieces.

Occasionally an actor is actually shaped quite differently from side to side, so much so that the pattern should not be evened but fitted very carefully on the body and marked so the pieces fit on the left will always be on the left, and so forth.

Constructing the costume

Basic sewing methods will not be discussed in this book since this type of information can be found in many other sources. Costume construction begins with the same type of sewing skills used in making regular garments, but, contrary to some beliefs circulated about the necessary quality of the work seen onstage, they often need to be sturdier because they get quite a workout during the run of a play and may be used over and over again as part of the stock of a continuing company.

Bodices and sleeves should be flat lined unless this will interfere with the drape of the primary fabric. Muslin can be used for economy, but a broadcloth is better because it is stronger, cleans more easily, and gives a neater appearance to the inside of the costume, particularly one that is used often. Seams should be sewn with a moderate-length stitch. A long stitch will be loose and may not hold; if alterations are necessary, removing short, tight stitches is time-consuming and may cause the fabric to be ripped in the attempt. Ample but not bulky seam allowances should be left wherever possible for future use, and the allowance finished in some way to keep it from raveling. Closings must be quite sturdy. Heavy-duty zippers should be used to hold together tight period bodices. Hooks and eyes should be of good size and very securely sewed. All grommeted edges should be interlined, and if they are under pressure the edges must be boned. Any stress points should be reinforced or they will need to be mended later.

Garments with complex pleating, tucking, or draping on the outside need a flat lining next to the body to hold the shape firmly in place. Large draped pieces should be carefully tacked to retain their shape. Complex sleeves should be built on a fairly tight undersleeve so they will not shift out of place and will be easy to put on.

Any trim applied to the costume must be attached firmly. Collars and cuffs that might get heavily soiled can be made as finished pieces that are attached for performance, then removed for laundering. The inner layer of all costumes that can't be washed regularly should be supplied with dress shields.

The key thought behind building any costume is quite simple. Construction should be careful and solid. A sloppy attitude toward the work and haphazard construction methods will show up in the quality of the finished product. There may be times when the method of working will vary from that found in a dressmaker's shop — a machine stitch may be substituted for handwork or on occasion even glue may be used — but careful craftsmanship must be employed if the result is to be successful. The most beautifully designed costume in the world, patterned and draped with precision, can look like a potato sack if seam lines are missed when it is sewed, the tension on the machine is wrong, and the pressing is haphazard.

One extremely important ingredient for a well-built costume is a crew that really cares about the work. It's up to the designer and the head of the shop to integrate all those who work with them into the production and to let them know how vital their input is to the success of the show. The designer should present the show to the entire shop, explain his or her ideas, display the fabrics and trims, establish the schedule that must be followed, describe any special problems that must be solved, and in general let everyone know what is going on so each can see how he or she fits into the picture. It is true that some workers will be more skilled than others, but all are vital to the success of the costume construction. Let them know what is happening. Encourage their work. Be kind and constructive with criticism. Designers can't be cheerful every moment, but those who try most of the time will be forgiven a few cranky periods and the crew will be more inclined to put extra effort into building the show. If the designer is not prepared and has careless work habits, this attitude may soon pervade the entire crew and the results can be devastatingly lackluster.

The costume shop

The costume shop can almost become home during a busy show. If it is a well-equipped, well-organized, pleasant place, the push to get things done will not seem too much like drudgery.

The size and location of shops varies considerably. The area is seldom too large, and often is smaller than ideal, so careful thought needs to go into the layout for the most efficient use of the available space. (Hopefully it's not in the basement, though for some strange reason it often is. This gives the crew the feeling they are turning into moles, but there is one advantage. No wall space is lost to windows.)

BASIC SEWING EQUIPMENT

The basic sewing supplies needed in a costume shop are similar to those found in most professional sewing situations. The following is a list of items most commonly used, with indications where costume use may be different from other situations.

Thread. Some shops use only black, white, and gray tones, blending the value rather than the color. If the audience is close to the stage the right colors are best for top stitching. Heavy-duty thread and button thread are also needed.

Machine needles. A medium size is satisfactory for most sewing, but lightweight and heavy needles should be available for special problems. Double needles can be used on machines with a dual tension set up for pin tucks. Leather needles are available for leather work.

Hand needles. A variety of sizes of needles with long eyes are the most useful. Heavy-duty upholstery needles and curved needles are occasionally necessary and should be kept around so the prop department will know where to go when it needs to borrow some.

Straight pins. Medium-size rustproof pins are most commonly used, but longer, heavier pins are desirable for heavy fabrics. Try very hard to keep them separate. It's a terrible nuisance to grab a giant, clunky pin when a small one is needed.

Safety pins. All sizes are needed in quantity. Large ones are most often used.

Tracing paper. At least four colors should be stocked, including white and probably blue, red, and yellow because they are easily distinguished from each other.

Tracing wheels. Regular tracing wheels are the most useful, but smooth and pointed ones are sometimes called for. The very pointed tracing wheels can mark most easily through heavy fabrics, but they can also rip up the surface of the table top.

Seam rippers. Small ones are the easiest to use. Some people prefer razor blades. These are fine in skilled hands but can be very dangerous to the fabric if the wielder is not careful.

Shears and scissors. Bent-handled shears with 8- to 10-inch or even 12-inch blades are used for most cutting chores. Good shears are expensive and generally worth it, for they keep a better edge. Fabric shears should be used only on fabric; other materials will dull the blades. A supply of inexpensive shears and smaller scissors should be available for nonfabric use. Mark the different types carefully. An inexperienced crewperson often thinks anything that cuts can cut anything. Leather shears will be a welcome tool for heavy-duty cutting;

pinking shears are not commonly used any more, as alternative methods are available to finish seams and pinking shears do not stay reliably sharp.

Tape measures, yardsticks, hem guages, plastic rulers. All measuring devices should be of a fairly good quality. Cheap ones, or free ones with a bit of advertising included, are sometimes calibrated inaccurately, and the yardsticks are inevitably warped. The measuring tools should be marked on both sides with the numbers reversing so the handiest end may be used. Large aluminum rules 48 and 72 inches long are convenient for laying out skirt and cape patterns. The tailor's square, tailor's curve, and French curve can be used for drafting patterns.

Tailor's chalk. Both wax and clay can be stocked, in white and colors. Clay brushes out of fabric, while wax will melt off with the iron and may stain some synthetic fabrics.

Fasteners

HOOKS AND EYES. All sizes may be used. The larger, size 3 or 4, are better for closings. Very large or skirt hooks and eyes are often needed.

SNAPS. All sizes should be stocked, from extra-small to the big, heavy "whopper poppers."

VELCRO. Available in 12-yard rolls, both white and black are useful. The white can be dyed, though one side takes much better than the other. This is a bit expensive, but when it is needed it is often needed fast.

ZIPPERS. Specific zippers will probably be bought for the show, but a good store of emergency zippers should be available.

Twill tape, seam binding, bias tape. Twill in 1/4-, 1/2-, and 1-inch widths, both black and white, can be an asset to the well-equipped shop.
Seam binding can be used to stay seam lines or face seams, though finishing the edge with an overlock stitch is often better if the machine is available. Bias tape can be stocked in black and white spools.

Elastic. This is needed in widths of quarter-inch to inch in both black and white. Elastic thread is also available for special problems.

Thimbles. Often resisted by many, they can speed up sewing with practice and are essential for some heavy materials. A thimble is really preferable to holes in the middle finger.

Hangers. Both wire and wooden are needed. Wooden hangers are particularly useful for heavier garments that lose their shape if supported by only the thin wire. While wire hangers seem to breed in the home closet, the reverse is true in the costume shop. A sign asking for donations usually helps solve the problem, though new ones can be purchased from the cleaners.

Most of these materials can be purchased from tailor's suppliers and wholesalers in bulk. This should be done whenever possible since the savings can be quite significant.

LARGER EQUIPMENT

Sewing machines. A number of good, sturdy, straight-stitch machines are invaluable, such as the old black metal Singers. These are almost indestructible, no matter how inexperienced the user. A modern zigzag machine such as the Elna, Bernina, or Viking is necessary for specialty stitches. If money is available for the more specialized machines the most useful is the overlock or serger, which finishes the edges of the fabric (Figure 8-67). A heavy-duty walking foot machine can make its way through practically anything and might be shared with the scene shop. The blindstitch machine (Figure 8-68) only does hems, but it does them very rapidly and with a stitch that is easily removed.

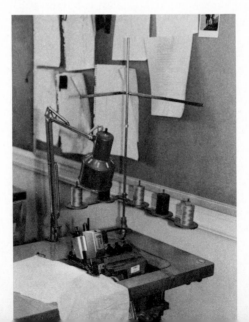

Figure 8-67   The overlock machine or serger is invaluable for finishing edges.

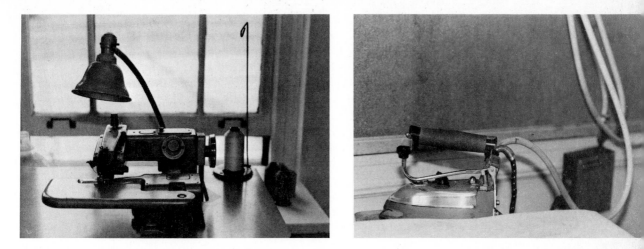

Figure 8-68   The blind stitch machine (above) can hem yards of fabric in a few minutes, and the hem can be easily removed if necessary.

Figure 8-69   Industrial irons (right) are efficient for the costume shop; they provide more steam and are heavier than household irons.

Irons. Industrial irons (Figure 8-69) are far superior to the domestic ones for they are heavier and deliver much more steam. As might be expected they are also much more expensive. This is a bit counterbalanced by a longer life span.

Ironing boards. Large, heavy-duty boards will minimize tipping accidents, which don't hurt the boards much, but are often tough on the irons.

Speciality ironing equipment. Sleeve board, needle board for velvets, pressing ham, clapper for pounding seams, distilled water to prolong iron life, and iron cleaner for the sole plate. Nothing gunks up an iron fster than pressing old costumes pulled from stock.

Steamer. The table model is useful for work on hats, the floor model good for large costumes and drapes.

Washing machine and dryer. These are vital for both maintaining the costumes and for dyeing fabrics. If one set is used for both purposes care must be taken to keep them clean so that the white garments don't spot. A good supply of liquid bleach is recommended to clean out both machines. The washer should top load and have a number of water levels and temperature combinations. The dryer could have an automatic senser, but also needs a timed dry cycle, permanent press, and air fluff. Large capacity, heavy-duty models are the best.

Hot plate or stove. Used for heating water to dye, the hot plate should be large and heavy duty. A 30-inch stove is even better if the money is available because it is sturdy with a large flat surface and has an oven available if it is needed.

Dye vat. Wonderful for dyeing large quantities, these can be extremely expensive. A soup kettle available from restaurant suppliers is still expensive but much less than a dye vat and can be used for the same purpose (see Figure 8-70).

Laundry sink. This must have two deep tubs and a mixer faucet.

Cutting tables. These should be 6 to 8 feet long, at least 42 inches wide, and 36 inches high. The top should be smooth enough to lay fabric out easily, but not so slick that the fabric slides to the floor the minute the cutter's back is turned. The surface should have a bit of give for easy marking. Upson board covered with vinyl can be quite practical. Cork coated with polyurethane makes an excellent, though more expensive, surface.

Figure 8-70   The dye vat below was actually a soup kettle and holds 40 gallons of water, which it can heat to boiling in less than 20 minutes.

Figure 8-71   A hanging dummy (right) is very useful for many construction problems.

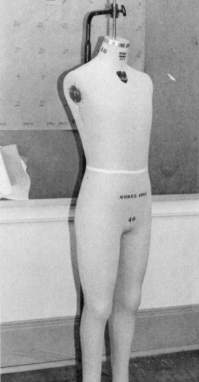

Dressmaker's dummies. Good dummies are expensive but can sometimes be found used or collected one or two a year when the money is available. A variety of sizes for both men and women can be used. New dummies can be purchased with detachable arms and collapsible shoulders, luxuries but very nice. A hanging dummy, which is a full figure (Figure 8-71), is even more expensive, but having something with legs around is a joy. Inexpensive home sewing dummies are useful only if nothing better is available. Those with adjustable pieces are almost more of a nuisance than they are worth; they are always crooked and every time something needs to be pinned to a surface the area is over a hole between the plates.

Figure 8-72 A small water distiller can provide a few gallons of distilled water each day.

Water distiller. Moderately expensive, but it's very handy to have a steady supply of water for the irons and steamers. (See Figure 8-72.)

GENERAL EQUIPMENT

Racks. Rolling racks with large casters are the most practical way to hang the costumes. One style, called the Z-Truck, is sturdy and good where space is a problem for the racks nest together well for storage.

Mirrors. A three-fold mirror is best for fittings, but a full-sized wall mirror can be used.

Hemming stand. Not essential, but certainly a boon to the person marking the hem, for it raises the actor about 12 inches off the floor.

Bulletin boards. These are necessary to hang up sketches, patterns, notes, trinkets, and other delights found while digging through trim boxes.

Brown paper and squared patterning paper

Muslin and other stock patterning fabric

Interfacing and lining fabrics

Buckram. This can be used in both regular and heavy weight for hats and other items that need a stiff base.

Cotton batting and wadding

Boning, both metal and plastic or feather boning

Wire. Milliner's wire in both medium and heavier weights is useful, as well as lightweight spool wire for jewelry and accessory work.

Basic tools. Hammer, screwdrivers, wrench, awl, wire cutters, rasps and files for distressing costumes, nails, screws, and anything else the scene shop might not want to lend

Hot glue gun and pellets

Flexible white glue, such as Sobo

Dress shields, bust pads, shoulder pads, and sleeve heads

Buttons. Always handy to have around, common types should be purchased in bulk whenever a sale is encountered

Laundry soap, starch, antistatic spray, bleach, clothes brushes, and lint removers

Cleaning fluid. Bought in bulk for economy, this is preferable in gallon cans with small, carefully marked glass bottles available for more easy use.

Dye and dye remover. These are much less expensive when purchased in bulk from a wholesaler.

Grommets and setters

Leather tools and dyes

Rhinestone setter

Paints, brushes, and sprays

Shoe polishes, brushes, and sprays

Plasticene or clay for molding shapes

Celastic and acetone. Acetone may be available in bulk from a chemical supply company or department of a university.

Scrap boxes. Medium to large boxes are needed, one for muslin pieces too large to throw away, and at least one for the scraps from the current show. These should be saved until the show closes, if possible, in case a repair should require that last 4 inches left from cutting the costume.

Combs, brushes, hair and bobby pins, dryers, curlers, and other wig and hair-setting materials. Wig blocks and hat stands.

Notebooks for measurement sheets and show organization

Filing system for catalogues, patterns, and reference materials.

All these items may not be necessary for every shop, nor can every shop afford them all. Many, many more items could be used, depending upon the project at hand. The size of the shop, the money available, and the type of production work usually done should be considered when deciding which items should be acquired first and what will be the most useful. Careful planning, which allows the shop to be stocked as well as possible under the given circumstances, has two definite advantages: work can be done more efficiently in a well-equipped space and items purchased in bulk are almost always less expensive.

The floor and ceiling of the costume space may not be as easy to alter as some of the other areas, but if there is a chance for input it is quite important that the floor be wood or cushioned tile, not cement! Many of those working in the shop spend a great deal of time on their feet, and a cement floor can cause tired and aching legs that definitely have a negative effect on the amount of work that gets done. The actual texture of the ceiling is not so important, but the light fixtures hanging from it are. A shop should have incandescent lighting, or at least a combination of incandescent and fluorescent lighting. Exclusively fluorescent light distorts the colors of the fabrics and trims. The dye area in particular must have incandescent illumination, and if possible both areas could use spotlights that have holders for color media so the tone of the light can be changed to approximate the light that will be used onstage.

A few more items are really quite essential, though they don't tie in directly to constructing costumes. There are often times when a number of people are spending a great deal of time in this area. A coffeepot can make life easier, as does a small refrigerator. Add to these the hotplate or stove in the dye area and the crew can camp out in the shop for days. And for a quick snack a hot-air popcorn popper can't be beat. No grease and it smells great.

Laying out the costume shop

Each space will have its own problems and its own potentials and will need to be considered with a good, logical eye to discern the best way to place the equipment for the most efficient use.

Cutting tables should be placed away from the walls so they can be approached from all sides. Shelves for fabric storage or scrap boxes can be kept beneath them. Sewing machines should relate to both the cutting tables and the irons and if possible should have sewing tables large enough for big costumes and lots of yardage. Tables and chairs should be available for those doing handwork.

A shelf unit can hold clearly labeled containers for all the small sewing equipment. Shelves near the ironing boards will organize all the ironing accessories. Deeper shelves can be used for fabrics and storage boxes of the trims and accessories most commonly used. Floor space needs to be allotted for racks and dummies. Dummies particularly have a terrible tendency to stand right in the way unless they have a specific home. The bulletin boards need to be on walls that can be easily reached. The mirror should be located in an area that allows maneuverability in front of it.

The dye area should be separated from the shop if at all possible because the moisture it produces can be hard on the machines and dyeing itself can be quite messy. A worktable is needed and storage shelves, as well as a space to hang fabrics that cannot go into the dryer. A floor drain is always best in this area. If the space is also used to spray costumes or if work with any toxic materials is done, it should have excellent ventilation. Many new materials can be quite hazardous to the health and should be used with extreme caution. Either the dye area or another separate space is needed for the costume craftwork such as the making of armor, shoes, jewelry, headdresses, and the like. This, too, can be very messy work involving different types of materials, tools, paints, and glues and is better done away from the regular costume construction. (See Figure 8-73.)

Filing cabinets are very convenient for pattern storage and catalogues. Large waste baskets located at regular intervals are a must for filing all those extraneous things that clutter up the corners if not disposed of promptly.

If no office is available in conjunction with the shop a desk will have to provide a headquarters area for the designer and costume shop foreman.

The arrangement of all the equipment that needs to go into a costume shop is seldom easy, often because there is not really enough area for all the equipment and space needed and because such a variety of activities are used when constructing costumes. A logical arrangement should be made and tried with an eye always open for an even better way of doing things. Sometimes it can be quite refreshing to rearrange the shop and try something different.

Figure 8-73 A separate area is necessary for the craft work since it is often messy and uses different types of tools and materials. Pictured are a table-top steamer and hat block.

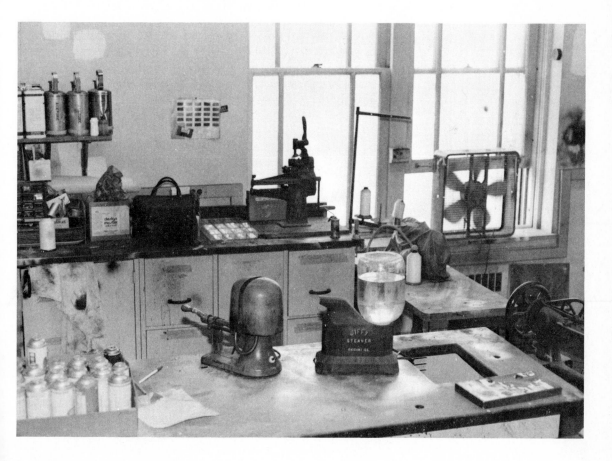

A clear system of methods and procedures is not a physical item used in the shop, but it must be established and understood by all who work in the space. There is seldom only one way to do anything, but there can be a way that is efficient and logical, one that all who are working together know and relate to. These can include work hours, sewing techniques, clean-up procedures, food policies; anything that will make life easier because those working together know what to expect of each other. Large signs full of prohibitions and directives are not recommended, however, for they can produce too much of a "Big Brother is watching you" atmosphere. Careful labeling and small, decorative signs are much friendlier. Remember, too, that because a method has been devised and written down does not mean that it may never be improved. Just as the physical space may sometimes need to be reorganized, new systems can be tried. If they improve the work or the result, so much the better; if not, little has been lost and the mind is in less danger of being locked in a rut because it has had the opportunity to try something different.

Flexibility can often be the key to both happiness and success in all phases of the costume field. One should not be in the profession if one wants a well-ordered world that does not change. Every show is a new challenge. New methods and techniques can continually be tried. It's an area where one can always learn and grow, from the first approach to the production to the last stitch on the costume.

APPENDIX A

A GUIDE TO COSTUME HISTORY

A knowledge of the history of clothing is an essential tool for the costume designer, who must be aware of the basic shapes as they develop and change through the centuries. This guide will help the designer to understand the development of the garments of the Western world. He or she will then be able to go to more detailed sources to do extensive research for a particular project and understand the information that is presented. The guide is not a research source in itself. No section of a book, or any single book, can provide enough information to truly familiarize a designer with an era. The principal forms are presented here to give a starting point. Other sources are suggested that can be used as the designer moves on to an in-depth investigation. This section can also be a brief overview, for no period in history should be thought of as an island but must be considered in the way it develops from that which came before it and in the way it affects that which comes after it.

The designer who begins a serious investigation of a period may discover that the terminology varies from source to source. There are few fixed definitions, and many different languages have contributed to the nomenclature of costumes. Various costume-history books use different terms for the same garment. This is not really a problem. What is important is an ability to comprehend the source material and to interpret it in a sketch that will communicate ideas successfully.

The four basic types of costumes

In terms of construction, all clothes fall into four basic types. These categories delineate the costume by the way it is worn on the body, or cut to fit the body contours.

THE DRAPED COSTUME

In this style the fabric remains in the rectangular shape in which it was woven. The draped costume can provide the wearer with great freedom of movement if the fabric is suspended from the shoulders or waist, or greatly constrain the wearer if the garment is wrapped around the body in such a way that the arms must hold it in position.

THE SEMIFITTED COSTUME

Semifitted costumes are generally cut simply — trousers are loose and shirts, tunics, and dresses are constructed in a T-shape.

THE FITTED COSTUME

The fitted costume, which is more complex to construct than the draped or semifitted, does not appear often in history. This is not because of construction difficulty but because it reveals so much of the actual body shape. The youthful figure is much more suited to this type of treatment than one beginning to show the usual effects of age.

THE ARTIFICIAL SILHOUETTE

A costume can create an artificial silhouette in which the body may be corseted or padded, and the fabric interlined, wired, or stiffened to create the shape of a particular historical fashion. Most costumes for the stage fall into this category because certain construction techniques can better realize the line of the design and create the best shape for the actor.

FOUR BASIC TYPES OF COSTUMES

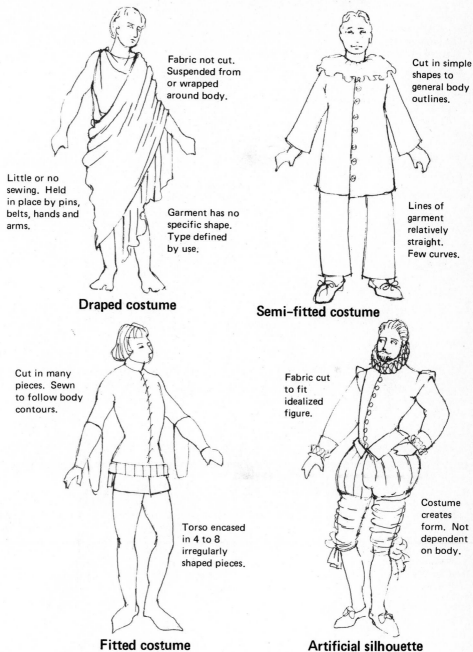

Fabric not cut. Suspended from or wrapped around body.

Little or no sewing. Held in place by pins, belts, hands and arms.

Garment has no specific shape. Type defined by use.

Draped costume

Cut in simple shapes to general body outlines.

Lines of garment relatively straight. Few curves.

Semi-fitted costume

Cut in many pieces. Sewn to follow body contours.

Torso encased in 4 to 8 irregularly shaped pieces.

Fitted costume

Fabric cut to fit idealized figure.

Costume creates form. Not dependent on body.

Artificial silhouette

GREEK

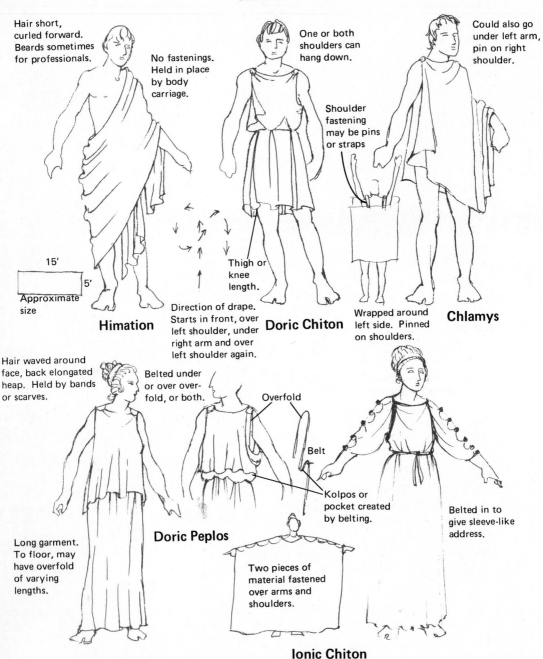

Hair short, curled forward. Beards sometimes for professionals.

No fastenings. Held in place by body carriage.

15'

5'

Approximate size

Himation

Direction of drape. Starts in front, over left shoulder, under right arm and over left shoulder again.

One or both shoulders can hang down.

Shoulder fastening may be pins or straps

Thigh or knee length.

Doric Chiton

Could also go under left arm, pin on right shoulder.

Wrapped around left side. Pinned on shoulders.

Chlamys

Hair waved around face, back elongated heap. Held by bands or scarves.

Belted under or over overfold, or both.

Overfold

Belt

Kolpos or pocket created by belting.

Doric Peplos

Long garment. To floor, may have overfold of varying lengths.

Belted in to give sleeve-like address.

Two pieces of material fastened over arms and shoulders.

Ionic Chiton

Greek costumes

The Greek costume required almost no cutting. Rectangular pieces of fabric were draped to become particular garments, distinguished by the way they were worn. They wrapped around or were suspended from the body, held in place by pins, belts, hands, or arms. A well-formed body was the ideal, with drapery used to enhance its contours.

The Greek "business suit" was the *himation,* an important garment that could be worn alone. Its method of draping could restrict movement, so it was impractical and not used by the lower classes. The *himation* had no fastenings, so was always held in place by the way the body was carried and for men could be the only garment worn. For women, the *himation* was only an outer drape. A simple tunic form could be used to cover the torso and legs of both men and women. For men the most common was the Doric *chiton,* a garment usually thigh- or knee-length with the waist most often belted in, but the girdle was neither ornamental nor too conspicuous. The women's most common tunic form was the Doric *peplos,* which was similar to the *chiton* but much longer. The garment was floor-length and often had an overfold at the top. It was belted at the waist, sometimes both under and over the overfold, and often had a blousing over the belt called the *kolpos.* The Ionic *chiton* was a tunic-type garment worn by both sexes, though principally by women and older men. It was usually made of linen or a crepelike material that was crinkled or finely pleated. The garment was girdled in around the slightly raised waist and over the shoulders in such a manner that it gave the appearance of sleeves, but no sleeves were cut in.

Wools, cottons, and linens in a variety of thicknesses were used in many colors, although only women wore yellow. Dyed and bleached fabrics were worn by the upper classes; the lower classes wore garments in natural tones. The fabrics were decorated with embroidered borders and sometimes all-over spotting. Headbands, necklaces, bracelets, earrings, pins, and narrow functional belts were common. Worked metals, such as bronze, comprised Greek jewelry; few precious stones were used. Sandals were worn outdoors, no footwear was worn indoors, and boots were worn for hunting. Hats were worn only for travel and work, though women often donned veils.

ROMAN

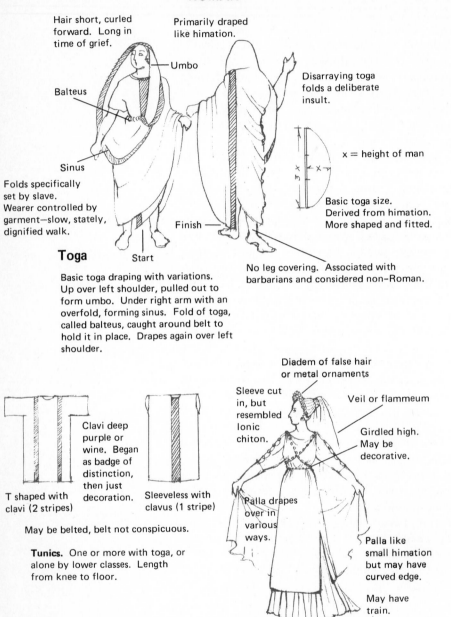

Hair short, curled forward. Long in time of grief.

Primarily draped like himation.

Umbo

Balteus

Disarraying toga folds a deliberate insult.

Sinus

x = height of man

Folds specifically set by slave. Wearer controlled by garment—slow, stately, dignified walk.

Finish

Basic toga size. Derived from himation. More shaped and fitted.

Toga

Start

No leg covering. Associated with barbarians and considered non-Roman.

Basic toga draping with variations. Up over left shoulder, pulled out to form umbo. Under right arm with an overfold, forming sinus. Fold of toga, called balteus, caught around belt to hold it in place. Drapes again over left shoulder.

Clavi deep purple or wine. Began as badge of distinction, then just decoration.

T shaped with clavi (2 stripes)

Sleeveless with clavus (1 stripe)

May be belted, belt not conspicuous.

Tunics. One or more with toga, or alone by lower classes. Length from knee to floor.

Diadem of false hair or metal ornaments

Sleeve cut in, but resembled Ionic chiton.

Veil or flammeum

Girdled high. May be decorative.

Palla drapes over in various ways.

Palla like small himation but may have curved edge.

May have train.

Roman matron in one or more tunics which may or may not have sleeves

Roman costumes

The traditional founding date of Rome is 753 B.C. For the first six or seven centuries, Roman garments were similar to those of the Greeks, although without the same reverence for the well-developed body. The more truly Roman style existed from the first century B.C. to A.D. 200. More garments were used to complete the costume, more cutting was needed, and there were more costume differences between men and women.

The most important male garment was the *toga*: a costume of distinction required in formal situations and worn by all Roman aristocrats and free men. It was denied to peasants and foreigners, though possibly bestowed as an honor on visiting dignitaries. The toga had a curved edge and was cut according to the size of the wearer with the width at the deepest part of the curve equal to the height of the man and the length three times as long. Draped around the body in a fashion similar to the *himation,* the folds were very specifically set in place by a slave to give dignity to the wearer, who was controlled by this garment that required he stand erect and move with a slow stately walk. Disarraying the folds of a gentleman's toga could be a deliberate insult, a slap in the face. The several types of togas varied in color and material, but not in shape, and were worn over a *tunic.* The tunic was usually belted in an inconspicuous manner and might be decorated by a deep wine-colored stripe down the center front or over each shoulder. Women, too, wore one or more tunics, with the top one referred to as the *stola* and the undertunic called the *tunica interiore.* Over these the *palla* might be draped, but not the *toga,* which was exclusively a male garment.

The *lacerna* and *abolla* were short cloaks similar to the short Greek cloak or *chlamys;* the *paludamentum* was a large purple cape of consequence, and the *paenula* was a protective overgarment similar to a modern hooded poncho. Fine wools, cottons, silks, and linens were used, sometimes woven with gold threads. Many real and false jewels were worn. Stones were round, not faceted, so produced a luster, not a sparkle. Sandals were the ordinary footwear both indoors and out and boots might have been seen on men.

Men's hair was worn short and brushed forward over the forehead with no part. Women's hairdressing could be quite elaborate, pulled to the back to elongate the head with the front raised in a diadem of artificial hair or metal ornaments.

Early Christian, Byzantine, and Romanesque costumes

Simple tunic, shirt, and mantle shapes predominated in Europe from the second to the twelfth centuries. The Roman Empire declined and power moved east to Constantinople and the Byzantine Empire. Western Europe was ruled by various barbarian nations who wore simple garments influenced first by Rome, then Byzantium. In the Early Christian era, the second to fifth centuries, the *toga* declined in popularity for regular dress and was worn only as a symbol of office. The *pallium* took its place as an overdrape and was considered something of a badge of learning, for it was associated with the Greek philosophers. The principal tunic styles were the *talaris,* with long tight sleeves; the *dalmatica,* based on the loose, flowing Asiatic tunic; and the loose and sleeveless *colobium.* Overgarments included the *paenula,* the larger *amphibalus,* and the *cuculla,* a rectangular poncholike garment with a hole in the middle for the head. Women's tunics were not particularly graceful as the three basic forms of the *dalmatica* were all rather large and ill-fitting. Jewelry, worn by both sexes, included pearls, polished stones, and goldsmith's work. Cosmetics were in general use.

The center of fashion and civilization moved to Byzantium from the sixth to twelfth centuries. The basic forms developed in the fifth and sixth centuries and stayed much the same throughout the entire period. The new state garment was the *paludamentum,* worn by men only except for the empress. It was seen in practically all colors on high officials, with imperial purple reserved for the emperor. Legcoverings were previously worn only by Asiatics and northern savages, but *hosa* now became part of regular clothing. They were cut and seamed from silk, wool, or linen, not knitted. Because of this, hose that fit the body tightly and smoothly could restrict movement. Women wore garments that were simple in form and rich in fabric. Jewelry had an Oriental influence, employing intricate goldwork with pearls, polished gems, and mosaic stonework. Pearls were sometimes sewn to the garments with gold threads.

Romanesque costumes were seen in Western Europe from the eighth to the twelfth centuries, developing from the simple wraps and skins of the barbarians. They were decorated with embroidered bandings and medallionlike trims, often in a mosaic style, reflecting the Byzantine influence. Both sexes wore layers of tunics and mantles; the quantity and quality of fabric varied with the occasion.

EARLY CHRISTIAN

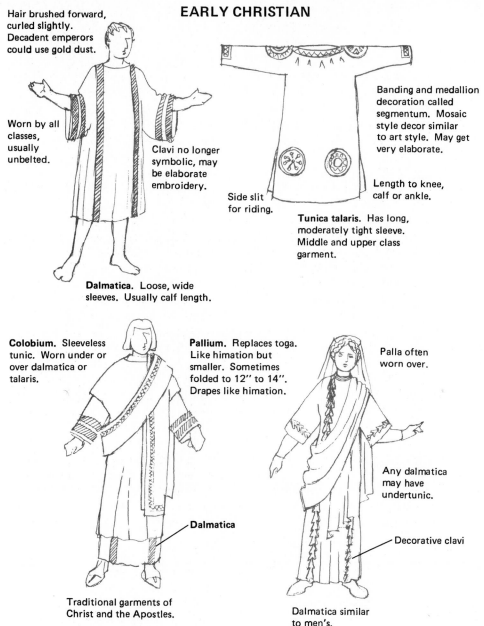

Hair brushed forward, curled slightly. Decadent emperors could use gold dust.

Worn by all classes, usually unbelted.

Clavi no longer symbolic, may be elaborate embroidery.

Dalmatica. Loose, wide sleeves. Usually calf length.

Banding and medallion decoration called segmentum. Mosaic style decor similar to art style. May get very elaborate.

Side slit for riding.

Length to knee, calf or ankle.

Tunica talaris. Has long, moderately tight sleeve. Middle and upper class garment.

Colobium. Sleeveless tunic. Worn under or over dalmatica or talaris.

Pallium. Replaces toga. Like himation but smaller. Sometimes folded to 12" to 14". Drapes like himation.

Dalmatica

Traditional garments of Christ and the Apostles.

Palla often worn over.

Any dalmatica may have undertunic.

Decorative clavi

Dalmatica similar to men's.

EARLY CHRISTIAN

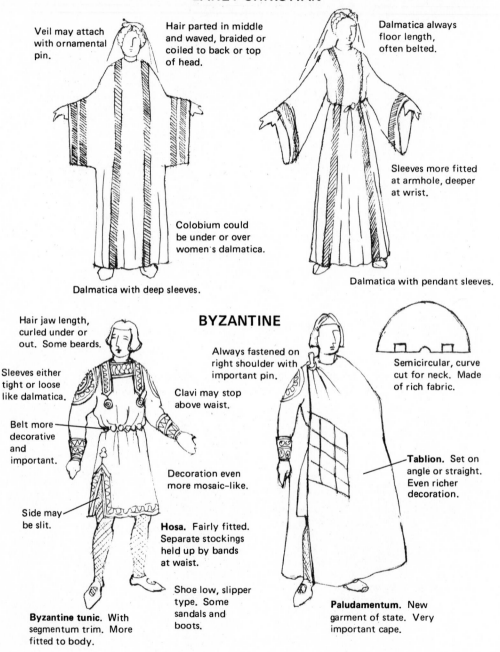

Veil may attach with ornamental pin.

Hair parted in middle and waved, braided or coiled to back or top of head.

Dalmatica always floor length, often belted.

Sleeves more fitted at armhole, deeper at wrist.

Colobium could be under or over women's dalmatica.

Dalmatica with deep sleeves.

Dalmatica with pendant sleeves.

BYZANTINE

Hair jaw length, curled under or out. Some beards.

Sleeves either tight or loose like dalmatica.

Belt more decorative and important.

Side may be slit.

Always fastened on right shoulder with important pin.

Clavi may stop above waist.

Decoration even more mosaic-like.

Semicircular, curve cut for neck. Made of rich fabric.

Tablion. Set on angle or straight. Even richer decoration.

Hosa. Fairly fitted. Separate stockings held up by bands at waist.

Shoe low, slipper type. Some sandals and boots.

Byzantine tunic. With segmentum trim. More fitted to body.

Paludamentum. New garment of state. Very important cape.

BYZANTINE

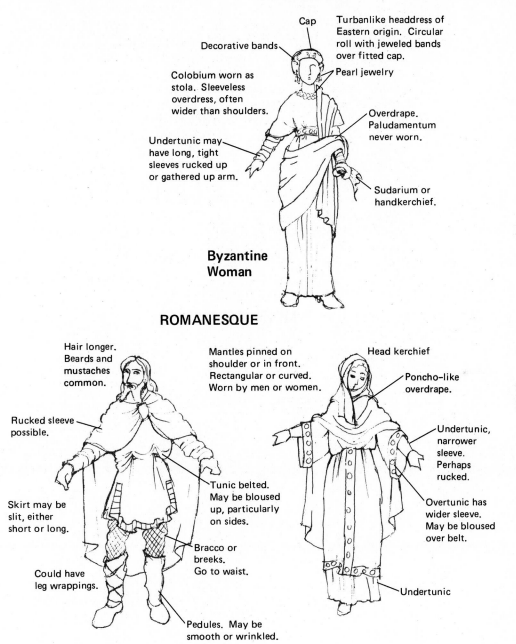

Cap

Turbanlike headdress of Eastern origin. Circular roll with jeweled bands over fitted cap.

Decorative bands

Pearl jewelry

Colobium worn as stola. Sleeveless overdress, often wider than shoulders.

Overdrape. Paludamentum never worn.

Undertunic may have long, tight sleeves rucked up or gathered up arm.

Sudarium or handkerchief.

Byzantine Woman

ROMANESQUE

Hair longer. Beards and mustaches common.

Mantles pinned on shoulder or in front. Rectangular or curved. Worn by men or women.

Head kerchief

Poncho-like overdrape.

Rucked sleeve possible.

Undertunic, narrower sleeve. Perhaps rucked.

Skirt may be slit, either short or long.

Tunic belted. May be bloused up, particularly on sides.

Overtunic has wider sleeve. May be bloused over belt.

Could have leg wrappings.

Bracco or breeks. Go to waist.

Undertunic

Pedules. May be smooth or wrinkled.

Thirteenth-century costumes

The costumes of both sexes in thirteenth-century France and England used an excess of material to reveal a sober grandeur with long, flowing lines. Elaborate bandings were gone and class distinction was revealed in the quantity and quality of fabric. Men's costumes consisted of layers of tunics with new variations developing in the overtunic or supertunic. Mantles were both small and very long and ample. Both sexes were quite adept at handling the large draperies. The most common men's headgear were the coif and hood. Hose were still separate pieces tied to the waist, and a purse was often attached to the belt. Women also wore tunics in a new form called the *kirtle,* shaped more to the body. Stockings were gartered above the knee and close-fitting slipper-style shoes were worn. The hair was parted in the middle and braided around the head or curled in ramshorn fashion on each side. The headdresses often employed veiling, which tended to formally encase the woman.

THIRTEENTH CENTURY

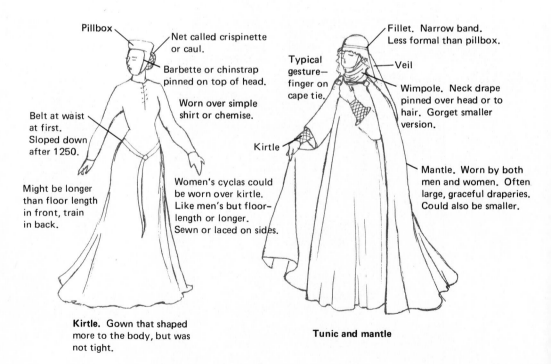

Pillbox

Net called crispinette or caul.

Barbette or chinstrap pinned on top of head.

Worn over simple shirt or chemise.

Belt at waist at first. Sloped down after 1250.

Might be longer than floor length in front, train in back.

Women's cyclas could be worn over kirtle. Like men's but floor-length or longer. Sewn or laced on sides.

Kirtle. Gown that shaped more to the body, but was not tight.

Fillet. Narrow band. Less formal than pillbox.

Typical gesture—finger on cape tie.

Veil

Wimpole. Neck drape pinned over head or to hair. Gorget smaller version.

Kirtle

Mantle. Worn by both men and women. Often large, graceful draperies. Could also be smaller.

Tunic and mantle

THIRTEENTH CENTURY

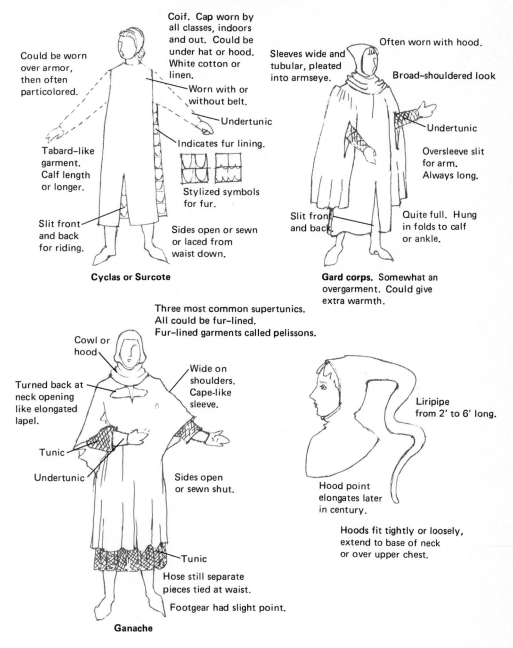

Could be worn over armor, then often particolored.

Coif. Cap worn by all classes, indoors and out. Could be under hat or hood. White cotton or linen.

Worn with or without belt.

Undertunic

Indicates fur lining.

Tabard-like garment. Calf length or longer.

Stylized symbols for fur.

Slit front and back for riding.

Sides open or sewn or laced from waist down.

Cyclas or Surcote

Often worn with hood.

Sleeves wide and tubular, pleated into armseye.

Broad-shouldered look

Undertunic

Oversleeve slit for arm. Always long.

Slit front and back

Quite full. Hung in folds to calf or ankle.

Gard corps. Somewhat an overgarment. Could give extra warmth.

Three most common supertunics. All could be fur-lined. Fur-lined garments called pelissons.

Cowl or hood

Turned back at neck opening like elongated lapel.

Wide on shoulders. Cape-like sleeve.

Tunic

Undertunic

Sides open or sewn shut.

Tunic

Hose still separate pieces tied at waist.

Footgear had slight point.

Ganache

Liripipe from 2' to 6' long.

Hood point elongates later in century.

Hoods fit tightly or loosely, extend to base of neck or over upper chest.

Fourteenth-century costumes

The height of the fourteenth century in England and France, from 1325 to 1375, was a time of extravagant and eccentric styles. Garments were cut and shaped closer to the body as the fitted style gained popularity. Flowing robes were still worn for ceremony and by the elderly, but aristocratic attire accentuated the physique and emphasized youth. The man's *doublet* was now an undergarment padded to give a deep-chested look. The *hosen,* still separate pieces, tied to the waist of the doublet with strings called *estaches* that ended with decorative tips, *poynts.* The process of pulling the hose up tightly to give a smooth, fitted leg was called *trussing the poynts* and produced a tension from shoulder to foot. The *cotehardie* replaced the supertunic for the gentry and was worn over the doublet. This was a tight-fitting garment that conformed quite snugly to the padded chest, waist, and hips, often so tight that a man required assistance getting it on. The cotehardie was belted at the hipline, often with the knightly *girdle,* which consisted of a series of ornamental plaques made of worked metal and jewels. Women also wore a version of the cotehardie that fit the upper body smoothly and fell into fullness. The neckline was moderately low and wide, stressing the horizontal, and the garment could button or lace up the front or back. The new headdress style also emphasized the horizontal, with the hair parted in the middle and brought to the sides of the head, where it was drawn through jeweled metal ornaments that created a square shape. The positioning of the headdress, the bodice neckline, and the weight of the garments encouraged the development of the "Gothic slouch": chin tucked in, shoulders back, and pelvis thrust forward.

Colors were bright, fabrics rich with embroideries, damasks, and silks. Heraldic motifs were common in particolored garments that followed the colors of a noble house. Many decorative elements adorned these costumes. Any edge might be cut in a tonguelike shape called *dagging,* rows of small buttons were regularly seen, and ornamental garters were often worn, sometimes supporting a row of small *folly bells* — which could also be worn on a band over the shoulder.

FOURTEENTH CENTURY

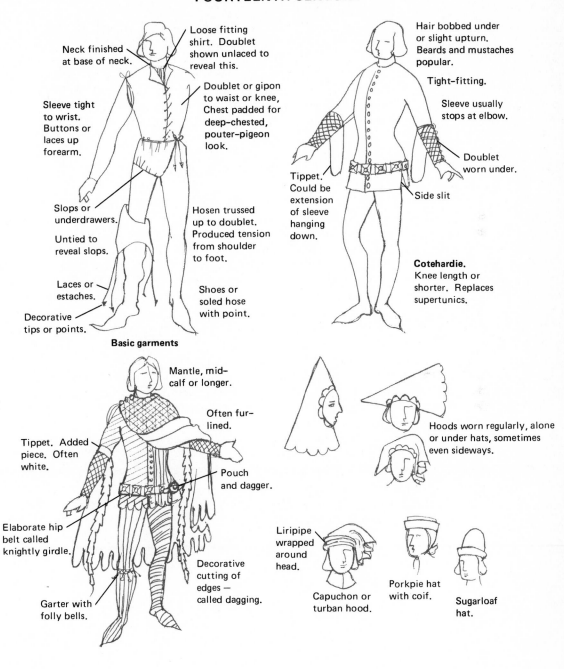

Neck finished at base of neck.

Loose fitting shirt. Doublet shown unlaced to reveal this.

Doublet or gipon to waist or knee, Chest padded for deep-chested, pouter-pigeon look.

Sleeve tight to wrist. Buttons or laces up forearm.

Slops or underdrawers.

Untied to reveal slops.

Hosen trussed up to doublet. Produced tension from shoulder to foot.

Laces or estaches.

Decorative tips or points.

Shoes or soled hose with point.

Basic garments

Hair bobbed under or slight upturn. Beards and mustaches popular.

Tight-fitting.

Sleeve usually stops at elbow.

Doublet worn under.

Tippet. Could be extension of sleeve hanging down.

Side slit

Cotehardie. Knee length or shorter. Replaces supertunics.

Mantle, mid-calf or longer.

Often fur-lined.

Tippet. Added piece. Often white.

Pouch and dagger.

Elaborate hip belt called knightly girdle.

Decorative cutting of edges — called dagging.

Garter with folly bells.

Hoods worn regularly, alone or under hats, sometimes even sideways.

Liripipe wrapped around head.

Capuchon or turban hood.

Porkpie hat with coif.

Sugarloaf hat.

FOURTEENTH CENTURY

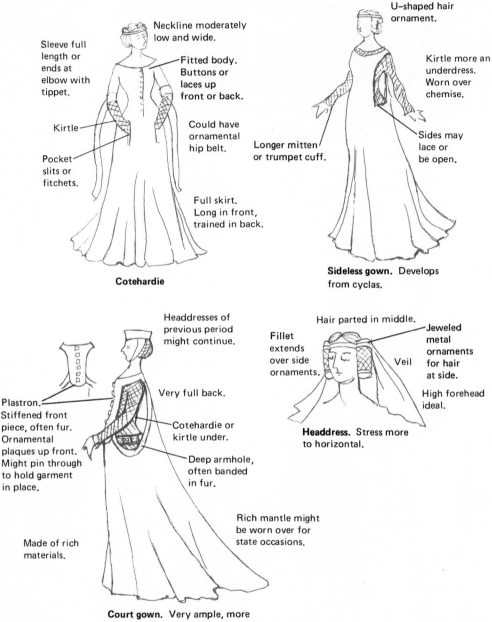

Neckline moderately low and wide.

Sleeve full length or ends at elbow with tippet.

Fitted body. Buttons or laces up front or back.

Kirtle

Could have ornamental hip belt.

Pocket slits or fitchets.

Full skirt. Long in front, trained in back.

Cotehardie

U-shaped hair ornament.

Kirtle more an underdress. Worn over chemise.

Longer mitten or trumpet cuff.

Sides may lace or be open.

Sideless gown. Develops from cyclas.

Headdresses of previous period might continue.

Plastron. Stiffened front piece, often fur. Ornamental plaques up front. Might pin through to hold garment in place.

Very full back.

Cotehardie or kirtle under.

Deep armhole, often banded in fur.

Made of rich materials.

Rich mantle might be worn over for state occasions.

Court gown. Very ample, more elaborate version of sideless gown.

Hair parted in middle.

Fillet extends over side ornaments.

Jeweled metal ornaments for hair at side.

Veil

High forehead ideal.

Headdress. Stress more to horizontal.

Fourteenth- and early-fifteenth-century costumes

The years between 1375 and 1425 saw a transition from the styles of the fourteenth century to those of the fifteenth century. The young still continued to reveal the figure with tight-fitting garments while a stately robe more suitable to the older figure became popular. The man's doublet was now definitely an underdress, stopping at the waist. The body might be cheaper fabric than the sleeves, which showed through the overgarment. Hose took on a new shape to accommodate the rising hemline of the overgarments and were joined together in back and laced up the front with a baglike piece called the *codpiece* tied over the lacing.

The new garment that developed was the *houppeland,* a gown for both men and women that was worn for both state and ordinary occasions. This was a very ample gown that fitted to the shoulders and top of the chest, then fell away in a funnel shape, becoming fuller as it approached the hem. It was caught at the waistline in formal or casual pleats by a belt no longer so ornamental as that of the preceding period. Made of wool, velvet, satin, or damask, the houppeland was usually lined and frequently had dagged edges or fur borders. Hoods were still occasionally worn, as were many styles of caps and hats, including the fez, porkpie, and sugarloaf. The distinctive headwear of the period was the *chaperon.* Shoes that fit close to the ankle, soled hose, or long laced boots were worn, all having a point that could extend out in front of the foot. Occasionally this point became so long that it needed to be attached by a gold chain to the garter. This period was known more for rich fabrics than a great amount of jewelry, but jeweled collars were worn at the base of the neck, or long chains were worn over the shoulders. The pouch and dagger were usual accessories, with folly bells still seen.

Women continued to wear the gowns stylish in the fourteenth century as well as the *houppeland.* The neck opening might reveal the *kirtle* or a more decorative insert piece called the *stomacher.* The silhouette continued to display the "Gothic slouch." Headcovering became even more elaborate, as this time began a period of extraordinary fantasy in headdresses. The accent remained on the horizontal; the hair was generally concealed and sometimes shaved off the forehead, with eyebrows plucked to a thin line or shaved off. Many headdresses were based on the *templers,* metal and jeweled latticeworks that began at the temples and covered the ears. The more intricate headcoverings were common in England and France, while in Italy braided and twisted hairstyles interwoven with jewels were more often seen.

FOURTEENTH TO FIFTEENTH CENTURY

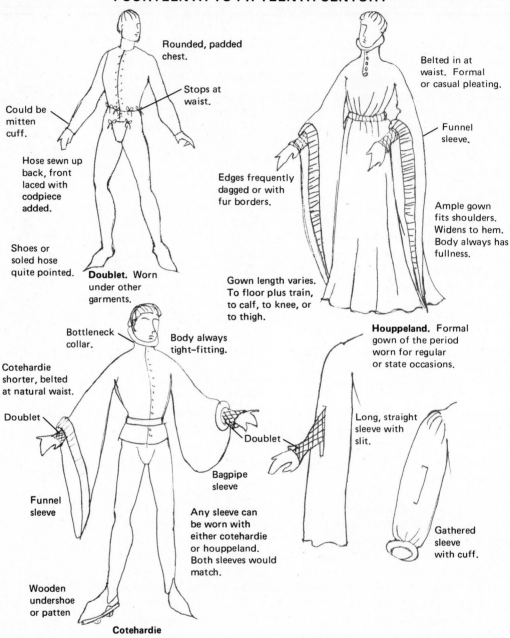

Rounded, padded chest.

Stops at waist.

Could be mitten cuff.

Hose sewn up back, front laced with codpiece added.

Shoes or soled hose quite pointed.

Doublet. Worn under other garments.

Belted in at waist. Formal or casual pleating.

Funnel sleeve.

Edges frequently dagged or with fur borders.

Ample gown fits shoulders. Widens to hem. Body always has fullness.

Gown length varies. To floor plus train, to calf, to knee, or to thigh.

Houppeland. Formal gown of the period worn for regular or state occasions.

Bottleneck collar.

Body always tight-fitting.

Cotehardie shorter, belted at natural waist.

Doublet

Doublet

Long, straight sleeve with slit.

Bagpipe sleeve

Funnel sleeve

Any sleeve can be worn with either cotehardie or houppeland. Both sleeves would match.

Gathered sleeve with cuff.

Wooden undershoe or patten

Cotehardie

FOURTEENTH TO FIFTEENTH CENTURY

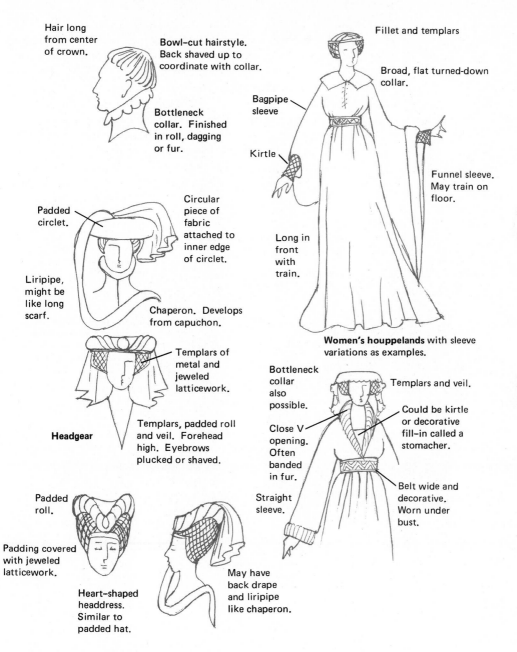

Hair long from center of crown.

Bowl-cut hairstyle. Back shaved up to coordinate with collar.

Bottleneck collar. Finished in roll, dagging or fur.

Fillet and templars

Broad, flat turned-down collar.

Bagpipe sleeve

Kirtle

Funnel sleeve. May train on floor.

Long in front with train.

Padded circlet.

Circular piece of fabric attached to inner edge of circlet.

Liripipe, might be like long scarf.

Chaperon. Develops from capuchon.

Women's houppelands with sleeve variations as examples.

Templars of metal and jeweled latticework.

Headgear

Templars, padded roll and veil. Forehead high. Eyebrows plucked or shaved.

Bottleneck collar also possible.

Templars and veil.

Close V opening. Often banded in fur.

Could be kirtle or decorative fill-in called a stomacher.

Straight sleeve.

Belt wide and decorative. Worn under bust.

Padded roll.

Padding covered with jeweled latticework.

Heart-shaped headdress. Similar to padded hat.

May have back drape and liripipe like chaperon.

Mid- to late-fifteenth-century costumes

The height of this period in France and England was from 1450 to 1485. The elite costume was rich, dignified, elegant, mannered, brilliantly colored, and elaborately patterned. The masculine stress was basically vertical with broad shoulders, deep chest, narrow waist, and fine legs. The feminine stress emphasized the vertical curve with a high waist. Fantastic headdresses were worn. This style began the artificial silhouette that continues more or less to this day. The new man's garment was the *jerkin*, which featured full sleeves to give a broad shoulder. The long gown was similar to the jerkin and remained an upper-class garment until the late sixteenth century. It then added a hood and became an official costume of dignitaries. It is the model for the legal

FIFTEENTH CENTURY

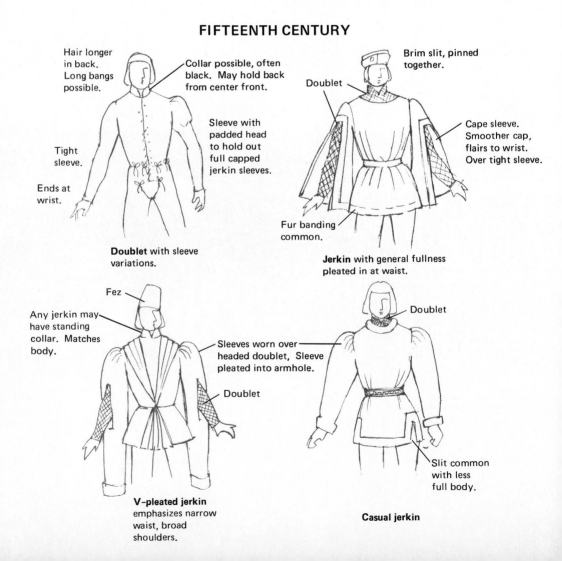

Hair longer in back. Long bangs possible.

Collar possible, often black. May hold back from center front.

Sleeve with padded head to hold out full capped jerkin sleeves.

Tight sleeve.

Ends at wrist.

Doublet with sleeve variations.

Brim slit, pinned together.

Doublet

Cape sleeve. Smoother cap, flairs to wrist. Over tight sleeve.

Fur banding common.

Jerkin with general fullness pleated in at waist.

Fez

Any jerkin may have standing collar. Matches body.

Doublet

Sleeves worn over headed doublet, Sleeve pleated into armhole.

Doublet

V-pleated jerkin emphasizes narrow waist, broad shoulders.

Slit common with less full body.

Casual jerkin

FIFTEENTH CENTURY

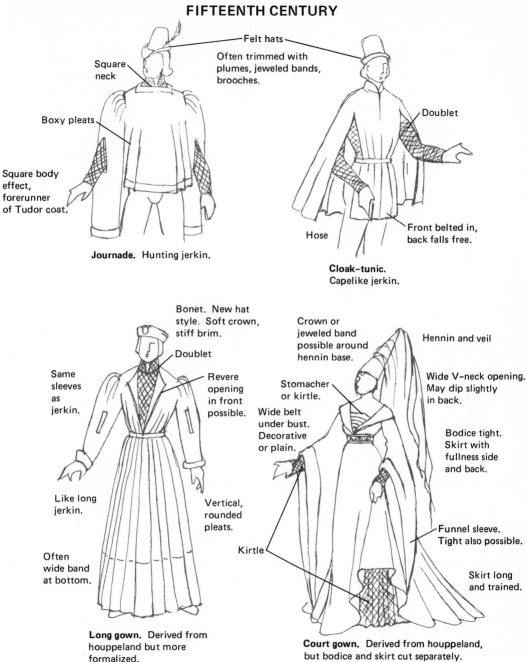

Felt hats

Often trimmed with plumes, jeweled bands, brooches.

Square neck

Boxy pleats

Square body effect, forerunner of Tudor coat.

Journade. Hunting jerkin.

Doublet

Hose

Front belted in, back falls free.

Cloak–tunic. Capelike jerkin.

Bonet. New hat style. Soft crown, stiff brim.

Doublet

Same sleeves as jerkin.

Revere opening in front possible.

Like long jerkin.

Vertical, rounded pleats.

Often wide band at bottom.

Long gown. Derived from houppeland but more formalized.

Crown or jeweled band possible around hennin base.

Hennin and veil

Stomacher or kirtle.

Wide belt under bust. Decorative or plain.

Wide V-neck opening. May dip slightly in back.

Bodice tight. Skirt with fullness side and back.

Kirtle

Funnel sleeve. Tight also possible.

Skirt long and trained.

Court gown. Derived from houppeland, but bodice and skirt cut separately.

and academic gowns. Hose and shoes were as before; the toe point was quite long in the 1560s and 1570s. *Pattens* were worn under the shoe for protection from mud, and delicate walking sticks and gloves were important accessories. The extraordinary part of the woman's style was the *hennin* (also called steeple headdress), which varied from truncated to long and pointed. It was made of stiff, buckramlike material covered with decorative fabric. It had no visible fastening, though the black U-shaped wire on the forehead may have provided support.

FIFTEENTH CENTURY

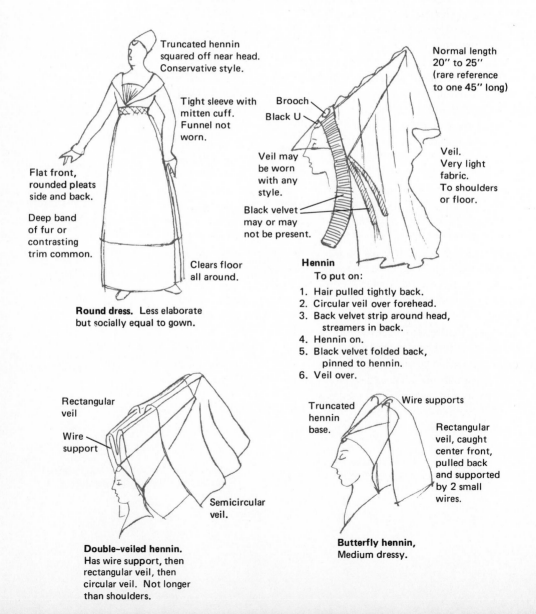

Truncated hennin squared off near head. Conservative style.

Tight sleeve with mitten cuff. Funnel not worn.

Flat front, rounded pleats side and back.

Deep band of fur or contrasting trim common.

Clears floor all around.

Round dress. Less elaborate but socially equal to gown.

Brooch

Black U

Veil may be worn with any style.

Black velvet may or may not be present.

Normal length 20" to 25" (rare reference to one 45" long)

Veil. Very light fabric. To shoulders or floor.

Hennin

To put on:

1. Hair pulled tightly back.
2. Circular veil over forehead.
3. Back velvet strip around head, streamers in back.
4. Hennin on.
5. Black velvet folded back, pinned to hennin.
6. Veil over.

Rectangular veil

Wire support

Semicircular veil.

Double-veiled hennin. Has wire support, then rectangular veil, then circular veil. Not longer than shoulders.

Wire supports

Truncated hennin base.

Rectangular veil, caught center front, pulled back and supported by 2 small wires.

Butterfly hennin, Medium dressy.

Fifteenth- to sixteenth-century costumes

At this time, from about 1485 to 1515, men's costume had a more casual air with less emphasis on the vertical line. The silhouette emphasized an irregular, shorter line; the costume looked a bit as if it were falling apart and the stress started toward the horizontal. Women, however, became even more encased and nunlike. The men's costumes in England and France were very much influenced by the Italian fashions, while women's costumes reflected the feeling of the northern countries.

Men's garments had a generally casual air, with shirts important, low necks, open sleeves, loose casual coats, and long flowing hair. The doublet now became street dress, often worn merely with hose and perhaps a short cape. For the most part, padding was gone from the chest. The shirt became more important now, for much more of it was seen. Made of fine cottons or silks, it was cut full and gathered into the neck opening, which was often square, and into bands at the wrists. Hose became more decorative, with particoloring, and the upper part, around the hips, was often trimmed in contrasting braid. This was the first sign of what was to become a separation of the upper leg covering and lower leg covering. The hose were trussed up to the doublet with very decorative lacings and the shirt was sometimes allowed to puff out between the two garments. An important decorative element was called *cuttes*, the slashing of the outer garment to allow the shirt or other material (such as lining fabric at the hips) to show through. The ornamental costume feeling was enhanced by heavy metal and jeweled shoulder collars, massive chains, brooches, pendants, and rings.

The basic silhouette of the women's garments changed from a mannered elegance and a striking effect to one that was restrained, reserved, and subdued. Before there had been an upward, outward movement; now it was tightly encased, closing in. Under the gown the woman wore a stiffened corset, a lightweight shift, and petticoats or underdresses with the top one made of rich fabric since it would show as the skirt was lifted to move. The boned hoop, which was in common use by the Spanish nobility, began to be seen in France and England. Hair was generally parted in the middle, then pulled back, perhaps with a slight wave over the temples, to be covered by a headdress that could be quite enclosing.

FIFTEENTH TO SIXTEENTH CENTURY

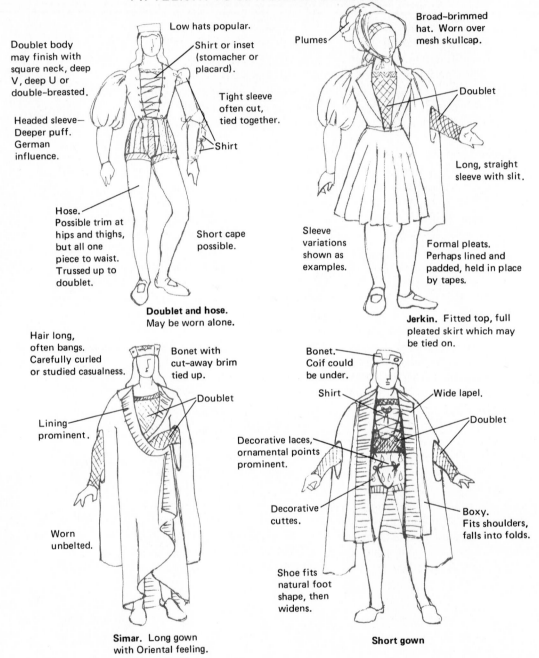

Low hats popular.

Shirt or inset (stomacher or placard).

Doublet body may finish with square neck, deep V, deep U or double-breasted.

Tight sleeve often cut, tied together.

Headed sleeve— Deeper puff. German influence.

Shirt

Hose. Possible trim at hips and thighs, but all one piece to waist. Trussed up to doublet.

Short cape possible.

Doublet and hose. May be worn alone.

Broad–brimmed hat. Worn over mesh skullcap.

Plumes

Doublet

Long, straight sleeve with slit.

Sleeve variations shown as examples.

Formal pleats. Perhaps lined and padded, held in place by tapes.

Jerkin. Fitted top, full pleated skirt which may be tied on.

Hair long, often bangs. Carefully curled or studied casualness.

Bonet with cut–away brim tied up.

Doublet

Lining prominent.

Worn unbelted.

Simar. Long gown with Oriental feeling.

Bonet. Coif could be under.

Shirt

Wide lapel.

Doublet

Decorative laces, ornamental points prominent.

Decorative cuttes.

Boxy. Fits shoulders, falls into folds.

Shoe fits natural foot shape, then widens.

Short gown

FIFTEENTH TO SIXTEENTH CENTURY

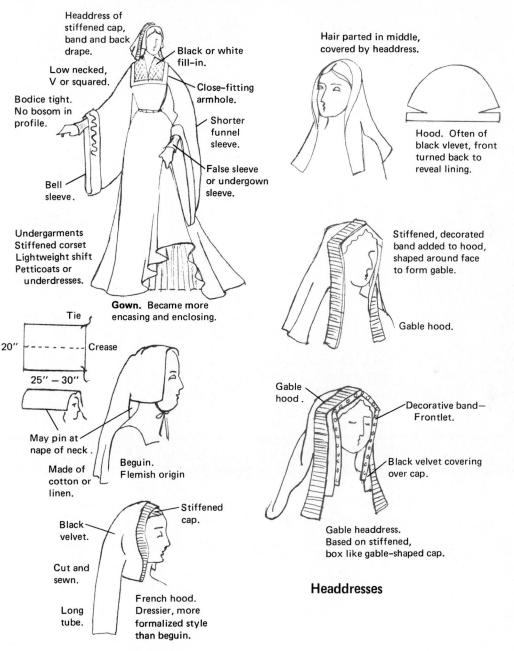

Headdress of stiffened cap, band and back drape.

Black or white fill-in.

Low necked, V or squared.

Close-fitting armhole.

Bodice tight. No bosom in profile.

Shorter funnel sleeve.

False sleeve or undergown sleeve.

Bell sleeve.

Undergarments Stiffened corset Lightweight shift Petticoats or underdresses.

Gown. Became more encasing and enclosing.

Tie

20"   Crease

25" — 30"

May pin at nape of neck.

Made of cotton or linen.

Beguin. Flemish origin

Stiffened cap.

Black velvet.

Cut and sewn.

Long tube.

French hood. Dressier, more formalized style than beguin.

Hair parted in middle, covered by headdress.

Hood. Often of black vlevet, front turned back to reveal lining.

Stiffened, decorated band added to hood, shaped around face to form gable.

Gable hood.

Gable hood.

Decorative band— Frontlet.

Black velvet covering over cap.

Gable headdress. Based on stiffened, box like gable-shaped cap.

Headdresses

Early sixteenth century — Tudor costumes

The period from 1515 to 1545 in France and England was one of German influence. Fairly clear outlines gave a feeling of solidity and bulkiness. There was a squareness and breadth for men and a cone shape for women. The gentlemen were massive, strong, broad-shouldered, and arrogantly masculine. Women became enclosed, inactive, and protected.

The men's costume tended to extend away from the body on the horizontal plane. The doublet again became an undergarment and was not worn alone. It might have been padded, though men seemed to follow the trend set by Henry VIII and were heavier. Trunk hose developed from the prominent decoration around the hips of the hose. The embroidered bands became separate pieces called *panes* that opened to reveal the contrasting material beneath. The codpiece was still present, but no longer functional. It was now padded and trimmed, and considered almost obscene in its own time. Panes, lining, and codpiece were permanently attached to the full hose underneath, with and all tied to the doublet as one unit. More and more embroidered banding was used as a decorative element on the costume, and *cuttes*, commonly seen, were more formally set, with the backing material carefully puffed out, surrounded by embroidery and jewels. Hair was bobbed and moderately long until the 1530s, then cut short till past the end of the century. Beards were squared off and mustaches followed natural growth. Hats were characteristically flat, with feathers following the horizontal line. Heavy, wide, jeweled collars were very common, worn out on the shoulders further to stress the horizontal. Jewels were cut and faceted to add sparkle to the costume.

The women's costume continued many of the shapes used in the previous period, but they seem frozen into a rigid form. Much stiffening and unyielding underpinnings produced a figure that moved as if on wheels, with little flow to either fabric or body. The rigid effect of the female costume owed a great deal to the conical hoop or Spanish *farthingale*, and the *corset*, which was stiffened with bone or even constructed of thin iron bands made in two parts and hinged on the side. Hair was still encased by the headdress.

EARLY SIXTEENTH CENTURY—TUDOR

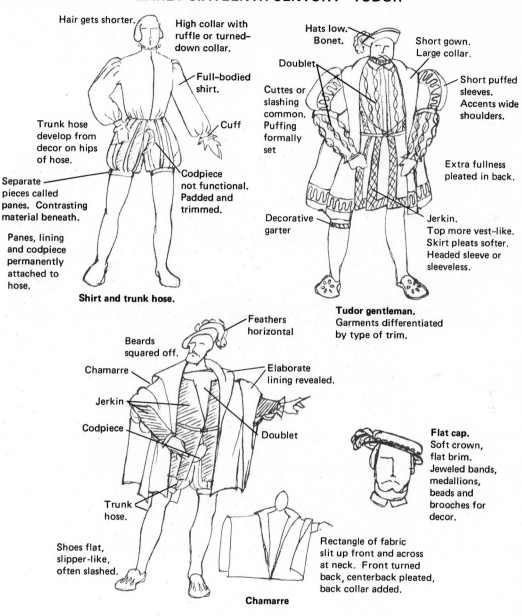

Hair gets shorter.

High collar with ruffle or turned-down collar.

Full-bodied shirt.

Cuff

Trunk hose develop from decor on hips of hose.

Codpiece not functional. Padded and trimmed.

Separate pieces called panes. Contrasting material beneath.

Panes, lining and codpiece permanently attached to hose.

Shirt and trunk hose.

Hats low. Bonet.

Doublet

Cuttes or slashing common. Puffing formally set

Short gown. Large collar.

Short puffed sleeves. Accents wide shoulders.

Extra fullness pleated in back.

Decorative garter

Jerkin. Top more vest-like. Skirt pleats softer. Headed sleeve or sleeveless.

Tudor gentleman. Garments differentiated by type of trim.

Feathers horizontal

Beards squared off.

Chamarre

Jerkin

Codpiece

Elaborate lining revealed.

Doublet

Trunk hose.

Shoes flat, slipper-like, often slashed.

Flat cap. Soft crown, flat brim. Jeweled bands, medallions, beads and brooches for decor.

Rectangle of fabric slit up front and across at neck. Front turned back, centerback pleated, back collar added.

Chamarre

EARLY SIXTEENTH CENTURY—TUDOR

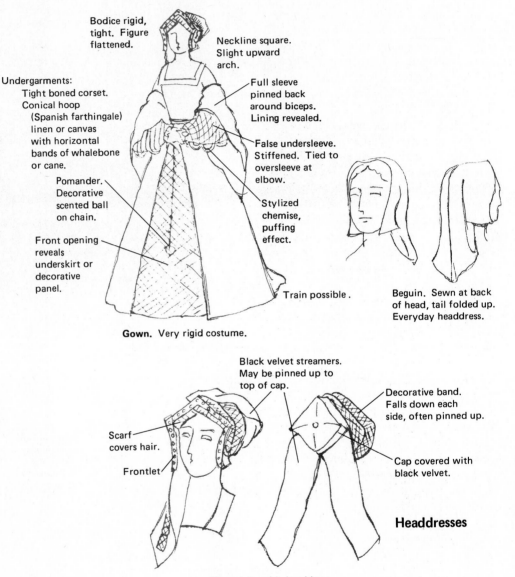

Bodice rigid, tight. Figure flattened.

Neckline square. Slight upward arch.

Undergarments:
Tight boned corset.
Conical hoop
(Spanish farthingale)
linen or canvas
with horizontal
bands of whalebone
or cane.

Full sleeve pinned back around biceps. Lining revealed.

False undersleeve. Stiffened. Tied to oversleeve at elbow.

Pomander. Decorative scented ball on chain.

Stylized chemise, puffing effect.

Front opening reveals underskirt or decorative panel.

Train possible.

Beguin. Sewn at back of head, tail folded up. Everyday headdress.

Gown. Very rigid costume.

Black velvet streamers. May be pinned up to top of cap.

Decorative band. Falls down each side, often pinned up.

Scarf covers hair.

Cap covered with black velvet.

Frontlet

Headdresses

New–style gable headdress. Based on stiffened cap.

Mid-sixteenth to early seventeenth century — Elizabethan costumes

Western European costume now followed the lead of Spain, thus the Elizabethan style was one of Spanish influence. As Spain declined as a world power so did its influence wane in clothing styles. The Elizabethan costume developed from 1545 to 1570, was in full flower from 1570 to 1595, and declined from 1595 to 1620. The chief characteristic was extreme rigidity achieved by *bombast,* the padding used to fill out garments. Bombast also included all the stiffening, padding, starching, and wiring used to achieve the epitome of the artificial silhouette. The costume created a shape of its own. As the period declined, the bombast declined and the silhouette wilted.

The ideal gentleman once again had a vertical emphasis, accenting a narrow waist, broad shoulders, and long legs. The shapely leg was now more readily enhanced by the knitted stocking, available because of the invention of the stocking frame. These fit the leg well and still allowed flexibility. The focal point of the costume was the *ruff* worn at the neck. Overgowns similar to academic gowns were sometimes donned for ceremonial or professional reasons. Gauntlets and regular gloves were commonly worn, ornamental handkerchiefs and delicate walking sticks carried, and masks used by both sexes for incognito situations. The military steel collar, or *gorget,* was sometimes seen with civilian dress. Elaborate jewelry was worn and gems, both false and real, covered garments and hats. Long boots were used for riding.

The rigid woman's costume emphasized a frontal perspective. Bombast created the ideal stiffness and a gliding walk was used, so the fabric had very little flow or movement. The corset was extremely confining and gave the foundation for the long-waisted bodice to extend to a deep point in the center front. The three principal skirt shapes were supported by the funnel farthingale, the cartwheel farthingale, or the bolster and petticoats. Pendant sleeves could be attached behind the regular sleeve for ceremonial occasions. An asymmetrical jewel-and-sash arrangement might be draped over the bodice. Quite a bit of makeup was used.

MID-SIXTEENTH TO EARLY SEVENTEENTH CENTURY—ELIZABETHAN

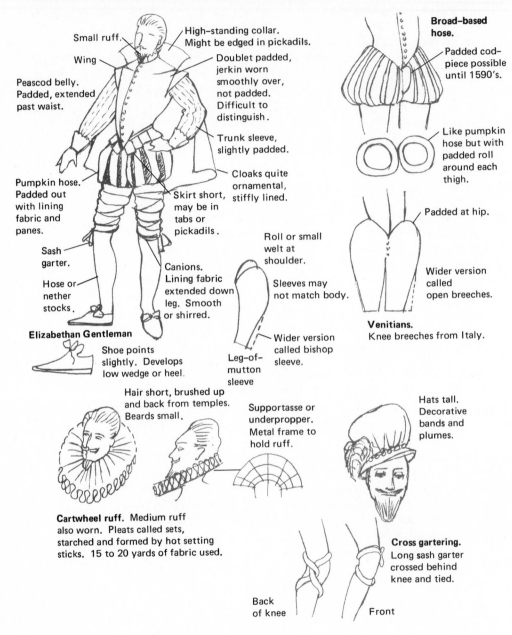

Small ruff.

Wing

Peascod belly.
Padded, extended
past waist.

High-standing collar.
Might be edged in pickadils.

Doublet padded,
jerkin worn
smoothly over,
not padded.
Difficult to
distinguish.

Trunk sleeve,
slightly padded.

Cloaks quite
ornamental,
stiffly lined.

Skirt short,
may be in
tabs or
pickadils.

Pumpkin hose.
Padded out
with lining
fabric and
panes.

Sash
garter.

Hose or
nether
stocks.

Canions.
Lining fabric
extended down
leg. Smooth
or shirred.

Elizabethan Gentleman

Shoe points
slightly. Develops
low wedge or heel.

Roll or small
welt at
shoulder.

Sleeves may
not match body.

Wider version
called bishop
sleeve.

Leg-of-
mutton
sleeve

**Broad-based
hose.**

Padded cod-
piece possible
until 1590's.

Like pumpkin
hose but with
padded roll
around each
thigh.

Padded at hip.

Wider version
called
open breeches.

Venitians.
Knee breeches from Italy.

Hair short, brushed up
and back from temples.
Beards small.

Supportasse or
underpropper.
Metal frame to
hold ruff.

Hats tall.
Decorative
bands and
plumes.

Cartwheel ruff. Medium ruff
also worn. Pleats called sets,
starched and formed by hot setting
sticks. 15 to 20 yards of fabric used.

Cross gartering.
Long sash garter
crossed behind
knee and tied.

Back
of knee

Front

MID-SIXTEENTH TO EARLY SEVENTEENTH CENTURY—ELIZABETHAN

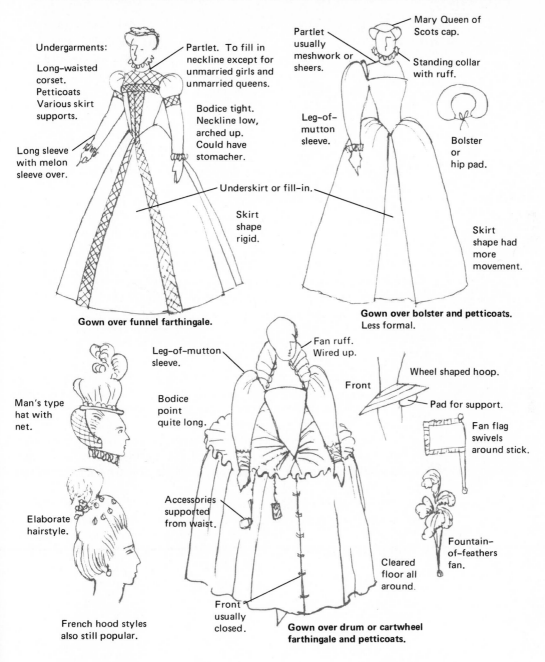

Undergarments:

Long-waisted corset. Petticoats Various skirt supports.

Long sleeve with melon sleeve over.

Partlet. To fill in neckline except for unmarried girls and unmarried queens.

Bodice tight. Neckline low, arched up. Could have stomacher.

Underskirt or fill-in.

Skirt shape rigid.

Gown over funnel farthingale.

Partlet usually meshwork or sheers.

Mary Queen of Scots cap.

Standing collar with ruff.

Leg-of-mutton sleeve.

Bolster or hip pad.

Skirt shape had more movement.

Gown over bolster and petticoats. Less formal.

Man's type hat with net.

Elaborate hairstyle.

French hood styles also still popular.

Leg-of-mutton sleeve.

Bodice point quite long.

Accessories supported from waist.

Front usually closed.

Fan ruff. Wired up.

Front

Wheel shaped hoop.

Pad for support.

Fan flag swivels around stick.

Cleared floor all around.

Fountain-of-feathers fan.

Gown over drum or cartwheel farthingale and petticoats.

Early seventeenth century — Cavalier costumes

The clear, rigid Elizabethan outline became more broken and casual in the Cavalier period, especially for men. The feeling was domestic rather than formal. Spain's domination of the fashion world diminished with its loss of power and France began to regain prestige. Fashion centered in Paris and stayed there to a degree to the present day, though England led in men's clothes after the eighteenth century. The Cavalier period, from 1620 to 1655, showed the influence of the Thirty Years' War fought in Europe during much of this time. Civilian dress reflected the constant presence of soldiers. During the first twenty years of the century, as the Elizabethan costume declined, the shapes stayed much the same but the feeling of bombast was less evident. The Cavalier period seemed to have the starch taken out of it; the costume had a flow, a movement not allowed to happen previously, a feeling for "swashbuckle" associated with the gentleman soldier.

The doublet became easy-fitting and slightly high-waisted, with little or no padding except over the stomach, where belly pieces were the interlinings used to help the garment retain its shape. The jerkin was no longer fashionable and was discarded by 1630. The only remnant was the leather jerkin, or *buff coat,* which was of military origin and popular until about 1665. Many types of breeches were worn during this time, though the style that might be thought most typical was the long-legged breeches or *Spanish hose.* Two forms not illustrated were *trunk slops,* which were short and quite full, and *open breeches,* which were like long-legged breeches but wider at the knee. Collars and cuffs came in various sizes and shapes but were usually fairly large and decorative. One new form was the *whisk* or *golilla,* a standing-band type with embroidery and lace that lay flat on the tilted wire frame, or underpropper. The image of the dashing gentleman soldier was enhanced by his accessories, such as sword, baldric, broad military sash, gorget, and gauntlets.

The women of the Cavalier period had a soft, round line and — though the corset was still present — the feeling of extreme rigidity was gone. The waist was raised and the neckline featured a low décolletage with the bosom pushed up by the corset to create a cleavage that was very much a part of the costume. Elaborate lace collars were also quite prominent. Hairstyles began to have a horizontal feeling.

EARLY SEVENTEENTH CENTURY—CAVALIER

Large, broad-brimmed hats. Ostrich plumes.

Love lock.

Doublet. Easy fitting. Slightly high waisted.

Capes long, full, fluid. Worn with swashbuckle.

Shirt full.

Baldric to support sword.

Moderate sleeve, open in front.

Sword

Long-legged breeches most typical. Pleats in seat.

Sash garter.

Cavalier gentleman. With leg variations.

Spur or gingler.

Ribbon loops.

Lace-topped boot hose.

Bucket-top boot.

Standing collar

Wing and shoulder line droops.

Waist straighter, slight point. Padding gone.

Fitted forearm.

Skirt may have side and back vents.

Doublet with slashed chest and sleeves. Could reveal shirt or lining.

Hair longer. casual curls.

Face clean-shaven or small beard and mustache.

Falling ruff. More casual.

Military gorget under collar.

Large falling band collar, lace edge.

Doublet with implied high waist.

Hand fall or cuff.

Fuller breeches. To above or below knee.

Galligaskins or cloak-bag breeches.

Dress shoe for formal occasions. Might have an elaborate shoe rose.

Spur leather.

Boots most popular footwear. Developed from higher boot — folded down, then back up. Wide top encouraged rolling gait.

EARLY SEVENTEENTH CENTURY—CAVALIER

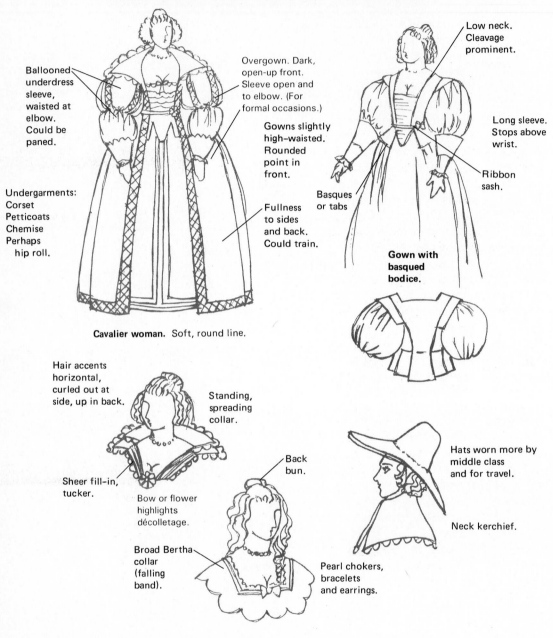

Ballooned underdress sleeve, waisted at elbow. Could be paned.

Overgown. Dark, open-up front. Sleeve open and to elbow. (For formal occasions.)

Gowns slightly high-waisted. Rounded point in front.

Undergarments:
Corset
Petticoats
Chemise
Perhaps
  hip roll.

Fullness to sides and back. Could train.

Cavalier woman. Soft, round line.

Low neck. Cleavage prominent.

Long sleeve. Stops above wrist.

Ribbon sash.

Basques or tabs

Gown with basqued bodice.

Hair accents horizontal, curled out at side, up in back.

Standing, spreading collar.

Sheer fill-in, tucker.

Bow or flower highlights décolletage.

Back bun.

Broad Bertha collar (falling band).

Pearl chokers, bracelets and earrings.

Hats worn more by middle class and for travel.

Neck kerchief.

Mid-seventeenth century — petticoat breeches

The forms of the garments worn by the men of 1655 to 1680 were fairly simple, but a gentleman could become almost useless because of the profusion of detail applied to the shapes, particularly in the French court. The doublet became quite short and skimpy, in some instances almost a bolero. The shorter sleeve could be either plain, open on the front seam, or paned. Much of the shirt could show, so it was very full and made of fine fabric, often with ruffles at the wrist and down the front. Legs might be covered by the Spanish hose, open breeches that were now even looser around the knee, or *petticoat breeches*. Baggy underbreeches that gathered into a band above the knee could be worn with the latter.

The coat and vest, prototypes of those worn today, began to be seen in the mid 1660s. The coat had very little shaping as it fit the shoulders and tapered out somewhat to hang loosely to about the knee. It was first worn over the doublet, then the vest. Cloaks were less commonly seen after 1670 and were often replaced by an overcoat. Boots were less fashionable and worn more for riding. The shoe had a high, square heel, square toe, and squared tongue. Hair was worn long, to the shoulders, till about 1660, when wigs came into fashion and were an essential part of dress. If a gentleman was not rich enough to have a wig he would dress his hair to look like one. The most popular color was blond, appropriate for those living in the court of the Sun King, Louis XIV. In the boudoir turbans were worn over shaved heads. Hats were fairly large and plumed, but not as dashing as before. As the wigs got bigger the hats became less important and were often carried. In addition to all the trim, accessories might include gloves, handkerchiefs, sashes, mirrors, combs, snuff boxes, beauty patches, and paint. There was, however, very little jewelry.

The women of this time were rather regulated and subdued compared to their male counterparts. The bodice was again long-waisted, close-fitted, and boned with a medium-low, horizontal neckline that had a somewhat off-the-shoulder look. The skirt was closely gathered in small, carefully set pleats that flared out at the hips and provided fullness at the sides and back. The pearl choker necklace and drop earrings continued to be the most popular jewelry, and a few ribbon loops might be used. The fabrics used by women did tend to be more ornamental, since less trim was added.

MID–SEVENTEENTH CENTURY — PETTICOAT BREECHES

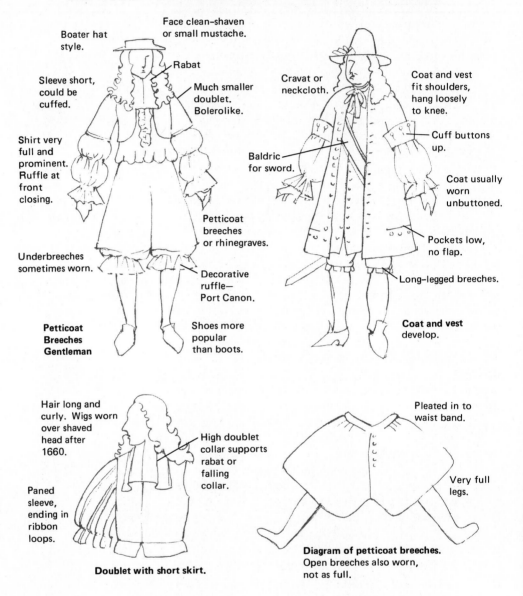

Boater hat style.

Face clean–shaven or small mustache.

Rabat

Sleeve short, could be cuffed.

Much smaller doublet. Bolerolike.

Shirt very full and prominent. Ruffle at front closing.

Petticoat breeches or rhinegraves.

Underbreeches sometimes worn.

Decorative ruffle— Port Canon.

Petticoat Breeches Gentleman

Shoes more popular than boots.

Cravat or neckcloth.

Coat and vest fit shoulders, hang loosely to knee.

Cuff buttons up.

Baldric for sword.

Coat usually worn unbuttoned.

Pockets low, no flap.

Long–legged breeches.

Coat and vest develop.

Hair long and curly. Wigs worn over shaved head after 1660.

High doublet collar supports rabat or falling collar.

Paned sleeve, ending in ribbon loops.

Doublet with short skirt.

Pleated in to waist band.

Very full legs.

Diagram of petticoat breeches. Open breeches also worn, not as full.

MID-SEVENTEENTH CENTURY—PETTICOAT BREECHES

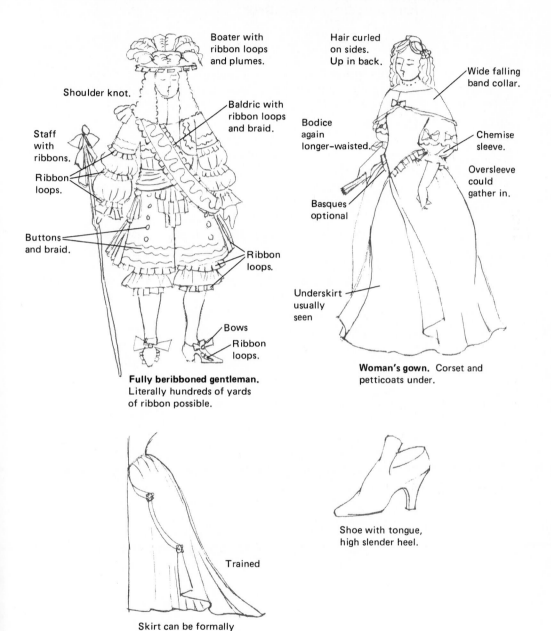

Boater with ribbon loops and plumes.

Shoulder knot.

Staff with ribbons.

Ribbon loops.

Buttons and braid.

Baldric with ribbon loops and braid.

Ribbon loops.

Bows

Ribbon loops.

Fully beribboned gentleman. Literally hundreds of yards of ribbon possible.

Hair curled on sides. Up in back.

Wide falling band collar.

Bodice again longer-waisted.

Chemise sleeve.

Oversleeve could gather in.

Basques optional

Underskirt usually seen

Woman's gown. Corset and petticoats under.

Trained

Skirt can be formally caught back.

Shoe with tongue, high slender heel.

Late seventeenth to early eighteenth century — Restoration costumes

The Restoration costume, prominent from about 1680 to 1715, had a heavy opulance and deep, rich colors, similar to the Baroque art of the time. The primary garments for men were the coat, vest, and breeches, which became much more tailored. The art of tailoring developed during this century as clothes were cut and interfaced to maintain a particular shape, no longer relying on the heavy padding and bombast of undergarments to create the form.

The coat was now more fitted and conformed to the chest, defined the waist, then flared out over the hips in pleats that were controlled at the top by stitching hidden by a large button. The vest was cut similarly to the coat though the back panel, usually hidden, could be much shorter than the front and might be made of cheaper material. The shirt was not nearly so prominent in this costume and was often only seen in the heavy lace ruffle that came to the knuckles. Breeches were now closer-fitting, though still with fullness in the seat, and came to below the knee where they buttoned, buckled, or tied. Capes were not as popular as before; when worn they were full, to the knee or calf, and often had rounded collars. Fabrics varied from simple wools to very rich brocades. Rich bandings were used to edge the front opening, cuffs, and pockets. Baldrics, hip sashes, and muffs were common, and snuff was used extensively, causing spots of discoloration on the jabot.

Women's garments stressed the vertical and took on a feeling of authority and aggressiveness. A bustle was added to silhouette and a great deal of ornamentation was used. The long-waisted bodice was worn over a very tight corset and the stomacher in the center front extended to a point at the waist. The gathered and trained full overskirt was often turned back and fastened to reveal the rich lining or the inside of fabric that had been woven to be reversible. The primary headdress was the *fontange*. The costume was one of rich embroidery but used very little jewelry, with pear-shaped pearl earrings and a single strand of pearls at the neck the most popular. Very elegant aprons were sometimes worn and the folding fan was a definite part of the ensemble. Parasols and muffs were carried outdoors and the mask was always appropriate for any incognito situation. Elbow length gloves complemented the shorter sleeve.

LATE SEVENTEENTH TO EARLY EIGHTEENTH CENTURY—RESTORATION

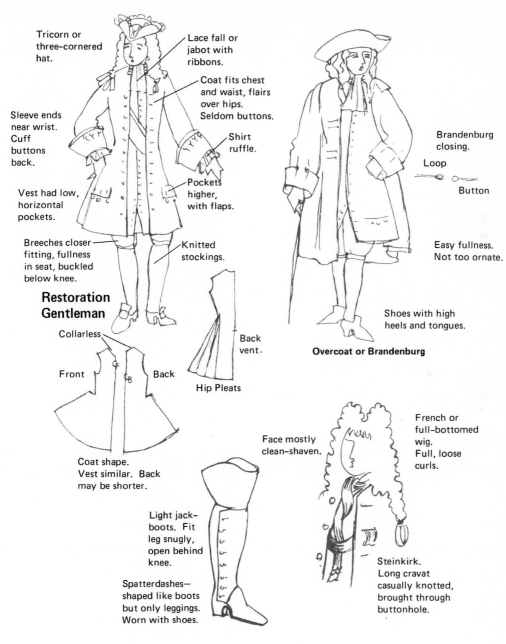

Tricorn or three-cornered hat.

Lace fall or jabot with ribbons.

Coat fits chest and waist, flairs over hips. Seldom buttons.

Sleeve ends near wrist. Cuff buttons back.

Shirt ruffle.

Vest had low, horizontal pockets.

Pockets higher, with flaps.

Breeches closer fitting, fullness in seat, buckled below knee.

Knitted stockings.

Restoration Gentleman

Collarless

Front   Back

Back vent.

Hip Pleats

Coat shape. Vest similar. Back may be shorter.

Brandenburg closing.

Loop

Button

Easy fullness. Not too ornate.

Shoes with high heels and tongues.

Overcoat or Brandenburg

French or full-bottomed wig. Full, loose curls.

Face mostly clean-shaven.

Light jack-boots. Fit leg snugly, open behind knee.

Spatterdashes—shaped like boots but only leggings. Worn with shoes.

Steinkirk. Long cravat casually knotted, brought through buttonhole.

LATE SEVENTEENTH TO EARLY EIGHTEENTH CENTURY—RESTORATION

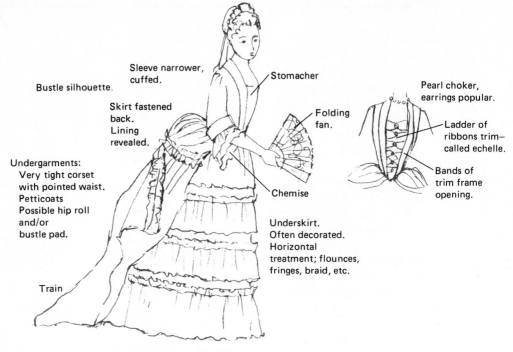

Bustle silhouette.

Sleeve narrower, cuffed.

Stomacher

Skirt fastened back. Lining revealed.

Folding fan.

Undergarments:
Very tight corset with pointed waist.
Petticoats
Possible hip roll and/or bustle pad.

Chemise

Pearl choker, earrings popular.

Ladder of ribbons trim—called echelle.

Bands of trim frame opening.

Underskirt.
Often decorated.
Horizontal treatment; flounces, fringes, braid, etc.

Train

Woman's gown. Vertical stress.

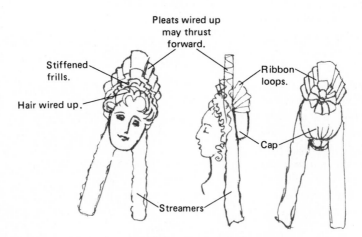

Pleats wired up may thrust forward.

Stiffened frills.

Hair wired up.

Ribbon loops.

Cap

Streamers

Fontange. Primary headdress.

The first half of the eighteenth century — Rococo costumes

The heavy Baroque grandeur gave way to the more informal, intimate atmosphere of the Rococo with its lighter, buoyant silks and cottons in subtle and lighthearted colors. The general mood was much more soft and reclining as opposed to the heavy, upright opulence of the period before. The basic thrust of this early-eighteenth-century feeling continued to about 1755, though there were no really striking changes until closer to the end of the century. Social pressures at this time had a strong influence on the clothing, for the lower classes became less satisfied with their lot and sought to climb the ladder of society. The dress of the higher ranks was still restrictive, but as the result of social changes there was more mobility of forms between the classes. The dress coat was made of linens, silks, velvets, and brocades, sometimes shot with metallic threads. The frock coat was mostly wool. Cloaks were occasionally worn, often with a collar, buttons down the front, and slits for arms. Queue wigs became popular, so named because the back hair was longer and controlled in a particular way. For example, the back hair of the bag wig was caught in a black fabric bag. The front hair of the wig, called the foretop or toupée, was brushed back from the forehead and perhaps padded up a bit. The side hair might be curled or frizzed in front of the ears. Another non-queue style was the bob wig with bushy, curly hair that came to the jawline or shoulder. Wigs were made of human or animal hair and usually powdered white or gray for dress. A gentleman might style his own hair, but this was not the fashionable thing to do. Common accessories included gloves, sashes, handkerchiefs, muffs, swords, canes, watches, and snuff boxes. Women's garments were also made of more light-weight fabrics and became softer and less formal, with a horizontal feeling. Short capes or large scarves were the most common type of outer garments. Accessories included elegant aprons, ribbon neck bands, ribbon bows, narrow belts, elbow-length gloves, small muffs, handkerchiefs, and folding fans. Necklaces of three or four rows of pearls or gems might be worn at the neck. Makeup and beauty patches were prominent. Outdoors the lady could wear hoods or hats. Shoes were pointed and had high, slender heels that might be waisted — that is, shape in from the heel of the shoe, then widen again at the base.

FIRST HALF OF THE EIGHTEENTH CENTURY—ROCOCO

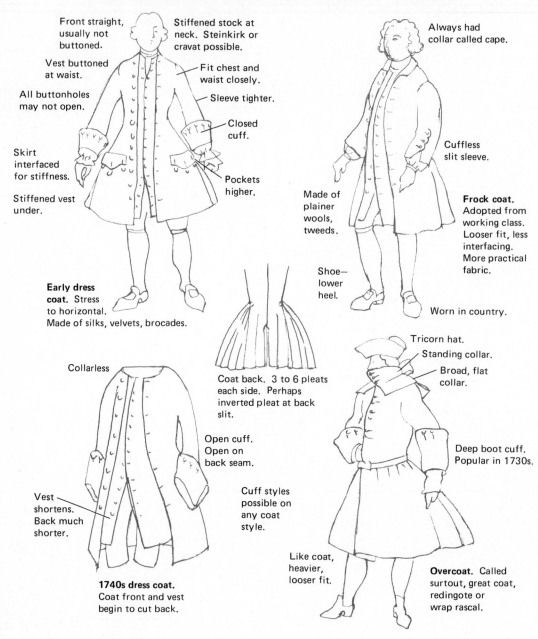

Front straight, usually not buttoned.

Vest buttoned at waist.

All buttonholes may not open.

Skirt interfaced for stiffness.

Stiffened vest under.

Early dress coat. Stress to horizontal. Made of silks, velvets, brocades.

Stiffened stock at neck. Steinkirk or cravat possible.

Fit chest and waist closely.

Sleeve tighter.

Closed cuff.

Pockets higher.

Always had collar called cape.

Cuffless slit sleeve.

Frock coat. Adopted from working class. Looser fit, less interfacing. More practical fabric.

Made of plainer wools, tweeds.

Shoe—lower heel.

Worn in country.

Collarless

Vest shortens. Back much shorter.

1740s dress coat. Coat front and vest begin to cut back.

Coat back. 3 to 6 pleats each side. Perhaps inverted pleat at back slit.

Open cuff. Open on back seam.

Cuff styles possible on any coat style.

Tricorn hat.

Standing collar.

Broad, flat collar.

Deep boot cuff. Popular in 1730s.

Like coat, heavier, looser fit.

Overcoat. Called surtout, great coat, redingote or wrap rascal.

FIRST HALF OF THE EIGHTEENTH CENTURY—ROCOCO

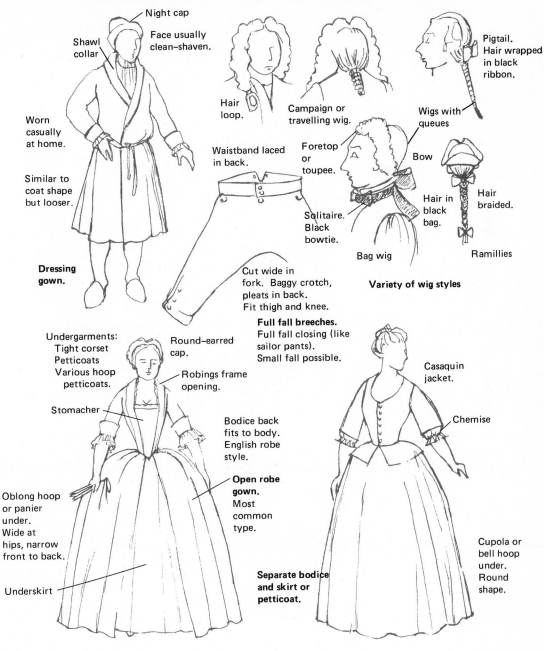

Night cap

Shawl collar

Face usually clean-shaven.

Worn casually at home.

Similar to coat shape but looser.

Dressing gown.

Hair loop.

Campaign or travelling wig.

Waistband laced in back.

Foretop or toupee.

Solitaire. Black bowtie.

Cut wide in fork. Baggy crotch, pleats in back. Fit thigh and knee.

Full fall breeches.
Full fall closing (like sailor pants). Small fall possible.

Pigtail. Hair wrapped in black ribbon.

Wigs with queues

Bow

Hair in black bag.

Bag wig

Hair braided.

Ramillies

Variety of wig styles

Undergarments:
Tight corset
Petticoats
Various hoop petticoats.

Stomacher

Round-earred cap.

Robings frame opening.

Bodice back fits to body. English robe style.

Open robe gown.
Most common type.

Oblong hoop or panier under. Wide at hips, narrow front to back.

Underskirt

Casaquin jacket.

Chemise

Cupola or bell hoop under. Round shape.

Separate bodice and skirt or petticoat.

FIRST HALF OF THE EIGHTEENTH CENTURY—ROCOCO

Shorter jacket version (thigh-length) called petenlair.

Both gowns have French robe back.

Relatively unfitted.

Robings to hem.

Straight sleeve with cuff.

Wing cuff. Pleated in front.

Front and side skirt and bodice cut separately.

Chemise sleeve.

Closed robe front not open to reveal petticoat.

Fan hoop under. Flairs from hip to hem. Narrow front to back.

Early sacque (or sack) style.

Later sacque style.

French robe back.

Fullness in box pleats, falling freely shoulder to hem.

Called Watteau back.

Hair up in back.

Small head effect.

Day caps. Worn indoors, white, lace-edged.

Round-earred cap

Pinner

Mob cap

Lappets tie under chin. Possible on any cap.

Straw hat

The mid-eighteenth century—Georgian costumes

The period from 1755 to 1780 showed a continuation of the trends that began earlier. The men's dress coat fit closer to the body and the frock coat became even more acceptable and was seen everywhere but at court. The skirt of the frock coat was likely to be shorter, especially for sport and riding. The vest was now much shorter than the coat and the breeches, which were more visible, fit the leg quite well while still cut with fullness in the seat. The most popular type of outerwear was the large overcoat called the *surtout, great coat,* or *caped coat* that could finish at the neck with one, two, or three broad falling collars or capes. Wigs without queues were not common, though the full-bottomed wig was used by dignitaries. In the 1770s the foretop of the wig was padded up. Jockey boots with a tight turned-down cuff were the most fashionable boot style.

The dandies of the period, called Macaronis, took all fashion elements to extremes. They wore their clothes cut quite tight, their coattails quite short, their shoes very low and slipperlike, and in the 1770s they often had the foretop of the wig padded to excessive heights, topped with a tiny tricorn.

Women's gowns in this period had a great many variations. The sack was still quite popular, but now worn as an open robe with robings that framed the bodice opening and continued down the skirt front to the hem. The skirt on any gown might be caught up in some way to reveal more of the underskirt. The new-style gown was the *Polonaise*, which had the overskirt permanently sewed up in three puffs and the underskirt shorter—a style that was particularly popular with Marie Antoinette, who found it most suitable for gamboling in her gardens at Versailles. Women's hair also went to extremes in the 1770s and the height of the toupée often exceeded the length of the face and was achieved with such additives as false hair, pads, lard, and pomantum liberally coated with powder and topped with some ingenious decoration. These concoctions might be left in place for a month or two, revealing some unpleasant surprises when dismantled. The Salisbury *Journal* in 1777 advertised "nightcaps made of silver wire so strong that no mouse or even a rat can gnaw through them," being sold because of "the many melancholy accidents that have lately happened in consequence of mice getting into ladies hair in the night time." Shoes continued to have high, slender, waisted heels that might be placed forward under the instep to give the appearance of a tiny foot peeking out from under the ruffled skirt.

MID-EIGHTEENTH CENTURY—GEORGIAN

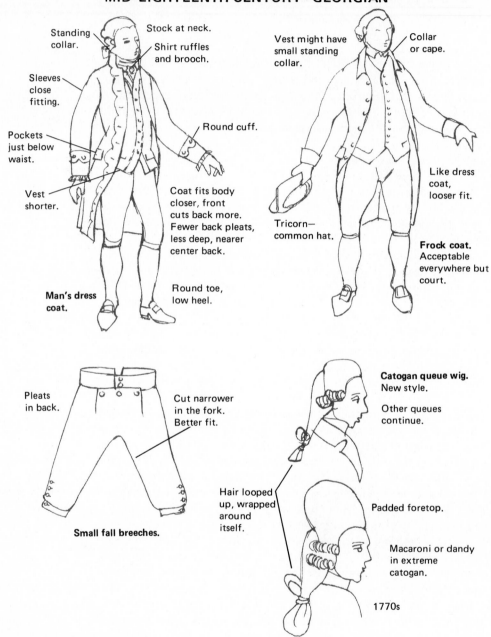

Standing collar.

Stock at neck.

Shirt ruffles and brooch.

Sleeves close fitting.

Pockets just below waist.

Round cuff.

Vest shorter.

Coat fits body closer, front cuts back more. Fewer back pleats, less deep, nearer center back.

Man's dress coat.

Round toe, low heel.

Vest might have small standing collar.

Collar or cape.

Like dress coat, looser fit.

Tricorn— common hat.

Frock coat. Acceptable everywhere but court.

Pleats in back.

Cut narrower in the fork. Better fit.

Small fall breeches.

Hair looped up, wrapped around itself.

Catogan queue wig. New style.

Other queues continue.

Padded foretop.

Macaroni or dandy in extreme catogan.

1770s

MID-EIGHTEENTH CENTURY—GEORGIAN

Dress turban.

Gathered or ruched robings.

Straight sleeve with matching flounce.

Echelle

Engageants or frills.

Overskirt could be casually hitched up in some manner.

Watteau back.

Open robe sacque.

Petticoat

1750s

Small head.

Hair up in back.

1770s

Hair padded up. Pearls and decor added.

Lard, pomantum and powder used to lighten.

Mob cap with lappet.

Day caps very large—1770s.

Exaggerated hairstyle.

Dormeuse. French cap. 1770s

Bodice diverging from bust to waist.

Zone or vest fill-in.

Round cuff

Chemise

Fabric shirred up seams.

Ankle length.

Skirt back sewn in place. Loops added.

Bell hoop under. Flatter in front, curved in back.

New style gown—Polonaise. Skirt formally set in three puffed sections.

Front

Back

Calash. Boned hood which extended up over high hairstyles.

Could also be worn with bustle pad or false rump.

END OF THE EIGHTEENTH CENTURY

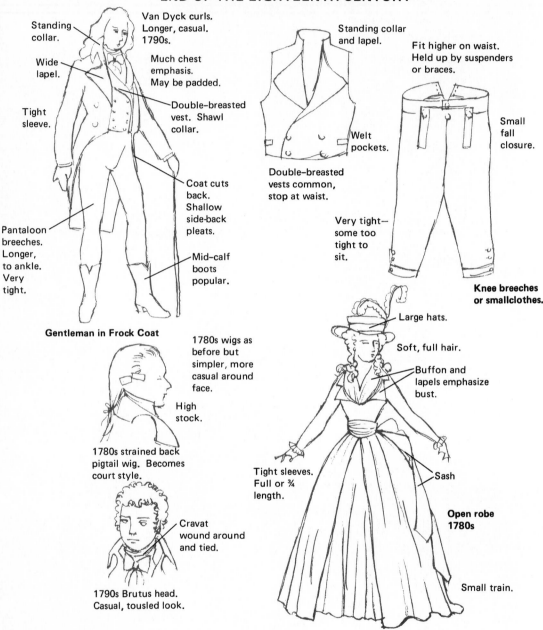

Standing collar.

Van Dyck curls. Longer, casual. 1790s.

Much chest emphasis. May be padded.

Wide lapel.

Tight sleeve.

Double-breasted vest. Shawl collar.

Pantaloon breeches. Longer, to ankle. Very tight.

Coat cuts back. Shallow side-back pleats.

Mid-calf boots popular.

Gentleman in Frock Coat

Standing collar and lapel.

Fit higher on waist. Held up by suspenders or braces.

Welt pockets.

Small fall closure.

Double-breasted vests common, stop at waist.

Very tight— some too tight to sit.

Knee breeches or smallclothes.

1780s wigs as before but simpler, more casual around face.

High stock.

1780s strained back pigtail wig. Becomes court style.

Cravat wound around and tied.

1790s Brutus head. Casual, tousled look.

Large hats.

Soft, full hair.

Buffon and lapels emphasize bust.

Tight sleeves. Full or ¾ length.

Sash

Open robe 1780s

Small train.

END OF THE EIGHTEENTH CENTURY

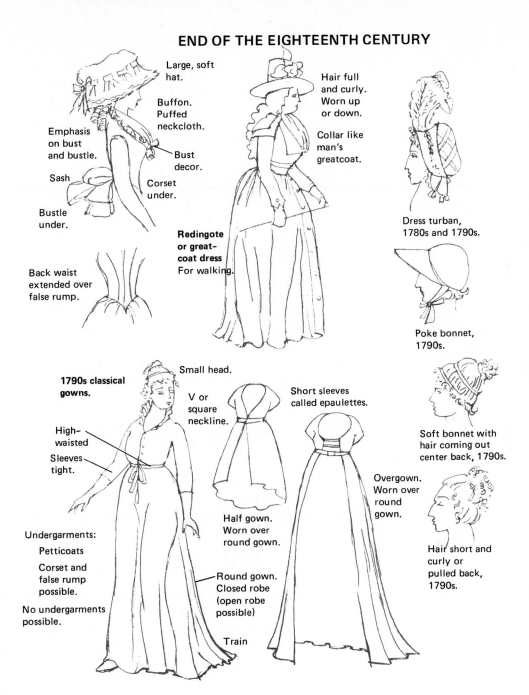

Large, soft hat.

Buffon. Puffed neckcloth.

Emphasis on bust and bustle.

Bust decor.

Sash

Corset under.

Bustle under.

Back waist extended over false rump.

Hair full and curly. Worn up or down.

Collar like man's greatcoat.

Redingote or great-coat dress For walking.

Dress turban, 1780s and 1790s.

Poke bonnet, 1790s.

1790s classical gowns.

Small head.

V or square neckline.

Short sleeves called epaulettes.

High-waisted

Sleeves tight.

Undergarments:

Petticoats

Corset and false rump possible.

No undergarments possible.

Half gown. Worn over round gown.

Round gown. Closed robe (open robe possible)

Train

Overgown. Worn over round gown.

Soft bonnet with hair coming out center back, 1790s.

Hair short and curly or pulled back, 1790s.

Costumes at the end of the eighteenth century
(see pp. 354 – 355)

The end of the eighteenth century brought a basic change in men's clothing. This change began in the 1780s and was even more evident in the 1790s. Men ceased to be colorful peacocks and status was shown by clothes that were tailored to perfection out of very good wool cloth, considered the most suitable for the tight styles that became popular. Men's dress became more somber and social superiority was expressed in a much more subtle fashion. The figure accented the chest and shoulders with a small waist and long leg. Underwaistcoats were sometimes worn to give the gentleman three layers to emphasize his chest. Hats included a form of tricorn called the *fantail,* the *bicorn,* and a round hat with a tall, straight crown and small brim.

The styles of the women changed more rapidly than those of the men. The silhouette of the 1780s was quite different from that of the 1770s, and the 1790s had yet another look. In addition to the 1780s styles shown, a chemise gown, which slipped over the head and was casually sashed in at the waist, was worn. The separate jacket and skirt was again quite popular, with the jacket bodice fitting snugly to the waist and flaring to the thigh or knee. False rumps were present under all styles of gowns. Indoor caps and turbans continued. Hats developed into wide, sweeping, plumed millinary masterpieces. During the 1790s classical-style gowns became the fashion. White dresses of muslin, cambric, and calico were common. Though the fashion was thought to be very Greek, it was actually quite diluted by many elements retained from the previous period. Shoes were low slippers or sandals and shawls and stoles were the regular outdoor garments.

Nineteenth-century costumes (see pp. 358 – 359, 361 – 363)

The nineteenth century was a time of rapid changes in both society and clothing styles. A great many books and periodicals were printed and are still available. Detailed sources are not difficult to find and in most cases can be easily understood. During this time the Industrial Revolution had its effect on costume as the political, social, and moral power shifted toward the middle class, and the soot and dirt from smokestacks and factories required more practical fabrics. The first twenty years, known as the Regency, were based on classical lines. The rest of the century is thought of as Victorian and the various styles are considered Gothic.

Men's clothes became less and less distinguished as the century wore on, but in the first two decades the true gentleman was concerned with fine fabric, expert cutting, and skillful tailoring. The emphasis was still on the deep chest, trim waist, and long leg. The neck linen was worn very high, framing the chin and brushing the earlobes. All styles of legwear were high-waisted. The most popular overcoat was the *Garrick,* with many deep collars or capes and a standing collar. During the decade between 1820 and 1830 the Age of Romanticism began, highlighting a pinched waist, rounded hips, and full chest. To aid this look a gentleman might have worn a corset and padding. In the mid-twenties a new style of frock coat became popular, one with a straight front that did not cut back at the waist. It continued to be important throughout the century, with the tailcoat relegated to evening and formal wear by the 1850s. A few gradual changes took place from 1830 to 1840, and during the decade from 1840 to 1850 the last vestiges of the true dandy began to disappear. Rich colors, pleated frills, and smart tailoring faded away and color seemed to be restricted to the vest and tie. In the late 1840s the more conservative suit coat began to appear and for daywear the gentleman could have chosen between it and the frock coat. The smoking jacket was also introduced. Both fitted and loose overcoats were worn. Fitted cloaks were also seen, which could have an overcape. Wellington boots were the usual daywear; low shoes were worn for evening dress. The period between 1850 and 1860 was one in which the matched suit of coat, vest, and trousers became widely worn. Called the *ditto suit,* the coat or sack coat was square and boxy. The top hat was still popular and soft felt and straw hats began to appear. The suit from 1860 to 1870 had a smaller collar. *Knickerbockers,* loose breeches gathered into a kneeband, began to be worn for sports. Overcoats could be single- or double-breasted. The cloak, called the *Inverness* or *Ulster,* fit fairly closely with a circular overcape and two long openings for the arms. The deerstalker cap in plaid or tweed was used for sports.

The 1870s began an era when more and more factory-produced clothes could be found, with a corresponding decrease in the quality of the garments. Despite the general inelegance that was affecting men's fashions there was a considerable amount of dandyism in the 1880s. For evening wear the swallowtail coat was worn and the dinner jacket or tuxedo introduced. A casual jacket worn at sporting occasions was the belted *Norfolk,* usually made of tweeds. No strong changes occurred in the last decade of the century. Suits had a fairly easy cut and trousers were of comfortable proportions. The clean-shaven look prevailed; mustaches were worn by those who were more conservative and beards were grown only by older men.

NINETEENTH-CENTURY MEN

1810

Round hat. Beginning of top hat.

Much chest emphasis. Vest could be colorful.

Slight kick.

Sleeve tight

Very High Neckwear

Tight pantaloons.

Shorter tails.

Knee breeches also possible.

Gaiters

Boots also worn.

1820

Top hat larger.

Kick at shoulder.

Shawl collar.

Double-breasted look.

Might not fasten.

Tight at forearm.

Pleats, peg top trousers.

Tails long, narrow.

Full-length trousers

Strap under foot.

1826

Leg-of-mutton sleeve

Tight forearm. Mitten cuffs.

Small waist

Trousers most common.

Tails widen.

Boots under trousers.

1836

Sleeve less full.

Vest single-breasted. With or without lapels.

Frock coat for day wear. Tail coat at night.

Short Wellington boots under.

1846

Hair rather long, short sidewhiskers.

Vest under. Single- or double-breasted.

Trousers wider. Fly front closing.

Frock coat. Long-waisted look.

No strap under foot.

NINETEENTH–CENTURY MEN

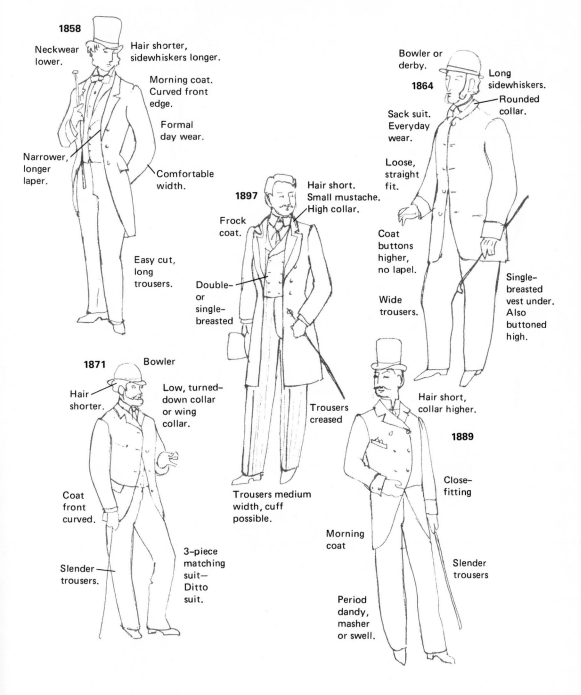

1858

Neckwear lower.

Hair shorter, sidewhiskers longer.

Morning coat. Curved front edge.

Formal day wear.

Narrower, longer laper.

Comfortable width.

Easy cut, long trousers.

1864

Bowler or derby.

Long sidewhiskers.

Rounded collar.

Sack suit. Everyday wear.

Loose, straight fit.

Coat buttons higher, no lapel.

Wide trousers.

Single-breasted vest under. Also buttoned high.

1897

Frock coat.

Hair short. Small mustache. High collar.

Double- or single-breasted

Trousers creased

Trousers medium width, cuff possible.

1871

Bowler

Hair shorter.

Low, turned-down collar or wing collar.

Coat front curved.

Slender trousers.

3-piece matching suit— Ditto suit.

1889

Hair short, collar higher.

Close-fitting

Morning coat

Slender trousers

Period dandy, masher or swell.

During the first ten years of the century the chief characteristics of the fashionable woman included a tall, slender, willowy silhouette with a high waistline and light, supple, clinging fabrics, low shoes without heels, scarves, and stoles. Evening gowns were elaborately trimmed. An overcoat, the *pelisse* or *redingote,* could be worn, as well as a short jacket. Gloves, handkerchiefs, and purses were common accessories. The period between 1810 and 1820 was one of transition, with the high waistline continuing but the classical line forgotten in the increasing use of Gothic ornamentation. For walking, a woman could wear a pelisse or woman's Garrick. Gloves were important. In the years between 1820 and 1830 the waistline lowered and the accent moved more to the horizontal as the skirt and sleeves got fuller. Hats, fans, muffs, parasols, and quite a bit of jewelry were usual accessories. The styles of the 1820s continued to expand in the 1830s, reaching their peak in about 1836. There was a buoyancy and feeling of outward extension that changed to one of drooping restraint as the years moved toward 1840 and the costume lost its horizontal emphasis with both sleeves and skirt declining. For outer wear, the pelisse-robe or coat dress was often worn as a walking costume. Three-tiered cloaks were also seen, as well as shaped shawls. From 1840 to 1850 the fashionable young woman was quite demure in a fairly controlled costume, though her skirt was still quite full. The evening bodice was worn off the shoulders and usually had some form of deep collar, pleats, or ruffles to accent the horizontal neckline. Shawls and half capes were common overgarments, and some fitted overcoats were worn. Shoes or boots had a low heel. The decade between 1850 and 1860 was prosperous and the silhouette of the day was dominated by the skirt, which was now a large bell shape that increased in size because the hoop petticoat again became popular. Amelia Bloomer introduced her new practical garment for ladies, long, full trousers cuffed at the ankle, but they were not received favorably. Capes were shaped to the waist and flared over the skirt, as were fitted overcoats. Shawls were also used. The pale complexion was proper. The years between 1860 and 1870 continued the extravagant skirt shape, though the excess material gradually moved to the back of the figure. The new bonnet style was the spoon bonnet, which had a peak that raised over the hair with trim inside. Small hats were popular later. The gowns of the 1870s were quite incredible because of the amount of detailing on the skirt. The long molded bodice developed by the middle of the decade and was still present at the end, when the bustle was practically gone and the silhouette was quite slim and tubular. The skirt of the late 1870s, which might be so narrow at the hem that only small steps were possible, was still intricately detailed and swagged toward the back. The slim silhouette that ended the decade did not stay long, for by 1881 the bustle had

NINETEENTH-CENTURY WOMEN

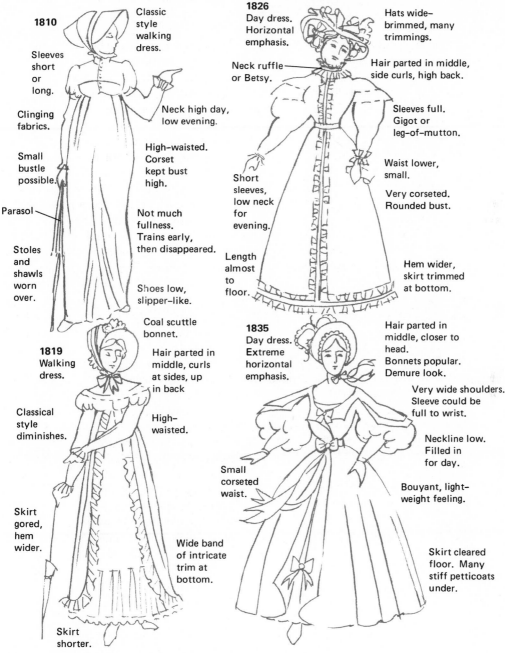

1810

Classic style walking dress.

Sleeves short or long.

Clinging fabrics.

Small bustle possible.

Parasol

Stoles and shawls worn over.

Neck high day, low evening.

High-waisted. Corset kept bust high.

Not much fullness. Trains early, then disappeared.

Shoes low, slipper-like.

1826
Day dress. Horizontal emphasis.

Neck ruffle or Betsy.

Short sleeves, low neck for evening.

Length almost to floor.

Hats wide-brimmed, many trimmings.

Hair parted in middle, side curls, high back.

Sleeves full. Gigot or leg-of-mutton.

Waist lower, small.

Very corseted. Rounded bust.

Hem wider, skirt trimmed at bottom.

1819
Walking dress.

Classical style diminishes.

Skirt gored, hem wider.

Skirt shorter.

Coal scuttle bonnet.

Hair parted in middle, curls at sides, up in back

High-waisted.

Wide band of intricate trim at bottom.

1835
Day dress. Extreme horizontal emphasis.

Small corseted waist.

Hair parted in middle, closer to head.
Bonnets popular. Demure look.

Very wide shoulders. Sleeve could be full to wrist.

Neckline low. Filled in for day.

Bouyant, light-weight feeling.

Skirt cleared floor. Many stiff petticoats under.

NINETEENTH-CENTURY WOMEN

1840
Promenade
dress.

Controlled,
demure
hairstyle.

Ruffle
on
bonnet.

Drooping
shoulder.

Bodice
tight and
simple.
V trim
to accent
small,
corseted
waist.

Tight
sleeve.

Long-
waisted
look.

Often
highly
decorated.

Costume
less bouyant,
more
downward
feeling.

Skirt to floor.
Bell-shaped.
5–6 petticoats
under.

Evening
bodices
very low.
Short
sleeves.

Hair fuller.
Back could
be in snood.

1860 Day dress.

Bodice just to
waist. May have
slight point.

Skirt-and-
blouse look
possible.

Extravagant
skirt over
large hoop.
Fullness in back.

Could have
train.

1850
Day costume.

Bonnet smaller.
Set back to
reveal hair.

Under-
sleeve.

Sleeve
widens
to wrist.

Not as long-
waisted.

Full skirt,
often 2 or
3 flounces.

Hooped
crinoline
and
petticoats
under.

Long
drawers
worn
under.

1870
Day dress.

Hair piled high.
Small hats popular.

Bodice to waist,
point in front.

Bustle high.

Many
details
like
1770s.

Large wired
bustle and
petticoats under.

Overskirt–underskirt
effect common.

Excessive,
complicated
draping and
trims used.

Trained

NINETEENTH-CENTURY WOMEN

1876 Day dress.

Hair up. Hats small.

Corset under, hour-glass figure ideal.

Cuirass bodice molded down over hips.

Jacket bodices popular.

Smaller bustle.

Skirt highly decorated.

High-heeled shoes or boots under.

Trained

1895 Day dress.

Hair piled softly on head. Hats larger.

High boned collar.

Large gigot or leg-of-mutton sleeve.

Very horizontal emphasis at mid-decade.

Some blousing possible.

Fitted over forearm.

Small, corseted waist.

Skirt springs smoothly over hip.

Side and back pleats possible.

Length to floor.

Wide at hem.

Petticoats under.

1886 Tailored costume.

Hair up. Small hats.

Bodice molded tightly over top of hips. Long-waisted look.

Sleeve tight.

Bustle squared out. Lower than 1870s.

Skirt draping simpler.

Could clear floor. Long for evening.

1900 Tailor-made costume.

Hair up and soft. Hats large.

Corseted figure emphasizes full bosom and hips.

Slimmer silhouette.

Skirt fits hips smoothly, flares lower.

Trains in back.

reappeared. The tailor-made costume appeared during this decade, a businesslike ensemble tailored of wool with masculine touches, which was more appropriate for the woman who was now venturing forth into the practical world. Fashions at the end of the century tended to indicate that women were leading a more active life, though many restrictions were still present. In less than thirty years women would have completely shed the layers of clothing and rigid bonings that had confined them for centuries, but in the 1890s they were still very much in evidence. The accent was to the horizontal in the middle of the decade and more vertical by the turn of the century. The ideal figure was somewhat S-shaped: the bosom curved out above the waist and the hip line curved out behind below the waist.

APPENDIX B
SOURCE LISTS

The chronological list of source materials and the list of useful costume source books are provided to start the designer on more extensive research in a particular period. The chronological list gives the dates of the periods, including some of the people and events of the time, and the type of source material available for primary research. From the thirteenth century on, some of the painters who worked with clothed figures are listed with their nationality and birth and death dates, to give the designer an idea of the range of material that was painted by each. Some of the painters were associated with more than one country, but are only included here once.

The book list should guide the designer toward the many types of sources that are available for research. Included are general costume surveys, specialty books, and specific sources for the periods of history. An indication of the time span of the material covered is also included with each entry. The books cited can guide designers to the sections of the library and bookstore that have potential for their purposes, and they can easily search out other related books that may be useful. A purposeful browse can be extremely rewarding for the designer. A number of these books are published in paperback editions. A good personal library can slowly but surely be acquired at moderate prices if designers keep their eyes open whenever they are in a bookstore or read a book sale catalogue.

Chronological list of source materials

Greek

Age of Pericles or Golden
Age   480–400 B.C.
Fourth Century   400–320 B.C.
Hellenistic   320–100 B.C.

Sculpture
Architectural
Statuary
Relief
Vase painting

Roman

Monarchy   750–500 B.C.
Republic   500–31 B.C.
Empire   31 B.C.–A.D. 323

Sculpture
Portrait busts
Reliefs
Triumphal arches
Statuary
Painting
Walls
Portrait heads
Mosaics
Coins

Early Christian

323–604

Mosaics

Byzantine

400–1100
Sack of Rome by Alaric   410
Charlemagne crowned Emperor
at Rome   800
Alfred the Great   870–901
Norman Conquest   1066
Crusades:
First   1095
Second   1144
Third   1187–1192

Ivory carvings
Manuscript miniatures
Romanesque churches
Sculpture
Tapestries
Frescoes

Romanesque

900–1200

Thirteenth Century

Early Gothic   1200–1350
Richard the Lionhearted   1189–
1199
Magna Charta   1215
Marco Polo's voy-
ages   1260–
1295
Manuscript miniatures
Stained glass
Small wood, ivory, and stone
carvings
Statuary
Tapestries
Frescoes

Painters
Italian
Cimabue   1240–c. 1302
Ducchio   c. 1255–1318
Giotto   c. 1266–1337
Simone Martini   1284–1344
Pietro Lorenzetti
active   1320–1345
Ambrogio Lorenzetti
active   1319–1347
Francesco Traini—active   c.
1321–mid.1300s
Andrea Orcagna   1308–1368

Fourteenth Century	Middle Gothic 1350–1425	Italian
	Edward III of England 1327–1377	Massaccio 1401–1428
	Books of Hours	Fra Angelico 1387–1455
	Panel paintings	Antonio Pisanello c. 1395–1455
	Brasses and rubbings	Fra Filippo Lippi c. 1406–1469
	Tomb sculptures	Paolo Ucello c. 1396–1475
	Richard II of England 1377–1399	Flemish
	Henry IV of England 1399–1413	Jan van Eyck— active 1422–1441
	Henry V of England 1413–1422	
	Charles VI of France 1380–1422	
	Joan of Arc martyred 1431	
	Medici power begins	

Fifteenth Century   Late Gothic   1425–1485

Edward IV of England   d. 1483
Richard III of England   d. 1485
Cosimo de Medici   from 1434
Lorenzo de Medici   d. 1492
Louis XI of France   d. 1483

Italian

Andrea Verrochio   1435–1488
Piero della Francesco
  c. 1410/20–1492
Domenico Ghirlandaio
  1449–1494
Cosimo Tura—
  before 1431–1495
Ercoli Roberti   c. 1450–1496
Piero Pollaiuoli   1441–1496
Antonio Pollaiuoli   1432–1498
Benozzo Gozzoli   1421–1497
Alesso Baldovinetti   1426–1499
Filippino Lippi   1457–1504
Andrea Mantegna   1431–1506
Gentile Bellini   1429–1507
Cosimo Rosselli   1437–1507
Sandro Botticelli   1447–1510
Giorgione   1476–1510
Bernardino Pinturicchio
  c. 1454–1513
Giovanni Bellini   1430–1516
Leonardo da Vinci   1452–1519

Early Renaissance France ⎫
Early Tudor England   ⎬ 1485–1520
High Renaissance Italy   ⎭

French
  Jean Fouquet   c. 1420–1480
Flemish
  Roger van der Weyden
    c. 1400–1464
  Dirk Bouts   c. 1415–1475
  Hans Memling   c. 1430–1495
Italian
  Raphael   1483–1520

Luca Signorelli   c. 1445–1523
Perugino   c. 1445–1523
Vittore Carpaccio—active
   1490–c. 1526
Andrea del Sarto   1486–1531
Lorenzo di Credi   c. 1458–1537
Michelangelo Buonarroti   1475–
   c. 1564
German
   Matthias Grünewald
      c. 1470/80–1528
   Albrecht Dürer   1471–1528
   Hans Baldung   c. 1484–1545
   Lucas Cranach   1472–1553
Flemish
   Gerard David   d. 1523
   Quentin Matsys   c. 1464–1530
French
   Jean Clouet   c. 1485–1540
   François Clouet   c. 1510–1572

Sixteenth Century   Tudor England   1520–1547
   Henry VIII of England   d. 1547
Renaissance France and Germany
   François I of France   d. 1547
   Martin Luther of Germany
      d. 1546

Italian
   Giovanni Baptista Rosso   1494–
      1540
   Francesco Parmigianino
      1503–1540
   Sebastiano del Piombo
      1485–1547
   Jacopo Pontormo   1494–1556
   Francesco Primiticcio
      c. 1504–1570
   Paris Bordone   1500–1571
   Agnolo Bronzino   1503–1572
   Georgio Vasari   1511–1574
   Titian   1487–c. 1576
Flemish/Dutch
   Guillim Stretes—active   1530s
      to 1550s
   Anthonis Mor   c. 1517–1576
   Pieter Brueghel   c. 1525–1569
German
   Barthel Bruyn   c. 1492–1555
   Christoph Amberger
      c. 1500–1561
   Hans Holbein   c. 1497–1543

Elizabethan   1545–1620   Italian
   Elizabethan and Jacobean England   Giovanni Battista Moroni   1525–
   Late Valois and Early Bourbon   1578
      France   Paolo Veronese   1528–1588

Renaissance Germany and Spain
Elizabeth I of England   1558–1603
James I of England   1603–1625
Shakespeare   1564–1616
Sculpture
Brasses
Engravings
Miniatures
Tapestries

Cavalier or Early Baroque   1620–1660
Charles I of England   1625–1649
Oliver Cromwell   1599–1658
Thirty Years' War

Jacopo Tintoretto   1518–1594
Michelangelo Merise de Caravaggio   1573–1610
English
Hans Eworth—active   c. 1545–1574
Federigo Zuccari   c. 1540–1609
Isaac Oliver—active   1590–1617
Nicholas Hilliard   1547–1619
Marcus Gheeraerts   1561–1636
Flemish
Pieter Pourbus   1523–1584
Peter Paul Rubens   1577–1640
Spanish
Alonzo Sanches-Coello   c. 1531–1588
El Greco   1548–1614
Flemish/Dutch
Adriaen Brouwer   c. 1605–1638
Anthony van Dyck   1599–1641
Cornelis de Vos   1584–1651
Nicholaes Elias   c. 1590–1654
Franz Hals   1580–1666
Jan Miensz Molenaer   c. 1609–1668
Rembrandt van Rijn   1606–1669
Gerard Terborch   1617–1681
Adriaen Ostade   1610–1684
French
Jacques Callot   c. 1592–1635
Antoine Le Nain   1588–1648
Louis Le Nain   1593–1648
Simon Vouet   1590–1649
George de La Tour   1593–1652
Philippe de Champaigne   1602–1674
Abraham Bosse   1602–1676
Mathiew Le Nain   1607–1677
Jacob Jordaens   1593–1678
Spanish
Diego Velázquez   1599–1660
English
Daniel Mytens   c. 1590–before 1648
Gerard S. van Honthorst   1590–1656
Cornelius Johnson   1593–1661
Wenzel Hollar   1607–1677

Petticoat Breeches, Restoration, or
Middle Baroque   1660–1685
    Charles II of England
    1630–1685
    Louis XIV of France
    1638–1715

Italian
    Carlo Dolci   1616–1686
Flemish/Dutch
    Gabriel Metsu   1629–1667
    Bartholomeus van der
      Helst   1613–1670
    Jan Vermeer   1632–1674
    Pieter de Hooch   1630–1677
    Jan Steen   1626–1679
    Gerard Terborch   1617–1681
French
    Charles Le Brun   1619–1690
    Pierre Mignard   1612–1697
Spanish
    Bartolome Esteban Murillo
    1617–1682
English
    Sir Peter Lely   1618–1680
    Jacob Huysmans   1633–1696
    Sir Godfrey Kneller   c.
    1646–1723

Restoration and Late Baroque
1685–1715
    James II of England
    1685–1688
    William and Mary of
      England   1688–1702
    Anne of England   1702–1714

French
    Antoine Watteau   1684–1721
    Antoine Coypel   1661–1722
    John Baptiste Joseph Pater
    1695–1736
    Nicholas Lancret   1660–1743
    Hyacinthe Rigaud   1659–1743
    Jean Baptiste van Loo   1684–1745

Eighteenth Century

Nicholas de Largilliere
    1656–1746
Jean Francois de Troy   1679–1752
Carle van Loo   1705–1765
Jean-Marc Nattier   1685–1766
Francois Boucher   1703–1770
Louis-Michel Van Loo
    1707–1771
Louis Toque   1696–1772
Francois Hubert Drouais   1727–
    1775
Jean Baptiste Simeon Chardin
    1699–1779
Jean-Baptiste Perroneau
    c. 1715–1783
Quentin La Tour   1704–1788
Jean Baptiste Greuze   1725–1805
Jean Honoré Fragonard
    1732–1806

Early Georgian England
Rococo France   1715–1755
    George I of England 1714–1727
    George II of England
    1727–1760
    Louis XV of France   1715–1774
    Benjamin Franklin   1706–1790
    George Washington
    1732–1799
    Catherine the Great of
    Russia   1729–1796

Italian
    Antonio Canaletto   1697–1768
    Giovanni Battisti Tiepolo   1692–
      1769
    Pietro Longhi   1702–1785
    Francesco Guardi   1712–1793
English
    William Hogarth   1697–1764
    Francis Cotes   1725–1770
    Joseph Highmore   1692–1780
    Allan Ramsey   1713–1784
    Arthur Devis   c. 1711–1787
    Thomas Gainsborough
      1727–1788
    Joshua Reynolds   1723–1792
    George Romney   1734–1802
    Johann Zoffany   1733–1810

Middle Georgian
George III of England
1760–1820

German
    Daniel Chodowiecki   1726–1801
Flemish
    Raphael Menge   1728–1779
Swedish
    Alexandre Roslin   1718–1793
American Colonies and United
States
    Robert Feke   1705–1750
    Joseph Blackburn   1700–1765
    Joseph Badger   1708–1765
    John Hesslius   1728–1778
    Ralph Earle   1751–1801
    John Singleton Copley
      1737–1815
    Benjamin West   1738–1820

Late Georgian England
Louis XVI of France
1774–1792

French
    Jean Michel Moreau (le jeune)
      1741–1814
    Paul-Pierre Prud'hon
      1758–1823
    Antoine Vestier   1740–1824
    Theodore Géricault   1791–1824
    Jacques-Louis David   1748–1825
    Antoine Jean Gros   1771–1835
    François Gerard   1770–1837
    Louise Elizabeth Vigée-
      Lebrun   1755–1842
    Jean-Auguste-Dominique
      Ingres   1780–1867
Spanish
    Francisco de Goya   1746–1828

England—
Regency
France—
Directoire and Empire
Germany—
Biedermeier
United States—
Federal

} 1790–1815

English
George Morland   1764–1804
John Opie   1761–1807
John Hoppner   1758–1810
Isaac Cruikshank   c. 1756–c. 1811
Robert Dighton   1752–1812
James Gilray   1757–1815
Samuel Cotes   1734–1818
Thomas Rowlandson   1756–1827
Thomas Lawrence   1769–1830
Scots
Henry Raeburn   1756–1823
United States
Edward Savage   1761–1817
Charles Wilson
Peale   1741–1827
Gilbert Stuart   1755–1828
John Trumbull   1756–1843
French
Horace Vernet   1789–1863
Eugène Delacroix   1798–1863
Garvarni   1804–1866

Nineteenth Century—
Victorian Era

Romantic Age   1815–1848
Daguerreotype invented   1839
(Louis Daguerre   1789–1851)

Crinoline Period   1845–1868

Bustle Period   1868–1890

Fin de siècle   1890–1900

French
Jean-François Millet   1814–1875
Gustave Courbet   1819–1877
Honoré Daumier   1808–1879
Edouard Manet   1832–1883
Constantin Guys   1805–1892
English
Henry Alken   1784–1851
Robert Cruikshank   1789–1856
John Leech   1817–64
George Cruikshank   1792–1878
H. K. Browne (Phiz)   1815–1882
Aubrey Beardsley   1872–1898
United States
Samuel Waldo   1783–1861
Thomas Sully   1783–1872
Samuel Morse   1791–1872
William Jewett   1792–1874
French
Henri-Marie-Raymond de
Toulouse Lautrec   1864–1901
Edgar Degas   1834–1917

Pierre-Auguste Renoir 1841–1919
Claude Monet   1840–1926
United States
  Thomas Nast   1840–1902
  James McNeil Whistler
    1854–1903
  Winslow Homer   1836–1910
  Thomas Eakins   1844–1916
  John Singer Sargent   1856–1925
  Charles Dana Gibson 1867–1944

Useful costume source books

Coverage in some of these volumes extends to the periods preceding and following the time span noted.

GENERAL COSTUME SURVEYS

Barton, Lucy. *Historic Costume for the Stage.* Boston: Walter H. Baker, 1938.
  Ancient Egypt to 1914.

Batterberry, Michael and Ariane. *Mirror, Mirror.* New York: Holt, Rinehart and Winston, 1977.
  Ancient Near East through 20th century.

Boucher, François. *20,000 Years of Fashion.* New York: Harry N. Abrams, 1967.
  Prehistoric times to 1914.

Braun and Schnieder. *Historic Costume in Pictures.* New York: Dover, 1975.
  Antiquity to 19th century.

Brooke, Iris. *Western European Costume.* London: George G. Harrap, 1939.
  13th to 17th centuries.

Bruhn, Wolfgang and Max Tilke. *A Pictorial History of Costume.* New York: Praeger, 1955.
  Antiquity through 19th century, including national costumes.

Clinch, George. *English Costume from Prehistoric Times to the End of the Eighteenth Century.* London: A. & C. Black, 1909.

Contini, Mila. *Fashion from Ancient Egypt to the Present Day.* New York: Odyssey, 1965.

Cunnington, C. Willett and Phillis and Charles Beard. *A Dictionary of English Costume: 900–1900.* New York: Barnes & Noble, 1960.

Cunnington, Phillis. *Costume in Pictures.* New York: Dutton, 1964.
  Middle Ages through first half of the 20th century.

Davenport, Millia. *The Book of Costume.* New York: Crown, 1948.
  Antiquity to the 1860s.

Dorner, Jane. *Fashion.* London: Octopus Books, 1974.
  14th century to modern day.

Garland, Madge. *The Changing Face of Beauty.* New York: M. Barrows and Company, 1957.
  Ancient Crete to 20th century.

Gorsline, Douglas. *What People Wore.* New York: Bonanza Books, 1952.
  Antiquity to 20th century.

Hansen, Henny Harald. *Costumes and Styles.* New York: Dutton, 1956.
  Antiquity to 20th century.

Hill, Margot Hamilton and Peter A. Bucknell. *The Evolution of Fashion: 1066–1930.* New York: Drama Book Specialists, 1967.

Huyghe, René (ed.). *Larousse Encyclopedia of Renaissance and Baroque Art.* London: Hamlyn, 1964.
13th through 18th centuries.

Kelly, Francis M. and Randolphe Schwabe. *Historic Fashion: A Chronicle of Fashion in Western Europe, 1490–1790.* New York: Scribner, 1925.

Kelly, Francis M. and Randolphe Schwabe. *A Short History of Costume and Armor: 1066–1800.* London: Batsford.

Kemper, Rachel H. *Costume.* New York: Newsweek Books, 1978.
Antiquity to 1970s.

Kohler, Carl. *A History of Costume.* New York: Dover, 1963.
Antiquity to 1870.

Kybalova, Ludmila, Olga Herbenova, and Milena Lamarova. *Pictorial Encyclopedia of Fashion.* London: Hamlyn, 1968.
Antiquity to 1960s.

Lister, Margot. *Costume: An Illustrated Survey from Ancient Times to the 20th Century.* Boston: Plays, Inc., 1968.

Laver, James. *The Concise History of Costume and Fashion.* New York: Harry N. Abrams, 1969.
Antiquity to 1960s.

Laver, James. *Costume Through the Ages.* New York: Simon & Schuster, 1963.
Ancient Rome to 1930.

Payne, Blanche. *History of Costume.* New York: Harper, 1965.
Ancient Egypt to 20th century.

Pistolese, Rosana and Ruth Horsting. *History of Fashions.* New York, Wiley, 1970.
Antiquity to 20th century.

Piton, Camille. *Le Costume Civile en France du XIIIième au XIXième Siècle.* Paris: Flammarion, 1926.

Racinet, M. A. *Le Costume Historique.* Paris: Librairie de Firmin-Didot, 1888. 6 volumes.
Antiquity to early 19th century; includes national costumes.

Rosenberg, Adolph. *Geschichte des Kostums.* New York: E. Weyhe, 1905–1923. 5 volumes.
Ancient Greece to 20th century.

Selbie, Robert. *The Anatomy of Costume.* New York: Crescent Books, 1977.
Antiquity to 20th century.

Squire, Geoffery. *Dress and Society.* New York: Viking, 1974.
1560–1970.

Walkup, Fairfax Proudfit. *Dressing the Part.* New York: F. S. Crofts and Company, 1947.
Ancient Egypt to 1930s.

Wilcox, R. Turner. *The Dictionary of Costume.* New York: Scribner, 1969.

Wilcox, R. Turner. *The Mode in Costume.* New York: Scribner, 1958.
    Ancient Egypt to 1947.

Yarwood, Doreen. *The Encyclopaedia of World Costume.* New York: Scribner, 1978.

Yarwood, Doreen. *European Costumes: 4000 Years of Fashion.* New York: Bonanza Books, 1975.

GENERAL SURVEY SPECIALITY BOOKS

Accessories

Lester, Katherine Morris and Bess Viola Oerke. *Accessories of Dress.* Peoria, Ill.: Charles A. Bennett Company, 1954.

Arms and heraldry

Allcock, Hubert. *Heraldic Design.* New York: Tudor, 1962.

Fox-Davis, Arthur Charles. *The Art of Heraldry: An Encyclopaedia of Armory.* New York: Arno Press, 1976.

Fox-Davis, Arthur Charles. *A Complete Guide to Heraldry.* New York: Bonanza Books, 1978.

Hart, Harold H. (ed.). *Weapons and Armor.* Compiled by Robert Sietsema. New York: Hart Publishing, 1978.

Nickel, Helmut, Stuart W. Pyhrr, and Leonid Tarassuk. *The Art of Chivalry.* New York: Metropolitan Museum of Art, 1982.

Norman, Vesey. *Arms and Armor.* London: Octopus Books, 1972.

Reid, William. *Arms Through the Ages.* New York: Harper, 1976.
    Neolithic Age to modern times.

Stone, George Cameron. *A Glossary of the Construction, Decoration and Use of Arms and Armor.* New York: Jack Brussel, 1961.
    Antiquity to 20th century.

Banking

Caline-Stephanelli, Elvira and Vladimir. *Two Centuries of American Banking: A Pictorial Essay.* Washington, D.C.: Acropolis Books, 1975.
    18th, 19th, and 20th centuries.

Children

Brooke, Iris. *English Children's Costume Since 1775.* London: A. & C. Black, 1930.

Cunnington, Phillis and Anne Buck. *Children's Costume in England.* London: A. & C. Black, 1965.
    4th through 19th centuries.

Worrell, Estelle Ansley. *Children's Costume in America, 1607–1910.* New York: Scribner, 1980.

Church

Haverstick, John. *The Progress of the Protestant.* New York: Holt, Rinehart and Winston, 1968.
> 15th to 20th centuries.

Rice, Edward. *The Church: A Pictoral History.* New York: Farrar, Straus and Cudahy, 1961.
> Early Christian Era through 19th century.

Collars

Colle, Doriece. *Collars, Stocks, Cravats.* Emmaus, Pa.: Rodale Press, 1972.
> Men's neckpieces from 1655 to 1900.

Corsets and underwear

Ewing, Elizabeth. *Dress and Undress: A History of Women's Underwear.* New York: Drama Book Specialists, 1978.

Ewing, Elizabeth. *Underwear: A History.* New York: Theatre Arts Books, 1972.

Waugh, Norah. *Corsets and Crinolines.* New York: Theatre Arts Books, 1970.
> 16th century to 1925.

Everyday life

Brosse, Jacques, Paul Chaland, and Jacques Ostier. *100,000 Years of Daily Life.* New York: Golden Press, 1961.

Cunnington, Phillis and Catherine Lucas. *Occupational Costume in England.* London: A. & C. Black, 1967.
> 11th through 19th centuries.

Lister, Margot. *Costumes of Everyday Life: An Illustrated History of Working Clothes.* Boston: Plays, Inc., 1972.

Hats and hair

Amphlett, Hilda. *Hats: A History of Fashions in Headwear.* Chalfont St. Giles England: Sadler, 1974.
> 1st millennium A.D. to 20th century.

Corson, Richard. *Fashions in Hair: The First Five Thousand Years.* London: Peter Owen, 1971.

Kilgour, Ruth Edwards. *A Pageant of Hats, Ancient and Modern.* New York: Robert M. McBride, 1958.

Severn, Bill. *The Long and Short of It: Five Thousand Years of Fun and Fury Over Hair.* New York: David McKay, 1971.

Wilcox, R. Turner. *The Mode in Hats and Headdresses.* New York: Scribner, 1959.
> Antiquity to 1944.

Jewelry

Black, J. Anderson. *A History of Jewelry: Five Thousand Years.* New York: Park Lane, 1981.

Frank, Joan. *The Beauty of Jewelry.* New York: Crescent Books, 1979.
Primarily 18th, 19th, and 20th centuries.

Fregnac, Claude. *Jewelry: From Renaissance to Art Nouveau.* London: Octopus Books, 1973.

Hart, Harold H. (ed.). *Jewelry.* Revised edition by Robert Sietsma. Text by Nancy Goldberg. New York: Hart, 1978.

Medicine

Margotta, Roberto. *The Story of Medicine.* New York: Golden Press, 1968.
Primitive man to modern times.

Shoes

Wilson, Eunice. *A History of Shoe Fashion.* London: Pitman, 1969.
Pre-Roman Britain to 1960s.

Sport

Arlott, John and Arthur Daley. *The Pageantry of Sport.* New York: Hawthorn, 1968.
14th through 19th centuries.

Stained glass

Lee, Lawrence, George Seddon, and Francis Stephens. *Stained Glass.* New York: Crown, 1976.
11th to 20th centuries.

Tailoring

Waugh, Norah. *The Cut of Men's Clothes, 1600–1900.* London: Faber & Faber, 1964.

Tapestries

Hulst, Roger Adolf d',A. *Flemish Tapestries from the 15th to 18th Centuries.* New York: Universe Books, 1967.

Jarry, Madelein. *World Tapestry, from Its Origins to the Present.* New York: Putman, 1969.
Primarily 14th through 18th centuries.

Jobe, Joseph. *The Art of Tapestry.* London: Thames and Hudson, 1965.
Primarily 14th through 18th centuries.

Thomson, Francis Paul. *Tapestry: Mirror of History.* New York: Crown, 1980.
Primarily 11th through 18th centuries.

ANCIENT GREECE TO THE TWELFTH CENTURY

Abrahams, Ethel. *Greek Dress.* London: John Murray, 1908.

Amiet, Pierre. *Art in the Ancient World: A Handbook of Styles and Forms.* New York: Rizzoli, 1981.
  Ancient Mesopotamia to Rome.

Bonfante, Larissa. *Greek-Etruscan Dress.* Baltimore: Johns Hopkins, 1975.

Chamoux, François. *Greek Art.* Greenwich, Conn.: New York Graphic Society, 1966.

Charbonneaux, Jean, Roland Martin, and François Villard. *Classical Greek Art.* New York: Braziller, 1972.

Field, D. M. *Greek and Roman Mythology.* New York: Chartwell Books, 1977.

Graber, André. *Byzantine Painting.* Geneva: Skira, 1953.
  5th to 14th centuries.

Graber, André. *Early Medieval Painting from the 4th to the 11th Centuries.* New York: Skira, 1957.

Hale, William Harlan (ed.). *The Horizon Book of Ancient Greece.* New York: American Heritage, 1965.

Hanfmann, George M. A. *Roman Art.* Greenwich, Conn.: New York Graphic Society, 1964.

Heuzey, Léon. *Histoire du Costume Antique.* Paris: Librarie Ancienne Honoré. Champion, 1922.
  Greek and Roman costumes.

Hope, Thomas. *Costume of the Greeks and Romans.* New York, Dover, 1962.

Houston, Mary. *Ancient Greek, Roman and Byzantine Costume.* New York: Barnes & Noble, 1947.

Huyghe, René (ed.). *Larousse Encyclopedia of Byzantine and Medieval Art.* London: Hamlyn, 1963.

Maiuri, Amedeo. *Roman Painting.* Geneva: Skira, 1953.

Norris, Herbert. *Costume and Fashion,* Vol. I. London: J. M. Dent, 1947.
  Greece to the 11th century.

Oakeshott, Walter. *The Mosaics of Rome, from the Third to the Fourteenth Centuries.* Greenwich, Conn.: New York Graphic Society, 1967.

Pfuhl, Ernst. *Masterpieces of Greek Drawing and Painting.* New York: Macmillan, 1926.

Rice, Talbot. *The Art of Byzantium.* New York: Harry N. Abrams, 1959.

Richter, Gisela M. A. *Attic Red-Figured Vases.* New Haven: Yale University Press, 1958.

Robertson, Martin. *Greek Painting.* Geneva: Skira, 1959.

Robertson, Martin. *A Shorter History of Greek Art.* New York: Cambridge University Press, 1981.

Robinson, H. Russell. *The Armor of Imperial Rome.* New York: Scribner, 1975.

Shoder, Raymond V. *Masterpieces of Greek Art*. Greenwich, Conn.: New York Graphic Society, 1960.   /

TWELFTH THROUGH FIFTEENTH CENTURIES: GOTHIC

Ashley, Maurice (ed.). *Dawn of a New Era: Milestones of History*. New York: Newsweek Books, 1974.
1209–1402.

Baker, John. *English Stained Glass*. London: Thames and Hudson, 1960.
12th to 16th centuries.

Bise, Gabriel. *Medieval Hunting Scenes*. Geneva: Minerva, 1978.
14th century.

Boehn, Max von. *Die Mode: Menschen und Moden im Mittelalter*. Munich: F. Bruckmann, 1923.

Brooke, Iris. *English Costume of the Early Middle Ages*. London: A. & C. Black, 1936.
10th to 13th centuries.

Brooke, Iris. *English Costume of the Late Middle Ages*. London: A. & C. Black, 1935.
14th and 15th centuries.

Clayton, Muriel. *Brass Rubbings*. London: Victoria and Albert Museum, 1968.

Cunnington, C. Willett and Phillis. *The Handbook of English Medieval Costume*. Boston: Plays, Inc., 1969.

Cunnington, Phillis. *Medieval and Tudor Costume*. Boston, Plays, Inc., 1972.
11th to 16th centuries.

Delaisse, L. M. J. *Medieval Miniatures*. New York: Harry N. Abrams, 1965.
11th through 15th centuries.

DuPont, Jacques. *Gothic Painting*. Geneva: Skira, 1954.
14th and 15th centuries.

Evans, Joan (ed.). *The Flowering of the Middle Ages*. New York: McGraw-Hill, 1966.
11th through 15th centuries.

Formaggio, Dino and Carlo Passo. *A Book of Miniatures*. New York: Tudor, 1962.
11th through 15th centuries.

Gaborit, Jean René. *Great Gothic Sculpture*. New York: William Morrow, 1978.
12th through 14th centuries.

Graber, André. *Romanesque Painting from the 11th to 13th Century*. New York: Skira, 1958.

Hindley, Geoffrey. *The Medieval Establishment*. New York: Putnam, Sons, 1970.
1200 to 1500.

Houston, Mary. *Medieval Costume in England and France.* London: A. & C. Black, 1939.
  13th, 14th, and 15th centuries.

Lacroix, Paul. *The Arts in the Middle Ages and the Renaissance.* New York: Frederick Ungar, 1964.
  13th to 16th centuries.

Lacroix, Paul. *France in the Middle Ages.* New York: Frederick Ungar, 1963.
  12th to 16th centuries.

Lacroix, Paul. *Military and Religious Life in the Middle Ages and the Renaissance.* New York: Frederick Ungar, 1964.
  12th to 16th centuries.

Lassaigne, Jacques and Giulio Carlo Argan. *The Fifteenth Century.* New York: Skira, 1955.

Laver, James. *Early Tudor: 1485–1558.* London: Harrap, 1951.

Meiss, Millard. *French Painting in the Time of Jean de Berry.* London: Phaedon, 1969.
  Late 14th century.

Meiss, Millard. *The Great Age of Fresco.* New York: Braziller, 1970.
  Primarily 14th, 15th, and early 16th centuries.

Newton, Stella Mary. *Fashion in the Age of the Black Prince: a Study of the Years 1340–1365.* Woodbridge, England: Boydell Press, 1980.

Norris, Herbert. *Costume and Fashion,* Vol. II. New York: Dutton, 1940.
  11th to 15th centuries.

Platt, Colin. *The Atlas of Medieval Man.* New York: St. Martin's, Press, 1980.
  11th through 15th centuries.

Pognon, Edmond. *Les Très Riches Heures du Duc de Berry.* New York: Crescent Books, n.d.

Porcher, Jean. *Medieval French Miniatures.* New York: Harry N. Abrams, 1960.
  11th through 15th centuries.

Stirton, Paul. *Renaissance Painting.* New York, Mayflower Books, 1979.

Wagner, Eduard, Zoroslava Drobna, and Jan Durdik. *Medieval Costume, Armor and Weapons.* London: Hamlyn, 1958.
  1350 to 1450.

Williams, Neville (ed.). *Expanding Horizons: Milestones of History.* New York: Newsweek Books, 1974.
  1415–1516.

Williamson, Hugh Ross. *Lorenzo the Magnificent.* New York: Putnam, 1974.
  1449–1492.

SIXTEENTH CENTURY

Blum, André. *Early Bourbon: 1590–1643.* London: Harrap, 1951.

Blum, André. *The Last Valois: 1515–90.* London: Harrap, 1951.

Boehn, Max von. *Die Mode: Menschen und Moden im sechzehnten Jahrhundert.* Munich: F. Bruckmann, 1923.

Brooke, Iris. *English Costume in the Age of Elizabeth.* London: A. &. C. Black, 1936.

Cunnington, C. Willett and Phillis. *Handbook of English Costume in the 16th Century.* Boston: Plays, Inc., 1970.

Fraser, Antonia. *King James.* New York: Knopf, 1975.
  The 16th to early 17th centuries.

Hay, Denys (ed.). *The Age of the Renaissance.* New York: McGraw-Hill, 1967.
  Primarily 15th and 16th centuries.

Kelly, F. M. *Shakespearean Costume for Stage and Screen.* Boston: Walter H. Baker, 1938.

Laver, James (ed.) *Le Costume des Tudor à Louis XIII.* Paris: Horizon de France, 1950.
  1485 to 1643.

Morse, H. K. *Elizabethan Pageantry.* London: The Studio, 1934.
  1560 to 1620.

Norris, Herbert. *Costume and Fashion,* Vol. III. Book 1, 1485–1547. Book 2, 1547–1603. New York: Dutton, 1938.

Plaidy, Jean. *Mary Queen of Scots.* New York: Putnam, 1975.
  Mid- to late 16th century.

Ross, Josephine. *The Tudors.* New York: Putnam, 1979.
  1485 to 1603.

Schoenbaum, S. *Shakespeare: The Globe and the World.* New York: Oxford University Press, 1979.

Trevor-Roper, Hugh, (ed.). *The Age of Expansion: Europe and the World 1559–1660.* New York: McGraw-Hill, 1968.

Vecellio, Cesare. *Vecellio's Renaissance Costume Book.* New York: Dover, 1977.

Venturi, Lionello. *The Sixteenth Century.* New York: Skira, 1956.

Williams, Neville. *All the Queen's Men.* New York: Macmillan, 1972.
  1533 to 1603.

Williams, Neville. *Life and Times of Elizabeth I.* Garden City, N.Y.: Doubleday, 1972.

Williams, Neville (ed.). *Reform and Revolt: Milestones of History.* New York: Newsweek Books, 1974.
  1517–1600.

SEVENTEENTH TO EIGHTEENTH CENTURIES

Boehn, Max von. *Die Mode: Menschen und Moden im achtzehnten Jahrhundert.* Munich: F. Bruckmann, 1923.

Boehn, Max von. *Die Mode: Menschen und Moden im siebzehnten Jahrhundert.* Munich: F. Bruckmann, 1913.

Brooke, Iris and James Laver. *English Costumes of the 18th Century*. London: A. & C. Black, 1945.

Brooke, Iris. *English Costume of the 17th Century*. London: A. & C. Black, 1934.

Cresswell, Donald H. *The American Revolution in Drawings and Prints*. Washington, D.C.: Library of Congress, 1975.
   1765 to 1790.

Cunnington, C. Willett and Phillis. *Handbook of English Costume in the 18th Century*. Boston: Plays, Inc., 1972.

Cunnington, C. Willett and Phillis. *Handbook of English Costume in the 17th Century*. Boston: Plays, Inc., 1972.

DuPont, Jacques and François Mathey. *The Seventeenth Century*. New York: Skira, 1951.

Fosca, François (George de Traz). *The Eighteenth Century*. Geneva: Skira, 1952.

George, M. Dorothy. *Hogarth to Cruikshank: Social Change in Graphic Satire*. New York: Walker, 1967.
   18th and 19th centuries.

Grafton, John. *The American Revolution: A Picture Sourcebook*. New York: Dover, 1975.

Hesketh, Christian. *Tartans*. New York: Putnam, 1961.
   Primarily 18th and 19th centuries.

Hibbert, Christopher (ed.). *The Pen and the Sword: Milestones of History*. New York: Newsweek Books, 1974.
   1601 to 1698.

Hibbert, Christopher (ed.). *Twilight of Princes: Milestones of History*. New York: Newsweek Books, 1974.
   1713 to 1799.

Hogg, Ian V. and John H. Batchelor. *Armies of the American Revolution*. Englewood Cliffs, N.J.: Prentice-Hall, 1975.

Ketchum, Richard M. (ed.). *The American Heritage Book of the Revolution*. New York: American Heritage, 1971.

Kinnaird, Clark. *George Washington: The Pictorial Biography*. New York: Hastings House, 1967.

Laver, James (intro.). *17th and 18th Century Costume*. London: Victoria and Albert Museum, 1951.

Masters, John. *Casanova*. New York: Bernard Geis Associates, 1969.

McClellan, Elisabeth. *Historic Dress in America*, Vol. 1. Philadelphia: George W. Jacobs, 1904.

Mollo, John and Malcolm McGregor. *Uniforms of the American Revolution*. New York: Macmillan, 1975.

Peterson, Harold L. *The Book of the Continental Soldier*. Harrisburg, Pa.: Stackpole, 1968.

Preston, Antony, David Lyon, and John H. Batchelor. *The Navies of the American Revolution*. Englewood Cliffs, N.J.: Prentice-Hall, 1975.

Schönberger, Arno and Halldor Soehner. *The Rococo Age.* New York: McGraw-Hill, 1963.
18th century.

van Thienen, Frithjof. *The Great Age of Holland, 1600–1660.* London: Harrap, 1951.

Walker, Stella A. *Sporting Art.* New York: Clarkson N. Potter, 1972.
England 1700–1900.

Warwick, Edward, Henry C. Pitz, and Alexander Wyckoff. *Early American Dress.* New York: Bonanza Books, 1965.
17th and 18th centuries.

Weigert, Roger-Armand. *Personnages de Qualite.* Paris: Editions Rombaldi, 1956.
1680 to 1715.

Whitney, David. *The Colonial Spirit of '76.* Chicago: J. G. Ferguson, 1974.

NINETEENTH CENTURY

Beebe, Lucius and Charles Clegg. *The American West.* New York: Dutton, 1955.

Blay, John S. *After the Civil War: A Pictorial Profile of America from 1865 to 1900.* New York: Bonanza Books, 1960.

Blay, John S. *The Civil War: A Pictorial Profile.* New York: Bonanza Books, 1958.

Blum, Stella. *Ackermann's Costume Plates: Women's Fashions in England 1818–1828.* New York: Dover, 1978.

Blum, Stella. *Victorian Fashions and Costumes from Harper's Bazar: 1867–98.* New York: Dover, 1974.

Boehn, Max von. *Modes and Manners of the 19th Century.* 3 volumes. New York: Dutton, 1909.

Brander, Michael. *The Victorian Gentleman.* London: Gordon Cremonesi, 1975.

Brooke, Iris and James Laver. *English Costume of the 19th Century.* London: A. & C. Black, 1929.

Cone, Polly (ed.). *The Imperial Style: Fashions of the Hapsburg Era.* New York: Metropolitan Museum of Art, 1980.
Primarily 19th century.

Croonborg, Frederick T. *The Blue Book of Men's Tailoring.* New York: Van Nostrand Reinhold, 1977.
Early 20th century.

Cunliffe, Marcus. *The Age of Expansion.* Springfield, Mass.: G. & C. Merriam, 1974.
1848 to 1917.

Cunnington, C. Willett and Phillis. *Handbook of English Costume in the 19th Century.* Boston: Plays, Inc., 1970.

Evans, Hilary and Mary. *The Victorians.* New York: Arco, 1974.
Mid- to late 19th century.

Gibbs-Smith, Charles H. *The Fashionable Lady in the 19th Century.* London: Victoria and Albert Museum, 1960.

Gillard, David. *The New Illustrated History of the World: Industrial Revolution 1848–1917.* London: Hamlyn, 1970.

Harter, Jim. *Women: A Pictorial Archive from Nineteenth Century Sources.* New York: Dover, 1978.

Holland, Vyvyan. *Hand Colored Fashion Plates.* London: Batsford, 1955.
    1770 to 1899.

Jensen, Oliver (ed.). *The Nineties.* New York: American Heritage, 1967.

Kraus, Michael and Vera. *Family Album for Americans.* New York: Grosset & Dunlap, 1961.
    late 18th and 19th centuries.

Kunciov, Robert. *Mr. Godey's Ladies.* New York: Bonanza Books, 1971.
    1830s to 1870s.

Laver, James. *Manners and Morals in the Age of Optimism, 1848–1914.* New York: Harper, 1966.

Lucie-Smith, Edward and Celestine Dars. *How the Rich Lived.* London: Paddington Press, 1976.
    1870 to 1914.

Lucie-Smith, Edward and Celestine Dars. *Work and Struggle.* London: Paddington Press, 1977.
    1870 to 1914.

McClellan, Elizabeth. *Historic Dress in America,* Vol. 2. Philadelphia: George W. Jacobs, 1910.
    1800 to 1870.

Norris, Herbert and Oswald Curtis. *Costume and Fashion,* Vol. VI. New York: Dutton, 1933.
    1800 to 1900.

Palmer, Alan (ed.). *Nations and Empires: Milestones of History.* New York: Newsweek Books, 1974.
    1854–1900.

Pitz, Henry C. *The Gibson Girl and Her America.* New York: Dover, 1969.

Pyne, W. H. *Rural Occupations in Early 19th Century England.* New York: Dover, 1977.

Raynal, Maurice. *The Nineteenth Century.* New York: Skira, 1951.

Sears, Stephen W. (ed.). *Century Collection of Civil War Art.* New York: American Heritage, 1974.

Simpson, Jeffrey. *The American Family: A History in Photographs.* New York: Viking, 1976.
    Late Victorian to modern times.

Weymouth, Lally. *America in 1876: The Way We Were* New York: Vintage Books, 1976.

NINETEENTH-CENTURY PERIODICALS

American Magazine (1876–1956)
Bon Ton and *Le Moniteur de la Mode* (1851–1927)
Bon Ton, Journal des Modes (1834–1881)
Gallery of Fashion (1794–1803)
The Gentleman's Magazine (1828–1894)
Godey's Lady's Book (1830–1898)
Good Housekeeping (1885–present)
Harper's Weekly (1857–1916)
Harper's Bazaar (1867–present)
Illustrated London News (1842–present)
L'Illustration (1843–1944)
Ladies Home Journal (1883–present)
Life Magazine (1883–present)
Mode Illustré (1843–1873)
Peterson's Magazine (1846–1898)
Vogue (1892–present)

BIBLIOGRAPHY

General theatre and basic design approach

Adams, J. Donald. *Naked We Came.* New York: Holt, Rinehart and Winston, 1967.

Bell, Quentin. *On Human Finery,* 2nd ed. New York: Schocken Books, 1978.

Binder, Pearl. *Muffs and Morals.* London: Harrap, 1953.

Bland, Alexander. *A History of Ballet and Dance.* New York: Praeger, 1976.

Brockett, Oscar G. *History of the Theater,* 4th ed. Boston: Allyn and Bacon, 1982.

Brockett, Oscar G. *The Theatre: An Introduction,* 4th ed. New York: Holt, Rinehart and Winston, 1979.

Burian, K. V. *Story of World Opera.* London: Peter Nevill, 1961.

Clark, Kenneth. *The Nude.* Princeton, N.J.: Princeton University Press, 1956.

Clark, Mary and Clement Crisp. *Design for Ballet.* New York: Hawthorne, 1978.

Dodd, Craig. *Ballet and Modern Dance.* New York: Elsevier-Dutton, 1980.

Hiler, Hilaire. *From Nudity to Raiment.* Paris: Groves & Michaux, 1929.

Hollander, Anne. *Seeing Through Clothes.* New York: Viking, 1975.

Horn, Marilyn J. *The Second Skin,* 2nd ed. Boston: Houghton Mifflin, 1975.

Jones, Robert Edmund. *The Dramatic Imagination.* New York: Theatre Arts, 1941.

Komisarjevsky, Theodore. *The Costume of the Theatre.* New York: Benjamin Blom, 1968.

Langner, Lawrence. *The Importance of Wearing Clothes.* New York: Hastings House, 1959.

Laver, James. *Clothes.* London: Burke, 1952.

Laver, James. *Costume in the Theatre.* London: Harrap, 1964.

Laver, James. *Drama: Its Costumes and Decor.* London: Studio Publications, 1951.

Laver, James. *Taste and Fashion.* London: Harrap, 1945.

Lurie, Alison. *The Language of Clothes.* New York: Random House, 1981.

MacGowan, Kenneth and William Melnitz. *The Living Stage.* Englewood Cliffs, N.J.: Prentice-Hall, 1955.

Nagler, A. M. *A Source Book in Theatrical History.* New York: Dover, 1959.

Newton, Stella Mary. *Health, Art and Reason: Dress Reformers of the 19th Century.* London: John Murray, 1974.

Nicholl, Allardyce. *The Development of the Theatre,* 5th ed. London: Harrap, 1966.

Nicholl, Allardyce. *Mimes, Masks and Miracles.* London: Harrap, 1931.

Nicholl, Allardyce. *Stuart Masques and the Renaissance Stage.* London: Harrap, 1937.

Oenslager, Donald. *Scenery Then and Now.* New York: Norton, 1936.

Orrey, Leslie (ed.). *The Encyclopedia of Opera.* New York: Scribner, 1976.

Parsons, Frank Alvah. *The Psychology of Dress.* Garden City, N.Y.: Doubleday, 1920.

Scholz, Janos (ed.). *Baroque and Romantic Stage Design.* New York: Dutton, 1962.

Simonson, Lee. *The Art of Scenic Design.* New York: Harper, 1950.

Strong, Roy. *Festival Designs by Inigo Jones: Drawings for Scenery and Costume.* International Exhibition Foundation, 1967–1968.

Unger-Hamilton, Clive (ed.). *The Entertainers.* New York: St. Martin's, 1980.

Veblen, Thorstein. *The Theory of the Leisure Class.* New York: New American Library, 1953.

Volland, Virginia. *Designing Woman.* New York: Doubleday, 1966.

Methods and materials

Berry, William A. *Drawing the Human Form.* New York: Van Nostrand Reinhold, 1977.

Birren, Faber. *Color: A Survey in Words and Pictures.* New Hyde Park, N.Y.: University Books, 1963.

Birren, Faber. *Creative Color.* New York: Van Nostrand Reinhold, 1961.

Birren, Faber. *Light, Color and Environment.* New York: Van Nostrand Reinhold, 1982.

Bridgman, George B. *Bridgman's Complete Guide to Drawing from Life.* New York: Sterling Publishing Co., 1952.

Burris-Meyer, Harold and Edward Cole. *Scenery for the Theatre.* Boston: Little, Brown, 1971.

Dalley, Terence (ed.). *The Complete Guide to Illustration and Design: Techniques and Materials.* Secaucus, N.J.: Chartwell Books, 1980.

Dobkin, Alexander. *Principles of Figure Drawing.* Cleveland: World, 1948.

Edwards, Betty. *Drawing on the Right Side of the Brain.* Los Angeles: J. P. Tarcher, 1979.

Hiler, Hilaire. *The Painter's Pocket Book.* London: Faber & Faber, 1970.

Itten, Johannes. *The Elements of Color.* New York: Van Nostrand Reinhold, 1970.

McCandless, Stanley. *A Method of Lighting the Stage,* 4th ed. New York: Theatre Arts Books, 1973.

Mayer, Ralph. *The Artist's Handbook of Materials and Techniques.* New York: Viking Press, 1982.

Mayer, Ralph. *The Painter's Craft.* New York: Van Nostrand, 1948.

Motley. *Designing and Making Stage Costumes.* New York: Watson-Guptill, 1975.

Nicolaides, Kimon. *The Natural Way to Draw: A Working Plan for Art Study.* Boston: Houghton Mifflin, 1975.

Parker, W. Oren and Harvey K. Smith. *Scene Design and Stage Lighting,* 4th ed. New York: Holt, Rinehart and Winston, 1979.

Peck, Stephen Rogers. *Atlas of Human Anatomy for the Artist.* New York: Oxford University Press, 1956.

Pecktal, Lynn. *Designing and Painting for the Theatre.* New York: Holt, Rinehart and Winston, 1975.

Pilbrow, Richard. *Stage Lighting.* New York: Drama Book Publishers, 1979.

Pope, Arthur. *The Language of Drawing and Painting.* Cambridge, Mass.: Harvard University Press, 1931.

Richmond, L. and J. Littlejohns. *Fundamentals of Water Color Painting.* New York: Watson-Guptill, 1978.

Ross, Denman Waldo. *On Drawing and Painting.* Boston: Houghton Mifflin, 1912.

Ruby, Erik A. *The Human Figure: A Photographic Reference for Artists.* New York: Van Nostrand Reinhold, 1974.

Russell, Douglas A. *Stage Costume Design: Theory, Technique and Style.* Englewood Cliffs, N.J.: Prentice-Hall, 1973.

Traphagen, Ethel. *Costume Design and Illustration.* New York: Wiley, 1932.

Fabrics and construction

Arnold, Janet. *A Handbook of Costume.* London: Macmillan, 1973.

Arnold, Janet. *Patterns of Fashion.* Volume 1: 1660–1860; Volume 2: 1860–1940. New York: Drama Book Specialists, 1972.

Barazani, Gail Coningsby. *Safe Practices in the Arts and Crafts: A Studio Guide.* The College Art Association of America, 1978.

Basic Tailoring. New York: Time-Life Books, 1974.

Bernstein, Aline. *Masterpieces of Women's Costume of the 18th and 19th Centuries.* New York: Crown, 1959.

Buchman, Herman. *Stage Makeup.* New York: Watson-Guptill, 1971.

Corbman, Bernard P. *Textiles: Fiber to Fabric.* New York: McGraw Hill, 1975.

Corson, Richard. *Stage Makeup,* 6th ed. Englewood Cliffs, N.J.: Prentice-Hall, 1981.

Cowan, Mary L. and Martha E. Jungerman. *Introduction to Textiles.* New York: Appleton-Century-Crofts, 1969.

Croonborg, Frederick T. *The Blue Book of Men's Tailoring.* New York: Van Nostrand Reinhold, 1977.

Dryden, Deborah M. *Fabric Painting and Dying for the Theatre.* New York: Drama Book Specialists, 1981.

Editors of American Fabrics and Fashions Magazine. *Encyclopedia of Textiles,* 3rd ed. Englewood Cliffs, N.J.: Prentice-Hall, 1980.

Ewing, Elizabeth. *Dress and Undress: A History of Women's Underwear.* New York: Drama Book Specialists, 1978.

Hollen, Norma and Jane Saddler. *Textiles.* New York: Macmillan, 1979.

Ingham, Rosemary and Elizabeth Covey. *The Costumer's Handbook.* Englewood Cliffs, N.J.: Prentice-Hall, 1980.

Labarthe, Jules. *Textiles: Origins to Usage.* New York: Macmillan, 1964.

McCann, Michael. *Artist Beware.* New York: Watson-Guptill, 1979.

Taylor, Al and Sue Roy. *Making a Monster.* New York: Crown, 1980.

Waugh, Norah. *Corsets and Crinolines.* New York: Theatre Arts Books, 1970.

Waugh, Norah. *The Cut of Men's Clothes: 1600–1900.* London: Faber & Faber, 1964.

Waugh, Norah. *The Cut of Women's Clothes: 1600–1930.* New York: Theatre Arts Books, 1968.

Wingate, Isabel B. *Textile Fabrics and Their Selection,* 7th ed. Englewood Cliffs, N.J.: Prentice-Hall, 1976.

INDEX

Page numbers in **boldface** type indicate illustrations.